The History of Civilization
Edited by C. K. Ogden, M.A.

Life and Work in Modern Europe

(*Fifteenth to Eighteenth Centuries*)

Life and Work in Modern Europe

(Fifteenth to Eighteenth Centuries)

By

G. RENARD

AND

G. WEULERSSE

With a Foreword by
EILEEN POWER, M.A., Lit.D.

LONDON
ROUTLEDGE & KEGAN PAUL LTD.

First published in Great Britain 1926
by Kegan Paul, Trench, Trubner & Co. Ltd

Reissued 1968

by Routledge & Kegan Paul Ltd
Broadway House, 68-74 Carter Lane
London, E.C.4

Printed in Great Britain
by Lowe & Brydone (Printers) Ltd, London

TRANSLATED BY
MARGARET RICHARDS, Ph.D.

SBN   7100   6137   4

CONTENTS

CONTENTS

CONTENTS

CONTENTS

CONTENTS

LIST OF ILLUSTRATIONS
(at end of book)

FOREWORD

An increasing interest in social and economic problems has
been one of the most marked characteristics of the twentieth
century, and has led, among other things, to an increasing
demand for books dealing with the economic history of the
past. It is perhaps true to say that all the great movements
of history have had an economic side, masked more or less
completely by other and more picturesque motives and often,
no doubt, outweighed by them. But in the modern world
economic motives have tended to drop the mask and to
become steadily more powerful; and almost all the serious
problems with which society finds itself faced to-day are in
their essence economic. For this reason it is difficult not to
feel an interest in their historical evolution, and, indeed,
dangerous to be wholly ignorant of it.

In general, however, the interest in economic history
in England has tended to confine itself entirely to the British
Isles, and the increased study of European political history,
which has been so marked of late years not only in schools and
universities but among the general public, has rarely been
extended to the study of European economic history, at any
rate prior to the nineteenth century. This is to some extent,
though less so, true also of the study of economic history in the
United States. That it should be so is in many ways unfortunate. On the one hand, just as modern industrial and
commercial problems are largely international in scope and
cannot properly be understood except on an international basis,
so the economic problems of the past usually require for their
right understanding to be studied internationally. It is
true that the sixteenth century ushered in an era of national
states, whose violently egocentric policies, wars, and balances
of power kept Europe in turmoil; but at the same time that
developed and self-conscious nations thus appeared upon the
stage of history, there also appeared a developed and equally

self-conscious international money market and an international commerce, which bound those nations together even while it set them at grips both in Europe and in the new-found worlds of America and the East. Moreover, the social revolution which agitated England in the sixteenth century was by no means peculiar to this country, and was indeed only the repercussion of a similar movement which was shaking the whole of Western Europe and adding to the general ferment caused by the Renaissance, the Reformation, and the great discoveries. The evolution of the English poor law, one of the most characteristic achievements of English municipal and governmental authority during the sixteenth century, owed much to experiments in Germany and the Low Countries. As to the rise of a science of political economy, that, like the rise of mathematics and the natural sciences, was the work of European thinkers, in which German reformers, English merchants, and French statesmen and philosophers all played a part.

There is another reason also which makes the study of her national history in isolation particularly misleading in the case of England. For the first centuries of the modern era (with which this book is concerned) England was not the teacher but the pupil, not the leader but the follower, and only by degrees the rival of other European Powers. The centre and leader of the economic world in the sixteenth century was Spain, with her great commercial and industrial province of the Netherlands and her empire in America and (after the annexation of Portugal) in the East. Antwerp was then the money market of the Western world. It was this which made Philip II so great a danger to the faith and liberty of the Protestant States. The revolt of the Netherlands and her own economic incapacity wrested her supremacy from Spain at the end of the sixteenth century, but in the seventeenth the new state of Holland took her place, and Amsterdam inherited the financial hegemony of Antwerp. From both these Powers England learned valuable lessons; throughout the seventeenth century, indeed, Holland was her taskmistress in agriculture, in irrigation, in many branches of industry, in banking, and in the carrying trade. In the struggle against both she found her own feet, and her rivalry played a foremost part in the fall of each. London at last took the place of Antwerp and of Amsterdam as the money market and commercial centre of the world, but not until after a protracted struggle with a third great Power, France, a struggle which, like those against Spain and Holland which preceded it, was economic as well as political in its aims and methods. The state commercial and economic policy, which was so carefully developed by the Restoration and Whig Governments of the late seventeenth and eighteenth centuries, was practised by all the European states and notably by France, so much so that Cunningham, in his work on *The Growth of English Industry and Commerce* describes the English form of the policy as Parliamentary Colbertism, after the great French minister who was its most active and logical exponent. Indeed, there is something at once ironical and tragic in the spectacle of the great Powers striving so hard to destroy each other, while bound together by a hundred economic ties and dependent upon each other for a hundred economic lessons, and in the wastage by ruinous warfare of the inestimable treasures of wealth built up in Europe by the inventions and the enormously increased production of the new age.

Apart from these wider considerations, innumerable interesting questions arise in English history alone, which only a knowledge of European economic history can answer. Why was the English East India Company the successful midwife of an empire and the French East India Company almost from its inception a failure ? Why is France a land of small peasant proprietors and England one of landless labourers ? Why were Italy and Germany, the leading commercial and financial powers of the Middle Ages, whose Lombards and Hansards played so signal a part in English economic history, comparatively unimportant in the modern world ? Why was England able to attract and immeasurably profit by the skilled artisans of the Netherlands in the sixteenth century and of France in the seventeenth ? Who financed the great wars ? How did the history of gild organisation differ in England and on the Continent ? It is to provide

an answer to some of these questions and to fill a notable
gap in the books available for English and American readers
that this book (the only one to deal comprehensively in English
with European economic history during the first three centuries of the modern age) has been translated. Beginning
with a sketch of the great revolutions which were changing
the face of society in the sixteenth century, it ends with the
beginning in England and France of the great revolutions
which were to change its face in the nineteenth. The authors
deal in turn with the four great economic Powers of the period,
Spain and Portugal, Holland, England, and France, as well
as with the great economic powers of the Middle Ages, Italy
and the German States, now in the background, and other
countries which played a still less prominent part in the
economic world, but the development of which is yet interesting and important. They trace the chief characteristics of
the history of labour and social life from 1500 to 1800, the
gradual disappearance of medieval survivals, the development of a national economy, the progress of capitalism, the
evolution of new economic classes, and the increasing intervention of the Government in all sides of economic life.
They give us thus a *coup d'œil* over the whole of Europe
during the pregnant period in which the contemporary world
was growing, a *coup d'œil* which is not only interesting in
itself, but essential to the proper understanding of our own
national history.

It should be added that footnotes to which the initials
M. R. are appended have been added by the translator,
where they seemed necessary to explain allusions or technical
terms which might have been strange to English readers.
All other footnotes are by the authors.

EILEEN POWER.

LIFE AND WORK IN MODERN EUROPE

INTRODUCTION

THE ECONOMIC AND SOCIAL REVOLUTION AT THE BEGINNING OF THE MODERN ERA
(FIFTEENTH AND SIXTEENTH CENTURIES)

THIS volume will deal with the economic and social changes which took place in Europe between the second half of the fifteenth century and the last quarter of the eighteenth. This long period was an age of growth and expansion, and of every kind of material progress. After the Turkish attack, which submerged Constantinople, the Balkans and Greece, and even for an instant washed the walls of Vienna, this continent was never again the victim of foreign invasion. Henceforth it was Europe which, like an inexhaustible reservoir of men and of vigour, overflowed the rest of the globe, whose peoples became the conquerors and colonisers of the world, supreme on land and sea, carrying their civilisation to every corner of the earth.

At the opening of our period Christian Europe was divided into two quite distinct worlds: the East, where peoples, still semi-barbaric, acted as a rampart against the Mussulman power advancing from Asia, and thus played a part as useful as it was heroic; and the West, which, thus protected, could develop in peace, and repay the Eastern peoples in ideas and in culture what it owed them in security. But it is in the West that we find a fruitful and creative life, and there that we must follow and study it.

§ 1. Three revolutions precede or accompany the economic revolution; they determine and explain it.

The first was a *political revolution*. It was characterised by two essential facts—the formation of powerful states, and the establishment in these states of a central authority strong enough to guarantee order and tranquillity. Weary of feudal anarchy, which kept the whole country in arms and made peace an accident, the nations of the modern world awoke to consciousness of themselves, and national states were formed. France felt herself French as a result of her long and bitter struggle with England; the long crusade against the Moors gave the Spanish people their soul; and everywhere this work of relative unification, of territorial and administrative simplification, was carried out to the profit of the monarchy, and at the expense of those social classes which had been wont to share territory and sovereignty with it.

In the Middle Ages, Western Europe was united in religion, but politically split up into fiefs and free towns. In the new society the reverse was the case.

The Church, which had been the guardian of men's souls, trustee of education and storehouse of learning, and which had, moreover, controlled vast domains and revenues, was now menaced on all sides, alike in authority, privileges and possessions. In France, the concordats made by Louis XI and Francis I put all the wealth and dignity of the Church at the disposal of the sovereign. In Spain, kings, who called themselves Catholic, forced the Pope to grant them the right of nomination to all great ecclesiastical offices, made themselves Grand Masters of the most famous monastic Orders, and converted the Hermandad into a sort of spiritual militia, vowed to their service. But more than all this, since Luther had rebelled against the Holy See, Rome had lost half her followers; her seamless cloak was rent. North Germany and the Scandinavian countries had broken the yoke of dogma; the King of England had proclaimed himself Supreme Head of a national Church; Switzerland, France and Scotland were all more or less the prey of heresy; and wherever the Reformation had triumphed, ecclesiastical property had been confiscated, or, as it was termed, secularised.

The lay powers of feudalism, like the clergy, suffered terrible blows. In France, the downfall of the House of Burgundy showed that there was no longer any vassal strong enough to oppose the king. Half a century later, the great nobility preferred the gilded domesticity of the court to a barren and sullen opposition, while the squirearchy, driven from their eyries by hunger or by force, disputed among themselves for the honour and profit of serving in the royal armies. In England, the great families were decimated by the Wars of the Roses, and their lands were bestowed upon the docile servants of the victorious dynasty. In Spain, Ferdinand and Isabella destroyed many castles and took advantage of the fact that the nobles did not pay taxes to forbid the most powerful of them to attend the Cortes. This was the end, if not of the pretensions, at least of the domination of the greater and lesser nobility.

The free cities and independent communes, which had been strongholds of liberty in the midst of the general oppression, succumbed almost everywhere, conquered by adventurers, lulled to sleep by merchant-princes, or ruined by the jealousy of kings. Louis XI nominated the mayors and aldermen of all his good towns, as well as the captains of the town militia, and he made the masters of the gilds take an oath of fidelity to his person. In Spain, town administration fell entirely into the hands of the kings, who suppressed municipal rights. In England, civic independence was only a memory, and under the despotism of the Tudors, the House of Commons was as weak as the Lords. In Germany, the imperial cities, which were to all intents and purposes independent, were reduced to impotence by their divisions and their isolation. The decay of Genoa and Florence marked the decline of the brilliant and restless Italian republics. Venice among her lagoons, the Swiss among their mountains, and later the Protestants of the Low Countries among their marshes, alone offered a partial resistance to the current which was sweeping all European nations towards the system of strong centralised government.

The crown strengthened its position by making an alliance with the wealthy middle class, whose interests also lay in the maintenance of order, which had too long been disturbed by the strife of town against town and castle against castle. Kings, such as Louis XI and Edward IV, took the merchant class under their protection, and in return were furnished with money, the sinews of war and of government. Kings needed money to establish a standing army. Maximilian of Austria, in his hereditary dominions, replaced the feudal levy by a regular army of lansquenets and reiters. All countries needed vast financial resources to pay professional soldiers, and to maintain a costly artillery. Taxes became permanent, like the army; but this was not enough. In addition to the ever-increasing returns of the *Gabelle*, the *Aides*, the *Taille*, and to the product of the customs and the crown lands, Francis I found it necessary to raise money by new registration fees, lotteries, loans, and the sale of offices. In England, the wealth confiscated from the nobles and the monasteries put a huge sum at the disposal of the Tudors. Being unable to raise enough money by regular taxation, they procured the additional sums needed by other means—if necessary, by the lucrative sale of monopolies.

This was the Golden Age of Absolutism in France, in Spain, in England and in Russia. Nevertheless, England, isolated within the silver girdle of her sea, managed to preserve, though with difficulty, her peculiar system of parliamentary government, which was destined to spread over the greater part of the world.

This political revolution, itself of great importance, was accompanied by an *intellectual and moral revolution* which expressed itself in two ways.

It was, in the first place, the Renaissance. Greek and Roman antiquity, like a Sleeping Beauty, awoke once more in Italy, after centuries of slumber. Those who welcomed and admired it when it rose from its living tomb, looked, like Janus, both backwards and forwards. On the one hand, they returned to the past, accepting its traditions, its pagan ideal, its *joie de vivre* and its untroubled enjoyment of the fruits of the earth and of the refinements of luxury. On the other hand, through Antiquity, they rediscovered Nature; they freed the individual from the fetters which were strangling him, and encouraged initiative, invention, observation and science.

In the second place, this new spirit expressed itself in the Reformation, which originated in Germany. The Reformation may be defined as a Christian Renaissance, and it, too, faced both past and future. It exalted primitive Christianity over medieval Catholicism, St. Paul over St. Thomas Aquinas, the Bible over the decrees of popes and councils. But at the same time it also emancipated or half-emancipated the individual, for although he was subject to the authority of a book, he was allowed to interpret it in his own way, and he was encouraged to discuss and to form his own opinions. It contained the germ of the principle of free criticism, and in urging those who could to read the Scriptures, the Reformation gave a vigorous impulse to popular education.

These two movements, the one beginning in the North and the other in the South, met, as it were in mortal combat, in the intermediate lands. But it seemed as though those countries from which the movements started must pay for the honour of being in the advance-guard, for both of them declined rapidly.

Italy did not achieve unity. The Pope and the Emperor continually fomented disunion, for, rivals and enemies as they were, they always patched up peace in time to prevent the small states of the Peninsula from uniting against them. The people of Italy had no common fatherland; they were citizens of dead cities, like Athens or ancient Rome, of the world, of the republic of letters or of art. Incapable of defending their soil against invaders, they were condemned to three hundred years of foreign domination. But, as in the case of Greece, when she was conquered by the Romans, Italy assimilated her conquerors. She beguiled and tricked and sometimes corrupted them. She communicated to them her fashions and her love of beauty, her vices and her refinement. She gave them a taste for pictures and statues, perfumes and silk stockings, satin doublets and brocaded gowns, laces and mirrors, tessellated pavements and carved ceilings. She made them long to possess and to be able to make all these things, and she furnished them with the means of fulfilling their desires. It was like a transfusion of Italian blood into the veins of Europe, and the operation has left the unhappy Italy weak and anæmic to the present day.

Germany was split up in exactly the same way, and it was not without reason that it was then known as 'the Germanies.' The central government was no more than a shadow; princelings and free towns swarmed; between North and South the clash of interests made a deep gulf, soon to be widened by the religious question. At the end of the Middle Ages, Germany unquestionably had a brilliant reputation. She gave the art of printing to the world; the clocks of Nuremberg spread the fame of her industries; the bankers of Augsburg and the fleet of the Hanseatic League were a proof of her commercial prosperity.   United to Spain under Charles V, she could dream again her imperial dream of world empire.   But the furies of religious war, unchained by the restless piety of her people, embroiled Lutherans, Anabaptists and Catholics in bitter strife, strewed the countryside with smoking ruins, and left Germany for many years in an exhausted condition.   She could take no part in overseas conquest, but, like Italy, had to wait for several centuries before she achieved unity.

Meanwhile other nations, which at the beginning of the period had received their inspiration from Italy and Germany, were fortunate or clever enough to resolve all the warring elements in their states into harmony.   This successful concentration of their strength gave them a great advantage over their neighbours in the race for supremacy.   It was France and Great Britain which in this way were able to assume the leadership.

At the same time, a *geographical revolution* greatly modified the accepted idea of the relative importance of European powers.   Christopher Columbus, sailing west in search of a new route to the Indies, found America.   Vasco da Gama, searching eastwards for these same Indies, coasted down Africa, and found the route round the Cape of Good Hope. Unknown lands opened up to the curiosity and the greed of those who found them.   The axis of the old world shifted, and moved to the West.   The Mediterranean, hitherto bitterly disputed between Turks and Christians, ceased to be the centre of maritime activity, and gave place to the Atlantic, which became the miraculous path on which all hopes and all desires were set.   Those countries which had direct access to it—Spain, Portugal, France, England and the Low Countries—were by that fact alone in a strong position for creating a colonial empire.

Naturally such changes must have had profound and manifold results upon the economic and social conditions of the peoples of Europe, results which can hardly be overemphasised, for they indeed mark the beginning of a new age.

§ 2.   The first result of the political and geographical revolution was the widening of both domestic and foreign markets. The barriers imprisoning each little community within narrow limits had now been thrown down, and the frontier of a man's country was pushed further and further away, to the top of a mountain, to the banks of a wide river, to the shores of the sea, or even across the seas to countries which he did not know and could hardly imagine.

This expansion brought in its train a change in the economic system, which had grown up empirically and spontaneously and without any precisely formulated principles in the course of the Middle Ages. Whether on the domains of the nobles or within the walls of the free towns, it was essentially a *local* system, restricted in aim and in area. The object of the nobles was to maintain large bands of retainers and to produce enough to feed, clothe, and arm them; and most of the towns also were primarily concerned with producing for themselves and the districts under their rule, and keeping themselves well provided with the necessities of life. Some few towns, however, such as Florence or Venice, Bruges or Ghent, had wider ambitions, and were already industrial and financial centres. They manufactured cloths, silks and glass, they did a big trade in luxuries, they were the headquarters of powerful banks. Their trade was of every kind, they had customers in the most distant parts of the known world, and carried on an inter-regional traffic, as well as trading at the fairs which were the ordinary centres of commerce. The economic policy of these active and wealthy towns was usually a mixture of free trade and protection. They allowed the free importation of the products of the country and of the raw materials necessary for their manufactures, but they prohibited the import of manufactured articles which might compete with theirs, and they forbade the export of anything necessary to the life and work of the people, even the export of the secrets of the different crafts and of the artisans who practised them.

Now when a *national* economy began to prevail in the world of great states, it was in some ways strikingly similar to the old *urban* economy, and in others strikingly different from it. It was impossible, henceforth, to legislate for one city alone, to sacrifice one city to another, or the countryfolk to the townsfolk. All the subjects of a prince, diverse as their interests might be, began for the first time to feel, however slightly, that they were members of one body. Customs duties still hampered trade between the provinces, but in spite of this, intercourse became easier in a united kingdom, for the confusion caused by varying systems of laws and regulations, currency and weights and measures was gradually swept away. Paris was brought into touch with Bordeaux and Marseilles, London with Bristol; the spirit of the parish pump gave place to wider interests. At the same time, across the seas in America, in India and in Africa, new markets were being opened up, Eldorados rich in promise. Idealists, adventurers and merchants all worked together to extend the narrow limits of the known world. They brought into subjection new lands, which, regarded simply as sources of profit, were exploited in a fashion undreamt of by the men of the Middle Ages.

These changes are sufficiently striking, even to the superficial observer, and they demand close and careful analysis.

Commerce, which throughout this period was of primary importance, sprang into life and splendour under this new spur. In every peaceful state the roads were safer, and merchants could travel in reasonable security. Freed from the fear of war and the necessity of preparing for it, men could now devote themselves to the productive works of peace. Populations, no longer decimated by constant wars, increased rapidly, and at the same time began to demand a far higher standard of living. The courts themselves showed unusual splendour. In France, Francis I vied in magnificence with Henry VIII at the Field of the Cloth of Gold. In the first half of the sixteenth century, according to a contemporary, pride increased in every estate. Citizens wished to look like gentry, gentry aped princes. " The ploughman," wrote Bernard Palissy, " wants his son to be a burgher. The workman wants to eat meat like the rich."[1] In Germany, likewise, " the clodhopper aspires to equality with the noble." In England and in Holland the national passion for domestic comfort asserted itself; every room had its chimney and its windows, every bed its pillow, every meal its beer or wine.

The merchant class, created to satisfy these new demands,

[1] Emile Levasseur, *Histoire des classes ouvrières en France avant 1789*, vol. ii, p. 8.

at once sprang into fame and power. Merchant-princes, like Jacques Cœur, were admitted to the councils of kings. Later, Colbert, a merchant's son, was to be the great peace minister of Louis XIV. It was the age of bold adventurers, who set up factories on the coasts of India or America, or conquered for the king, their master, territories so vast that the sun never set on them. It was the age of the great chartered companies, whose task it was to civilise this or that corner of the world.

The political economy of the period is, with reason, called *mercantilism*. States took as their models firms of wholesale merchants; they measured their prosperity by what they called the balance of trade, and counted themselves successful if their exports exceeded their imports.

Banking kept pace with the development of business. The whole paraphernalia of modern finance, private and public banks, exchanges, financiers and speculators, treasurers and farmers general, sprang up on every side. At the end of the fifteenth century precious metals were growing scarce in Europe. The few known mines were almost worked out; great quantities of gold and silver were tied up in the coffers of the Church, the nobles, or the Jews; there was the daily loss of wear and tear; and the Eastern trade caused a constant drain. But, from 1545 onwards, the galleons of Spain brought every year from Mexico and Peru about 300 tons of silver, and within fifty years the amount in circulation was quadrupled. The results of this influx of precious metal were an increased facility of exchange, an improvement in the system of credit, and the progressive lowering of the rate of interest, which Calvin, unlike earlier theologians, recognised as legitimate. The trading class benefited, and wealth poured freely into their coffers; but two classes of the community—the nobles, and, at the other end of the social scale, the artisans—suffered by the general rise of prices which resulted. The nobles could not increase their income by raising their tenants' rents, which were fixed by custom; while the artisans' wages rose much more slowly than prices. Thus the end of the sixteenth century saw a monetary crisis which nearly brought about a social crisis.

The rapid development of trade was accompanied by changes in its organisation. Throughout Western Europe fairs declined in importance, for they represented a stage that was past, a time when merchants had to carry their goods from place to place at fixed times in order to secure custom. Now traffic was regular, even daily in the leading countries. Only in Germany and in Russia did fairs preserve or acquire their importance. The Hanseatic League owed its downfall as much to its superannuated methods as to the internal divisions which set Catholic and Protestant towns at each other's throats.

On the other hand, maritime trade made a great advance. Hitherto merchants in their oared galleys had not ventured far from land, and had been content with coastal trade. But now they aimed at oceanic trade, and a new type of vessel resulted. Speed was essential in crossing great tracts of water; therefore, in order to catch every breath of wind, they lengthened the masts, increased the number and size of the sails, and varied their shape and their setting. Then they had to increase the size of the ships and strengthen their framework so that they could stand the increased pressure of canvas and meet more dangerous storms. They launched caravels of 1,100 tons, about the size of our coastal tramps, but gigantic in their eyes. These ships in turn caused the decay of many of the old shipping centres, which had been built as far as possible from the reach of foreign invasion and as near as possible to the markets of the interior, and had no channel deep enough to float the new type of ship. Henceforward, " instead of hiding themselves up estuaries or in lagoons, many ports came down boldly to the sea." Neither national rivalry, which was as strong at sea as on land, nor piracy, which was a permanent menace to sailors in the Southern hemisphere, and sometimes even in European waters, had power to check the expansion of maritime trade. Merchant fleets, escorted by men-of-war, unceasingly crossed the newly conquered oceans.

While commerce advanced, industry did not stand still. To satisfy the demands of a growing number of customers all over the world, production must be increased. But that could not be done without changes both in the methods of manufacture and in its organisation.

Increase of business almost necessarily entailed increased

division of labour. Already, during the Middle Ages, a certain amount of specialisation had crept into the various crafts, which, at first united, had gradually split up into separate and independent sections. The iron industry, for example, was split up into blacksmiths, nail-makers, cutlers, chain-makers, and armourers. But this was not enough. Though the master of a small workshop, who did his work himself or with the help of a few journeymen and apprentices, might have to perform personally all the successive operations necessary to the manufacture of the article he sold, he no longer did so when business increased and he employed more men. After that, there was division of labour between different sets of workmen. This had existed for some time in towns where goods were manufactured on a large scale; the same piece of cloth passed, stage by stage, through the hands of a whole series of workmen; a single suit of armour was produced by several sets of men working in concert with each other. In some industries the point was even reached when manufacture was split up into a regular series of simple movements, always the same, repeated indefinitely, and becoming in time almost mechanical. From this highly divided and productive manufacture, it was only a step to the use of machinery.

For at the same time the spirit of invention was at work in the West. The Renaissance encouraged economic development in two ways. In the first place, men no longer followed the medieval ideal of ascetic Christianity. They learned to enjoy life and to look for happiness in this world, as well as in the next, and were concerned to increase their mastery of everything necessary for their material comfort and prosperity. Secondly, the Renaissance broke the fetters of tradition and routine, and urged men to penetrate the secrets of Nature and to use her forces for their own purposes. It was the age of ' supermen,' like Michael Angelo and Leonardo da Vinci, who were painters, architects, inventors and chemists in one, and already dreamt of the conquest of the air and the transmutation of metals.

The only industrial machinery known in the Middle Ages was the mill, worked by wind or water. But from the middle of the fifteenth century the printing-press, which made use of the two older inventions of movable type and paper made

from rags, began to supersede the laborious copying of manu-
scripts by hand. It was printing which gave wings to human
thought, allowed it to spread far and wide and to reproduce
itself unceasingly, and thus multiplied its power and its
chances of immortality. From the beginning printing was
done by machinery, and therefore depended on capital. From
the first it displayed all the characteristics with which the
development of machine industry has made us familiar: the
continual improvement of machinery; the enormous economy
of time and labour; the cheapness and uniformity of production, which seemed so marvellous that the first printers
were accused of being in league with Satan; the violent and
yet vain struggle of the copyists, representing hand labour,
against the diabolical machines which robbed them of their
livelihood and reduced them to starvation; great workshops
where workmen were soon numbered by hundreds and already
began to wield the weapon of the strike.[1]

Printing was the mother-invention, the common ancestress
of the great industrial inventions which were to be the glory
of modern times. It supplied the passionate demand for
books and for knowledge created by the Renaissance and the
Reformation. Its development was very rapid. The Mainz
Psalter, the first book whose date we know, was printed in
1457; in 1500 there were already over a thousand printing-
presses in Germany, without taking into account those in
convents, castles, and the houses of the wealthy. Although
it began as a German art, it became European almost immediately, and Venice and Florence, Paris and Lyons, rivalled
Frankfort and Leipzig. Printers were exempt from taxation,
and were allowed to practise their craft without being hampered by gild restrictions, for printing was held to be a liberal
art escaped from the bonds of medieval routine. But the
business man, as well as the scholar, realised the use which
could be made of the new discovery. The first newspapers
were started quite as much in the interests of commerce as of
politics, and were largely composed of advertisements.

This technical change, of which we have chosen the most
striking example, was accompanied by a change in industrial
organisation.

In the first place, a distinction grew up between commerce

[1] H. Hauser, *Ouvriers du temps passé*, p. 177. Paris, F. Alcan.

and industry. Then in many cases a third person intervened
between the maker and the retailer of manufactured goods,
a man who called himself a manufacturer, but who was really
an *entrepreneur*. He was a daring innovator, " as devoted to
the conquest of fortune as was the humanist to the knowledge
of the ancients, as unscrupulous as the politician educated
in the school of Machiavelli."[1] The workshop, henceforth
distinct from the shop, grew to resemble the modern factory
in size and organisation. The class gulf between masters and
men widened rapidly, and the workers found themselves
in a subordinate position, forced to submit to a discipline
which was merciless in the interests of increased production.

Thus the workers of the nation were gradually divided
into two classes, separated by a wide gulf and yet inseparable,
whose interests were both identical and opposite.

At the top were the wealthy bourgeois, great financiers,
merchants or manufacturers, who aspired to noble rank and
often attained it. Not only did they buy great town houses,
but they also acquired the estates of a ruined and effete
nobility. Rich and intelligent, they ousted from their offices
in the law and the Church the ignorant and lazy sprigs of
nobility who had hitherto held them. In luxury they completely outshone the old nobility of birth, unless, indeed, they
condescended to regild this or that coat-of-arms by the gift
of a daughter-in-law, whose lack of ancestry was overlooked
in consideration of the size of her dowry.

At the bottom of the scale were the workmen, who suffered both in the conditions of their life and in public esti-
mation. In the first place, their work was much more ar-
duous. The Reformation had lessened the number of holidays,
while Catholics and Protestants united in condemning the old
methods of indiscriminate charity. Henceforth, therefore,
the impotent poor must go to the workhouse, the able-bodied
to the factory. The age when all must needs work was
beginning, and when the poor were, indeed, driven to work
by law. Those who had no capital must give up all hope
of becoming masters and resign themselves to be for ever
the servants of the more fortunate. Moreover, they began
to suffer from legal disabilities. In many cases these
mechanics, as they were scornfully called, were excluded

[1] Pirenne, *Les Anciennes Démocraties des Pays-Bas*, p. 252.

from municipal offices. The proletariat of the future was in sight.

In the second place, the workers suffered from the aristocratic spirit of the Renaissance. The system of education established by the Renaissance had for its basis a knowledge of Greek and Latin, and thus set an insurmountable barrier between the children of the rich and of the poor. Moreover, a division grew up between the artist and the craftsman, who should have been inseparable. One became a great man, the friend of princes and bankers, while the other dropped into the ranks of the ordinary workmen. Artists dissociated themselves from the daubers of the Brotherhood of St. Luke; architects felt themselves superior to master-masons, the despised and fallen heirs of the men who had built the cathedrals. The idea that there was something degrading in manual work was so generally accepted, that it was only in a few state industries, such as the Gobelin tapestries, that the melancholy divorce between artist and craftsman was avoided. " Only men of noble birth can attain perfection. The poor, who work with their hands and have no time to cultivate their minds, are incapable of it."[1] Such was the opinion of Lorenzo de' Medici, all the more significant because he himself was the son of *parvenu* merchants. Roman law, the oracle of the new age, consecrated this new convention, since, while asserting the absolute power of the king and the absolute prerogative of the proprietor, it said nothing of the rights of the worker.

Between these two classes, at the opposite poles of the industrial world, there still, however, existed a third, which was gradually disappearing. Traders and craftsmen on a small scale still dragged out an obscure and precarious existence. They were the last representatives of the gilds, which, admirable as they were when towns and industry were in their infancy, were useless and out of place in a flourishing state. Attacked by princes jealous of all independence, and by merchants impatient of every obstacle, undermined, to boot, by their own internal weaknesses, by the quarrels between journeymen and masters or between rival gilds, by their claim to possess the monopoly of a craft and by their harass-

---

[1] Georges Renard, *Histoire du travail à Florence*, vol. ii, ch. xx.

ing regulations, they were on the way to extinction. For a time they retained their outward forms, but the life had gone out of them, and the future lay in other hands.

It remains to consider agriculture, which presents a picture of the greatest diversity, so widely did climate, crops, methods of cultivation, conditions of tenure, and the social position of the cultivators vary from country to country. It is impossible to generalise among so many local peculiarities; but, nevertheless, agriculture felt the repercussion of the great changes which were taking place around it.

The discovery of new lands led to a useful exchange of products between Europe and her colonies. The Old World gave to the New the horse, the ox, the sheep, poultry, and many vegetables and fruit-trees. In return, she received from America the potato, tobacco, cocoa, vanilla, the tomato, dye-woods and cabinet woods, and certain flowers. Besides this, many of the products of the East, such as coffee, sugar-cane, cotton and indigo, which had hitherto been the luxuries of the wealthy, came within everyone's reach when they were transplanted to the West Indies and Brazil.

Agriculture learnt a great deal from the scientific irrigation and cultivation of Italy and even Spain. French landowners, on their return from expeditions across the Alps, followed the example of the Tuscan and Milanese nobles who devoted their lives to the improvement of their estates. Among the artists and craftsmen whom Charles VIII brought back with him from Italy, as well as perfumers, embroiderers and tailors, there were several gardeners, and even " an inventor skilled in the breeding of fowls."

New markets were opened to agricultural produce. Provence competed with Sicily in supplying Rome and Florence with corn. Brittany provided part of the corn-supply of Northern Spain. Baltic grain supplemented the home crops in England.

Two further points to be emphasised are the extension of land under cultivation and the increase of sheep-farming. Forests were cleared, land was reclaimed from the sea by the Dutch, and in countries where the Reformation had been accepted the secularisation of Church lands brought vast estates into the market.

As a result of the high price of wool, which was in great demand by a population anxious to be better clad, these reclaimed lands were devoted, not to arable farming, but to pasture. Sheep drove out men in consequence, for only a few shepherds were needed to run the farms, and the labourers were forced into the towns. This movement spread from the Spanish plateaux to the Swiss mountains, from the Roman Campagna to the plains of Schleswig-Holstein.[1] It was strongest in England, where the highways swarmed with beggars, and the outskirts of the towns with cheap labour.

Thomas More, in his *Utopia*,[2] says that the discharged retainers of the nobility are not the sole cause of the prevalence of vagabondage and theft. " There is an other, whych, as I suppose, is proper and peculiar to you Englishmen alone. . . . Your shepe that were wont to be so meke and tame, and so smal eaters, now, as I heare saye, be become so great devowerers and so wylde, that they eate up and swallow downe the very men them selfes. They consume, destroye, and devoure whole fieldes, howses, and cities." The condition of the peasants varied greatly. In Eastern Europe serfdom survived and even increased, but in the West and the centre it was disappearing. There, forced labour and military service were no longer exacted from the peasants, as feudalism gave way to a new political system. Instead, the peasants held their land on condition that the lord received a certain proportion of the profits (*métayage*), or they became lease-holders for a term of years at a fixed rent. The old landowners were replaced by members of the wealthy middle class, who bought up the land taken from the nobles or the clergy, and henceforth possessed the greater part of the landed wealth of the nation as they had already acquired almost all its movable wealth.

To sum up, three great developments were prefigured and outlined at the beginning of modern times. First, the preponderance of Europe was established, and her people began to swarm over other continents.[3] Secondly, the increase of commercial prosperity gave wealth and ease to the peoples of

---

[1] *Cf.* Ch. Jannet, *Grandes époques de l'histoire économique*, pp. 301-302.

[2] Book I.

[3] This overflow of the population of Europe into other parts of the world was partly the result of the Turkish invasion.

the West, and encouraged science and art. Thirdly, the middle classes, supreme in finance and industry, rose to power.

After this general survey there arises the question of the order in which we shall take the various countries as we study them more closely.[1] Several arrangements are possible, though none is perfect. After consideration, we have decided to arrange the nations in the order of their development and supremacy. Since the nations of the West have been the leaders of civilisation, we shall begin with Western Europe and examine in turn Spain, Portugal, the Low Countries, England and France. Then passing to Central Europe, we shall meet, going from south to north, Italy, the Empire, i.e. the Germanies and Austria, with Switzerland, which come into its economic sphere of influence, and the Scandinavian countries. We shall finish up in Eastern Europe with Poland and Russia.

BIBLIOGRAPHY

CUNNINGHAM: *Western Civilisation in some of its Economic Aspects.*
    Vol. ii. Modern Times. 1900.
JANNET: *Les grandes époques de l'histoire économique.* Paris, 1897.
OPPEL: *Natur und Arbeit.* 1904.

---

[1] A political arrangement is essential in this period, which marks the triumph of national economy.

CHAPTER I

SPAIN AND PORTUGAL

§ 1. Spain.

Summary of political development—Short period of prosperity; causes of decline—Royal fiscal system counteracts advantages offered to national trade by new facilities—Short-lived boom in industry; lack of economic sense; introduction of foreign manufactures and workers—Agricultural prosperity ruined by the expulsion of the Moors, by the growth of great estates, by the encouragement of sheep-farming, and by the fiscal and commercial policy of the Government—Depopulation; widespread poverty; wretched condition of the working classes—Slight increase in national prosperity in the eighteenth century.

THE history of Spain in the period we are studying falls into three periods. Up to the last thirty years of the sixteenth century she was the first country in Europe; from that time until about 1730 her power declined; but the last part of the eighteenth century saw her partial restoration.

At the beginning of the modern era Spain possessed vast dominions in Europe; she had crossed the Pyrenees and hemmed France in on all sides; in Italy she already possessed some territory and laid claim to still more; she was proud of her infantry, which passed for the finest in the world. United to Austria by the succession of Charles V, she was a menace to the balance of power in Europe. Meanwhile overseas she was conquering a vast empire whence her galleons returned laden with silver. Her prestige suffered slightly when Philip II succeeded the Emperor-King, but even so his court was the most luxurious and stately in Europe. He prided himself on being the defender of Christianity against the Turks, over whom his brother, Don John, won the naval victory of Lepanto in 1571. He was the champion of the Counter-Reformation, in the interests of which he launched his famous and ill-fated Armada against England, seized Portugal, dreamt of securing the throne of France, and laboured to crush political and religious freedom in the Low

18

Countries.   While Madrid was thus the centre of a policy of limitless ambitions, it was at the same time the scene of a brilliant Renaissance of art and literature.   Cervantes, Lope de Vega, Calderon, Velasquez, Ribera, to mention no others, are as famous in their own spheres as Ignatius Loyola or St. Theresa in theirs, and bear witness to the creative genius of their race at that time.   It is true to say that for nearly a hundred years Spain was the dominant nation, to be imitated and admired, to be feared and to be fought.

Such a position could not possibly have been won without an accompanying development in the economic life of the nation, and, in fact, Spain in those days was very far from being the impoverished country which we, with our knowledge of her later history, too easily picture her.

She was rich in actual bullion; her doubloons, which bought her allies and paid her fleets and armies, were current throughout the whole of Europe; from 1545 onwards her mines in Mexico and Peru produced on an average about 300 tons of silver a year.

As a result of her natural position, commanding both the Atlantic and the Mediterranean, she had two navies, one stationed at Cadiz, the other at Barcelona.   Ferdinand and Isabella opened their ports to the vessels of other nations and encouraged them in various ways.   They abolished the barbarous right of wreckage, which gave the salvage of a wrecked ship to the inhabitants of the shore on which it was wrecked and made the coasts of Spain as perilous as those of the Barbary pirates.   They also freed from customs duties such foreign ships as put into their ports for anchorage and not for trade.   But at the same time they did their best to protect their own ships and shipowners.   An edict of September, 1500, on the same lines as the Navigation Act which Cromwell drew up later, forbade all merchants, Spanish or otherwise, to give any cargo to a foreign ship if a ship flying the royal flag were available.   Indeed, for about a hundred years, the Spanish navy was really prosperous; at the beginning of the sixteenth century it numbered a thousand vessels. Barcelona carried on a prosperous trade with Alexandria, Naples, Sicily and even the Barbary States, and though it gradually declined as a result of the raids of the Turkish pirates and the growing importance of the trans-Atlantic discoveries, trade with America more than compensated Spain for her loss in the Mediterranean. On the north and west the Castilians maintained a flourishing trade with Flanders, London, Nantes and La Rochelle through their ports on the Gulf of Gascony, and Seville shared with Bilbao the valuable monopoly of trade with America.

Industry was no less prosperous. The leather of Cordova, the weapons of Toledo, the paper and silk of Jaen and other places still retained their old reputation. After the reunion of the crowns of Castile and Aragon, Ferdinand and Isabella had wisely encouraged manufactures, and since 1484 had attracted many Italian and Flemish craftsmen to Spain by offering them exemption from taxation for ten years. Such an appeal to the foreigner was then not a symptom of decadence but of progress. They had protected young and struggling industries against the disastrous attacks of foreign competition, and it was in pursuance of this policy that for two years the importation of cloth had been forbidden in Murcia and of Neapolitan silk thread in Granada. During the first half of the sixteenth century the textile trades flourished: linen and silk at Toledo, cloth at Saragossa, where 16,000 looms were at work, and at Barcelona and Valencia. Ocana became famous for its soap, and still more for its gloves, which were known throughout Europe. Seville, Cadiz and Valladolid manufactured articles designed to meet the needs of the colonies.

Agriculture at first seemed to be quite as successful as trade or industry. The Spanish climate was dry, but provided that the farmers would take the trouble to overcome this defect, Spain was well suited to the production of oil, wine, fruit and even grain. The Moors, a race of skilled cultivators, trained in irrigation in a harsher climate, had settled in Spain and had transformed vast stretches of parched land into marvellous gardens and made of Andalusia a fertile and prosperous country, which was a model to all Southern Europe. Even when pitiless fanaticism had driven 400,000 of them from the kingdom of Granada (1492), those who remained were still a source of profit to the heartless country which persecuted them. In remote districts of the Betic Mountains a few of them succeeded in keeping themselves alive, and even to-day you may see the results of their patient and scientific toil in the greater fruitfulness of these places. Until the beginning of the seventeenth century[1] twenty-two thousand Moorish families continued to occupy the plain of Valencia, which they succeeded in turning into the *huerta* or model garden. There the science of irrigation was brought to perfection, and the waters of the Guadalaviar, jealously husbanded, had enabled them to develop plantations of sugar-cane, as well as ordinary Mediterranean products like the mulberry and the orange. Thus during the greater part of the sixteenth century agriculture preserved throughout the kingdom some measure of the prosperity given it by the Moors. The magnificent olive plantations of Andalusia were at their best; the tithe on oil at Seville reached the considerable sum of 32,000 ducats, while the yield was big enough to supply important soap-works. Other crops, unknown to the Moors or avoided by them for religious reasons, were also cultivated: such as flax in the damp northern regions, or, in hot Castile, the vine, which even encroached on cereals. The heavy wines of the uplands found a profitable market in America, while all Europe sought after the famous wines of the south such as Alicante, Malaga and Xeres.

Nevertheless, Spain, in spite of her command of two seas, in spite of the advantage she gained in being the first of the powers to carve out an empire in the New World, suffered a rapid decline. The reasons for this are to be found both in the political and moral life of the country, and in external and internal affairs. It resulted not only from the competition of neighbouring countries, such as Holland, England and France, whose people were more active and industrious and whose policy was more enlightened, but also from a series of mistakes in the conduct of Spanish affairs.

In the first place, the sovereigns did not realise the economic unity of the countries under their sway. Ferdinand and Isabella, indeed, at the end of the fifteenth century, did suppress some of the burdensome seignorial tolls, though only such as had been established in recent years, and in 1496 they issued a decree urging the adoption of a single system of weights and measures. But the natural formation of the

---

[1] Some of the Moors established in this district had perished in the violent agrarian revolt of 1519, when the sailors, workmen and Christian peasants had risen against the big landowners and their Moorish serfs.

peninsula, cut up as it is by rugged mountain ranges, the marked variation in climate from district to district, as well as historical tradition, made their task difficult, and the provincial separatism of Spain has lasted almost to our own times. It was not until Philip V introduced the French idea of big public works that a network of highroads, radiating from Madrid, made communication between the chief cities a little easier.[1] Soon, however, the kings themselves, burdened by the expenses of gigantic wars and a luxurious court, found themselves forced to raise in their own interests the barriers which their predecessors had tried to break down in the interests of commerce. From the reign of Philip II the internal customs duties multiplied, and the *alcabala*, an indirect tax on all purchases and sales, which it was not always possible to escape by means of a contract, was scarcely less harmful to merchants than to artisans. Smuggling spread rapidly, and only served to increase the demand of the royal revenue. Ferdinand and Isabella at least kept their currency from depreciating, but Philip III, when he wanted money, did not hesitate to debase the coinage.

In the second place, the absolute power of the king was used in the interests of the Catholic Church, and this clerical despotism had disastrous results on national life. Philip II, like an Asiatic king, kept majestically aloof in his gloomy palace of the Escurial, built on the model of the gridiron of St. Lawrence. He swept away what remained of seignorial and civic liberty, and pursued his policy of extravagant expenditure, war and intrigue without restraint. He followed his ideal of religious unity to the death, both in Spain and elsewhere, saying, " I would rather reign in a desert than in a country peopled with heretics." Thus the Holy Inquisition, with its attendant train of idle monks and auto-da-fé, triumphed disastrously in Spain. The intellectual life of the nation received a permanent check, since all those who bought, sold or read forbidden books were condemned to lose all their property and be burnt alive. Moreover, all suspected books were seized at the frontier, and thus a sort of intellectual customs barrier was created, which effectively cut Spain off from all contact with foreign culture. Those who followed the teaching of the Reformation were ruthlessly put to

[1] See Saint-Simon, *Mémoires*, vol. xviii, p. 415.

death. Commerce and agriculture declined after the expulsion of the Jews and the persecution of the Moors. In the Low Countries there was a long struggle against the Calvinists and Lutherans, who were destined to shake off the yoke and to become on the sea the most redoubtable enemies of their old lords. Even outside his hereditary dominions, in England, in France and in Sweden, Philip II attempted to impose the rule of the Holy Office, and in pursuit of this fantastic and fanatic ambition he spent the vital force and fortune of his people.

As is usual in such cases the people had their share in responsibility for the general impoverishment. The Aragonese and Castilian nobles were essentially soldiers, whose mission it had been to reconquer Spain from the Moors. This done, it was beneath the dignity of these *hidalgos* to work with their hands or even to employ their money in business; that had been the affair of these Mussulmans and Israelites whom they had driven out, and would still provide employment for the subject populations whom they had freed from the despotism of the Crescent. The eldest sons of the nobility lived in idleness on the revenue of their estates, which were subject to the law of primogeniture; the younger sons, with only their pride for their fortune, were ashamed to work when their elder brothers lived in noble idleness, and preferred to vegetate in noble poverty. If the heads of the great families happened to have any money to dispose of, they did not dream of risking it in business, but dignity—or prudence—counselled them to lend it to the State, in which case it could be entailed. But the worst of all was that the *pecheros*, the descendants of the people liberated by the *hidalgos*, quickly grew to share the prejudices of their new masters. Since they were despised and loaded with taxes like the land-tax, it became the sole aim of the richest and cleverest of them to enter the *hidalguia*. At the end of the seventeenth century there were 625,000 nobles in Spain, at least four times as many as there ever were in France, which had a far larger population; and when at last in 1682 the government decided to issue a proclamation declaring that industry was not degrading, it was too late. The poor found a refuge for their idleness in the monasteries, which increased in number incessantly, and always supported a whole train of beggars. Craftsmanship itself became rare as the population decreased, and the enforced idleness of the too numerous religious festivals reduced still further the amount of effective work that could be obtained from a working class already too few in number.

Spain still had a source of wealth in her colonies, but from them she received little more than precious metals. The treasure was first accumulated in the celebrated Golden Tower, and later made its way to the treasury of the capital by an old Roman road, which is still called to-day the *Camino de la Plata*. The real trade in exotic products was soon to fall into the hands of the Dutch and the English, established at Curaçao and Jamaica, who bought cheaply at Carthagena and Porto-Bello Peruvian bark, indigo and cotton. As to the manufactured articles which Spain sent to America, the consignments were very irregular and depended entirely on the number of ingots which the Indians brought to the factories of the New World; it was useless to attempt to impose upon them a fixed amount of purchases. Moreover, privateers of other nations, Dutch, English and French, intercepted the galleons. In the second half of the seventeenth century Cadiz succeeded to the diminished heritage of Seville, the great city of the Guadalquivir, which was said at certain periods to have had 300,000 inhabitants, of whom 130,000 were workmen. Cadiz tried for a time to increase her trade with the Adriatic and Levantine coasts, but all the foreign trade of the kingdom was hampered by the almost prohibitive duties which the Madrid government, usually for purely fiscal purposes, levied on imports and exports. What chance had trade under these conditions ?

It seemed at first that an important and influential class of rich merchants would grow up in the country, and in fact towards the end of the sixteenth century the merchant-princes of Seville were marrying their daughters to gentlemen. On the other hand, nobles were invited to take a share in great trading ventures, and an edict of 1626 proclaimed that it was not derogatory for a noble to be connected with trade, provided that he did not buy and sell himself or carry on business in his house. But the terrible exactions of a government as ambitious as it was impecunious crushed without pity those who had, at their own risk and peril, grown rich in overseas trade. The government policy was really confiscation; they cloaked it by handing over government stock in exchange, though they usually forgot not only to pay back the capital but even to make up arrears of interest. The officials, who had to be bribed, exerted still further pressure on these voluntary taxpayers; if they were Portuguese Jews they got no mercy. Thus the upper-middle class of Spain died almost as soon as it was born, and that at a time when the country stood in dire need of its ability and its wealth.

Spain was forced to rely instead upon foreigners, against whom, in the early years of the sixteenth century, a whole series of laws had been passed forbidding them to engage in retail trade or to act as middlemen or brokers. Then foreigners had been feared as competitors; now they were regarded as indispensable allies. The king, always in want of money, was the first to welcome the aid of Genoese or German bankers, who demanded in return not only a high rate of interest but also privileges which were still more remunerative. For example, the Fuggers, the celebrated Augsburg bankers, extorted the monopoly of exporting wool, timber and iron; in the same way, in 1700, the town of Santander signed a special agreement with English shippers. The English, following in the track of the Germans and the Dutch, had long since obtained the right to create a special commercial court at Seville or at Cadiz. Five-sixths even of the internal trade had passed out of Spanish hands. When the seventeenth century opened, 160,000 foreigners were already monopolising the large-scale trade, and soon were to seize upon the large-scale industries of the kingdom.

The growth of industry had closely followed the reunion of the crowns of Aragon and Castile. But even during its brief period of prosperity it soon found itself lacking every necessity —capital, middlemen, labour. Not only was manual labour despised, but industry was hampered by a series of laws such as might be expected from an assembly of *hidalgos* entirely lacking in economic knowledge. The Cortes of Castile and Aragon would not have tolerated the presence of a merchant in their midst, and cared only for one thing, to keep down the price of those articles which were necessary to maintain themselves in luxury. Such things they taxed very lightly. At the risk of destroying one of the most important industries in the kingdom, they prohibited the export of fine cloth; and in

Charles V's reign they even went so far as to forbid its manufacture outright, simply in order to oblige the merchants
to import it from Flanders. These men, fanatically devoted
to the military glory and the religion of their country, seemed
in economic affairs to have no conception of the national
interest. Following the luxurious fashion of the day, they
deliberately preferred cloth from Holland, carpets from
Brussels, linen from Antwerp, brocades from Florence, lace
from Paris, plush from Tours—all the finery of France. At
the same time the impoverishment and decreasing numbers of
the working classes caused the home market to shrink still
further. Moreover, the gilds were breaking down under the
weight of the so-called free gifts and contributions, the products of the big manufactures were overwhelmed with exorbitant taxes, and the artisan, harassed by the exorbitant
assessment of the *alcabala,* often found idleness more profitable than work. Under these conditions it is hardly surprising that the expansion of Spanish industry was followed by
a sharp decline.

The woollen industry, which seemed the most firmly
established, was the first to suffer. As early as 1545 the
merchants of Seville could only meet the demands of Porto-
Bello, Carthagena and Vera Cruz by reserving for six years
ahead such quantity of the national production as was
available for disposal abroad. At the end of the sixteenth
century there were no looms at work in Cuenca, and even
Seville, which had gathered up the remnants of its fallen
rival's trade, had only four hundred looms, a total which soon
fell to sixty. The amount of wool woven in the kingdom was
reduced to one-fifth. The silk industry fared rather better.
About the year 1640 Saragossa still had four thousand looms
at work, and Murcia and Valencia also retained their activity.
Seville, Granada and Cordova continued to make luxurious
materials. But already no less than nine-tenths of the total
amount of manufactured articles sent to Mexico and Peru
came from abroad.

Thus the wealth of Spain, except when it was hoarded
in churches or palaces, flowed out of the country to the
foreigner.[1] The gold and silver of the New World simply
passed through Spain, and gave to the land of the *conquista-*

---

[1] See Saint-Simon, *Mémoires*, vol. xviii, pp. 345, 409.

dores only a false and fleeting appearance of wealth. The decadence of native industry soon showed itself in the enormous increase of foreign imports from France, England, Holland, Italy and even from Hamburg, and thus hastened the ruin of those businesses which still survived. Lille and Arras flooded the kingdom with their point lace and tanned leather, Forez and Limousin with their hardware, while the irresistible competition of the foreigner killed the sugar-works of Andalusia and the earthenware manufactories of Talavera.

After the manufactured products came the invasion of the manufacturers themselves. There were many places to be filled, many needs to be supplied in this empty kingdom, among a people who lulled themselves to sleep with dreams of past splendour and of gilded ease. From all sides foreigners swarmed in and settled. First came the Genoese, who, profiting by their strong financial position, bought up, among other big concerns, the soap-works and silk factories of Granada, in spite of the belated and inconsequent protests of the Cortes. Everywhere the foreigners penetrated into the old gilds and corporations, or else formed new ones for themselves alone. The Italians and the French for the most part preferred to fill the places of ordinary artisans. The Italians were usually carpenters, masons or cordwainers, while the men of Limousin or Auvergne were pedlars, ironmongers or water-carriers, and the Béarnese were brickmakers. " I had no difficulty," wrote Gourville[1] towards the end of the seventeenth century, " in discovering that these people were at the same time extremely lazy and extremely vain. There are workmen who make knives, but there would have been none to sharpen them were it not for great numbers of Frenchmen, whom we call ' knife-grinders,' who are spread all over Spain." In 1700 in the capital alone the French colony numbered 40,000 persons, the population of an average town. In spite of the influx of these half-million workers from across the Pyrenees or from the Western Mediterranean, Spain still kept vast resources of wealth hidden and unexploited in her soil. Biscay was rich in ore, but though workmen might be found to mine it, there were none who could smelt it; therefore, iron goods came ready-made from Milan. Chili, the New Spain, had important copper-mines, but the Spanish government had no

[1] Gourville, *Mémoires* (Collection Petitot, 2nd series), vol. lii, p. 411.

foundries capable of providing her with the artillery she needed. Even the wax used in the churches came from England or Holland, or from Morocco by the agency of French merchants,[1] although the flowery meadows of Castile offer so fair a booty for the honey bee. But (if we may press home the metaphor) the Spain of those days was no land for busy bees.

Agriculture suffered as much as industry. In 1609 such Moors as remained in the peninsula were expelled by a royal edict, and fled for refuge to Africa, Asia, and even to France. Whole provinces were depopulated by this new victory of religious fanaticism, and the inhospitable soil which had grown fertile under their care again lay waste. The gravity of the disaster was soon apparent. Two things had contributed to the success of the Moors in agriculture. In the first place, they had constructed a complete system of reservoirs and canals, which they kept in good repair and regulated by an elaborate code of laws. But more especially they had relied upon a system of small-holdings, which were particularly fitted for intensive cultivation. Now the government tried to replace the small Moorish proprietors by farmers from other provinces of Spain. Twelve thousand five hundred families came from Castile and the Asturias, and even from Galicia, to take possession of the abandoned farms of Granada; each of them was given a piece of cultivable land and a share in the vineyards and orchards, on condition that they kept them cultivated and did not alienate them. The government also tried to colonise the deserted plain of Valencia with peasants from Catalonia and the Pyrenees, and some cities, like Jaen, tried in the same way to repeople their empty suburbs. But these experiments were not carried far enough, or only half succeeded, for these barren lands needed hard and unremitting toil, and the toilers were lacking. Many small farmers shrank from the heaviness of the task, or were crushed by the competition of the big landowners.

Spanish society, indeed, was still in a semi-feudal state, which secured the preponderance of the great landowners. The custom of entailing estates, which originated at the end of the fourteenth century, led to the almost indefinite growth

[1] See *Bulletin de la Société d'Histoire moderne* (November, 1913). Article by M. Albert Girard.

of the estates of the great families; the Medina-Cœli estates, for example, were as big as a principality. The uninhabited districts of Lower Andalusia had been, for the most part, distributed in enormous holdings to a small number of great nobles. These rich proprietors hardly ever lived on their estates; they preferred the life of the court. They made no attempt to increase their revenues by improved methods of cultivation, because the worst methods produced enough to support them in luxury, and if by chance the revenue fell short, their government pensions made good the loss. The government attempted to check this evil: Philip III promised noble rank and exemption from military service to any Spaniard who cultivated his land scientifically and profitably, while Philip IV tried to make the nobles live on their estates by abolishing some of the useless posts which kept them at court. But these measures had no success.

The property of the Church, which owned twice as much as the lay nobles, was another factor in the decline of agriculture. The Church had too much power in Spain. She had played so decisive a part in the reorganisation of the nation that the crown could never even have dreamed of secularising any of her possessions. But now that her historic work was done the kings could at least seek to put a stop to any extension of her domains; but when in the eighteenth century they tried to forbid the laity to leave any land to the Church without their permission, they found themselves face to face with relentless opposition. At the end of the seventeenth century the Church owned a sixth of the land of Castile, and showed herself as indifferent to the scientific cultivation of her estates as were the nobles. Moreover, she hoarded capital which otherwise would have been in general circulation, for many rich men on their death-beds left the whole of their fortunes to the Church. The convents, to the exclusion even of all creditors, received the treasures thus invested in the next life.

The extension of big and ill-cultivated estates, the scarcity of labour, the high price of wool throughout Europe and the fineness of the *merino* fleeces in that dry atmosphere—all these causes united to bring about an excessive development of sheep-farming, the only form of farming which could prosper on the barren Spanish uplands. Even so, the flocks of New

Castile had to move up the hills as far as the boundaries of
the Asturias and Leon every summer in search of food and
water, and in the autumn had to move down, sometimes even
as far as Andalusia and Estramadura, to avoid the severe
winter. Natural conditions had prescribed for Spain this
system of migratory pasturage, and historical conditions had
emphasised the necessity. The kingdom of New Castile for
centuries had been no more than a frontier zone, where there
must be no obstacle to check the flight of the cattle in the
event of a sudden raid. Hence the old prohibition to enclose
even the cultivated lands, a prohibition which was gradually
extended to the whole country as the conquest progressed.

As early as the middle of the fourteenth century sheep-
farmers had formed the powerful and celebrated association
known as the *Mesta*, and had obtained privileges which had
twice been confirmed and made general by the crown in 1511
and in 1566. A special strip of land, the *canada*, linking up
the summer and winter pastures, was reserved for them,
so that their flocks could cross the country with adequate
supplies of water and grass. They were, indeed, warned not
to trespass on the crops or meadows which they passed here
and there on their journey and which were intended to provide
food for the working oxen, nor were they allowed to feed
among the vines or olive-trees, at any rate until after the
harvest. But on the track itself and all along the line of the
moving flocks all cultivation and enclosure were absolutely
forbidden, with heavy penalties for disobedience. The prohibited area was gradually enlarged, while the sheep-farmers,
protected by severe laws against the reprisals of the peasants,
strongly organised, rich and in close touch with the government, could ignore all complaints. In the end the *Mesta*
became almost an autonomous government, a state within
the State, with a council and courts of first instance and of
appeal, and the interests of agriculture were mercilessly sacrificed to it.

For more than a century the Spanish kings acted as though
the production of wool were the sole source of their greatness.
They gave shepherds exemption from taxation, and in answer
to the requests of the Cortes, which was dominated by the
sheep-farmers, they took every precaution to stop the " encroachment " of tillage. From 1550 to 1630 edict after edict

was issued ordering that public and municipal land which
had been cleared should be allowed to relapse into its natural
state, under the pretext of maintaining the low price of wool,
leather and meat, and of securing raw material for the cloth
manufactures and the success of the principal export of the
kingdom.   In 1580 this war against cultivation was carried
into private estates: all land which had been pasture at any
time during the previous twenty years, whatever it had been
used for since, must return to pasturage.   Moreover, in order
to prevent in future any mischievous extension of cultivated
land, it was stipulated that " land could not be sold without
stock "—that is to say, that henceforth no land could be alienated unless it was to be used for sheep-farming.   In the same
year also a purely nominal sum was made the fixed charge for
the use of pastures, thus giving to the sheep-farmers what
was, to all intents and purposes, free access to private pastures.

People realised, rather late, that the production of cereals
was endangered by this curious system, and proposed measures
to avert the danger.   First they tried severity: in 1558
Philip II ordered every husbandman to sow his land at least
once in three years.   When this failed they tried encouragement: in 1594 it was made illegal to seize farmers' cattle or
their machinery or their cornfields, except for debts to the
State or to the proprietor who had advanced them money.
Moreover, the insolvent farmer must not be imprisoned during
the second six months of the year; he must get in his harvest
first and pay his penalty afterwards !   In 1619 a further
concession was made.   The sheep of the small farmers, which
provided the manure indispensable for cultivation, were
exempt, up to the number of a hundred, from confiscation,
except for the payment of tithes.   But these protective
measures could help agriculture but little, when the whole
trend of the fiscal and commercial policy of the government
was opposed to it.

To relieve the distress of the Treasury, indirect taxes were
multiplied, and in order to obtain a sufficient return and at
the same time to make contraband trade more difficult, articles
of general consumption—that is, agricultural products such as
wine, oil, leather and meat—were taxed over and over again.
When Philip III on his accession demanded an extraordinary
subsidy of eighteen million ducats spread over eight years

these articles again bore the burden. The government prevented the farmer from putting any part of his burden on to the consumer, by taxing his products directly, by fixing the selling price and by surrounding their sale with innumerable restrictions. But in order to secure, nevertheless, a cheap supply of the necessities of life they deliberately forbade the export of grain, leather and even of wool—except the finest varieties which only foreigners could sell—and of native silks, although, in this article at least, free import was allowed.

Meanwhile the home market was becoming more restricted every day, for the fall in population resulted in decreased demand. Moreover, the decline of the woollen industry reacted on sheep-rearing. About 1480 the successful competition of imported cloth had reduced the number of sheep in Murcia from 50,000 to 8,000 head. In Philip II's reign the all-powerful *Mesta* saw their flocks reduced from seven million head to two, and although at the beginning of Philip III's reign fine wool was exported in larger quantities than before, this increase was merely another symptom of the decay of home manufacture. It was small wonder if in the end the farmers lacked both the means and the courage to continue so ruinous a business.

Such, in fact, was the case. In the western and north-western provinces, which were more suitable for stock-breeding, the peasants continued to use oxen for ploughing, but in Castile they began to employ mules, which were both quicker and cheaper. The trouble was that these animals, whose price, moreover, rose rapidly, were no use for deep ploughing. Only horses, in fact, can plough both quickly and deeply, and since in central Spain the use of horses for this purpose was unknown, their ploughing merely scratched the surface of the ground. Equally inadequate were their methods of clearing the soil. In the north the farmers attacked the thistles three or four times a year, but the Castilians only once. As a result their crops were very poor. Everywhere the irrigation canals fell into disrepair, even round Toledo, where the farmers were reduced to depending upon the scanty rainfall which a charitable west wind might bring them, while in Aragon the irrigated land was a mere oasis in an arid desert. On the other hand, in places where the marshes might have been drained, as in the Avila district, no one thought of doing it. Save for a narrow strip of country along the coasts, the whole peninsula began to look deserted, and this appearance was heightened by the wastage of such scanty woods as nature had given to this parched country. The sheep-farmers of the *Mesta* had the right of cutting all the wood they needed for making bridges or for any other purpose, and they probably abused their privilege. And if some miserable little copse had managed to survive among the fields, the peasant hastened to cut it down, on the pretext that its shade interfered with the ripening of his crops and that it attracted thieving birds from all the ends of the sky.

Wider and wider stretched the gloomy pall of the steppes. In 1688 it was shown that near Segovia there existed an entirely uninhabited *despoblado*,[1] sixty miles in circumference. In Philip III's reign it was calculated that in the province of Salamanca the numbers of cultivators and of head of stock had both decreased by half. Even at the beginning of the seventeenth century the country could not feed its population, which, however, was not increasing, and the government was obliged to give permanent permission for the importation of grain. In the next century it was necessary to promise exemption from taxation to the bakers who supplied Seville. While the population of the Atlantic coasts almost entirely neglected the resources offered them by the great northern fisheries, on the shores of the Mediterranean the mulberry groves were dying and the yield from the olives decreased year by year.[2] Moreover, in spite of all the privileges offered to them, the farmers did not marry and settle down, but sometimes even left the country. Some enlisted in the army and went to fight in the outlying domains of the king, in Italy or Flanders. There they were killed or won promotion; in either case they did not return. Others embarked on the galleons bound for America. In 1681, 6,000 went out in one convoy, "driven by necessity, since they could not make a living in Spain." In some years the total emigration of all kinds reached the enormous total of 50,000

[1] A district which used to be inhabited and has since become a sort of desert.

[2] The people of the Mediterranean coasts did, however, gather great quantities of sea-weed rich in soda. The export of the ashes was worth about £1,000,000 a year.

persons, almost all young men of marriageable age. Of those who remained too many found a refuge from an active and useful life by becoming beggars or monks. As early as 1618 the Cortes had protested in vain against the excessive number of monks, and had asked that the age for taking the final vows, and even for entering the noviciate, should be raised. At the end of the century the clergy, taken as a whole, formed at least a thirtieth part of the population. Thus agriculture, like industry, suffered from a shortage of workers, and Spain in future had to rely even for her food supply on foreigners, especially on the French. " Guienne and other provinces," wrote Gourville, " send many men to Spain to reap and thresh the grain. These men are called *gavaches* by the Spaniards, who despise them heartily. Nevertheless, they carry off the greater part of their employers' money to France."[1] Moreover, by pretending to be Walloons or Burgundians, they even escaped the tax on foreign labour.

This almost universal neglect of the economic life of the nation finally resulted in widespread poverty and the loss of political energy. As early as 1621 the Cortes had sounded the alarm: " If this evil continues, there will soon be no peasants to work on the land, no pilots on the sea, none to marry. The kingdom cannot possibly survive another hundred years unless some effective remedy be found." The kingdom did survive, but only as a shadow of its former self. On the morrow of the Peace of the Pyrenees (1659) Philip IV could only muster 15,000 men against the Portuguese, and Italians or Flemish formed the bulk even of this insignificant army. Under Charles II the Mediterranean coasts were so ill defended that the Moors took courage and began their raids again. Segovia, in 1669, was almost deserted, the population of Madrid itself at the end of the seventeenth century had fallen from 400,000 to 150,000, while the population of the whole kingdom was only five millions.

What was the position of the working classes in the midst of this disaster ? In considering this question a distinction must be made between the small farmers and the wage-earners in town and country. The farmers, who formed a very necessary but rapidly decreasing class, obtained some tardy relief from the government. They were allowed to delay the pay-

[1] Gourville, *op. cit.*

ment of their rent, and, in some provinces, after the harvest
had been valued, they were even allowed some relief in the
conditions of their leases. Many, moreover, possessed long
leases, and profited by the increased prices of their products,
which resulted from the general decay of agriculture. Moreover, the excess of money was equivalent to a corresponding
fall in rents, in cases where these were fixed once and for all.
Thus one section of the working class preserved a relative
prosperity. But what was the case of the day-labourers ?
Most of them did not possess even a small patch of ground;
on the plains of Lower Andalusia they lived in big villages like
those of South Italy. Moreover, there were too many of
them; at the end of the seventeenth century there were
150,000 voluntary or involuntary loafers roaming about the
country. The competition of foreign labour beat down their
claims. As a general rule, the price of living rose much more
quickly than the nominal rates of wages, and when, as a result
of the depreciation of money and the heavy imports, the price
of bread and wine was almost trebled, wages were scarcely
doubled. In this wretched country, where even the rich were
needy, the poor were miserable.

In the eighteenth century, however, it seemed that the time
of recovery had come. In the reign of Philip V the economic
situation improved, and this improvement was shown in new
activity and some return even of external splendour. But
it was especially in the reign of Charles III (1759–1788) that
two energetic ministers, Campomanes and Florida Blanca,
undertook the enormous task of regeneration. The cloth
industry was established anew at Guadalajara and at San-
Fernando, a great linen factory at San Ildefonso, a royal
armament factory at Toledo, which sought to revive the
former industrial fame of the old capital. But as was
natural they turned their energies chiefly to the revival of
agriculture. Labourers were brought from Switzerland,
Flanders and Bavaria to repeople and recultivate the deserts
of the Sierra Morena, and in a few years nearly sixty villages
had arisen on the abandoned lands. To encourage agricultural science sixty or more societies were founded, and the
Bank of St. Charles was created to make advances to poor
farmers. The privileges of the *Mesta* were attacked at last.
The Imperial Canal, begun by Charles V to water the valley

of the Ebro above Saragossa, was finished; canals were opened at Mancanares, Guadarrama and Murcia. Even then the kingdom could not do without foreign corn, but it was estimated that, during this vigorous reign, the population increased from seven to eleven millions, and the public revenue was trebled.

Unhappily the accession of Charles IV (1788) was to open for Spain a new era of decadence and misfortune.

§ 2. Portugal.

The heroic age: commercial and colonial expansion—Seizure by Spain; victorious rivalry of the Dutch; economic protectorate of England.

In the dawn of modern history Portugal seemed destined to play a great part. Checked on land by Spain, who hemmed her in on all sides, she launched forth on her only free frontier, the Atlantic. Hers was the glory of discovering the western coast and indeed the whole continent of Africa, and it seemed that she must be the first to profit by it.

Indeed, throughout the fifteenth century, the Portuguese continued the adventurous voyages of discovery which the merchants of Genoa and Dieppe had already undertaken, to the Canaries and the Azores, and even to the Ivory and Gold Coasts. While King John II was completing the foundation of an absolute monarchy (1481–1495), Prince Henry the Navigator was launching from Cape St. Vincent, where he had established his Academy, his school of explorers, methodical expeditions which, going a little further each time, skirted the coast of the mysterious African continent and in the end sailed round it. In 1487 the Cape of Storms was doubled and became the Cape of Good Hope. At Lisbon in those days high hopes were cherished. Spain alone was to share these unknown worlds. An imaginary line passing 270 leagues west of the Azores was to be the boundary between the two powers. In 1498 Vasco da Gama, having sailed up the eastern coast of Africa, braved the Indian Ocean and reached Malabar. Columbus might have discovered unsuspected lands, but this was the direct route to the spice country. It was certainly longer than the Mediterranean and Red Sea route, of which the Arabs and the Venetians had long been

masters, but it had the advantage of needing no tranship-
ment and no middleman, and it was to become the highroad
for European shipping. Once they had conquered the
Egyptian fleets which Venice sent against them in the Sea of
Oman, the Portuguese were masters of the Indian waters.

Year after year discoveries and conquests succeeded each
other. In 1500 Alvarez Cabral was driven by a storm on to the
coasts of Brazil, which the government peopled with exiled
Jews and convicts. Then Ormuz and Socotra were occupied, and relations opened with Persia. Portuguese adventurers crossed the Straits of Malacca and penetrated as far as
Java and the Moluccas, the country of pepper, cinnamon
and ginger. They ventured as far as China (1517), whose
only means of communication with the West hitherto had
been by a long and dangerous journey across Asia. They
reached Japan, where they had a friendly reception. As they
advanced further east they were astonished in 1528 to meet
the Spaniards who had reached the same point by the opposite western route, and a new line was necessitated, a line of
demarcation this time, to divide the globe between these
two nations who found themselves neighbours again in the
Antipodes.

In their advance to the Far East the Portuguese had not
found, like the Spaniards, countries which were semi-bar-
barous and easy of conquest; they had had to deal with peoples
who were highly civilised, rich, and concentrated in great and
populous cities. Therefore, except in Brazil,[1] their system of
colonisation differed widely from that of Spain. They took
possession of some promontory, island, or place which could be
easily defended, and created along the Coasts of the countries
where they gained a footing, a chain of factories and forts,
often separated one from another by great distances. The
important point for them was to have markets where they
could barter their European goods for the eastern products
of the surrounding population. The governors of these
scattered posts often suffered terrible attacks, which they
repulsed with desperate energy.

It was the heroic age of Portugal, the age which has been
celebrated by her famous poet, Camoëns. " Lisbon the
Great," which dethroned Venice, was magnificent in its

---

[1] See *Le Travail en Amérique avant et après Colomb*, by L. Capitan.

luxury, its pride and its wealth. " The man who has not seen Lisbon has seen nothing beautiful," says a contemporary proverb. It was the enchanted city of the West. This small nation, which had created a vast empire, had its moment of splendour.

But the nation was indeed too small to furnish for long the men necessary for the administration and defence of these immense and distant possessions.

The long struggles against the Moors and the Castilians had weakened her. Alemtejo, the province immediately south of the Tagus, was half deserted, and packs of wolves roved throughout the country. As early as 1505 one of the ships in Almeïda's great expedition was manned by a crew of rustics who could hardly tell port from starboard. Soon convicts and negroes were enlisted, and in 1538 a free pardon was offered to all condemned men who would embark for the Indies. Of the thousands who went out, not one in ten returned; the rest perished, or deserted, or disappeared on strange adventures. Plague and famine also did their work, and, added to this curse of excessive emigration, reduced the population, during the sixteenth century, from two millions to hardly more than one. To supply the lack of labour in the country of the south, slaves had been introduced. This discredited agricultural work, and the husbandmen sold their farms and crowded into the towns. The plague of the *latifundia*[1] spread, and this new infusion of African blood debased the race itself. Moreover, the ports had behind them too narrow a strip of territory to maintain a big trade. The wool of Algarve and the wines of Oporto were not enough to provide permanent freight for vessels, while the mountain ores were not worked and industry scarcely existed on Portuguese territory.

In her colonies the State claimed the absolute ownership of all newly discovered lands, and for some time even restricted the right of trading to government ships. This was not done to hasten the growth of a mercantile marine, for the Portuguese themselves did not distribute the exotic cargoes on which they made such enormous profits. At first they had carried them as far as Antwerp, but soon they waited for their customers to come to Lisbon to fetch them. The

[1] Big estate run by slave labour.—M. R.

Dutch took over this profitable business, and at the same time brought with them manufactured articles from Europe, so that the Portuguese spent the greater part of the profits of their Indian trade on paying for foreign imports.   The crowning misfortune was that the governors and officials of the colonies, who were changed frequently lest they should show any signs of independence, devoted themselves to getting rich quickly and traded on their own account.   The slave-trade, in which the Portuguese specialised, enriched individuals, but did not suffice to keep up a steady flow of commerce.

Then, at the very moment when Holland was breaking away from the Spanish domination, Portugal suffered conquest and annexation at the hands of Spain, who was to drag her down in her own fall (1580).   Their union simply offered a wider field and an easier prey to their enemies.   The new masters of the country forbade their subjects to hold any intercourse with the rebellious Dutch, who at once attacked the ill-defended Portuguese colonies.   The Jews were expelled and carried their money to Holland and France.   The Inquisition was carried abroad to inflame the natives by persecution and to provoke revolts and wars by the indiscreet zeal of its missionaries.   Thus in 1637 the Portuguese were expelled from Japan as a result of the trouble caused by the Jesuits, to whom these old civilisations did not offer the same opportunities as did the indolent and ignorant inhabitants of Paraguay.   In the mother-country the demands of a luxurious Church absorbed the greater part of the treasures amassed by the government.

Thus year by year the Portuguese Empire was torn to shreds.   English privateers plundered her galleons and even Lisbon itself.   Dutch fleets seized islands and factories, reducing the Portuguese possessions in the Indian Ocean to a few small stations, and even seizing a part of Brazil (Guiana).

When, after sixty years, the little state recovered her independence, she no longer had the means to re-establish her short-lived prosperity.   Delivered by the help of France, it was not long before she fell under the economic protectorate of England. In 1703, by the Methuen Treaty, England agreed to buy her wines from Portugal, on condition that Portugal should purchase her manufactured goods, as far as possible, from England. The demand for port and madeira became so great that almost the whole productive activity of the country was concentrated on this trade and on the exploitation of the forests of cork-oak. Emigration ceased in the wine-growing provinces of the north, but such little manufacturing activity as the country had ever possessed soon disappeared, and the kingdom became dependent on its tyrannical protectors even for its food supplies.

For fifty years Portugal lay dormant. She still possessed one big colony, Brazil, where since 1680 the gold mines had been worked, and where in 1729 diamond mines had been discovered. Thence also she received three times a year a fleet of a hundred sailing vessels, laden with valuable cargoes of sugar, tobacco, precious woods, cocoa and indigo. But very few of these riches touched Lisbon. Her splendid bay held more ships than any other port in Europe, except London and Amsterdam, but they belonged to the shipowners of England, Holland, Italy, Hamburg, Sweden, Spain or France. The Portuguese nation received no profit from this trade to which they gave protection; and although the royal Treasury derived considerable sums from it, in spite of fraud, by customs dues, royal tolls and monopolies, they were swallowed up by the all-powerful Church. The country was drained of gold coinage; it was with Portuguese gold that the English, notably, paid their debts all over the world. This explains the excitement of all Europe at the news of the earthquake which, in 1755, destroyed three-quarters of this splendid international market, the El Dorado of the West.

At last a daring minister exerted himself to awaken Portugal from this deadly torpor. Pombal broke the ecclesiastical yoke and tried to shake off the heavy tutelage of England. In spite of the Methuen Treaty he set up powder, sugar and silk manufactures (1750–1752), and about 1760 he established cloth, paper and glass works. The economic principles which inspired this energetic reformer may seem old-fashioned, but when he forbade the exportation of precious metals, circumstances justified this apparent return to the narrowest mercantilist practices. When he created the Company of the Upper Douro (1756), to which he gave the monopoly of the port-wine trade, it was in order to break up the burdensome monopoly hitherto enjoyed by an association of English traders. When he founded the privileged Company of Upper Para and of Marañon, it was in order to restrain the mischievous power exercised over the whole administration of Brazil by the Jesuits.[1]

But Pombal had aroused too much enmity. He was overthrown in 1777, and only part of his work survived him. Portugal enjoyed no more than a moderate degree of prosperity until she was involved, like Spain, in the Napoleonic upheaval.

BIBLIOGRAPHY[2]

SPAIN

ALTAMIRA Y CREVEA: *Historia de España y de la Civilisâçion española,* vol. iii. Barcelona. 2nd edition. 1909-1911 (4 vols.).

HUME, M. A. S.: *Spain, its Greatness and Decay.* 1898.

MARIÉJOL: *L'Espagne sous Ferdinand et Isabelle.* Paris, 1892.

RANKE: *Histoire de l'Espagne sous Charles-Quint, Philippe II, et Philippe III* (translated into French, 1873).

WEISS, CH.: *L'Espagne depuis le règne de Philippe II jusqu'à l'avènement des Bourbons.* Paris, 1844 (2 vols.).

PORTUGAL

BOUCHOT: *Histoire du Portugal.*

GASTINEL: *Le désastre de Lisbonne.* (Revue du xviiiᵉ siècle, 1913.)

---

[1] Note also the foundation of a company of the fishermen of Algarve (1753), and the creation of a School of Commerce (1759).

[2] Our thanks are due to M. André Paul, *diplomé* of the École des Chartes, who has given us very valuable assistance in the preparation of this chapter.

CHAPTER II

THE NETHERLANDS

The Netherlands, in the Middle Ages, had been among the richest and most industrious countries in Europe. Thickly populated and studded with communes jealous of their independence, they were as famous for their cloth manufacture as were the Italian cities, and during the fourteenth century they had even, thanks to their regular communications with the Levant, introduced the manufacture of cotton. Bruges had been a great centre of commerce and of banking. Ghent and Liège had had gilds as active as those of Florence. The country had been a huge market, the meeting-place of the people and products of North and South, and was quite ready to profit by the great geographical discoveries which marked the end of the fifteenth century.

But, during the period we are studying, a division hitherto latent was to come to light. The South, where French and Flemings shared the country, was an industrial and commercial district; there were many prosperous towns, and the influence of the French and English was predominant. In the North the mouths of the Scheldt, the Meuse and the Rhine formed an inextricable network, and the country consisted of canals, islands, marshes and land reclaimed from the sea and constantly menaced by it. Here the people were fishermen and stock farmers, amongst whom German influence was strongest.

Moreover, the religious question, which in the sixteenth century cut Europe in two, caused a similar division in the Low Countries. In the end the South remained Catholic and subject to the King of Spain, the heir of the house of Burgundy. This settlement was only reached, however, after a struggle, after revolts had been cruelly suppressed, and local liberties crushed. The North, protected by the waters which surrounded and even, in time of need, covered it, maintained for thirty-seven years a heroic struggle against Philip II, the most powerful prince of the time. Protestants and Republicans, the inhabitants of Holland, Friesland, and the Seven United Provinces, won for themselves liberty of conscience and self-government. The " Beggars of the Sea," as they were called, drove their enemies back. William the Silent, Prince of Orange, the incarnation of the Puritan and patriot spirit, was assassinated, but he left behind him a free people, flushed with victory and still thrilled with the excitement of battle.

There was thus a deep division between the two regions which composed the Low Countries, and they must be considered separately.

§ 1. The Spanish Netherlands (later Austrian).

Extension of foreign commerce: Antwerp, the chief international market and financial centre of the sixteenth century—Creation of great industrial concerns: growth of the proletariat—Increase of urban population—Rapid decay at the end of the sixteenth century.

It is most convenient to begin with those provinces which remained Spanish and which, in view of their past, were in a position to take immediate advantage of the shifting of the commercial centre of Europe.

Between 1550 and 1566 alone the volume of their trade increased twofold with Spain, threefold with Portugal, France and Germany, and more than tenfold with England. This rapid growth of foreign commerce, combined with the excellence of the roads and waterways which intersected the plains of the interior, brought about the concentration of trade in one or two privileged places. Bruges tried to maintain her former supremacy on a new basis, but in vain did she insist on her old rights as a staple town and her privilege as the port of entry for imported wool. Her port, which was becoming silted up, was deserted by ships, and the new merchant fleets made Antwerp their centre. Antwerp, placed in a commanding position on the mouths of the Scheldt, increased in size until her population numbered 200,000. Soon it was said that Antwerp did as much business in one month as Venice in two years. In the town there were about a thousand business houses, while every week fifty vessels sailed into port, not to speak of eight or nine hundred fishing-boats. Customs duties brought in 726,000 florins a year. About 1550, however, the lawless city of Ghent, equipped with a new constitution, appeared as a rival of this youthful metropolis. Ghent opened up independent communication with the sea by way of Ternewzen. Five hundred of her ships left her quays to carry cloth and linen to Norway, returning laden with timber; others sailed to Muscovy for furs or to the Guinea coast for salt. Others, again, took the haberdashery and ironmongery of Nuremburg to the Angola coast; there they traded them for slaves, who were easily exchanged in Brazil for sugar and dye-wood. At Brussels forty canal wharves were constructed, so that foreign wool could be disembarked at the very doors of the fabric factories. Brussels was also the centre of the system of imperial posts, which had been organised by Charles V, and which could be used by private individuals.[1]

But it was Antwerp which became the great market for all the products of the known world. London was still no more than a branch, where the merchants from the other side of the North Sea had opened magnificent shops instead of the humble brush and earthenware stalls of forty years earlier. Merchants from all over the world met in the new Flemish metropolis and found themselves welcome, a contrast with Bruges, which was already half dead behind the barriers with which she still bristled. Antwerp was the capital of a " world common to all nations," and already offered to international commerce all the facilities of modern life. Every year two great fairs were held there, each lasting twenty days; but in reality this city of 200,000 inhabitants presented the appearance and played the part of a universal and continuous fair. In addition to the merchants who bought and sold on their own account, there grew up a class of wealthy commission-agents, whose speculations tended to regulate prices. Money was naturally plentiful, and Antwerp, as well as being the chief centre of trade, became also the chief money-market of the time, and was the headquarters of the most powerful German and Italian banks. They tried, however, to reduce

[1] As early as 1504 Maximilian of Austria, Count of Flanders, had arranged with the family of Taxis, originally of Bergamo, to establish postal communications between the Low Countries and the courts of the Emperor, of France and of Spain. In 1516 his grandson Charles, before he became Charles V, extended this service to the courts of Rome and Naples. Couriers from Brussels took a fortnight to reach Naples, but only five or six days to Innsbrück, and thirty-six hours to Paris.

the export and import of bullion to a minimum, and used a system of notes of hand, which were the forerunners of our cheques. Vast enterprises were launched by men who had at their command ten or a hundred times as much capital as could have been mustered by the old burgess-traders, the *poorters.* The men who made these great fortunes were rarely the sons of the old merchant class, who, if they were not ruined by the progress of commerce, took refuge in the more peaceful, humble careers offered by government service and the liberal professions. Men of a new type, starting from the foot of the ladder, prepared to risk anything, true *conquistadores* of commerce, were needed to endure the feverish existence which led to the heights of wealth along the verge of the abyss of bankruptcy.

Capitalism, which had transformed commerce, also changed the conditions of industry. The old gilds clung jealously to their most strongly established privilege, the control of the municipal food supply. Further than this they could not go. The textile industry, which supplied an enormous and scattered market, escaped almost entirely from their control. New cloth factories were established in the town of Ghent itself, but it was only after 1540, when the gild organisation had been broken up. Following the example of the English clothiers, against whom the national industry was beginning to see the necessity of defence, great cloth manufactures, founded with the financial help of the wealthy burghers of Antwerp, were set up in the country, where they escaped all gild restrictions and where labour was plentiful. It was natural that the new manufactures of satin, ribbons, velveteen and glass should adopt without hesitation from the very beginning the more modern and freer of the two types of organisation between which they could choose. In the same way mining and metallurgical enterprises were undertaken in the neighbourhood of Liège, which was excellently situated at the cross-roads between Germany and the Netherlands, and was near Namur and in Hainault.

This brilliant industrial expansion expressed itself in magnificent feasts and merrymaking,[1] but the mass of ordinary workpeople obtained no benefit from it. Although the journeymen of the old crafts had lost all hope of becoming

[1] See Taine, *Philosophie de l'Art dans les Pays-Bas*, p. 96.

masters, a rank which was barred to them by exorbitant fees, if by nothing else, they had at least lived with their masters in a sort of domestic familiarity, and the kindness with which they were usually treated made up for the growing inefficiency of the old system of relief, which ceased to operate as the gilds fell into debt. The new working class, on the other hand, was left entirely without support or protection. The big manufacturer could please himself as to the conditions under which they worked and the rate of their pay. He could recruit his labour from any part of the countryside indiscriminately; indeed, workers offered themselves, superabundantly and on all hands, an inorganic mob, whose very numbers were a source of weakness, and who were incapable of uniting to offer a serious resistance. The factories pressed into their service beggars, the sons of paupers who had learnt a trade at some charitable institution, and even children five or six years old.

The workmen often emigrated from the town in order to live at the gates of a factory established in the suburbs. On the other hand, when the factory was built in the town, the workmen from the surrounding districts who were employed in it ceased to return every evening to their native villages. Altogether the number of towns, already considerable, increased still more.[1] The fate of this city proletariat became precarious, especially after 1550, when the price of food rose sharply without a proportionate rise in wages. Then for the first time was seen the width of the gulf which was henceforth to separate the mob of workmen, who had no resource but their wages, from the rich manufacturers, who lived like lords in a brilliant luxury. The difference between the two classes was so great that in some places there grew up an intermediate class of factors (*Winkelmeesters*), who directed on behalf of the urban employers the small country workshops employing between thirty and sixty workmen. They received the raw material from the employers, and every Sunday handed over to them the week's work. The excessive misery of the workers provoked some violent risings, but since the rioters were usually ill-armed, ill-fed and ill-led, the burgher militia had little difficulty in reducing them to order. The rich suffered only in so far as they had to rebuild a few

[1] " The whole of Flanders is one continuous town," wrote Guicciardini.

pillaged granaries and to allow a provisional reduction in
the price of bread.   When Calvinism was introduced, great
numbers of industrial workers accepted it, hoping to get some
advantage from any change in the established order.   But as
a result they seemed to gain, rather than lose, interest in the
economic and political struggle.   To shake off the tyranny of
the Duke of Alva they were ready to proclaim a general strike.

These social divisions, however, seemed to be the natural
price of progress, and would not have been enough to check
it had not Philip II's blindness brought about the decline of
the whole country at the end of the sixteenth century.   Religious persecution of heretics and the ferocious war to retain
the mastery at least of the wealthy southern provinces, caused
many people to emigrate, and covered the land with ruins.[1]
Antwerp was twice besieged, saw her port half choked by a
sea-wall, and was sacked; only her dead body remained for
Spain.   The fields were deserted, the towns depopulated;
wolves were seen even in the outskirts of Ghent.   The trade
of Antwerp received its death-blow when, in 1598, Philip II
prohibited merchants established there from all direct traffic
with America and the Indies.

Yet such were the native or acquired qualities of the
Flemish race, " its vital good sense, the fruitfulness which
was the result of continual labour," its ancient superiority
in the science of commerce, that the Spanish Netherlands
preserved some measure of prosperity.

After the death of Philip II they had a breathing-space
under the peaceful rule of the Archduke Albert and his
wife Isabella (1599–1633), who allowed provinces and towns
at any rate a shadow of autonomy.   They confirmed the
charters of the old gilds, but at the same time granted privileges and new manufactures.   Brussels and Malines stole
from Venice the secret of making fine lace.

The people continued to live luxurious, easy lives, careful
of their own comfort, and animated by an all-pervading good-
humour.   Round the tables of the inns, amid the smoke of
their pipes, they developed, now that peace had come again,
into a people at once Catholic and pagan, who united the
practice of an accommodating faith with the excesses of un-
bridled sensuality.   The paintings of Rubens, Jordaens and

[1] See Taine, *op. cit.*, p. 119.

Teniers represent to the life this motley civilisation, which was perhaps not remarkable for elegance and refinement, but which had a certain vulgar robustness and vigour. The towns doubtless did not recover their splendour and activity. At Antwerp, where, in 1602, the citizens had still been able to subscribe a great part of the shares of the Dutch India Company, the mania for gambling killed all fertile speculation and an English traveller declared that he had never seen forty people at once in one street. But comfort reigned inside the houses, while abundance had returned to the countryside. The fairs witnessed scenes of furious high spirits. In fact, if the satisfaction of material needs be accepted as the criterion of a people's happiness, it may be said that the Low Countries were again a happy land.

But then came the wars of Louis XIV, when the country was to be the battle-field between France and Austria. Vast strips of territory, including Lille, Douai, Valenciennes and Cambrai, were seized and became the possession of France, while the armies plundered and ravaged what remained. When, in 1714, the provinces passed under the domination of Austria, they were ruined, their spirit was broken, and they were subject to foreign, and especially French, influence. In vain did the Emperor Charles VI try to found at Ostend a great trading company (1723); English jealousy soon forced him to abandon the project. Joseph II was no more successful in winning from the Dutch the opening of the Scheldt, and Antwerp had to wait for the conquests of Revolutionary France before she revived her maritime life. Yet this tenacious people still preserved the memory of their ancient freedom and their industrial traditions, both of which were destined to bear fruit in our own times.

§ 2. The United Provinces.

Importance of the fishing-fleet; cheap freight—Amsterdam inherits the commercial supremacy of Antwerp; the Dutch, " carriers of Europe " —Foundation of a colonial empire—Accumulation of capital; development of industry—Progress of agriculture: intensive stock breeding, horticulture—General comfort—Decline at the beginning of the eighteenth century.

Economic supremacy passed to the Protestant Low Countries of the North, which, freed from Spanish domination, formed, in 1581, the United Provinces. At first the habits of the people were simple, education was more general there than elsewhere, and the citizens, careful of their own rights and respecting the rights of others, had that vital feeling of equality which should be characteristic of a republic. Work was regarded as honourable, and public opinion did not tolerate idleness. In the words of the Venetian ambassadors, " These people are so inclined to industry and toil that there is no task so difficult that they will not undertake to finish it. . . . They were born to toil and to deny themselves, and all do work in one way or another." " They dislike bad management and idleness so much," says another witness, Parival, "that there are places where the magistrates shut up idle vagabonds and people who cannot manage their own affairs, and there they are forced to work and earn their bread." Moreover, religious toleration, a new principle which was the clearest and best result of the religious wars, was widely practised in Holland, especially with regard to foreigners. The Jews, who elsewhere were persecuted or at least harassed and threatened, took refuge there in great numbers. It was the sanctuary of all dissenters. Descartes went thither from France in search of some retreat where he might elaborate without fear his method and his doctrine. Baruch Spinoza there professed theories which in any other country would have led him straight to the stake. Painting, like independent thought, flourished in this atmosphere, wherein every energy was employed.

Even before they had won their independence the Dutch had found a source of wealth in their fisheries. From the day when Beuzelzoon had invented a more practical way of preserving and packing herrings, his countrymen had begun actively to exploit the North Sea banks. They had carried their fish to the mouths of all the European rivers from the Vistula to the Seine, especially to the Rhine, the Meuse and the Scheldt. In the middle of the seventeenth century a fifth of the population made its living by this industry, and it used to be said that Amsterdam was " built on herringbones." Thus the Dutch had become the finest sailors in the world. An English vessel of a hundred tons needed a crew of thirty men to work her; in a Dutch ship of the same tonnage eight men were enough. Dutch freights, therefore, remained for a long time the cheapest in Europe, and as late as 1750 it was

3

estimated that the charges of Dutch shippers were twelve per cent. lower than those of the French. Moreover, the country itself, even though it did not directly produce the materials necessary for shipbuilding, was so situated that it could easily procure them from the northern states. Rich merchants, ready to take risks in more or less distant ventures, had alone been wanting, and these also were at hand. When the prosperity of Antwerp was disturbed by the Spaniards and the struggle they aroused, and when the fleets of Zealand succeeded in barring the mouths of the Scheldt, the merchants of that great metropolis had quickly emigrated to Amsterdam, which inherited its greatness. By the middle of the seventeenth century vast docks and big sheltered quays had been built, and this fishing port became the chief commercial centre of the world, with a population of about 300,000 persons.

In fact, by this time, the Dutch had become, to use the classic phrase, " the waggoners of the seas." In the first place, they were the agents of Europe; they were responsible for exchange of the products of the North, timber, corn, iron, hemp and furs, with the wine and spirits of more southerly countries. " Norway is their forest; Prussia and Poland their granaries; the Rhine, the Garonne and the Dordogne their vineyards; Germany, Spain and Ireland their sheep-fold." They went as far afield as Naples in search of silk, as far as Cyprus for fine wools. They could boast that they, " like the bee, sucked honey in every clime." As to the products of India, of the Far East and of America, they would doubtless have been content to fetch them from the quays of Lisbon, Cadiz and Seville, but these ports had been closed to them in 1580 by the stupidity of Philip II. Less than fifteen years after this interdict, Houtman, the first of a line of bold pioneers, reached distant Java. Several companies were formed among the former subjects of the King of Spain to exploit this new domain stolen from their former masters. The vigorous competition of these companies increased the price of commodities in the East and cheapened them in Europe, and therefore, in 1602, they united to form the great Dutch East India Company. A great part of the six and a half million florins of original capital was subscribed by the towns and provinces, so that the enterprise took on a national character.

The Company had the sole right of navigation in the Indian Ocean and in the Pacific, and also the right of making conquests there. At every renewal of the charter, the States-General claimed an increasing share in the profits of these conquests. The Portuguese colonial empire, attached for the time to the Spanish crown, was soon dismembered. In 1619 this new Holland took Batavia as its capital. Then the approaches of Malaysia were occupied; first Ceylon (1638), then Malacca, and lastly the Cape. Relations were established with Japan and China, where the newcomers obtained the " concessions " of Formosa and Canton. Three separate fleets shared the work of this profitable trade, two being employed on the European or Asiatic coasting trade, while a regular service of long-distance sailing ships linked up the colonial and European markets. The dividends soon reached an average of twenty-five per cent.

Founded nearly twenty years later (1621), the West India Company developed even more quickly than its predecessor. In a few years it had factories all along the Guinea coasts, it was established at Curaçao and at several other places in the Antilles, and had a footing on the coast of North America. But its prosperity was not to last, and it was not long before New Amsterdam was swallowed up by New England. About the year 1650, at the height of its splendour, the Dutch mercantile marine numbered more than ten thousand ships, manned by 168,000 sailors. Every year the shipyards of Holland turned out over a thousand ships; an excellent navy protected her shipowners in every quarter of the globe; and while her explorers tried to discover a new route to the Far East across the Polar seas of Northern Europe, her privateers boldly plundered the galleons of Mexico and Peru.

Capital accumulated in the hands of these great merchants of the little republic, whose grave manner and noble presence have been so magnificently reproduced by Rembrandt and Franz Hals. The growth of capital was all the more rapid because, for several generations, the sons of merchants who had made their fortunes persevered in their habits of hard work and rigid economy. Banks for deposits and securities, like those at Amsterdam (1609) and Rotterdam (1635), were organised to facilitate the working of the exchange, and these with the speculations set afoot by the Jewish colony, all contributed to liberate capital, so that on the Dutch Exchange interest had already dropped to the low rate of three or four per cent, which is usual in our own times. Add to this that public security was perfect, and that individuals, natives or foreigners, enjoyed complete freedom throughout the country, and it will be easily understood that industrial growth followed closely on the heels of commercial expansion. Moreover, the Spanish Netherlands freely furnished the United Provinces with the manufacturers and skilled workmen who were at first lacking there. It was these exiles, fugitives from Catholic oppression, who brought the cloth industry to Leyden and the linen industry to Haarlem. Three-quarters of a century later other exiles, victims of Louis XIV's intolerance, introduced the manufacture of silk and hats. The Dutch were no longer content to finish the undyed cloth which they used to bring from England in large quantities, but they began to make all kinds of cloth themselves. Utrecht velvet, for instance, soon made a name for itself. In other branches of industry their development was as marked. A clever imitation of Oriental china gave to Delft pottery the artistic character for which it was valued. The printing and bookselling trade, driven from Antwerp, where the house of Plantin had no successors, flourished in this country where almost everyone could read, where everything was discussed, and which was the home of the newspaper. The Dutch aptitude for patient and minute work was revealed as much in the faultless finish of the Elzevirs as in the delicate work of the diamond and lens cutters. Towards the middle of the seventeenth century Holland possessed more than 600,000 workmen, Amsterdam alone having 54,000. The progress of manufacture entailed the growth of towns, and the urban element soon formed two-thirds of the total population, an unusual, if not unique, proportion at that time.

The population itself had greatly increased, and agriculture profited by this enlargement of the home market. Even before they had had a fishing fleet, the Dutch had excelled in cattle-breeding and cheese-making, and at the end of the fifteenth century Dutch agriculture, taken as a whole, equalled that of Italy.[1] The rapidly increasing demands of

[1] See P. Boissonnade, *Le Travail dans l'Europe du moyen âge.*

the Northern Provinces hastened the perfection of agriculture.
By means of dykes and pumps worked by windmills, new land
was reclaimed from the sea, and as a result of the fruitfulness
of these *polders* and the careful way in which they were farmed,
breeding became more intensive. Many a village owned four
thousand cows, and bullocks weighing two thousand pounds
were no exception. Market-gardening prospered on the
outskirts of the towns, favoured by the damp soil and mild
climate, and the flower-gardens, enriched with exotic flowers
and carefully tended, were marvellous sights. Everyone knows
of the craze of the tulip fanciers, their rivalries and speculations and the follies into which they were led by the desire
to have the rarest and most beautiful blooms. It was the
ambition of all to create new varieties. People have ridiculed
the enthusiasm and the passions aroused by these horticultural wars, but it is certain that many processes of scientific
cultivation were discovered as a result of these persistent
experiments with soil and plants.

It is difficult to find out exactly how far the ordinary
workers benefited by the general increase of wealth. In
1533, at the call of the baker and prophet Mathiys, the workmen of the Haarlem district, and especially the workers in the
sedentary crafts, such as tailors and shoemakers, took part
in the mystical Anabaptist rising. Their claims were not
only communist but anarchist in spirit; there were to be no
masters, no property, no army, and even no law-courts. But
at that date Holland was a comparatively poor country; as
she grew rich the resources which she offered to labour were
greatly increased. Hospitals, orphanages, almshouses and
schools grew up at the same time as shops and factories. In
spite of the competition of foundling children brought up in
regular trade schools, it is difficult to believe that the working
class did not attain a certain measure of prosperity. In the
country, even if the bulk of the peasants did not approach the
fortune of those big farmers who could give their daughters
dowries of a hundred thousand florins and marry them to
princes, at least they were all free from the burdens of serfdom, and the fact that they were educated is a proof of their
prosperity. In some provinces, such as Groningen, the cultivators were practically the owners of the soil. They were
perpetual leaseholders, and only owed to the nominal owner

of the land a fixed rent which could not be increased. They could bequeath, sell and even sublet their holdings.

But towards the middle of the seventeenth century Holland was unhappily exposed to the rivalry of two powerful neighbours. First England closed her ports to Dutch vessels and challenged their command of the sea. The exploits of Tromp and Ruyter, Tromp's boast that he had swept the Thames with his broom, did not prevent their country from suffering. Then Louis XIV's armies invaded Holland. The little republic put up a splendid defence, but she emerged from the victorious struggle exhausted. Moreover, internally Holland was becoming softened and corrupted; the great wealth of the rich was matched by the great misery of the poor, and moral decadence resulted. In 1660 an eyewitness, Parival, noted the thirst of the Dutch for riches and their fear of violence: "They hate duels, assaults and quarrels, and commonly say that rich folk do not fight."[1] The heroes had developed into wealthy, peace-loving burghers; national energy had been sapped by luxury. Soon even civic virtue, the prop of republican government, failed, and Holland gave her destiny into the hands of a stadtholder, a prince; and when William of Orange became King of England in 1688, she was henceforth, in Frederick II's famous phrase, no more than "a little boat in the wake of a big ship."

Henceforth Holland played a secondary but still important part. It was through her that English ideas reached the Continent. After the revocation of the Edict of Nantes French exiles took refuge there, and it was by their means that new ideas, hostile to the absolute power of the king and the authority of the Church, penetrated into France. A quantity of pamphlets and books destined to make the round of the globe, beginning with the works of Bayle and ending with those of Rousseau, issued from the presses of The Hague and Amsterdam, where the Press was unfettered. Commerce was still active there. The bank of Amsterdam was still the greatest financial power of the day; it had credits in every country in Europe, and its investments had the reputation of being the best and safest. Up to the first quarter of the eighteenth century Holland was still disputing the maritime supremacy of England, and at the time of the Treaty of

---

[1] *Cf.* Taine, p. 165.

Utrecht her ships were as numerous as ever in the French ocean ports. Gradually, however, she had to give up the unequal contest and sink into obscurity, but not before she had set her mark on a period of world history. For a hundred years Holland had occupied in the world the place which England holds to-day.[1]

BIBLIOGRAPHY

PIRENNE: *Les anciennes démocraties des Pays-Bas.* Paris, 1910.
    Histoire de Belgique, t. iii et seq. Brussels, 1907.
TAINE: *Philosophie de l'art dans les Pays-Bas, t. i.* Paris, 1869.
LEFÈVRE-PONTALIS: *Jean de Witt, grand-pensionnaire de Hollande.* 1884 (2 vols.).
BRANTS: *La Belgique au xviie siècle.* 1910.

---

[1] See Taine, pp. 289-291.

CHAPTER III

ENGLAND

THE development of England during the three centuries we are studying can be summarised thus : After the Wars of the Roses there followed, in the sixteenth century, a period of peace and internal development under the despotism of the Tudors. The country became Protestant, and in the reign of the Virgin Queen Elizabeth entered on a period of rapid and splendid growth. In the seventeenth century, fighting at the same moment absolute monarchy and the renewed offensive of Catholicism, England became the revolutionary centre of Europe. Charles I was beheaded (1649), a Republic was proclaimed, and under Cromwell's dictatorship new advances were made. After a short-lived Restoration (1660) a second revolution took place, which gave the crown, in 1688, to a Protestant constitutional monarch. Throughout the eighteenth century the United Kingdom of Great Britain, as she had become after the union with Scotland, took the lead in economic progress and became the queen of the seas and the birthplace of modern industry, while politically she was the home of liberal ideas and the laboratory in which the Parliamentary system was worked out.

I.—TRADE

§ 1. Foreign Trade.

Extension of commercial intercourse; foundation of the British colonial empire—Change in the nature of imports and exports; modifications in commercial legislation—Development of the mercantile marine; Navigation Act of 1651; Trading companies—The chief ports: London, Bristol, Liverpool, Glasgow.

Accustomed as we are to thinking of England as the leading world power, we find it hard to realise that until quite recent times her commercial importance, even relatively speaking, was inconsiderable, and that the expansion of her trade was confined to a narrow circle of neighbouring countries. It is during the period which we are about to study that the amazing change took place.

France, it must be admitted, was a competitor rather than a customer. When economic relations between the two states were not interrupted by war they were, except at rare intervals, burdened with heavy restrictions which the British Government could enforce rigidly through England's insular position. Relations with the Low Countries were close and of long standing;[1] but after a period of considerable activity during the early part of the sixteenth century they suffered a check, first through the downfall of Antwerp, and later through Anglo-Dutch rivalry. It was in a wider sphere that progress of a decisive nature was taking place. In 1569, in spite of the opposition of the Hanseatic League, the Merchant Adventurers of London established themselves at Hamburg. It was already seventy years since a treaty with Denmark had opened up the Baltic and the Icelandic seas to British vessels. In 1533 a bold attempt to find a north-east passage to the Indies ended in the discovery of the port of Archangel and the opening of direct commercial relations with Muscovy. As early as the end of the fifteenth century Edward IV, who had the instincts of the true merchant, had sent his own ships to trade as far as the ports of the eastern Mediterranean, and in 1579 England had obtained official permission to trade directly with the Turkish Empire. With Italy her trade increased rapidly, notably with Venice, but also with Pisa and Florence. In the middle of the seventeenth century the long struggle with Catholic Spain ended at last, and England obtained the advantage of being treated as the most favoured nation by her late enemy. Moreover, the Methuen Treaty (1703) was to transform Portugal into the preserve of English commerce.

By that time English merchants had long since passed the limits of Europe, and by way of Asia Minor or Muscovy had reached Persia and the borders of the Indies. By the more indirect Cape route, which was less laborious if not less dangerous, more regular relations had been opened up with these regions of untold wealth. A Portuguese princess

[1] The first formal commercial treaty between England and Flanders was signed in 1496.

brought the Bombay factory as her dowry when she married Charles II (1664), and on the opposite coast of India the foundation of Madras (1639) and of Calcutta (1652) gave English merchants valuable bases from which, later on, they could undertake the conquest of the country. In 1608 English ships reached the Moluccas. The exploitation of Africa was begun; several factories were founded on the Guinea Coast, and in the eighteenth century they sent to Spanish America important cargoes of negro slaves, which England, by the *assiento* clause in 1713, had reserved to herself the right of supplying, while the " licensed ship " which was allowed by the treaty to be stationed at Porto-Bello was a reservoir of wealth, and opened the way to a profitable contraband trade with the vast Castilian colonies. Meanwhile, thanks to the buccaneers and Cromwell, England had taken a good part of the West Indies.[1] In the north of the New World Cabot discovered Newfoundland for her, and Walter Raleigh founded Virginia a century later (1584). Hardy pioneers, fugitives from an intolerant mother-country, created on the other shore of the Atlantic a New England (1620-40), which grew at the expense of New Amsterdam and later of New France. From the estuary of the St. Lawrence as far as the Great Lakes and the Mississippi there was to stretch a great English empire,[2] whose twelve hundred thousand inhabitants were all more or less closely attached to the country which had given them birth or had conquered them.

In 1763, after the signing of the Treaty of Paris which gave Canada and a large part of India to Great Britain, her supremacy spread over every sea. Moreover, in half a century, even before her triumph in the Seven Years' War, her foreign trade had already doubled.

A progressive and fundamental change in the nature of this trade and in the spirit of commercial legislation accompanied this remarkable expansion. Until the fifteenth century England had a large export trade in raw materials—tin, wool and cereals. But from the beginning of the sixteenth century, although Cornwall went on sending abroad a considerable proportion of her mineral output, the export of

[1] Occupation of Jamaica, 1655.
[2] See L. Capitan, *Le travail en Amérique, avant et après Colomb.*

English wool, particularly to Flanders, was forbidden, and for more than two hundred and fifty years, whatever Government was in power and in spite of the opposition of the sheep-farmers, the prohibition was strictly enforced; in fact, in the time of George III sheep-shearing was actually forbidden within a radius of five miles from the coast in order to stop smuggling.

It is true that during this same period the export of corn was encouraged. While Henry VII and Henry VIII had forbidden it as a matter of course, Elizabeth permitted it in certain circumstances; from 1663 the trade was carried on freely, and from 1690 it was encouraged by a system, revived from the fifteenth century, by which bounties were paid of varying value according to the market price. About eighty years later the increase in population combined with a succession of bad harvests caused the abolition of this system. Moreover, we must note that the favourable treatment given to exporters had had the effect of maintaining, if not of raising, the price level in England, rather than of stimulating the volume of exports.

It was in the export of manufactured goods, especially of cloth, that a notable and permanent increase made itself felt. In the sixteenth century the goods which England sent to Antwerp, to Bruges or to Hamburg were coarse or half finished; but soon her cloth was sufficiently fine and famous not only to invade the reserved market of Portugal, but even to compete with French cloth in the Levantine markets. Thus the cloth industry became one of the chief sources of national wealth, and even occasionally received assistance at the expense of the interests of the landed classes.

The laws regulating imports show equally clearly the development of a state which, without ceasing to be an agricultural nation, was inclining more and more to become an industrial power. Such things as Portuguese wines and Indian spices, which could not be produced in England, and which were increasingly in demand as the general standard of living rose, were imported free of duty. On the other hand, from the middle of the seventeenth century to about the middle of the eighteenth, heavy duties were put on imported corn, and for at least twenty-five years (1660-1685) insuperable barriers were raised against the Irish stock-breeders and against Irish cloth.   French fabrics were obstinately excluded; for instance, in 1700, brown holland was taxed at seventy per cent. of its value.   In spite of the demands of fashion and of public taste, the prohibition of Indian cotton goods, due to the pressure of the coalition between sheep-farmers and cloth manufacturers, lasted officially for more than fifty years (1721-1774).   In this period also the tanners joined with the owners of woodland to obtain the prohibition of all importation of pig-iron, even if it came from the colonies.

Yet amidst all these regulations, inspired now in the traditional interests of agriculture, and now in the new industrial interests, another and no less restrictive policy was making itself felt.   This policy sought to promote the interests of trade and aimed at making England a great world market.   It was for this reason that American colonial products—tobacco, rice, cotton and sugar—had to pass through the mother-country before they could be sold in Europe.

Even more amazing than the development of Great Britain's foreign trade was the growth of her mercantile marine.   Up to the end of the Middle Ages England had taken no advantage of the fact that she was an island, and most of her foreign trade had been in the hands of foreign agents, Lombards, Florentines, Dutch, and especially of the Hanseatic League.   But in the sixteenth century the public began to take an interest in this new way of making money, and, moreover, the necessity of protection against foreign invasion made them realise the usefulness of sailors.   Finally, in 1651, Cromwell's famous Navigation Act, which was made even stronger by the Restoration Governments (1660-1663-1672)[1] and the Glorious Revolution (1696), made it clear that England meant to win an honourable position on the seas for her national flag.   It was not enough that henceforth foreign goods might only be imported in English ships or in the ships of the country which produced the goods.   In addition, bounties were paid not only the great shipowners, but also the corn-exporters, who furnished them with profitable freights.   The colonies were encouraged to produce such

[1] Henceforth, in every ship flying the English flag, the captain and the majority of the crew must be English.

things as hemp for rope-making, so that the shipbuilders should have abundant materials. All sorts of expedients were resorted to in order to keep up the strength of the crews : foundlings were pressed as ship's boys, naturalisation was made easy for foreign sailors, help was promised to sick or aged sailors and to the dependents of those who died at sea. In order to give confidence to those who took part in the new national industry, powerful squadrons of ships of the line policed the seas, and on payment of a small premium an ingenious insurance system protected them even against the uncertainty of the weather. Moreover, the State was at pains to set up lighthouses in dangerous parts of the coasts and to improve marine charts. Ports were made deeper and wider, and ships were forbidden to throw their ballast overboard near harbour mouths.

At first the government had even tried to encourage maritime trade by granting more or less extensive privileges to associations of merchants. Henry VII granted official protection to the Merchant Adventurers. The reign of Elizabeth began the era of monopolist companies, institutions which had the threefold advantage of regulating trade, facilitating the collection of Customs dues, and reducing the risk entailed in distant expeditions. The East India Company, at its foundation in 1599, obtained a monopoly for fifteen years, which in 1609 was made perpetual, and a century later, in 1708, became absolute. The Muscovy Company and the Eastland Company, founded in the same reign, were also granted monopolies, as were the later companies established under the Stuarts, such as those formed to trade with Guinea, the Levant, Hudson Bay and the South Seas.

From the beginning, however, this system aroused the vigorous resistance of "interlopers," who never ceased to demand a share in the trade with the Far East. The London merchants had monopolised the right of trading with Muscovy, and therefore the merchants of the other ports protested violently against their exclusion. Under the Commonwealth foreign trade regained a measure of freedom; new companies were formed, but almost all of them were destined to fail or to coalesce with the old ones. After 1689 no new companies were created, and most of the existing ones had difficulty in maintaining their position. The idea began to spread that monopolies, instead of developing trade, restricted it, and that, except perhaps in the special case of Eastern trade, it would be better to allow competition under the control of a liberal government. From 1698 the Guinea Company opened its privileges to those who could pay for them, and allowed private traders to visit its factories on payment of certain duties. In 1750 it was transformed into a free association which could be joined by merchants from any English port on payment of a subscription. In 1753 the Levant Company's monopoly ended. It must be noted that the government had given no help to any of these enterprises, which had been floated solely with private capital, subscribed either by groups of shareholders or by the merchants themselves.

In any case the progress accomplished in two hundred years, whether it was the work of companies or of individuals, was amazing. The fishing fleets of the Channel ports, which had been strong enough to defeat the Invincible Armada, were certainly not capable of winning supremacy on the high seas. But Elizabeth had been able to muster fifteen thousand sailors, and London had furnished thirty-eight ships. During this great reign the Hansards, who had only just lost their exorbitant privileges, abandoned the Steelyard which they had held so long in the English capital. While English whalers sailed in increasing numbers to the Arctic Sea, English merchants no longer waited for the Venetians to bring them the products of Italy and the Levant, but, guided by pilots from Marseilles, they visited the Mediterranean ports for themselves. Then, for nearly a hundred years, Holland held the supremacy of the seas. In 1603 the English sent only about a hundred ships into the Baltic, while their rivals sent three thousand. In 1694 the English were still forced to defend their fisheries in their own waters against these formidable competitors. But Dutch power was beginning to decline. Already English vessels were bringing Spanish wines and Italian oil to France, and were taking an increasing part in the French coasting trade. After the wars of the middle of the eighteenth century the days of French competition were numbered and English supremacy was assured.

Maritime development naturally resulted in the development of new ports in an island which offered so many facilities for their establishment. From Yarmouth to Plymouth there was a succession of fishing harbours, to which we must add those of Cheshire and Ulster on the Irish Sea. Southampton lost the Venetian trade, but was compensated by its dealings in ivory and gold dust with the factories of Guinea. Boston and Hull seized their opportunity, between the decay of the Hanseatic towns and the rise of Dutch power, to extend their Baltic trade.[1] London, however, remained by far the most important town in the eastern and southern counties, and, indeed, in the whole kingdom. It was London which derived most direct benefit from the decline of Antwerp, many of whose merchants took refuge with her. At the beginning of the seventeenth century, before the extraordinary and short-lived prosperity of Amsterdam, she was the chief European market for the products of the Near and Far East. The old city was decimated by plague and almost destroyed by fire,[2] but a new city arose, finer and healthier, and the population increased. Even then London could hardly be called a brilliant city. About 1680 the proposal to put a street lantern on every tenth house was regarded as a daring innovation. The streets were badly paved, and down their midst ran a gutter which became a torrent in bad weather. The houses were not numbered, and from the upper stories slops were often emptied. Blackcock were shot where Regent Street now runs. Some quarters of the city were overrun by beggars and thieves, who ruled there supreme. But in 1685 London had outdistanced her new rival on the other coast of the North Sea; her tonnage was more than a third[3] of the total English tonnage, a higher proportion than she has to-day; and with more than half a million inhabitants she was the most populous capital of the West.

In the eighteenth century, however, as a result of the extension of trade with the New World, it was the ports on

[1] At the beginning of the eighteenth century Hull was the chief centre for the export of cereals and the import of iron.

[2] The first fire insurance companies seem to have been founded in London in 1710.

[3] About 70,000 tons. Less than a quarter of the present tonnage of Newcastle.

the west coast which increased most in size and wealth. Bristol's prosperity began as early as the fourteenth century when she came into close relations with Aquitaine. During the reigns of Elizabeth and James I the colonisation of Ireland and fishing expeditions to Newfoundland and Iceland[1] added to her wealth, so that, in 1685, with a population of 29,000 persons, Bristol was the second city in the country. Thence there set sail for New England hundreds of artisans recruited by a press-gang system, which resembled a white slave trade. Sugar was imported from Virginia and the Antilles, and a sugar-refining industry grew up. The passion for foreign trade touched even the little shopkeepers, who did not hesitate to send their humble wares to the West Indies. Liverpool, which in Charles I's reign was nothing but a swamp, and in Charles II's reign a small town of four or five thousand inhabitants, had become, a century later, a great market for coffee and cotton. Her merchants distributed these articles in Holland, Germany and the Baltic countries, while her shippers grew rich on the slave trade and on the profitable contraband trade with Spanish America. Meanwhile Glasgow, which benefited by the union of Scotland and England (1707),[2] became the great northern market for American tobacco. This change in the position of trade centres is a distant result of the great geographical discoveries made two and a half centuries earlier.

§ 2. Internal Trade.

Late development of means of communication—Maintenance of roads first left to neighbouring parishes; later system of tolls—Coasting trade and inland navigation: Manchester Canal and the Grand Trunk. Absence of restrictions in internal trade—Posts: mail-coaches; flying coaches—Fairs and markets; commercial travellers and hawkers—Privileged associations of merchants—Metal and paper coinage—The goldsmiths of Lombard Street and the Bank of England; joint-stock companies.

Although it is usually true that an expansion of foreign trade gives an impetus to the internal trade of a country, it

[1] The Cabots sailed from Bristol.

[2] Until that time, under the Navigation Act, no merchandise coming from the American colonies could enter Scotland unless it had first been unloaded in England and had paid duty. Moreover, it could not be reshipped in Scotch vessels.

can sometimes happen in a particular state that the extreme
ease of external communication delays for a time the development of methods of internal transport. Such was the case in
England. Her shores, cut up by deep estuaries washed by
strong tides, were so favourable for a coastal trade that for a
long time it seemed useless to go to the expense of creating
and maintaining a regular system of roads or canals.

Until the reign of Mary Tudor the upkeep of roads, like
most other public services, was left to private enterprise and
goodwill. But for more than a century this haphazard
method had been inadequate to meet the growing demands
of public necessity, and the crown stepped in and ordered
the parishes to maintain that part of the high-roads which
lay within their bounds. The peasants, summoned by overseers, were to give six days' work, and if this was not enough
they were to pay enough money to ensure the completion of
the work. This reform improved the position very little.
Forced labour is never economical except on the surface, and
some parishes were really incapable of fulfilling the heavy
task allotted to them. In particular the Great North Road,
which was the link between two rich districts, lay most of
the way through barren and thinly populated country, and
the adjoining parishes neither could nor would submit to
expense for the benefit of traffic from which they drew but
small profit in its passage. Thus about the middle of the
seventeenth century even the most important high-roads
were little more than mountain tracks, reduced in bad
weather to the width of a footpath, furrowed with ruts, beset
with quagmires, seeming at every turn to lose themselves in
the swamps and moors. A coach would not budge unless
drawn by four or six horses, and even then it often stuck in
the mud and had to be dragged out with the help of oxen.
Sometimes carriages would enter a village drawn along by
the peasants. Even in the flat country heavy carts were
always pulled by oxen, which are only used nowadays in the
remote mountain districts of the Continent.

At the Restoration it was decided that it would be more
just and more practical if those who used the roads contributed to their upkeep. Turnpikes were therefore set up at
intervals, and tolls, at first very moderate, were collected.
Light though they were, these tolls provoked discontent and

even riots. But these could not check the growth of a
system which was advantageous to everyone, even to those
short-sighted landowners who at first had opposed it, fearing
that easier communication with neighbouring markets would
lower the price of their produce and lessen their income.
After the alarm caused by the Jacobite march on London in
1745 the extension of the system was hastened for strategic
motives, and in 1773 for the first time a complete service for
the maintenance of high-roads was organised all over the
kingdom. A cart could now make the distance from the
Fens to London in two days and a night, and farmers loaded
whole flocks of geese into carts, and sent them up to the
London market, where they fetched a far higher price.
Cattle could come, for instance, from the Scotch mountains
to fatten on the plains of Norfolk and Suffolk. But even then
the great highways offered a striking contrast to the cross-
country roads, most of which were still only practicable for
pack-horses, which travelled in long files like desert caravans.

River traffic, for which England seemed to be fitted by
the comparative absence of mountains and by the slow
current of her rivers, was not organised until late in the
modern period. Until the middle of the eighteenth century
no important waterway was opened; the attempt was barely
made even to deepen a few rivers above the point at which
they ceased to be navigable. Coal, the chief article of inland
trade, was carried from the mines to the consumer by sea,
and was hence called sea-coal; but when the increasing use
of coal led to the working of mines out of reach of natural
waterways, artificial ones had to be constructed. Between
1759 and 1761 the Duke of Bridgewater had a canal cut
between his Worsley collieries and the Mersey, so that he
could send his coal to Manchester more cheaply. In 1766
Wedgwood, the great potter, undertook to link the Mersey
and the Trent by a canal, so that he might obtain more
cheaply the flint which he bought from the eastern counties
and the clay which he needed from Devon and Cornwall.
The Grand Trunk was finished in eleven years, and the rates
of transport for these heavy and cumbrous articles were
lessened by three-quarters. Before the end of the century
the " canal fever " had broken out and canals multiplied
rapidly. Not only raw materials, but manufactured goods

and food supplies, benefited by the opening of the new routes.

These vast undertakings, which often aroused the hostility of carriers and innkeepers, but which prepared the way for the development of industry on a large scale, were carried out entirely on the initiative and with the capital of private persons, great landowners or manufacturers acting alone or in groups. No authority, either local or central, attempted any longer to control or hinder the free circulation of all kinds of merchandise. Elizabeth herself from the first had allowed free trade in corn, the most valuable of all products, and England had never had a regular system of provincial Customs duties. Moreover, by the middle of the eighteenth century internal peace was firmly established, vagabondage was being rigorously repressed, highwaymen had almost disappeared from the great roads, and thus the safety of trade was guaranteed.

The means of transport which a merchant could command were, however, still primitive. After the Restoration the clumsy system of letter-post created by Charles I had been improved. Three times a week on all the chief routes horsemen, riding about five miles an hour night and day, carried their letter-bags. There was a daily service between London and the coast.[1] Private people could send their letters by these royal couriers, and travellers who were in a hurry could obtain relays of saddle-horses if they applied to the Post Office, which had the monopoly of this business. At the same time public conveyances became much quicker and more frequent. In 1669 the old stage-coach, which plied between London and Oxford and which offered travellers no greater comfort than trusses of straw, was replaced by a flying coach,[2] which took twelve hours, instead of two days, over the journey. Three times a week coaches left the capital for the chief provincial towns, going as far north as York,

[1] In London itself, as early as Charles II's reign, letters were delivered six or eight times a day for the charge of one penny.

[2] Like the railways later on, these swift coaches excited opposition. It was said that they would kill the art of horsemanship, ruin the makers of saddles and spurs, injure the health of travellers, be too hot in summer, too cold in winter and altogether too rapid. It was proposed to limit their speed to thirty miles a day, and a petition to this effect was presented to the authorities.

and as far west as Exeter. These rapid coaches, which only held six people, covered fifty miles a day in summer, but only about thirty in winter. The Universities were the first to enjoy the privilege of these flying coaches, and the public benefited by the rivalry between Oxford and Cambridge. Soon, however, the service became general. Waggons were also developed and by the middle of the eighteenth century had definitely taken the place of the pack-horse, at any rate on the chief high-roads.[1]

Up to this time the periodical fairs had kept their importance. Some, like the Stourbridge Fair, were held only once a year; men came to these from all parts of England and from Scotland, and the products of the whole country and even of the colonies were bought and sold there. Others, mere district fairs, were held more often, but even there all kinds of merchandise were on sale. Moreover, special fairs, held regularly at very short intervals, began to be organised. Such were the cloth fairs which every week overflowed from the market-places into the streets of Leeds, Bradford and Halifax. London by itself constituted an enormous continuous and cosmopolitan fair, and even in the smaller cities and boroughs the groceries were always open, with their varied store of provisions. About 1750 certain changes began to take place. The travelling merchants, who laboured along the bad roads from inn to inn and from fair to fair, with their large stocks of goods carried on pack-horses, began to disappear. Their place was taken by "commercial travellers," who bowled along the improved roads in their light carriages, taking with them only samples. They were content to take orders, and left the delivery of the goods to the carrier. Only along unfrequented roads did the pedlar continue to carry his wares from farm to farm on a single horse, or even on his own back.

Rich or poor, all English merchants were equally free. Each of them carried on his business without the intervention of any power either to help or to hinder him. The despotic

---

[1] Among other commercial organs developing about this time newspapers must be mentioned. They were still very small. They gave "in a year what *The Times* contains in two numbers" (Macaulay). But they were supplemented by news-letters, which, from the end of the seventeenth century, kept the provinces informed of what happened in the capital in the political and also in the business world.

Elizabeth had encouraged the formation of companies of merchants, which had been subject to state control, but at the same time had enjoyed exclusive privileges. It was possible to defend this system in the early stages of the development of trade, but nevertheless it aroused violent protests, and in 1601 the opposition of the Commons prevailed against the crown. Internal monopolies had had their day; national trade escaped from royal tutelage as it had already broken the bonds of the gilds.

On the other hand, from as far back as the fourteenth century a common system of weights and measures had been in force throughout the kingdom. The coinage also was uniform and stable and was in circulation throughout this relatively small state, which by the precocity of its economic and political organisation seemed already to be in advance of all other countries. In the seventeenth century paper money began to be used. The Lombard Street goldsmiths, who during the Civil War had undertaken the care of business-men's capital, had funds to back a considerable number of notes. Soon the Bank of England and the Treasury increased the issue, and paper money came into common use.

But it was not enough merely to facilitate exchange; it was also essential to encourage the application of capital to all sorts of undertakings. Already in Elizabeth's reign merchants had carried on their businesses with borrowed money, for although usury had long been condemned by the Church, and Luther had upheld its teaching in this respect, Calvin, on the other hand, declared that interest was legitimate. Moreover, the first deposit banks were opened in London, and among their clients were many men of small substance. The queen herself set an example to her subjects in preferring English to foreign banks. The Lombard Street goldsmiths were not long content with issuing notes to cover the funds entrusted to them. Happier than their medieval ancestors, they could invest them so as to bring in interest, and need not fear imprisonment or confiscation.

At the time of the Revolution of 1688, in order to provide the new constitutional monarchy with the money it needed, an association of capitalists was formed on the model of the Dutch and Genoese banks. In addition to the right of issuing notes, it was also granted the power to discount bills and to make loans. Thus was founded the Bank of England, which the new government regarded simply as a financial expedient, but which was to play a leading part in the economic growth of the country by rendering possible, within the next fifty years, the reduction of the rate of interest from eight to four per cent.

At the same time the direct distribution of capital in the different channels of economic activity was made possible by the formation of joint-stock companies of unlimited liability, whose growth was marked by a series of crises in speculation.[1] In 1566 Thomas Gresham had founded the Stock Exchange; in 1763 London was recognised as the chief financial centre of the world.

§ 3. The Commercial Aristocracy.

A new class was growing up, which was henceforth to be both socially and politically important. It was formed of men who were engaged in overseas trade, of heads of great private businesses, or shareholders in chartered companies, wealthy shipowners, rich merchants of London or Bristol, bankers and financiers. Even in Elizabeth's reign merchants had dazzled their contemporaries by the splendour of their houses. "The lofty houses of the wealthier merchants, their parapeted fronts and costly wainscoting, their cumbrous but elaborate beds, their carved staircases, their quaintly figured gables, not only contrasted with the squalor which had till then characterised English towns, but marked the rise of a new middle class which was to play its part in later history."[2]

A century and a half later their splendour was still more striking. It is estimated that in 1750 the merchants of the city of London "had a larger commercial income than the

---

[1] The scandal of the South Sea Company was almost exactly contemporary with the failure of Law's system in France. In 1720 there broke out in London a fever of gambling, speculation and stock-jobbing. Capital changed hands at an extraordinary rate. It was hoped to pay off the National Debt by issuing shares which rose in a month from £150 to £1,000. Hundreds of companies were formed. The madness ended in an epidemic of failures, lawsuits and suicides.

[2] Green, *Short History of the English People*, vol. ii, p. 791.

rents of the whole House of Lords and the Episcopal Bench."[1]
The great merchants rivalled the old aristocracy of blood. The
eldest sons of great families did not hesitate to associate with
these upstarts, provided that they could get a share in their
profits, and the younger sons no longer feared to disgrace
themselves by engaging in trade, the path to wealth of these
nouveaux riches. Poor noblemen's sons were not ashamed to
marry merchants' heiresses, while the merchants themselves,
having made their fortunes, were in a hurry to buy lands and
titles. With social influence went political power, and this new
aristocracy exercised an increasing influence on the government. The Revolution of 1688 marked the establishment of
this new class. " It was at the Guildhall that the Lords met
after the flight of James II. In the Parliament summoned
by the Prince of Orange the mayor and aldermen of the City
sat side by side with the old members of the House of
Commons. Finally the City advanced £2,000,000 to the
Treasury. This was the pledge of alliance between the new
monarchy and the merchants and financiers."[2] This alliance
between lenders and borrowers was especially profitable for
the former. The government laboured to win the supremacy
of the seas for British trade, and the merchants provided
the expenses of the conquest at interest. When the government wanted to make them bear too heavy a part of the
public burden, they had only to unite and the proposed tax
was abandoned.[3] Within the ruling aristocracy a constant
struggle was going on between the landed and agricultural
magnates and the commercial and industrial magnates,
between " green " England and " black " England. The
latter increased in power, and in the middle of the eighteenth
century was becoming supreme. Moreover, in the United
Kingdom the aristocracy of office was no more difficult of
entry than that of birth. Defoe wrote at the beginning of
the eighteenth century : " Commerce makes gentlemen. The

---

[1] Th. Rogers, *Six Centuries of Work and Wages* (1909 edit.), p. 473.

[2] Mantoux, *Revolution industrielle au XVIIIe siècle*, p. 78.

[3] This commercial prosperity had its bad side. The beginning of
the eighteenth century was a period when commercial standards were
supreme and everything had its price. Walpole retained power by
buying consciences and votes.

sons of merchants, or at any rate their grandsons, make as good members of Parliament, statesmen, Privy Councillors, judges, bishops, capable men of every calling, as the descendants of ancient families." To the foreigner the English merchant could proudly compare himself to the Roman citizen, for he carried with him the fortune of a new empire. He directed the labour which was the foundation of this vast power.

II.—INDUSTRY

In England, as in the rest of Europe, the development of commerce at home and abroad brought about the appearance of a new type of industry which was characterised by the concentration both of capital and labour, and also led to the growth of quite new industries. For instance, the cotton industry, which has transformed an obscure English county into one of the greatest manufacturing centres of the world, began by receiving, not only its raw material, but even its designs from foreign countries.

§ 1. Industrial Conditions.

Decay of the gilds—Development of large-scale industry—Privileged industrial companies—Capital provided by commerce or by the old industries; foreign capital—Labour: immigrants; ex-agricultural workers—Raw material, native and foreign—Markets: protective legislation.

The progress of industry necessarily led to a conflict with the gilds. Since the beginning of the fifteenth century the urban gilds had seen their power retreating before the advance of the woollen industry in the country, while the loss of their religious endowments, under Edward VI, had seriously reduced their social influence. But they did not accept their decline. In order to save as much of their power as possible, they allied with the new absolutism, and the monarchy for a time supported their pretensions. In 1556 the Weavers Act forbade any master clothier outside a corporate town to possess or to hire more than a certain number of looms. In order to check the country industry, an attempt was made to enforce the old law limiting the number of apprentices. At the beginning of Elizabeth's reign the Statute of Artificers, 1563, codified the confused mass of customs which had regulated industry during the Middle Ages. Indeed, for a few years the government did succeed in checking the exodus of industry from the corporate towns to the market towns and country districts. Still controlling many of the big towns, the gilds used their power to enforce in their restricted domain a series of regulations which were increasingly severe. More than once in the course of the seventeenth century, when new trades developed in the old centres, the town authorities and even the central government, swayed either by class interest or by the force of custom, obliged young and vigorous industries to fit themselves into the narrow and antiquated organisation of the gilds.

It was, however, quite clear that the gilds had ceased to justify their existence. It was two hundred years since they had exercised any effective control over the quality of articles offered for sale, and the purchaser had got into the habit of trusting his own judgment. For at least a hundred years the re-establishment of the royal authority and of internal peace had rendered unnecessary the mutual protection which had been afforded by the gilds to their members. They had become no more than monopolies, burdensome to the public and restrictive to the workmen. In 1623, therefore, James I had to promise to grant no more monopolies. Patents for fourteen years were to be granted as an encouragement or recompense to inventors. During the first half of the century the royal promise was not very strictly kept, but after the Restoration the crown voluntarily allowed the traditional legislation to fall into disuse. Even the heads of the City of London hardly succeeded in prolonging its application in the districts directly subject to their authority. Suburbs were growing up on all sides. An attempt was made to incorporate them in the Metropolis in order to make them subject to the old trade organisation, but it was unsuccessful. In the end it was the suburbs which, entering the struggle in spite of themselves, laid low the fortress of the gilds. In the other towns also the old trade gilds were quietly dying out. In the eighteenth century, in answer to general protests, Parliament formally suppressed them. In 1753 the statutes relat-

ing to stocking-knitters were abolished as being " vexatious
to manufacturers and harmful to industry," and " contrary
to reason and against the liberty of English subjects." The
new industry was to be allowed to grow in freedom.

But it would perhaps be possible to help its growth by
enabling it to procure capital, that chief essential and surest
pledge of its success. This at any rate was the opinion of
Elizabeth and the early Stuarts. The great queen was most
concerned with the interests of national defence; she thought
that England must have better artillery than Spain. Therefore it was expedient to grant privileges to companies
founded for the purpose of exploiting coal, iron or copper
mines. In reality, when they instituted these industrial
monopolies, the sovereigns were thinking also of enriching
their favourites and securing for themselves a supplementary
revenue which would enable them to escape from the watchfulness of Parliament. When Charles I granted to private
companies the monopoly of salt-mining and soap-making, he
may perhaps have been aiming only at the economic independence of the kingdom. But public opinion was from the
first violently opposed to such a policy. In 1601 Elizabeth
was forced by popular feeling to revoke all privileges of this
kind, and in 1623 Parliament forced James I to abandon the
system altogether. It was difficult to revive it even temporarily, when it was a question of encouraging some of the
valuable industries brought over by French refugees.

The new industrialism, therefore, was organised entirely
by private capital and owed nothing to governmental favour.
It has been shown already that, at the beginning of modern
times, a separation was effected between commerce and
industry, which, in the Middle Ages, had been regarded as
closely allied.[1] But commerce still exercised over industry
an influence which, though less direct, was none the less
powerful. It was natural that merchants should use their
money to promote the growth of that active industry for
whose birth they were responsible and on whose expansion
their own depended. In Henry VII's reign some rich drapers
of the northern and western counties did indeed set up workshops of their own, which they directed personally. Even

[1] See Introduction.

the big sheep-breeders employed the people in their own district to turn the wool of their flocks straight into cloth.

At the same time certain master-craftsmen from the towns, fleeing from the oppressive tutelage of the gilds which claimed to limit the number of looms and of workmen they could employ, found in the villages a means of making their unproductive reserves bear fruit. For as early as the fifteenth century there had appeared in England a new economic agent, the "capitalist artisan." Hitherto the farmer, landowner or noble, the monastery or lay corporation had bought the raw material and hired an artisan to work it. Gradually people got into the habit of buying ready-made articles. Thus it is clear that the artisans already had at their disposal sufficient capital to enable them to work with a view to the future needs of their customers.[1]

Then came the unexpected but valuable help of foreign capital. During the first half of the seventeenth century a large colony of Spanish Jews was established in London, and even Cromwell did not disdain to protect them. Although they were excluded from direct participation in certain trades, their money was used to promote big business concerns. Soon afterwards the richest of the French refugees brought to their adopted country not only their experience, but their wealth.

In the next century, it is true, industry protested against the drainage of capital which resulted from the unbounded extension of foreign trade by the energy of the chartered companies. But its complaints were exaggerated and often thoughtless. Commerce, on the whole, far from robbing it of money and power, was the chief instrument of its success. Moreover, the movement towards the growth of great estates, which was accentuated about 1750, provided industry with many new recruits who, having realised a little money by the sale of their land to the neighbouring great landowner, were ready to take part in the "industrial revolution."

As to labour, certainly no one protested if the government favoured so useful a type of immigration. Florentine workmen and cloth-workers from the town of Provins were the

---

[1] Thorold Rogers, *Six Centuries of Work and Wages*, p. 338.

first to come. The Flemish Protestant weavers and fullers, thirty thousand of whom crossed the North Sea between the years 1561 and 1570, were warmly welcomed,[1] as were also the metal-workers, glass-makers, ironmongers and cutlers who came from various lands to make the fortune of Birmingham. In 1585 England received the cotton-workers who fled from Antwerp. A century later she was the refuge of those excellent craftsmen who were driven from her rival, France, by the blindness of Louis XIV.[2] But even without any reinforcement from neighbouring countries the new manufacturers had discovered in the country districts not only freedom from gild regulations, but also an inexhaustible supply of labour. Great cloth-making workshops were set up almost in the open fields, and into these the agricultural changes which encouraged sheep-farming at the expense of tillage[3] threw the entire superfluous population of dispossessed small tenants and unemployed labourers.

Moreover, for two hundred years the increasingly restrictive regulations of the municipal crafts drove out many craftsmen, who shirked the prospect of long years of slavish and precarious apprenticeship. At the end of the seventeenth century nearly four-fifths of the population lived in the suburbs or in the country, and there the first factories grew up. In the second half of the eighteenth century, when industrial production went through a further process of concentration, the movement was reversed and a rural took the place of an urban exodus. The peasants, the small farmers, and even the yeomen were driven out by the continuous growth of big estates. They left their villages for ever, to go and seek a livelihood—as though in another America—in the country of the great factories, to crowd into industrial towns, offering their labour to the big employers.

The young woollen industry no longer ran the risk of a shortage of raw materials; abundant supplies were available. Its resources suffered little diminution even in the eighteenth

[1] An earlier immigration of Flemish weavers in 1544 had, however, provoked passing disturbances at Norwich.

[2] These French refugees were not always Protestants. Thus in 1681, following a quarrel with their masters, 4,500 linen weavers of Normandy, all good Catholics, went to enrich the industry at Ipswich.

[3] See the section on English Agriculture.

century when some of the land used for sheep-farming was converted again into arable land, and when the agricultural interest, again in the ascendant, created obstacles to the importation of Spanish and even of Irish wool. At this time one of the complaints against the East India Company was that it neglected to furnish the raw material needed by the new textile industries. But if there was an industry which may be said to have grown up in the teeth of existing legislation, it was the metallurgical industry. From the time of Elizabeth the development of ironworks had been hindered by the government's determination to preserve at least as much timber as would supply the shipbuilding yards. Since then an attempt had been made to limit the number of forges in certain counties, and after the Restoration master-founders were forbidden to use timber.

There remains the question of markets. On this point government intervention had been successful and popular. When Elizabeth and the early Stuarts had tried to found privileged industrial companies, they had protected them, not only from all English, but also, of course, from all foreign competition. When, about 1670, the East India Company began to import big cargoes of Eastern fabrics, there were strong protests; what were the secondary interests of overseas trade compared with the historic rights of the first national industry? In 1700 the importation of cotton goods was forbidden, and the prohibition was renewed in succeeding years with increasingly heavy penalties for disobedience. As a result of this prohibition the manufacture of printed cottons developed in the country itself. The woollen industry defended itself against this new attack on its traditional monopoly with equal energy. In Queen Anne's reign English cotton goods were taxed. But this was not enough, for these new fabrics were less than half the price of the old. Then, conscious that they were fighting for a time-honoured privilege which they had thought would last for ever, the cloth-workers stirred up riots, and ladies guilty of wearing these ruinous novelties were sprinkled in the streets with nitric acid. In 1720 all printed calicoes, even those made in England, were in turn forbidden, and this prohibition was officially maintained until 1774, at any rate in the case of pure cotton fabrics.

A heavy tariff was in force against the importation of French textile goods. After 1689, for motives which were not altogether the result of the new political order, these prohibitions were made stricter and were more generally applied. In addition to this, to encourage new industries, such as the silk industry, a system of drawbacks, or bounties on export, was established. In the first sixty years of the eighteenth century drawbacks were granted with equal freedom to manufactured and to agricultural exports. They could be obtained by Parliamentary bribery and by fraud, and many unscrupulous manufacturers made enormous fortunes at the expense of the nation. But they did serve to increase the volume of industrial interests and the amount of capital, which became available to build up new businesses and new fortunes.

§ 2. Sketch of Industrial Development.

Progress and extension of the cloth industry—Development of other textile industries: linen, silk, cotton—Mining: tin, copper, rock-salt, iron, coal—Metal trades: Sheffield steel, Birmingham iron-ware; exhaustion of fuel—Migration of various industries to the north-west.

In the middle of the fifteenth century England was not yet a great mercantile country and neither was she an industrial power. The cloth industry, the most important in the kingdom, had spread into the country districts, but still failed to use all the wool produced there. A great part of the wool was still exported in its raw state to various European markets, where it was greatly in demand on account of its extreme fineness. The Flemings bought large quantities of it, worked it into cloth, and in that form sold some of it back to the English, who then sent it to Florence to be dyed.

But in Elizabeth's reign, as a result of Flemish immigration, cloth-works, fulling mills and dye-works multiplied in Norfolk and the other south-eastern counties. Gradually in this district the farmers themselves began to work up the wool of their own sheep on rough looms into the country "home-spun." Further west, on the English Channel and the Bristol Channel, the important manufacture of fine cloth grew up. Throughout the seventeenth century the woollen industry remained the most important in the country, and in 1701 the export of cloth amounted to a quarter of the total exports of the kingdom. But its growth was flagging, and although it benefited, like the others, from the revival of prosperity which took place about 1750, its pre-eminence was more and more threatened by the rapid growth of the other textile trades.

Up to the time of Elizabeth the linen industry had not been important, but soon, thanks to the French refugees, English linens, notably those of Ipswich and later those of Ireland and Scotland, began to compete successfully with Dutch linens. Similarly in Elizabeth's reign the silk industry hardly existed, but French refugees, effectually supported by the government, established its success. Lastly, in the seventeenth century a new industry, which was later to be the most important in England, came into being. For a long time it had been considered that the few cotton weavers who, in 1585, came to England from Antwerp, had made but an unimportant contribution to the resources of their new country. The new manufacture depended on distant and very limited supplies. It could only count on the surplus products of the Levant, the Indies and China, or on the still uncertain products of the plantations in Brazil and the West Indies. But the success of Indian cotton goods showed the way to the Dutch weavers. Helped by French refugees, they established in the suburbs of London some of the first workshops for making printed calico. The Western workmen, however, could not rival the dexterity of their Indian masters, nor was their machinery good enough to compensate for this natural inferiority. It was the prohibition of foreign printed fabrics, foolishly urged by the heads of the woollen industry, which caused the growth of the native cotton industry by freeing it from competition. For more than fifty years the young industry was forced to use a mixture of flax and cotton or to seek contraband markets, in order to disarm the hostility of its enemies, who discovered their mistake too late. But this did not matter. It had caught the public taste and had besides the decisive advantage of extreme cheapness. Although in 1750 its total production was only worth about £60,000, and although in 1776

Adam Smith only mentioned it casually in his great book, the hour of its triumph was at hand.

Let us leave on one side the less important manufactures such as paper- and hat-making, both introduced by French Huguenots,[1] and pass on at once to the mining and metal-lurgical industries, which alone could claim to rival the importance of the woollen industry. Three thousand years after the Phœnicians, the Cornish tin mines still constituted one of the most precious sources of the mineral wealth of England. In Elizabeth's reign copper was also worked in the same peninsula, but the value of the Welsh copper mines was still unknown. Soon after the Restoration beds of rock-salt had been discovered in Cheshire, but the products which resulted from the rough system of dissolution and evapora-tion employed were so impure that the rich continued to get their supplies from the French salt-works. There were many iron mines, but the number of those being worked decreased every day as the forests were exhausted, as was necessarily the case so long as charcoal was the only known fuel for smelting.

The use of coal, which was found in abundance even on the surface, was not entirely unknown. For hundreds of years it had been used for domestic purposes. As early as the seventeenth century Newcastle, favourably situated near the coast, despatched a large proportion of its coal by sea, sometimes even to foreign countries, and Northumberland was deservedly called the "Black Indies." London especially received large quantities of sea-coal for the use of the glass-works, breweries, distilleries, sugar refineries, soap-works, dye-works and brick-works situated there. Coal was even used in forges for working iron, but it was no use for extracting the raw metal, because the sulphur which it contained made the cast-iron brittle.

Under such conditions only the smaller metal trades had flourished. Sheffield, which got its iron from Sweden through Hull, had been famous since the Middle Ages for its knives. This manufacture made the fortune of all the district round, where there were plenty of grindstones for everyone, and streams to turn them and to temper the

---

[1] It should be noted, however, that Venetian lace was first imitated in the workshops of Bedford, Buckingham and Dorset.

blades. All sorts of steel implements were produced there, but for fine steel, especially for surgical instruments, England was dependent on France until the use of the Huntsman process was introduced (1740).[1] Bristol and Gloucester manufactured pins. Birmingham furnished Cromwell's armies with swords and pikes, but later it made a speciality of hardware and iron toys and gewgaws. In the first fifty years of the eighteenth century its population had more than doubled.[2] Meanwhile the exhaustion of timber reserves, which was hastened by the growth of sheep-farming, had led to the decline of all the big iron manufactures. Even in Elizabeth's reign a number of furnaces in Sussex and Kent had been extinguished for want of wood to feed them. In 1720 only about sixty remained, and their total production was not more than a third of what one of our big iron-works produces to-day. About 1750 four-fifths of the iron used in the country came from Sweden.

As these different industries grew they tended to migrate to new districts. The cloth manufacture, hitherto most active in the eastern and south-eastern counties where the original Flemish cloth-workers had established themselves, had quickly been attracted to Bristol, as we have noted, by the commercial development of that great ocean port. Then towards the middle of the seventeenth century it began to spread north of the Mersey and the Humber, a district which, after the departure of the Romans, seemed to have fallen into an eternal sleep. There the spinners and weavers found that they could more easily procure certain kinds of wool. From that time the quilts of York and the cloth of Halifax and Leeds began to be known.[3] The oldest national industry seemed to confine itself mainly to the country districts of the West Riding, where it was spread about among the villages. This is not surprising, since it was only in the country that new manufactures on a large scale could develop in freedom.

As regards the more recent textile trades, the silk manu-

[1] This process consisted of plunging the steel into crucibles of black-lead, which gave the metal greater homogeneity.

[2] In 1696 its population was only 4,000; a hundred years later it had increased to 70,000.

[3] In 1696 Leeds had only 7,000 inhabitants, while Norwich had 30,000, the greater part of whom made their living by the cloth industry.

facture prospered chiefly in the immediate neighbourhood of London, where lived the rich population who at that time were its only customers, while the cotton industry tended to be localised in the north-west.   Thanks to the proximity of Liverpool which assured easy supplies, and to the humidity of the climate which made possible the working of fine thread, Lancashire became the principal seat of the cotton industry.[1]   The north-west also began to attract what remained of the heavy metallurgical industries, partly because more timber remained there than in the south-east, but especially because the more numerous water-courses could be used to provide power to work the furnace bellows.

§ 3. Technical Development.

The division of purely manual labour—The inventive spirit—Manufacturing regulations hostile to innovation—The stocking loom—The flying shuttle; the jenny (1765)—Coke used for smelting (1735); puddling (1784)—Water power: mallets for cloth fulling; the water-frame for cotton spinning (1767); iron rolling-mills (1783)—Pneumatic steam pumps of Savery (1698) and Newcomen.

The individual division of labour between workmen in the same workshop, which forms at once the simplest and most direct change brought about by industrial concentration, was clearly shown about 1750 in the small metal trades. Adam Smith's description of the processes employed in the pin-making factories has become a classic.   Progress there consisted of a more economical distribution of work.   Only manual labour was employed.   No mechanical force was used, nor even elaborate tools which, in proportion to their complexity, make the workman's task simpler.   The progress consisted in the greater technical skill which could be acquired by the specialised worker.

But the revived spirit of invention, which was one of the characteristics of the Renaissance, had shown itself earlier than this.   As early as the beginning of the seventeenth century the bold philosopher, Francis Bacon, had told his countrymen that " the universe was full of secrets of the highest importance to the happiness of man,"[2] and that the

[1] In 1696 Manchester had only 6,000 inhabitants.   In 1786 the population had increased to 30,000.

[2] Macaulay.

chief object of science was to discover them.' Half a century elapsed before this advice bore fruit, for England was disturbed, and absorbed in religious and political problems. It was only in the calmer and much less mystical age of the Restoration that experimental science won public favour. Charles II led the new fashion, or rather followed the fashion of the day, and the scientific society of London became the Royal Society (1662). Greenwich Observatory was built, Newton formulated the laws of astronomical science, Boyle laid the foundations of modern chemistry, and Woodward of mineralogy, while Grow and Malpighi made decisive discoveries in the physiology of plants. Naturally this spirit of observation and research was also widespread among the industrial workers. The era of industrial inventions of all sorts was at hand, but their application was to arouse the double resistance of the trade organisations and of the established powers.

Even in the preceding century the struggle between mechanical innovations and the established traditions of the manual workers had begun. In 1555 the gilds obtained from Parliament the prohibition of a new weaving-loom, the gig-mill. In 1598 the workers violently opposed the use of the stocking-loom. Two centuries later (1765) they tried to prevent the use of metal carding machines. At the beginning of the struggle, at any rate, the crown, in favour of uniformity and conservatism, used its authority to enforce old methods. The early Stuarts multiplied inspectors to oversee the manufacture of tin, lead, iron, cloth, silk and even of beer, under the pretext of suppressing drunkenness.[1] Sometimes, as in the case of the soap industry in Charles I's reign, the government entrusted this inspection to privileged manufacturing companies, who exercised it in such a way as to provoke incessant protests from their competitors. This system of official regulation fell into complete disuse at the Restoration, but for a long time public opinion remained hostile to free manufactures. People feared that the introduction of new processes would upset trade, that some of the workmen would be reduced to poverty, and especially that the quality of the products would not be so good.

[1] Real beer, made aromatic with hops, had not long been known in the country.

Nevertheless, progress was made, though slowly. The cloth industry, the oldest established in the country, did indeed for a long time remain faithful to old methods. Right up to the end of the period we are studying it preserved, for the most part, its domestic character and its primitive machinery. In George III's reign wool was still spun by a wheel or spindle, carding was done by hand, weaving on an antiquated loom. Each workman took his cloth to the public mill to be fulled and teaselled, and very often he sold it before it had been dyed and dressed. Yet the products of this primitive industry were exported to Holland and the Baltic countries, to the Levant and the American colonies. But the cloth industry was alone in its use of old methods, and in the woollen industry itself new machines were introduced, such as the stocking-loom, the use of which, from the seventeenth century onwards, began to give rise to the formation of big factories. In the cotton industry, which was of recent origin and therefore escaped the old regulations, mechanical changes took place much more quickly. It was in this industry that the *flying shuttle* was first used; it was pushed first in one direction, then in the other, by a double propeller worked by a handle. By its means the workman was saved time and trouble, and much wider pieces of cloth could be made. By 1760 it was used generally throughout the kingdom to such an extent that there was a risk of a shortage of thread for the weavers. But in 1765 Hargreaves invented the jenny, an improved spinning-wheel with which it was possible to spin several threads at once. Thus equilibrium was again established between spinning and weaving, and this invention alone would have made the fortune of Lancashire.

Moreover, the use of new chemical processes revived the heavy metal trade, which was suffering for lack of raw material, and hastened the development of the mining industry. After many unsuccessful attempts Darby succeeded, about the year 1735, in using coal, previously reduced to coke, for smelting iron. In 1760 Roebuck constructed the first modern blast furnaces. The cast-iron bridge thrown across the Severn in 1779 marks the awakening of the British iron industry. Its success was uncertain for a time, however, for no method was known by which the rough cast-iron could be easily and in large quantities converted into malleable iron. But coal again came to the rescue, and in 1784 *puddling*[1] was introduced. From that time dates the real growth of the iron industry and its concentration in those districts where it remains to the present day, no longer near forests or waterfalls, but in the immediate neighbourhood of beds of coal or iron ore. By chance both these were found close together in the counties which border the Pennine Chain. From 1776 onwards the English metal trades ceased to be dependent on foreign iron from Sweden, Russia, Ireland or America.

But it was not enough to increase the workman's skill by these clever appliances and to work more advantageous combinations of minerals. An increased use of natural power was necessary to give more rapid movement to the increasingly complicated machines, and to handle larger and larger quantities of raw material. Hitherto use had been made only of running water and wind, especially the former. The first thing to do was to adapt the old water-wheel to the needs of the new industry. From the beginning of modern times it had been used exclusively for working the mallets to full cloth. In the second half of the eighteenth century Wyatt invented an ingenious system of rollers and spindles for stretching and twisting cotton thread, and Arkwright, perfecting the invention of his unfortunate predecessor, constructed his famous *water-frame* (1767). Hydraulic power supplied the motive force for both these inventions, and redoubled the activity of this industry which, no longer limited to the resources of human strength, was destined to become the most important of all the textile industries.[2]

Water-mills were also used in metallurgy. In the fifteenth century they worked forge bellows; in the sixteenth century they worked the machines for hammering and cutting iron. Towards 1783, when rollers began to replace hammers, they were turned by water-mills. But this power contained in

---

[1] Puddling consists of getting rid of the excess of carbon in the cast-iron by subjecting it to a second heating under the action of a strong blast.

[2] After his spinning machine, Arkwright successively patented about 1775 a carding machine, and a mechanical moving comb and roving machine.

streams and waterfalls was chiefly made use of in pumping. When it was a question of getting rid of the water which collected in mines and threatened to flood them, or of filling the reservoirs which supplied the towns with water, or of raising the water of a river to a certain height so as to control its current, only hydraulic pumps possessed the necessary power, and for such purposes they were used from the sixteenth century onwards.

Steam-power was hardly dreamed of. Savery's fire pump, which dated from 1698, used air pressure at least as much as steam pressure. Newcomen's pump, a few years later, was an advance on Savery's, in that it had a safety-valve, but here, too, steam was used only for the vacuum caused by condensation. It was really a pneumatic rather than a steam engine. Such as it was, however, it did excellent service for half a century (1720-1770) until the day when James Watt's discovery (1769) gave to the world the most tractable and most powerful motive force ever known.

§ 4. Relations between the Different Industrial Classes.

A. The Aristocracy of Labour

Inequality within the gilds—Workmen of the small country industries, domestic and free—Change from scattered to concentrated manufacture—Industrial and commercial concentration.

We must now see what modifications these changes in the conditions of industrial production brought about in the respective positions of the different classes of men who took part in them.

There is no need to emphasise here the well-known fact of the hierarchy of the gilds. In England, sooner perhaps than in any other country, this characteristic medieval institution felt the effects of the changes which heralded modern times. It need only be noted that the division already apparent in the gilds between the big manufacturers and merchants on the one hand, and the small masters on the other, became more marked towards the end of the gild régime. The twelve Livery Companies of London, like the Six Corporations of Paris, formed a sort of middle class aristocracy. But at the same time, in the light metal trade, for example, there existed a class of masters of small workshops, who employed only one or two men and themselves helped in the work. They were becoming increasingly dependent on the merchants who had always bought their manufactures and who now, in many cases, supplied them with the raw material as well. As to the ordinary journeymen, most of them had abandoned all hope of ever becoming masters. Lastly, Elizabeth revived the old regulation which fixed seven long years as the term of apprenticeship in town and country.

But while the gild system was thus crystallising into castes, the decisive development was taking place outside it. Let us consider first the situation of the workers in domestic industry who had succeeded in escaping both from the bonds of the old system and from the lure of the new capitalist enterprises. In the fifteenth and sixteenth centuries these free workmen had emigrated from the old towns into the suburbs or country districts, and had succeeded in avoiding the current of industrial concentration. They were to be found chiefly in the woollen industry. In the seventeenth century the greater part of the cloth of the country was produced in these family workshops, where the daughters turned the spinning-wheel and the sons carded the wool. while the father worked the loom. The government protected them, knowing that they would never be a menace to public tranquillity; for in times of unemployment they could always live on the produce of their patch of land and their cow and their hens.

These free country weavers sold their undressed cloth a piece at a time to the merchants of the nearest town, and it was thought that the agency of these expert dealers was sufficient guarantee for the consumer. All these craftsmen were their own masters, and at first all enjoyed equal economic independence. But the very necessities of production were not long in causing slight differences in rank. The weaver sometimes used more wool than his children could full and card. Then he would buy the extra wool himself in a raw state, but would give it out to his neighbours to prepare. Thus even in the villages an aristocracy of labour grew up. But when England began to use more wool than she produced and in many counties the local supply became inadequate, these weavers experienced great difficulty in securing their raw material, and they had to rely on wealthy agents for their supply. This burden more than outweighed the small favours which the government still granted them, and was one of the causes of the decline of that patriarchal type of industry, which did not, however, disappear until mechanical looms, worked by water or steam, came into general use.

Moreover, even in the seventeenth century the domestic cloth-workers had fallen into more or less complete dependence on a more fortunate class. Many of them had found themselves too poor to buy their wool, and some rich Yorkshire landowner or merchant had provided them with the necessary material. In course of time these contractors had come to claim repayment in kind, in cloth not in money, and it was to them instead of to the other merchants that the workman sold the product of his labour. Insensibly the custom grew up of agreeing in advance on a fixed sum which the workman was to receive for each piece of cloth made. Thus he became the employee of the contractor. In most cases he still owned his machinery, but the slightest technical innovation was enough to rob him even of this. When the knitting-loom was introduced into the manufacture of stockings, very few of the domestic weavers could afford to buy it. The rest either had to go into the big workshops set up by the manufacturers and fitted with the new machinery, or else were obliged to hire a loom and pay *frame-rent;* and even then their position was in effect that of wage-earners. In the cotton industry the same changes took place, but much more quickly. Some improvements were made in the primitive machinery, but these were not enough to delay the inevitable issue of an unequal struggle in an industry which was destined from the first to be run on a big scale.

We must not linger, then, over the study of this free domestic manufacture, which represents only a transient stage in industrial evolution, but must pass at once to the great capitalist enterprises which are characteristic of modern times. Even as early as the fifteenth century we have seen that certain clothiers concentrated workmen in numbers varying from ten to one hundred in regular factories. Then for a time this development seemed to be interrupted. When the wealthy contractor reappeared, a hundred years later, it

was in the comparatively modest guise of the merchant who
bought unfinished cloth from the village weavers and dressed
and dyed it before selling it again.   But gradually it became
the custom for him to provide the wool for the country
workmen who, in future, worked solely for him.   In the
end he even hired out their looms to them.   The country
merchants became his employees.   Many, driven by choice or
necessity, gave up their bits of land in order to live in or
near a town.   For a time they continued to work in their
own homes, but in the end the big employer would concentrate all the spinners or weavers of the district in one
enormous factory.

In the first stage of this revolution the advantages of a
purely commercial management assured the success of big
business over individual and independent labour.   The man
who did business on a big scale could more easily adapt
himself to the fluctuations of the market, and he alone could,
at a given moment, deliver big consignments of goods to
meet the demands of his customers.   As he was both manufacturer and salesman, he could keep in touch with popular
demands much more easily than the merchant who was only
a middleman.   In short, the advantage of the new organisation was that it established—or re-established—contact
between the producer and the consumer.   As to the ultimate
change from the domestic to the factory system, the decisive
factor was the use of one set of machinery to work great
numbers of looms, a process which made it essential to have
all the workers in the same building.[1]

These various considerations applied even more closely
to the cotton and silk manufactures.   These two branches of
the textile industry had only recently been established in
the country, and therefore their traditions were less deeply
rooted and less tenacious.   Moreover, both depended on the
foreigner for their raw material, which, in one case, was very
expensive, and, finally, both offered exceptional facilities
for the development of machinery.   For all these reasons

[1] The jenny did not necessitate the use of big factories.   But the
introduction of the water-frame, which could work a great number of
machines, altered the situation.   Thus, from 1780 onwards, many
spinning-mills in Manchester employed six or seven hundred workpeople in the same building.

they were soon organised on the new plan, the principal features of which we have just described.

The heavy metal industry had, even in the Middle Ages, necessitated a certain concentration of capital, all the more because the two operations of extracting and smelting the iron ore, which to-day are quite distinct, were then almost always combined in one undertaking. In the sixteenth and seventeenth centuries the English ironmasters, who were at the same time mineowners, belonged for the most part to the great nobility. The coalowners were not long in rivalling them in wealth, and at the end of the eighteenth century these upstarts in the mining aristocracy initiated the bold policy of an employers' union to control mining and get better terms from the shipping companies.

Certain branches of the light metal industry, such as nail-making, did indeed preserve their domestic character. But even in this restricted area there was some commercial if no technical concentration. Many wealthy manufacturers found it advantageous to organise the production of several different articles at once. Thus some big ironmonger of Sheffield or Birmingham might manufacture bronze ornaments, metal buttons, watch-chains and snuff-boxes.

Still more industries were by degrees drawn into this movement, which was becoming universal. At Birmingham, in addition to the big ordnance factories, large glass and paper works were set up. This irresistible development was felt even in the small workshops which seemed to have escaped it. Alongside the old master-tailors who continued to work, like our dressmakers, in the house of the customer who furnished the material, were set up clothing establishments, where the customer could chose his cloth, and be measured and fitted for the suit, which was made for him by workpeople in the employment of the *entrepreneur*.

B. Condition of the Ordinary Workmen

Position of the journeymen—Position of workmen in big industrial concerns—The fixing of wages—Paupers forced to work; the poor rate (1601); the workman bound to his own parish (1662)—Three periods in the history of the workman: alternation between relative prosperity and great distress—Struggles between workmen and masters.

⊹ We must now consider how the position of the workers was affected by these changes in industrial organisation and management and particularly by the partial survival and gradual alteration of the gild system.

It is obvious that the Elizabethan laws which opposed the reduction of the term of apprenticeship did not improve the position of the journeyman, although they insisted on the traditional limitation of the number of apprentices. But on this point the new laws were not long respected, and the relative protection which they gave to the workmen soon ceased to be effective. For instance, in the seventeenth century the introduction of the knitting machine in the stocking industry made the work much easier, and employers were led to hire far more apprentices than were allowed by the regulations.

⊹ The new manufacturers were bound neither by custom nor, save in special cases, by law; and they were free to employ as many women, and even children, as they liked. At Norwich, in the seventeenth century, " a little creature of six years old was thought fit for labour. Several writers of that time, and among them some who were considered as eminently benevolent, mention, with exultation, the fact that, in that single city, boys and girls of very tender age created wealth exceeding what was necessary for their own subsistence by twelve thousand pounds a year."[1] Such competition seriously affected the position of the adult worker. The coming of the new industrial system did indeed free the workman from gild restrictions and gave him freedom of movement. But without capital he had no chance of becoming a master, and, go where he would, he would still be the victim of his poverty and of the over-

[1] Macaulay, *History of England*, vol. i, p. 420.

whelming numbers of his class. Even more than when he was under the protection of his craft would he suffer from periods of unemployment, which became more frequent and more serious as a result of the fluctuations of an ever-widening market. Moreover, he would be subject to harsh discipline in those huge workshops where machinery was coming into its own.

There was no custom to fix the wages of this new working class which was growing up outside the old institutions, and this uncertainty rendered legislative action both possible and necessary. Already in Richard II's reign, soon after the Black Death (1348), the state had intervened to fix wages, and Elizabeth followed this example. In her reign the Justices of the Peace were given the task of maintaining a reasonable balance between rates of wages and the price of necessities. Wages must not be too high or too low. The regulation of corn prices and the regulation of wages were strictly correlated. It goes without saying that in practice the magistrates usually fixed wages at a rate barely above the minimum subsistence level, but it is also clear that the government considered it a duty to preserve from extremity this mass of workers whose only capital was their labour, who did not possess economic independence, and had no industrial union to protect them against the future excesses of their employers' greed. Soon after the Restoration, however, this policy of protecting labour was abandoned.

Meanwhile, in the sixteenth century another principle which was destined profoundly to influence English administration and, in consequence, the condition of the workers, was making progress in Europe; this was the principle of forced labour for able-bodied paupers. Towards the beginning of Elizabeth's reign various circumstances, the compulsory dismissal of great numbers of retainers, the suppression of religious charitable institutions, the progress of enclosures and the division of the common lands, had caused a formidable increase of vagabondage. The first measures directed against this plague had been both cruel and useless. Then it was decided to meet the evil by extending to the whole country a system which had already been tried successfully in some of the big towns, and which consisted in setting vagabonds to work. This had the double advantage of bringing them under control and possibly of reforming them.

Among the hosts of paupers who lived at the public expense, an attempt was made to distinguish between the impotent and those who were able-bodied but idle. As a result of a series of edicts which were finally embodied in the Poor Law of 1601, parishes were henceforth obliged to confine the latter in Houses of Correction, where they were set to work. This original organisation went on developing throughout the seventeenth century. In 1723 it was carried still further, when local authorities were ordered to refuse relief to any pauper who would not enter the workhouse. These laws were doubtless not carried out to the letter; but it was only towards the end of the eighteenth century that the Workhouse Test began to be superseded by various kinds of public employment and that a little humanity tempered the harshness of a system which was not particularly successful even from an economic point of view. Yet it must be noted that the system was the result of a strong determination to uphold order and public security, and was inspired neither by blind hatred of the unfortunate nor by systematic hostility to the working class. The unemployed constituted a permanent danger. At moments of industrial crisis, when their number was likely to be increased, the government, especially in the time of the early Stuarts, did not hesitate to force employers to keep and pay their workmen just as in times of prosperity.

Nevertheless, there remained a numerous class of people who were reduced to poverty by an intermittent or perpetual shortage of work. They could neither be shut up in workhouses nor succoured in hospitals. To relieve their distress the Act of 1601 had ordered an obligatory rate to be collected in every parish instead of the old voluntary contributions. The justices or churchwardens, who were left to decide the amount of the rate, naturally fixed it as low as possible. As was just, it was paid by the rich, but in return they had henceforth at their disposal a great number of labourers who were ready, whenever the occasion presented itself, to do a great deal of work in order to supplement their resources by even the smallest sum. The existence of this reserve army of labour always at hand and semi-gratuitous, in addition to the workmen in regular employment, naturally lowered the position of the whole wage-earning class.

On the other hand, since the Civil War had increased the number of those dependent on the rates, some parishes tried to get rid of some of their paupers by passing them on to neighbouring parishes. To check this abuse the Act of Settlement of 1662 ordered that if any person who changed his abode seemed likely to become a charge on his new parish he might be sent back to that in which he was legally domiciled. After the Revolution of 1688 the list of all new-comers into the village had to be read publicly every Sunday after service. Thus labourers were bound like serfs to their parishes. In many places they were far in excess of the demand for their work and were condemned to live in wretched idleness; or, if some new business were set up there to profit by this supply of labour, they could only hope to obtain starvation wages.

Is it possible to estimate the real condition of the working classes as a whole in the midst of all these political and economic changes? At any rate, one can attempt to sketch it.

The fifteenth century and the first quarter of the sixteenth seem to have been a sort of Golden Age for the English working class. Wages rose, in spite of Acts of Parliament, while the price of necessities remained low. The Wars of the Roses, fatal to the nobility, had hardly any effect on the prosperity of the workers. But afterwards for more than a century, until about 1650, the condition of artisans and workmen became less favourable day by day. Like all persons depending on incomes the rate of which was fixed by contract, law or custom, they suffered from the debasement of the coinage to which both Henry VIII and Edward VI had recourse. Then, from about 1580, the effects of the natural depreciation of silver began to be felt in the country. During the next sixty years the price of necessities doubled, while wages only rose twenty per cent. Elizabethan wage legislation, by taking as the basis of the official rates the nominal rate of wages which was usual in the preceding period, only delayed and hindered the considerable rise which would have been necessary to maintain the workers in the same degree of real comfort. Thus there followed an increase of pauperism, and the evil was all the more serious since Edward VI's confiscations had deprived the workman of the help which the gilds might have given him. There was no one now who would lend him money without demanding interest, grant a pension to his widow or discharge the expenses incurred by apprenticing his children. Thus distress spread among the industrial population, especially in big towns, where wages were almost as low as in the country districts.

From 1650 until about 1770 the fortune of the workers seemed to improve. Even during the Civil War commerce and industry were developing. Domestic spinning, as we have seen, was spreading in rural districts, and most of the workers possessed a small holding of land as well, a fact which made it possible for them sometimes to take life easily, so that the masters denounced their indolence. Their needs, which at first were very few, increased in time, and a slight addition of well-paid work together with the low price of necessities enabled them to satisfy their new appetite for comfort. Barley bread was gradually replaced by wheaten bread on their tables, while meat and even tea became part of their usual diet. But this relative comfort was very precarious. The profound changes which were taking place or impending both in industry and in agriculture—on the one hand the introduction of machinery, and on the other the division of the common lands—were soon to destroy it.

It is therefore not surprising that there were many disputes between the different classes who took part in the work of manufacture.[1] Even in the gilds there had been collisions which grew daily more frequent as the barrier between journeymen and masters became increasingly difficult to cross. In the sixteenth century the journeymen incessantly demanded a strict limitation of the number of apprentices, and even an increase in wages. In 1710 the London stocking-knitters went on strike, enraged because their masters profited by the use of a new loom to employ an excessive number of apprentices. They broke machinery which did not belong to them, and the use of which threatened to ruin them.

[1] See a ballad which was sung in the streets (Macaulay, i, 419).

But the most decisive conflicts took place among the free workmen, who belonged to no gild and were unprotected. As early as the sixteenth century, in spite of legal prohibitions, there were some attempts to form workmen's unions among the workers engaged in the great industries. But long years passed before there appeared the first permanent organisations, humble ancestors of modern Trade Unions, founded to improve the condition of the wage-earners. At the beginning of the eighteenth century the wool-combers of the south-west, who were clever workmen, difficult to replace, fairly well paid and used to carrying on their work from town to town, profited by their advantages to establish an unchartered corporation, branches of which spread throughout the kingdom. The avowed aim of the society was to obtain by threats of strike, more than once put into execution with violence, the fixing of a minimum wage, and even the masters' promise not to employ workmen who were not members of the society. In London as soon as there appeared a new class of tailor-*entrepreneurs* distinct from the old masters, the latter, reduced to the position of workmen, formed an association to obtain better wages from their new employers. This movement for concentrating the forces of the workers became especially marked after 1760. Strikes had always been frequent among the coal-miners of Newcastle. In 1763 the watermen of the port formed some sort of definite organisation to force the mineowners to use measures recently fixed by Parliament. Nothing shows the progressive seriousness of these conflicts more clearly than the series of Acts passed to prevent them. In George I's reign all workmen's associations were formally forbidden. In George III's reign the masters were authorised to form associations in order to proceed against machine-breakers. This was the dawn which foretold the great social conflicts of our own day.

III.—AGRICULTURE

The progress of agriculture in England went hand in hand with the development of commerce and industry, and it may be said that the one was the natural consequence of the other. The various branches of economic activity helped instead of hindering each other; there were momentary discords, but these were soon resolved in harmony.

§ 1. Markets and Taxation.

At the beginning of the modern era England, from an agricultural point of view, was essentially a wool-producing country. The rise in the price of this article throughout Europe was so favourable to the English wool-growers that big manufactures were established, as we have seen, at the very gates of their sheep-runs. This saving effected on the carriage of the wool still further increased their profits. Thus during the first half of the sixteenth century sheep-farming became general throughout the country, while arable farming, threatened with the competition of Baltic corn and suffering still more from the relative costliness of labour, was on the decline.

But for reasons of public safety the government, from Henry VIII's time, did its best to check this development. Then, from about 1600 until 1760, the wealthy clothiers were powerful enough to prevent the export of raw material which they meant to buy themselves at the lowest possible price. Landed proprietors protested vigorously and incessantly, but as a matter of fact they did not suffer as much as might be imagined. They had many compensations. There was a flourishing contraband trade in wool, so that the official restrictions did not ruin them. New resources were opening to them in stock-breeding, which the government encouraged by a protective policy and even, in Charles II's reign, by the prohibition of competitors; in the export of butter and cheese; and later in horse-breeding, which the government encouraged most effectively by organising races. Moreover, they soon began to find a valuable compensation in the cultivation and sale of corn.

Under Henry VII and Henry VIII corn could only be exported by special permit, which had to be dearly bought, but Elizabeth allowed free export to everyone on payment of a regular duty. At the Restoration an import duty was fixed on cereals. This duty, which varied according to the market price of corn, remained in force until 1773, and protected the native grower from any risk of loss from foreign competition. Immediately after the Restoration (1689) the corn export trade, which was already flourishing, was encouraged by the methodical application of a system of bounties. This system remained in force during the first sixty years of the eighteenth century, and had the ultimate effect of raising the prices which it was intended to lower. Exporters who wished to earn the bounty had to load their grain in British vessels, but this did nothing to restrict the trade, and although for a long time selling prices were moderate, at any rate the nation's agriculture benefited uninterruptedly from a good vent and an easy market.

When, towards 1765, the export trade slackened, it was as a result of the increased demands of the home market. The development of industry caused a rapid increase in population (which was trebled in the space of one hundred and fifty years), an extraordinarily rapid growth of towns, and even an increase in general comfort. The natural consequence was a rise in the price of food, and since the days were far off when food regulations compelled farmers to empty their barns to relieve scarcity, prices became very high. Moreover, communications were easier, and thanks to the factors who were prepared to buy grain from samples and then take delivery direct from the granaries, internal trade was organised, and the value of land was greatly increased, for the very reason that prices were rising.

Add to this that the cultivator was quite secure from fiscal exactions, since the tax payable by him was completely abolished in 1698. The landowner himself had no need to fear that increasing taxation would rob him of the profits won from the progress of agriculture and of the trade in agricultural produce, for the land tax, based on the ancient assessment, was fixed in principle, and, indeed, during the peace and retrenchment of Walpole's ministry, it was actually reduced by a quarter.

Thus wide markets and light taxation combined to render possible the prosperity of English agriculture.

§ 2. Agricultural Production.

A. CAPITAL

Gentlemen farmers—The return of the aristocracy to the land; Lord Townshend—Big farmers and long leases.

There was no lack of land. In the sixteenth century there were enormous tracts of waste land, while the confiscation of the property of the regular clergy and of many of the great nobles offered a still easier field for the exploitation of new methods of cultivation. But what was needed was capital.

Among the rapidly growing class of rich merchants, however, there were sure to be some who would be wise enough to buy landed property and to farm it to the best advantage. Such a purchase was both a good investment and a means of rising in the social scale. These wealthy merchants, clothiers, goldsmiths, butchers and tanners could henceforth rival the landed aristocracy in influence and splendour, while at the same time they increased their fortunes. Thus was formed a new class, the gentlemen farmers. These new landowners were not obliged to live, more or less modestly, on the natural or traditional products of their land, nor were they bound by any inherited tradition. Their only aim was to get as much money as possible out of their estates by making them produce what would sell best at the neighbouring markets. Instead of the patriarchal routine of cultivation which aimed at supplying only domestic needs, they introduced the bolder methods of commercial agriculture producing for a market.

This change went on slowly until the last years of the seventeenth century, when, at the moment when it seemed as though the commercial and financial middle class was about to win, unopposed, the leading place in the state, the old nobility began once again to take an interest in the land. We have already seen that they could borrow the weapons of their successful rivals and go into business. They could command money with what still remained to them of political influence or social prestige, could demand bribes from ministers, or regild their coats of arms by a misalliance. But the most honourable and certain way of restoring their power and preserving their rank lay in improving the lands they still possessed, in order to get a larger revenue from them. Moreover, the gentleman who had gone into the brewing or woollen industry would find it very profitable to get rid of middlemen and grow his own barley and hops to make his beer, or to produce on his own land the wool used in his manufacture, just as, a hundred and fifty years earlier, the sheep-farmer had found it paid him to set up his own workshop for spinning and weaving. The dictates of fashion soon followed the counsels of self-interest, and the craze for kennels and stables was succeeded by a craze for agriculture.

In the first thirty years of the eighteenth century England became the model of Europe in all that concerned rural life; it was here that there began the great " Return to Nature " movement which filled the second half of the century. Thomson, twenty-five years before J.-J. Rousseau, preached in his poem, " The Seasons " (1726-30), the charms of simplicity, even of primitive savagery, and praised the beauty of lakes, meadows and forests.[1] The " English garden," with its paths, its dells, its lawns, broken by clumps of trees, its brooks winding through the green, replaced the geometrical regularity of avenues and bowers made to measure, round or square sheets of water, yew-trees cut in balls or pyramids, in a word, the rather formal architecture of the French garden. The park of Versailles had been the model of the seventeenth century. In the eighteenth century the Petit Trianon bore witness to the change of taste which had taken place. Following and hastening this movement, which was carrying everyone with it, the English nobles no longer spent more than a few months in London, and the rest of the year lived on their estates, on which they lavished their attention.

The signal for this " emigration " to the country was

[1] " Now from the town,
Buried in smoke and sleep and noisome damps,
Oft let me wander o'er the dewy fields
Where freshness breathes, and dash the trembling drops
From the bent bush, as through the verdant maze
Of sweet-briar hedges I pursue my walk."

And at each step he breaks into dithyrambs in praise of the state of nature.

given by some nobles of the Tory party, who were suspected of an indiscreet loyalty to the fallen dynasty and were unpopular at the court, which in any case had little attraction for them. In 1730 Lord Townshend, one of the most powerful men in the kingdom, quarrelled with Walpole, the Prime Minister. He retired to his Norfolk estates and devoted the rest of his life to great agricultural developments. As might be imagined, these examples were not wasted. "The pursuit was universal. Citizens who were engaged in London business five days in the week were farmers for the other two; men who had been brought up to other pursuits deserted them for a trade which appeared easy and independent. It was a by-industry with those who had other callings. Physicians, lawyers, clergymen, soldiers, sailors and merchants were farmers as well."[1] They gave to the land their leisure and, what was more important, their money.

More than this, however, the land demanded the unceasing care and experience of trained farmers. The great farmers who came into prominence in the eighteenth century provided both capital and the necessary technical organisation. They were wealthy men who had profited by the low rate of interest to stock their farms in the best market, financiers who owned as many as twenty ploughs and who could afford to spend a hundred pounds in improving a single acre of land.

It was essential that the farmer should be disposed to turn to the best advantage the capital which he could devote to the cultivation of the land. Up to 1527 it seems clear that the law did not officially guarantee him the full enjoyment of the rights conferred on him by his lease until the expiration of the contract,[2] and for a long time afterwards the ill-advised system of tenure at will continued to exist, not only in Ireland, but in England. In the seventeenth century, however, following the teaching of Gabriel Plattes, who had proclaimed the necessity of interesting the farmer in the improvement of the land, landowners ceased to cancel established leases without due reason. Moreover, they allowed their tenants to renew their leases in advance on payment of a fee, or granted them a long lease, sometimes even for life.

[1] Thorold Rogers, *op. cit.*, p. 470.
[2] See Ashley, *Economic History*, vol. i, part ii, p. 272 *et seq.*

The combined efforts of all these different social classes were necessary to finish the work of reclamation. It is difficult for us to realise that about the year 1685 cultivated land and pasture accounted for less than half the area of the kingdom; the rest consisted of moors, forests and marshes. Some districts were infested with foxes. In the Lowlands stags wandered through the woods, and a few wild bulls still haunted even the southern forests.[1] But now the waste land was encroached upon further and further every day, and while the total area under cultivation increased, so also did the productivity of each holding. Wild beasts were killed off or disappeared; the last wild boars were killed in Charles I's reign, the last wolves in Scotland at the end of Charles II's reign.

B. TECHNICAL IMPROVEMENTS

The first period of enclosures—Convertible husbandry—Progress of rotation of crops, roots for fodder, artificial grasses; Gabriel Plattes (1638)—Manures—Progress in horse and cattle breeding: Bakewell and sheep breeding—Second period of enclosures; redistribution of holdings in the open fields and division of the common land—Growth of big farms.

Until the close of the sixteenth century it may be said with some truth that English agriculture was still extensive in character. The conditions of the European market in the time of the early Tudors were such that wealthy landowners, old and new alike, were induced to increase the number of sheep on their estates, to the detriment of agriculture. But sheep-farming could only be practised on a grand scale and become the basis of rural economy if the flocks of each farmer could range over large and continuous stretches of enclosed land. The landowners therefore began by enclosing their woods to keep out the cattle belonging to the peasants of the district, while at the same time secularised or confiscated estates offered a field naturally suited for the operations of those who bought them. But on the whole the country still remained that mosaic of small holdings, so entangled one with the other that it was impossible to enclose them, which was the result of the *open field* system.

[1] Macaulay, *op. cit.*, p. 341.

If these scattered strips belonged to a single owner, he had no more pressing task than to unite them into one farm under his own direction. He had to buy up a few strips belonging to other people in order to round off his farm, and soon his pasture stretched almost out of sight to the new hedges which marked the distant bounds. The big sheep-farmers contrived to appropriate the greater part of the commons also, by means of legal division or rather by gradual encroachment, and these, too, they hedged to fold their sheep.

In Elizabeth's reign, however, commercial conditions altered and the plough became as profitable as the sheep. The progress of enclosures was checked, and in new enclosures part of the land was devoted to arable farming. It was the time of convertible husbandry, when the same piece of land was used now for pasture and now for crops. Landowners set themselves to improve their estates. They devoted part of their income to draining marshy ground, or building dykes to protect land threatened by the sea. The government made some attempt to undertake these costly works at public expense, but this failed and they were left to the initiative of private individuals, who sometimes formed associations to carry out the most important enterprises.

But, setting aside these preliminary works, many of which were destroyed during the Civil War, there was very little improvement in the actual processes of agriculture. Farmers still clung to the triennial rotation of crops, restricted to cereals and a few vegetables; one year wheat, the next oats, barley, beans, peas or vetch, and then a fallow year. Often, indeed, the fields lay fallow every other year. The tenant who could be turned out of his land at the owner's will, or the small farmer who had only secured a short lease, hesitated before going to the expense of liming or marling when he ran the risk of not reaping the benefit of his improvements. From idleness or poverty, rather than from design, small landowners also followed the same unintelligent routine. As for the common fields which remained undivided and were still farmed collectively, it may be imagined how small was their yield.

It was not until the reign of James I that, under the influence of Dutch agriculture, an advance took place in agricultural methods. The first improvements were introduced soon after the truce which had just guaranteed peace to the heroic republic (1609). Gabriel Plattes, the first theorist of modern agricultural science in Britain, whose chief work appeared in 1638, was undoubtedly Dutch in origin. Simon Hartlib, the friend of Milton, and one of the most active publicists of the new movement, was a naturalised Dutchman. In the eighteenth century Lord Townshend still drew his inspiration from the example of Dutch farmers.

Real progress was made in filling up the unproductive gap caused by the fallow year and keeping the land permanently under cultivation, by introducing, into the regular rotation of crops, new crops, which not only rested and recuperated the soil, but indirectly brought about an increased revenue. In the seventeenth century root crops such as the turnip, which since the time of the Renaissance had been grown in gardens, were chiefly used in this way. But for a long time these new crops were neglected in the same way as the old fields of peas and vetch had been. They were allowed to be overgrown by weeds, which exhausted the soil and came up stronger than ever the next year in the midst of the corn. The turnip, which could be sown immediately after the harvest to provide winter food for the cattle, did not become really important in English agriculture until after the publication of Jethro Tull's description of the new methods of cultivation (1731), which made it possible to grow much bigger roots, and until " Turnip " Townshend, as he was nicknamed, had proved its value.

The development of artificial grasses, which later reached such vast proportions, was still slower. Gabriel Plattes did indeed recommend sainfoin, and clover seed appeared in price lists at the end of the seventeenth century. But nothing was known about the selection of seeds and the use of the aftermath. In 1772, on the other hand, at least half the farmers used clover, and Arthur Young proposed a system of quinquennial rotation founded on the alternation of different kinds of cereals, roots and grasses.

Agricultural machinery was also improving. Plattes was the first to mention the drill; a hundred years later Tull recommended deep ploughing and harrowing, and Townshend again proved the value of these innovations. Gradually wooden ploughshares fell into disuse, and by about 1760 wealthy farmers such as Coke of Holkham owned collections of agricultural implements really worthy of the name. Not only did liming and marling receive great attention, but experiments were made with all sorts of mineral manures, with the ashes of heath, bracken, broom, stubble and pit-coal; everything was tried to promote the natural fecundity of the soil, old rags and scraps of cloth and malt dust. But animal manure still remained the chief fertiliser. Plattes urged the farmer to manure his land freely. It was not enough to pasture a flock of sheep on it from time to time, but it must be covered with rich farm manure from the stables and pig-sties. The development of the new fodder crops, whether hay or roots, served to furnish abundant supplies of food for the beasts in the stables.

Thus stock-breeding and agriculture advanced together to the stage of intensive production. The sixteenth century had seen great improvements in the breed of sheep. Then, in Charles I's reign, came the age of the Cavaliers with their passion for the turf. Barbary stallions were brought from Morocco to produce a breed of swifter and more nervous horses suitable for racing. At the same time the breed of draught animals was improved by the importation of strong grey Flanders mares.[1] As to oxen and cows, in the summer they were badly fed, and in the winter very few of them were kept. Until the middle of the seventeenth century it was the custom, since there was so little fodder for the winter, to slaughter most of them and salt the meat. For several months in the year the peasants and even the gentry in the provinces had no meat but " St. Martin's beef."[2] But as the hay harvest increased, or roots were grown to supplement it, English farmers took better care of their beasts. The Dutch had taught them the arts of butter- and fine cheese-making. The increased demand for fresh meat, which followed the rise in the people's standard of comfort, also helped stock-farmers and encouraged them to improve their herds, and the constant dampness of the climate was favourable to cattle farming.

[1] See Renard and Dulac, *L'évolution industrielle et agricole depuis cent cinquante ans*. Paris, 1912.

[2] Macaulay, *op. cit.*

At the end of the eighteenth century scientific methods of cross-breeding and selection were first tried by Bakewell at his well-known farm, Dishley Grange in Leicester. His object was no longer to produce sheep with thick fine wool or oxen with strong frames and muscles, but to breed both so as to produce as much meat as possible for the market. At the same time Colling bred his celebrated herd of Durham oxen. Between 1710 and 1795 the average weight of sheep or cattle more than doubled. These huge idle beasts, destined to pass from the cattle-shed to the slaughter-house, also contributed to the enrichment of the ploughlands, which were henceforth worked only by teams of horses and which also doubled their yield during the century.

Other new plants, besides the fodder crops, had been introduced. About 1550 the hop crossed the North Sea. In the next century " William Temple, in his intervals of leisure, tried many horticultural experiments and showed that many fruit-trees, natives of more favoured climates, could, with artificial aid, grow in English soil. Evelyn, with the authority of the Royal Society, issued instructions in the art of planting,"[1] and attention was given to silviculture. The potato, first introduced into Lancashire, doubtless direct from America, soon spread all over the country.

This development of intensive agriculture caused a revival of the movement for agricultural concentration and exclusive ownership which had seemed to be arrested in Elizabeth's reign. Already Plattes had shown the superiority of individual over communal agriculture, and the advantages which the farmer gained from a good hedge which sheltered him from all trespassers. In 1692 a third of the country was still occupied by commons, and of the rest the greater part was still under the domination of the open field system, which meant that a good deal of it was wasted in common pasture. In the interval between the two dates fixed by custom for harvest and ploughing, the proprietor ceased to be master of his land, over which all the flocks of the village could wander. If he were too early or too late he suffered. He must not infringe the laws of the customary routine. Even if he feared that his neighbour's cattle, by mixing with his, might bring disease, he had no right to exclude them. The rules of the

---

[1] Macaulay, *op. cit.*

traditional rotation applied uniformly to the whole parish. If the cultivator were bold enough to put into practice the new continuous rotation, he ran the risk of seeing his patch of lucerne or turnips, which was a mere speck in the midst of the wide fallow fields, treated exactly as if it, too, were fallow. If he complained, he was involved in endless law-suits.

Good hedges, on the contrary, excluded all these difficulties and prevented such damage. They checked at the edge of well-cultivated fields the invasion of weeds from the neglected land in the neighbourhood. They broke the force of the wind and afforded shelter from the sometimes excessive heat of the sun. But best of all they gave to each farmer freedom to exercise his own initiative and to reap the fruit of it. Therefore, in Anne's reign Parliament, in answer to numerous petitions from landowners, again began to author-ise enclosures. But it was especially after the accession of George III that enclosure Acts multiplied. Between the beginning and end of the century it was estimated that three million acres had been enclosed, and this transformation went on continuously until 1830.

But what was the use of authorising individuals to enclose their own fields, if farms remained subdivided into strips and inextricably entangled in the open fields, and if the common lands were still open to everyone? To assure the success of intensive agriculture it was necessary to redistribute the lands of every township, both commons and open fields. Such was, in fact, the procedure adopted by Parliament in the eighteenth century, and the division of the common lands, as well as the exchange of holdings between proprietors in the open fields, was always managed in such a way as to favour the big landowner at the expense of the small. Very often the small landowners, discontented with the new hold-ing assigned to them, preferred to give it up to a rich neighbour. Thus one man acquired huge estates which were both easy and profitable to enclose. This was the " promised land " of the new agriculture.

Unless the dimensions of these estates were too vast, the owner who had thus built them up out of many small hold-ings took very good care not to divide up their management among several farmers. Those whom he found established on the various scraps of his new domain he dismissed. It has been estimated that between 1740 and 1788 the number of separate farms was decreased by forty or fifty thousand. This union of farms made it possible to dispense with much labour and to economise on much useless expenditure. Moreover, the big farmer, better informed and richer than the others, would be able to choose the best seed and get the most perfect implements. He had the additional advantage of being able to store his crops till after Christmas, to await the rise in price which always came towards the end of the winter season. Moreover, in big farms, as in factories, the profitable system of division of labour could be introduced. There was only one important branch of rural economy in which small farms remained supreme and in which agriculture preserved in some measure a domestic character. This was poultry farming.

§ 3. Agricultural Classes.

Glance at Ireland—England: fortune of the big landowners—Vicissitudes of the yeomanry and the small farmers—Growing prosperity of the big farmers—Day labourers alternate between comfort and extreme want.

We have tried to explain how, during the three centuries we are studying, an enormous increase in the volume of English agricultural produce had been made possible. The widening of home and foreign markets, the encouragement of the government and public opinion, the increase of capital devoted to agriculture and the progress of agricultural science had all contributed to this. We must now see how this new wealth was shared between the different classes who took part in the business of agriculture and how each of them was affected by the commercial and technical changes.

It is convenient here to make special mention of Ireland. This unfortunate country, united to England by force, had been for centuries treated by her as a conquered country. The conquerors began by destroying the communal system of land-holding, which made all the members of the clan joint-owners of the soil and which has perhaps left a trace in the Irish custom which gives to the tenant any increment in the value of the land caused by his labour and his capital. But it was after the sixteenth century that the oppression and dispossession of the native Irish was carried to its highest pitch. The Irish, in the eyes of the English, were not only wrong in being of another race and speaking another language, but were guilty of professing another religion. They remained Catholic while their big neighbour became Protestant. Therefore they suffered confiscations, massacre, burning. In Elizabeth's reign Ulster, the most fertile part of their country, became a regular Puritan colony, where English nobles and city merchants shared the land taken from the primitive inhabitants.

In Cromwell's time Ireland, which had declared in favour of the absolute monarchy of the Stuarts, paid heavily for her loyalty to a defeated cause. It is estimated that five hundred thousand people were put to the sword, while a hundred thousand were sold as slaves in the colonies. The Catholics who remained were transplanted, by choice or by force, into the marshy districts of Connaught. The River Shannon acted as a boundary between these survivors and the newcomers, who took the places of those who had been killed or expelled.[1]

A little later, in and after the reign of William III, the Irish, despised, robbed, reduced to the condition of tenants at will on their own lands, excluded from the liberal careers, hampered by a thousand obstacles in commerce and industry, were indeed one of the martyred peoples of modern Europe, and the peasants, ignorant and starving, had no choice but to seek another country overseas. It is easy to understand what drove the vigorous pamphleteer, Swift, to paint in fiery words the misery of his countrymen, and to write that bitter lampoon, " A modest proposal for preventing the children of poor people from becoming a burthen to their parents or country " (1729). He showed there, with imperturbable gravity, the obvious advantages of turning such tender flesh into butcher's meat and making pies from these encumbrances.

In the eighteenth century, however, the situation of Ireland began to improve. An Irish Protestant, Henry Grattan, worked with all his energy for the repeal of the

---

[1] Barbe Gendre, *Études sociales*. Paris, 1886.

draconian legislation which ground down the Catholics, the pariahs of his nation, and in 1782 he succeeded in obtaining Home Rule. The lull, though only temporary, was very valuable, for it gave the Irish fisheries and woollen export trade a chance to recover, and, more than this, it gave hope for the future.

We must now return to Great Britain.

In the first rank of rural society came the landowners. But here a distinction must be made between the lords of huge estates and the modest owners of small holdings, whose futures were to be widely different.

The first class included the aristocracy of nobles, the squires who made up the gentry, and also the wealthy bourgeoisie who had bought land from them. Now, although it is obvious that the confiscation of the possessions of many of the old families and the secularisation of monastic lands had enabled the gentry to buy new property at a very cheap rate, it does not seem that up to the end of the sixteenth century the revenue of the soil, taking the kingdom as a whole, had really increased. Little progress had been made in the methods of agriculture, and the rise in price of all products, except wool, was purely nominal. The farmer who sold his produce at a higher rate had also to pay a higher price for the articles he needed.

But in the first half of the seventeenth century methods of cultivation began to improve, and the long peace enjoyed by the country was favourable to the sale of produce. Thus revenue from land increased, and the gentry, whose premature desire for luxury Elizabeth had tried to restrain, could henceforth indulge their splendid tastes without fear. The manor houses which date from that time show their wealth if not their good taste. The Civil War checked this prosperity, but it revived again after the Revolution. Agriculture had become more intensive, the bounties given by the state enabled farmers to sell their corn at a good price, and farm rents rose to a level twenty times higher than that of two hundred years ago.[1]

[1] Macaulay gives a picture of a squire about 1685. He notes especially the contrast between his homely appearance and manners and his aristocratic virtues and pretensions. Here we have the true country gentleman.

The wealthy landowners saw their revenues increasing, especially during the long and peaceful ministry of Walpole (1712-1742). The slight increase of indirect taxation of which they complained scarcely checked the growth of their fortunes. The increase in the rent of land was so continuous and regular that about 1750 its capitalisation rate fell as low as three per cent. Purchasers of land therefore put out their money at low interest in anticipation of a future increase. When a landowner became master of all the land in a parish, in order to reduce his expenses and increase his profits, he expelled all the agricultural labourers who lived there and destroyed their cottages. He could get all the labour he needed from the neighbouring parishes, which were already over-populated, and which had to bear the burden of this host of paupers while he remained the wealthy owner of an uninhabited estate.

Was the lot of the small proprietors or yeomen, who cultivated their land with the help of their families, equally fortunate? Under the early Tudors they had undoubtedly taken their share of the confiscated lands of nobles and monks, and for nearly two hundred years they had maintained their position. Towards the middle of the sixteenth century, indeed, they had for a time suffered from the attacks of a new competitor. At the time of the first extension of pastures, the new wealthy landowners, "greedy intruders who flung themselves from the town into the country,"[1] did not hesitate to attack the yeomen, whose established position was a check to their fierce ambition. Indirectly they injured them by the superiority of their equipment and organisation. More directly they tried to drive them out by a partial system of enclosures.

But the government intervened in favour of the threatened class. In Elizabeth's reign, at least, it appears that enclosure could not be carried out without the consent of all those affected. When it was accomplished thus by common consent the operation was to the advantage of all. "The result, so far as regards the main body of customary tenants, was only that they now obtained, instead of some thirty scattered strips, which they had been obliged to cultivate in a particular way, four or five fields of six or seven

[1] Boutmy, *Développement de la Constitution en Angleterre*, p. 202.

acres each, which they were free henceforward to employ as they pleased."[1] Moreover, the agrarian revolution was about to die down. Below the gentry, new and old, the yeomanry continued to " play an independent and semi-official part in the administration of the county." Supported by the throne, which regarded them as " the backbone of the army and the principal surety for taxation," and profiting, moreover, by a supplementary income drawn from rural industries, they prospered. About 1685 they numbered not less than one hundred and sixty to one hundred and eighty thousand families, forming a seventh of the population. At that time there were in the country more men farming their own lands than tenants upon those of others.

But in the eighteenth century the final decay of this interesting class set in. However attached he might be to his humble patrimony, whatever care he lavished on it, the small farmer had no capital to enable him to compete with the wealthy farmers and big landowners who alone could profit by the progress of agriculture. He could not sell at a low price, like these powerful competitors, without endangering his modest fortune. The burden of the poor rate grew daily heavier, and, as he hardly ever employed labourers, it was for him an unmitigated burden. He was no longer protected either by the government or by public opinion. He had no game rights even on his own land, while the lord's game devoured his crops unhindered. If he were forced to borrow the stock for his farm under a so-called livestock lease, the law in this case increased the severity of the right of seizure as against him.[2]

After 1750 his downfall became more rapid. Enclosures began again, and now it only needed the consent of those who owned four-fifths of the land to make the redistribution of land in the township obligatory. If the rich owners who had taken the initiative in demanding re-allotment did not reach this proportion themselves, they put pressure on the recalcitrant yeomen and almost always succeeded in extorting their consent. As soon as Parliament had passed the Act, the work of redistribution was carried out by a powerful commission, which was under the influence of wealthy

---

[1] Ashley, *Economic History*, vol. i, part ii, p. 273.
[2] Boutmy, *op. cit.*, p. 260.

landowners to such an extent that re-allotment amounted practically to confiscation. The lot assigned to each small proprietor was usually worth much less than the one of which he had been despoiled. When, towards the end of the century, an attempt was made to introduce rather more equity into these delicate operations, it was too late to save a class three-quarters of which had disappeared.[1]

The yeoman, half uprooted, and forcibly settled in a new holding of second-rate land, had been forced to share the expense of an operation which he had not desired and which had already cost him dear. He was then obliged immediately to enclose the farm of which he had become the unwilling owner. His share of the old commons, proportionate to the small number of his cattle, was of small help to him. Soon England ceased to export grain, and the price of cereals, henceforth determined by the fluctuations of the home market alone, underwent sharp changes after harvest. The wealthy farmer and the rich merchant could make profit out of this, but the yeoman, who was always in a hurry to sell, could only lose by it. There were no agricultural banks of credit to protect him from the terrible consequences of these crises of over-production, transitory though they might be.

If he had cherished any hope of being able to support these losses and meet these expenses by the help of domestic industries, the victorious growth of urban industry robbed him of this last means of safety. Then he sold his land, which his rich neighbours or purchasers from the town were only too ready to buy from him at a low price. Sometimes he went to seek his fortune across the Atlantic, where at least he might again own some land and make a competency. Sometimes he found employment for his strength and the little money he had saved from the wreck in the new industries. But often he fell into the ranks of the wage-earners.[2]

The same inequality was seen in the fate of the two chief classes of tenant farmers, where again the big grew at the expense of the small. But the small tenant farmers, on a

[1] See Mantoux, *op. cit.*, pp. 154-160.
[2] See Goldsmith's *Deserted Village* (1770). The Earl of Leicester used to say: " It is a sad thing to be alone in an inhabited country. I look around me and see no house but mine. I am the ogre in the fairy-tale, and I have eaten all my neighbours." See Mantoux, *op. cit.*, p. 168.

lower rung of the social ladder than the small freeholders, preceded them in the rapid decline which ended in the disappearance of both. Since the end of the fifteenth century they had suffered a series of attacks. Against the threat of enclosure they had no means of resistance either in fact or in law. The great landowner who wished to transform his ploughlands into pastures could turn them off his domain on the day on which he ceased to need their services. A long and hard-working occupation of the soil seemed to have given them a title to it which had almost been consecrated by custom, but it made no difference. In the absence of any formal agreement, the lord of the manor was free to evict them. Or, if he preferred to show some consideration to the old servants whom hitherto he had been anxious to keep, he waited for the death of the tenant and then refused to grant his son a renewal of the lease. Sooner or later these farmers, who had almost risen to be joint-owners of the lands they farmed, saw themselves pushed down into the class of wandering labourers, when they did not become vagabonds and beggars. If their lord consented to keep them on his land, they had to pay a rent at least twice as high as that fixed by custom; rack-rents date from the beginning of the sixteenth century. But the limited resources of the small farmers sometimes made it impossible for them to keep the terms of these burdensome agreements. The landlord then hastened to unite all his farms into one and put it in charge of a rich farmer.

This class would indeed have died out then, if the government had not taken steps to protect it. In Henry VIII's reign Wolsey had tried to restrict the expansion of sheep-farming. Elizabeth forbade any landowner to possess more than two thousand sheep. She tried to prevent excessive consolidation of estates by forbidding the demolition of the small farmhouses scattered over the countryside; for this was one of the economies aimed at by the landlords when they evicted the small farmers, since they considered that the upkeep of these buildings was costly and unnecessary. In the end, partly as a result of this protective legislation, but also for other reasons which we have indicated, this passion for consolidation, which was depopulating the countryside, subsided.

Those small farmers who survived this trouble profited by the enclosures, which, by rounding off their holdings, made farming easier and more productive. Competition between them was restricted to their own district and to a small group of buyers, and was not yet too keen. For another century they continued to enjoy a certain amount of comfort, but then they became the first victims of the commercial, agricultural and social changes which were to ruin them first, and then the small proprietors.

The men who profited by this revolution were the large landowners and farmers. In Elizabeth's reign many a rough wooden farmhouse was replaced by a house of brick and stone, while on the master's table glittered vessels of pewter or even of silver. But it was in the eighteenth century more especially that this new class prospered. Then these agricultural *entrepreneurs*, rich enough to rent a whole district at a high price and clever enough to get a long lease, made fourteen or eighteen per cent. on the capital they had invested lavishly in their farms. They lived in great style, kept good tables and offered their guests wine from France or Portugal. "They are rich enough," writes a traveller, " to have a taste for cleanliness, and have leisure enough to satisfy it. Always well clad, they never go out in winter without a greatcoat. Their wives and daughters are not content with simply clothing themselves, but dress luxuriously. In the winter they have little cloth cloaks to protect them from the cold; in the summer they have straw hats to shield them from the heat of the sun. It is rare to see them doing any hard work." These great capitalist farmers, who exploited land and labourers alike by industrial methods, held a much more important place in society than the small proprietors who existed alongside them. In the fifteenth and sixteenth centuries the general term of " yeomen " was used to describe the few rich tenant farmers as well as the small freeholders. " In the eighteenth century, on the contrary, the word ' farmers ' was used for both. The larger section of the class gave its name to the whole."[1]

The same vicissitudes which disturbed the upper classes of the agricultural world and made the fortunes of some

[1] See Boutmy, *op. cit.*, p. 232 *et seq.*

while the others were ruined, also affected the rank and file of agricultural labour. But the reaction was not always direct, and the position of the labourer did not necessarily follow the same curve of change as did that of his master.

The first period of their history in modern times may be said to last until the middle of the sixteenth century. As a result of the dépopulation which followed the Black Death (1349), wages had risen, and all the attempts of the government to restore the old wage rates had failed. But the suppression of livery and maintenance by Henry VII, and the dispersal of the bands of beggars hitherto dependent on the monasteries, threw into the market numbers of labourers whose competition tended to bring down wages. They were still further reduced by the extension of sheep-farming— itself partly caused by the rise in wages—for as the amount of arable land decreased, so did the amount of work offered to the labourers. As early as Henry VI's reign enclosures had caused violent riots among the peasants. The great landowners had not been content with turning superfluous labourers off their own land, but had encroached on the commons, and every day had narrowed down the land which could be used by the landless. Often they had not respected the humble cottages and patches of cultivated ground, which a time-honoured indulgence had allowed the cottagers to establish there. These cottagers had even lost the rights of pasture and of gathering acorns which the lords used to allow them to exercise in their woods. Thus there had been formed a floating population of labourers condemned to almost continual unemployment. Excessive misery sometimes forced them into insurrection, and it was against these men that the severity of the Statute of Labourers was aimed. Sir Thomas More, in his *Utopia*, protested vehemently against this agrarian tyranny and denounced the universal "conspiracy of the rich against the poor."

With Elizabeth's reign there began for this agricultural proletariat a better time which lasted almost two hundred years. Enclosures were somewhat rarer, and such common lands as had escaped the greed cf the sheep-farmer had henceforth a chance to survive. The cottagers were left in peace, and the queen decided that each of them might, for a very small payment, cultivate a space of four acres round his cottage. Most of the labourers having again taken possession of a small piece of land, were able to avoid the worst consequences of the change in the value of money. Although their wages did not rise in proportion to the fall in silver, they did not suffer unduly from the high price of food, because they could get part of their food from their own scrap of land.

It is true that the government, which had made it possible for them to return to the land, tried to keep them there. No one was allowed to leave his employment less than a year after he had been engaged, and he could not get other work without showing a certificate from his former master. Moreover, at harvest time local authorities could requisition workers *en masse*. But on the other hand a master was not allowed to dismiss a labourer within the minimum period required by the law, while the assessment of wages by a justice of the peace was a guarantee against the unfair claims of some masters. In fact, agricultural workers at the end of the sixteenth century seem to have enjoyed a position of relative comfort. They began to eat meat as well as salt fish; they only drank water, it was said, as a penance; they wore woollen clothes and seem to have been well provided both with household utensils and with agricultural implements. Moreover, the woollen industry offered them and their families a supplementary source of employment and of income; and if any of them could not make a living out of agriculture, even with the help of domestic spinning and weaving, the new factories which were springing up in the country districts offered them a last refuge, in spite of the regulations which aimed at forbidding it.

In the seventeenth century, and even during the first half of the eighteenth, economic and social conditions continued to be favourable to the labourers. Doubtless the Law of Settlement (1662) robbed some of them of the poor and uncertain possessions left them by the generosity of this or that great landowner. When he became owner of all the land in the parish he could rid himself of the expense entailed in housing his labourers on his own estate by demolishing the cottages he had allowed to be built. The labourers were forced to establish themselves in neighbouring parishes, which meant that they had to make a more or less difficult

journey every morning and evening between their house and
their work; and it was the neighbouring landlords who had
to pay the poor rate. Moreover, the official assessment of
wages tended, no doubt, to become merely an ingenious
method of keeping them at the lowest rate. Therefore, under
the first two Georges an attempt was made to grant aid
to able-bodied labourers in proportion to the size of their
families. In appearance this was a just measure, an honourable means of encouraging the growth of the population. In
reality it was a roundabout way of lowering the wages of
bachelors and childless couples, and thus, indirectly, the
market price of all labour.

But when intensive agriculture first began to make progress labour was once more in demand. At first the use of
the new processes demanded most careful attention, and
therefore more labour. On the other hand, the improved
returns and the increase in production, which for some time
exceeded the demand, meant that food was cheap. Moreover, the cottager, peacefully established on the common
land, made a profit out of his enclosure which he turned into
a kitchen garden or an orchard, while he kept his cow, pig
and a few fowls on the common pasture near by. Or if the
labourer were hired by a small farmer or landowner he was
boarded by his master and lived with the family. In one
way or another the agricultural worker's fare became more
substantial and less coarse. Wheaten bread replaced rye,
barley or oaten bread on his table. He ate cheese almost
daily and meat frequently. He drank beer, and even tea
was not unknown to him.

Towards 1760, however, all this changed. With the
revival of the enclosure movement the encroachment of the
big landowners on the commons and the war against cottages
began again.[1] Even the agricultural labourers who legally
possessed a scrap of land were forced willy-nilly to hand it
over to the rich neighbour who wished to round off his estate.
Even before sheep-farming came into favour again, agriculture had reached that point of perfection at which it could
economise in labour. The making of fences furnished the
labourers with but a transitory employment. When at

---

[1] Mantoux, *op. cit.*, p. 141.

length the population outgrew production and food became expensive, the difference between the cost of living and the rate of wages became daily greater. For the poorer classes of agricultural workers the iron age had come.

BIBLIOGRAPHY

MACAULAY: *History of England*, vol. ii.
GREEN: *Short History of the English People*, vol. i.
THOROLD ROGERS: *Six Centuries of Work and Wages*, 10th edit., 1909.
BOUTMY: *Développement de la Constitution de la Société politique en Angleterre.* 1898.
ASHLEY: *Economic History.* 1893.
CUNNINGHAM: *Growth of English Industry and Commerce. Modern Times*, vol. i.
MANTOUX: *La Révolution industrielle au XVIIIᵉ siècle.* 1905.

CHAPTER IV

FRANCE

ALTHOUGH the United Provinces and England had led the way in economic progress, France was not far behind them, and the size of her population made her in modern times the most important Western power. The history of French industry, therefore, demands full treatment, and in order to make that history more intelligible it may be useful to remind the reader of the sudden crises through which it passed.

The reign of Louis XII and the first years of that of Francis I (until 1525) offered an unusual spectacle of complete prosperity, the splendour of which lasted until about 1560, despite foreign wars and an extravagant Court. Then came the long and critical period of the Religious Wars, which lasted until the end of the century. The brilliant and rapid recovery which took place under the government of Henry IV was too soon interrupted by his death. From 1610 to 1661 was a long-drawn period of anxiety, disturbed by two outbreaks of civil war, when France seemed to be bending under the double weight of the growing power of her kings and of the political and military hegemony which they were attempting to establish for her. Then came the reign of Louis XIV, and a quarter of a century of dazzling magnificence (1661-1685). But a policy of oppression towards his subjects and of provocation towards foreign powers checked this expansion, and for the next forty years France ceased to increase in wealth and strength and even grew weaker (1685-1715). After that economic progress began again and continued until the Revolution, very active until 1740, checked by the great continental and maritime wars which followed each other from 1740 to 1763, and more secure again during the last years of the Ancien Régime. We shall have to consider later how far social progress followed the same curve during these three centuries of sudden revolutions of fortune.

I.—COMMERCE

§ 1. Foreign Trade.

Enlargement of the sphere of trade—Predominance of agricultural
exports; increase in manufactured exports; customs legislation in
protection of industry—Encouragement of native shipping; trading
companies; chief causes of their failure; vicissitudes of French
maritime trade—Chief centres of foreign trade.

Across the space of about three hundred years which we
have to cover, it is easy to see that the economic relations of
France with foreigners became closer as the sphere of her
foreign trade enlarged.

In the sixteenth century the Spanish monarchy, which
for a time included Portugal, annexed a huge empire. Spain
exported not only her own products, such as raisins and
wool, but also the produce of the Flemish weaver and spices
from beyond the seas. Soon, however, the Spanish New
World and the mother-country herself, half ruined by excess
of wealth too easily acquired, offered, directly or indirectly,
to the agriculture, the industry and the fisheries of France
a market which grew daily bigger. Without taking into
account the important contraband trade which was carried
on with South America through San Domingo, it has been
estimated that towards 1650 the share of France in the trade
of the Spanish Indies rose to about twelve out of the total of
forty million francs. In the seventeenth century, although
Spain was constantly at war with France, she was her best
customer.

During the same period almost as much trade was done
with Italy. Venice was on the decline, but Milan, Florence
and Rome took her place in importing silks, though not
spices. France, it is true, lost the profit of transport between
the Western Mediterranean and North-Western Europe.
When Henry III, in 1585, attempted to force all merchandise coming from the north, and bound for Italy or Eastern
Spain, to pass through the Customs-house of Lyons, Flanders
and England opened sea routes to both the Mediterranean
peninsulas, and the land route between North Italy and the
North Sea henceforth avoided French territory and passed
through Savoy, Franche-Comté, Lorraine and Luxemburg.[1]

[1] See Fagniez, *Économie Sociale*, p. 293.

On the other hand, French trade with Germany developed steadily. In exchange for their leather and ironware, the German states, where wealth was only just beginning to spread, bought every year from France increasing quantities of rich cloth and jewels. The Hanseatic League, with whom Henry IV concluded a treaty (1604) which was periodically renewed, came to her ports to buy the products of her vine-yards and salt-works, cloth, paper and spices, which they carried to Hamburg, Lubeck, Dantzig and Riga. The Scandinavian states also exchanged their timber and tar for the salt, wines and spirits of France. The commercial treaties made with Sweden and Denmark in 1604 were helped rather than hindered by political alliances.[1]

The relations between France and the United Provinces suffered many vicissitudes. In the second half of the seventeenth century friendship gave place to a mutual hostility which lasted until 1713, almost, in fact, until the decline of Dutch prosperity. This caused a complete cessation at any rate of official trade. Similarly, with regard to England, the liberal and friendly intentions which the French government showed on several occasions (1606 and 1713) were checked by the jealous exclusiveness of the English Parliament and Administration. But in spite of everything, when the two nations were not actually at war the trade which, from the nature of things, was bound to exist between them, grew constantly, and even during war a flourishing contraband trade triumphed over all restrictions.

From the sixteenth century onwards France did as much trade with the Levant as with Italy or Germany. The treaty concluded in 1536 between Francis I and Soliman gave all Frenchmen established in the Ottoman Empire the right to settle their civil or commercial differences before their own consuls in accordance with their own laws. The merchants of almost all other European nations had to accept the superior jurisdiction of the French consuls. These agents often abused their office and, conforming all too closely to the customs of the East, did not hesitate to obtain an illicit revenue at the expense of the people they were supposed to protect. But in spite of this abuse and of the competition

---

[1] In Richelieu's ministry Denmark was persuaded to lower the duty on French goods passing the Sound from 5 to 1 per cent.

first of the Dutch, and then of the English, French trade with the ports of the Eastern Mediterranean prospered. Cyprus and Greece sent wines; the Archipelago, sponges; Asia Minor, by way of Smyrna, Alexandretta, Tripoli or Beyrout, figs, carpets, silks and worked leather. In return these countries received from France silver, cloth and hosiery.

The building of the Bastion of France in 1560 marked the opening of regular relations with Barbary, and these were encouraged by the settlement of Jews exiled from Spain in Lower Languedoc. From Tripoli came ostrich feathers; from Tunis, oil; from Algiers (after 1603), coral and grain; from Morocco, leather and wool.

In North America New France was founded, and the ships of Normandy and Brittany fished for cod on the Newfoundland Bank, while Canada sent vast quantities of furs to the mother-country. Her colonists, who soon numbered eighty thousand, bought their provisions and manufactured goods from her, and when this market was closed to her the emancipation of the United States opened another, although for some time French industry was unable to make much use of it. By the middle of the seventeenth century, thanks to the privateers, seven thousand Frenchmen were established in the Antilles. Until the fall of the monarchy these islands furnished an increasing supply of exotic products, while they were ready to purchase, besides negro labour which was obtained from the Guinea Coast, all the articles necessary for the existence of the white population.[1] Nor was French commerce excluded from the East Indies. Her factories in India sent home pepper from Java or Malabar, cinnamon from Ceylon, Indian cotton goods, nutmegs and cloves from the Moluccas, and even tea and silks from Canton.

Thus in the " great century " France was already embarked upon what we should to-day call world commerce. Richelieu obtained permission for French merchants to pass through Muscovy on their way to Persia or Tartary. Colbert obtained from the Sultan the privilege of transit between the Mediterranean and the Red Sea, and he com-

---

[1] The white population of San Domingo alone rose to the total of 42,000.

bined the two companies of the Levant and the East Indies, with the object of making Alexandria once again the centre of Indo-European trade. Enterprising merchants advised Louis XIV to occupy Egypt, even to reopen direct communication between Asia and Europe by means of a canal. In the other hemisphere, only recently discovered and still half unknown, at the very time when France seemed on the point of foundering in the disasters of the War of the Spanish Succession, her sailors never ceased to cross the lonely Pacific from the Straits of Magellan to the Chinese seas, bringing to St. Malo or Port Louis the dazzling embroideries of the East. From the beginning of Louis XV's reign until the end of the absolute monarchy trade with the Far East increased in the proportion of one to six, while trade with Europe was more than quadrupled. It was not until nearly sixty years after 1789 that the sum of French foreign commerce once more attained—to surpass it rapidly, indeed—the total to which it had risen in the last years of the Ancien Régime.

We must now consider what were the principal articles of foreign trade, and what part royal intervention played in modifying the natural flow of exports and imports.

Throughout the whole of the period we are studying France remained predominantly an agricultural country. In 1787 the sum of its agricultural exports, counting, it is true, those which came from the colonies for re-exportation, exceeded its manufactured exports by a quarter.[1] Wine was the most common export, and although the government was not enlightened enough to free it from the burden of indirect taxation, its export was constantly encouraged, even at the expense of the interests of the industrial exports. France also exported to the northern countries, whose climate made it impossible for grapes to ripen or for salt to evaporate there, great quantities of salt. Prunes from Aquitaine and olive oil from Provence also found a market in England, Scotland and Flanders.

The exportation of cereals was intermittent. There were plenty of customers, for Spain and Portugal often suffered from a shortage, but corn was a very valuable food, and harvests were very uncertain. Trade, in fact, was under the control of a prohibitive policy, the descendant of the old

[1] According to Arnauld, 311 million livres against 231.

feudal or municipal regulations, the spirit of which was, at bottom, opposed to all export, especially that of food. For fear of famine grain could only be exported when there was a surplus. Although export was permitted temporarily by the ordinances of 1534 and 1539, and was free from 1601 to 1625, the tariff of 1664 imposed a heavy tax on it (22 livres a hogshead). From 1693 it was forbidden entirely, on pain of the galleys or even of death, and save for a short interval during the ministry of Choiseul (about 1764) the prohibition was not removed until the end of the Ancien Régime.

In the case of raw materials also, when France was ready to export them, the policy of prohibition was followed. Philip the Fair had already forbidden the export of wool, and this prohibition was renewed on several occasions during the second half of the sixteenth century, and at the beginning of the seventeenth was extended to flax, hemp and silk. The government sought to keep down the price of the raw materials of the textile industry, just as it kept down the price of bread, which was the chief food of the mass of the nation, especially of the artisans. On the other hand, the re-export of colonial produce, which began about 1670,[1] was always allowed, and after 1736 profited by complete freedom. In the course of the eighteenth century this trade trebled in value. In 1789 the sugar and coffee of the West Indies were among the most important exports of France. And the export of flour as well as of wines and spirits to the colonies was always allowed.

The only important manufactured article which France exported at first was coarse linen, but after the beginning of the seventeenth century she exported an increasing quantity of cloth and silk fabrics. Less important were ironware, jewellery and paper. Gradually industrial exports reached the point at which they outweighed agricultural exports. It is almost unnecessary to add that the government always favoured the former.

The list of the chief French imports and of the regulations applying to them naturally shows exactly the opposite tendency. Setting aside colonial produce, there was no constant or considerable importation of food; at most, corn

[1] Colbert wrote in 1670: "Foreigners no longer bring us sugar for our consumption, and we have even begun to send it to them."

in famine years and a few cattle or dried fish at certain times. The raw materials of the textile industries formed the bulk of the purchases. The government granted numerous privileges to importers of these two classes of goods. Corn had always entered free. At the end of Louis XIV's reign import duties on all cereals were reduced to an insignificant figure, and from 1740 to 1764 they were removed altogether. In times of national shortage the import of cereals was even encouraged by bounties. After 1687 the import duty on German sheep was reduced by five-sixths. Although during the seventeenth century France put prohibitive duties on Dutch and English herrings, this was a measure of reprisal rather than a manifestation of her general economic policy.

It was similarly expedient that the import duties on colonial produce should be reduced to a minimum. Such a measure was passed in 1717 under the influence of Law. From that time the French markets were flooded with the products of the West Indies, first tobacco and sugar, then coffee, and, towards the end of the century, cotton, besides less important articles such as cocoa, tortoise-shell, dye woods and wood for cabinet-making. The introduction of indigo was the only thing which caused any difficulty. In 1601, " in spite of the protests of the men of Lyons, who affirmed that this drug was preferable to woad for dark colours and that much less of it had to be used, woad, energetically championed by the men of Toulouse, who owed their fortunes to it, carried the day "[1] provisionally, and for a time the import of indigo was forbidden on pain of death.

The import of manufactured goods, on the contrary, was checked by many obstacles when it was not absolutely forbidden. In consideration of the vote of the States General in 1484 Francis I and his successors forbade the importation of fine cloth from Roussillon and Catalonia and of *sagetteries* from Flanders, while the Code Michau in 1629 renewed the prohibition against all foreign cloth. Then an attack was made on the cloth of gold and silver and silks with which the Italians were flooding the market. The reorganisation of the Lyons customs-house in 1540 made these imports more difficult, and soon protective duties were replaced by formal

[1] Levasseur, *Classes ouvrières*, vol. ii, p. 165.

prohibitions, which were continually renewed during the last years of the sixteenth century and the first of the seventeenth. The list of rates in 1667 was much more rigorous than that of 1664 and struck heavily at all fabrics coming from England and Holland, especially woollen stockings and caps and silk and cotton stockings. Louis XI had already forbidden the importation of Indian cotton goods, and this prohibition was renewed in 1686. Other products of foreign industry were the objects of similar measures. Henry IV opposed the import of English paper for the same reason that he prevented the export of rags. Louis XIV in 1669 and 1671 prohibited the import of Venetian glass and lace. The only question which puzzled the government was the import of mineral products, for although an abundance of fuel, such as coal and of various useful metals, was indispensable to the development of many native industries, it was nevertheless wise to protect native mining or metallurgical enterprises against foreign competition. For this reason English coal and Swedish iron were subject to various duties.

When a nation has considerable foreign trade and a long coastline, its interest lies in developing its mercantile marine so that it may not lose the profits of the ceaseless double traffic, henceforth an indispensable part of its economic life. Therefore the kings of France in the sixteenth century set themselves to organise and control this new national industry. An edict of March, 1584, laid down rules for the exploitation of fisheries and the armament of ships. No one could henceforth be captain of a ship without having passed special examinations and received the title of master, which conferred on him the right of commanding a ship. But above all it was necessary to protect native shipowners against foreign competition.

To encourage exporters an attempt was made to suppress foreign competition altogether. Louis XI ordered all his subjects engaged in maritime trade to employ French ships only. Richelieu forbade foreigners, on pain of confiscation of ships and cargo, to load their ships at French ports with any commodity save salt, unless no French ship were available. Although political necessities prevented the cardinal from applying his interdict rigorously, he did at least force the English to allow the import of Bordeaux wines on French ships. The exportation of grains, when it was allowed, was usually reserved to native shipowners.

It was impossible to create a similar monopoly for French shipping in the import trade, but at any rate it was possible to close French ports to foreign importers who were only middlemen. An edict of 1540, for example, directed against the merchants of Antwerp, forbade the import of spices unless they came direct from the country of production or at least from the *entrepôts* of Portugal, Italy or the East. The famous English Navigation Act was no more than a general application of the principle here laid down. And it was very easy to prejudice the chances of every foreign importer without distinction by making them all pay taxes from which native importers were exempt. Henry IV had already imposed an anchorage duty on all foreign ships entering his ports. In 1659, at the instigation of Fouquet, the celebrated proportional duty of fifty sous a ton was first levied. To get exemption from this it was not enough that the ship should belong to a French owner, but two-thirds of the crew must be Frenchmen also.

A more direct means of encouraging the national marine consisted in offering bounties for armament. Moreover, in order to compensate for the dearness of materials such as wood, iron, tar[1] and hemp, for which France was dependent on foreigners, Colbert granted five livres a ton on all ships built in French yards, but only two and a half livres on ships bought abroad. As for the plant and labour necessary for shipbuilding, they were not difficult to procure. Richelieu had ordered " all sailors, caulkers, rope-makers, sailmakers and fishermen employed abroad, under pain of loss of life and goods, to return to the kingdom and put themselves at the disposal of the king and his merchants." Colbert bribed the cleverest shipbuilders of rival maritime nations to enter French service.

But these rivals were so powerful and the field of trade so vast that it was almost hopeless for private individuals to enter the arena and engage in such a mighty struggle. The voyage from Europe to India, for example, lasted seven, nine or even twelve months on account of the equatorial

[1] Thanks to Colbert's efforts, the forests of the Landes began to compete with Norway in providing tar for the French navy.

calms, the monsoons and typhoons, not to mention the
storms round the Cape. Three years had to be allowed for
the voyage there and back. Even then the return was
always uncertain, for the perils of piracy were added to
those of the sea. English, Dutch, Spanish, Portuguese and
Arabs were all dangerous. In the Mediterranean itself the
English were as much to be feared as the Barbary pirates.
In the middle of the seventeenth century the danger was
still so great that insurance premiums on ships going from
Marseilles to the ports of the Levant were from forty to
forty-five per cent. of their value.

It was therefore not sufficient protection for every ship to
carry guns, but each ship must sail in a convoy with others
similarly armed. Therefore powerful companies were necessary, for they alone could organise such expeditions and take
part in these profitable but hazardous enterprises. It is
possible that such companies might have been formed even
without state encouragement, for at a period when French
merchants were ever ready for bold enterprises the merchants
of Rouen, in 1535, had spontaneously formed an unprivileged
association to carry on trade with India, and had thus fore-
stalled the Dutch and English companies by more than half
a century. But after the religious wars kings and ministers
were agreed that only official companies more or less directly
supported by the state, such as those which already existed
in neighbouring countries, would be able to enter into competition with them for this distant trade.

The first necessary step was to grant a more or less strict
monopoly to these new companies. Henry IV granted to the
second East India Association an exclusive monopoly of this
trade for a period of fifteen years. The monopoly granted by
Richelieu to the Company of the Antilles was renewed several
times, though in a modified form. The fur trade was
reserved for ever to the Company of New France, founded
in 1628. The great East India Company founded by Colbert
in May, 1664, was granted an absolute commercial monopoly
of all the coasts of the Indian Ocean and the Pacific for half
a century. The Company of the West Indies, founded three
months later, was given a monopoly for forty years over a
field of action stretching from Canada to the West Indies
and from Cape Verde to the Cape of Good Hope.

Several of these companies, such as the two India companies, the Company of the North (1669), and the Company of the Levant (1670), received bounties in addition. For the East India Company the rate was raised to fifty livres a ton on goods exported, and seventy-five livres on goods imported. They also benefited by big public grants. The king granted four million francs to the East India Company; he provided a tenth of the capital of the West India Company, and a third of the capital of the Company of the North, for the losses of which he made himself responsible during its early years. All these privileges were only granted with the object of encouraging private subscribers on whom the companies must necessarily depend for the bulk of their capital, and other means were used to the same end. Henry IV invited the nobles to join his Association of the Indies. In 1664 not only did the king subscribe himself to the great Company, but he made the queen and princes do the same, while Colbert recommended the affair to the Councils, to the Royal Courts, to the chief financial officers and to the towns. It was a way " of winning souls for God and subjects for the King," but it was also the best way of winning ministerial favour. All the officials rivalled each other in zeal; one intendant even went so far as to " call in the help of the dragoons."[1]

What was the result of all these efforts? If we consider the history of these companies we shall find nothing but a series of failures. The various societies founded by Henry IV disappeared before they had really begun to work. The East India Company of 1664, as far as it was a commercial enterprise, did nothing. The West India Company died within ten years, the Company of the North within three, while the Levant Company only struggled on for twenty years. It is important to trace the causes of this widespread failure, for although it did not ruin the national mercantile marine it did weaken it considerably. To begin with, especially in Henry IV's time, the municipal patriotism of the sea-ports was very strong and hostile to any national enterprise. The trade of Rouen, of St. Malo or of La Rochelle was more important than the trade of France.[2] Even in Louis XIV's

[1] Lavisse, *Hist. de France*, vol. vii[1], pp. 240-1.
[2] *Cf.* Pigeonneau, *Histoire du Commerce de la France*, vol. ii, pp. 346-347.

time the men of Bordeaux refused to join in the operations
of the Company of the North. In some ports there was so
strong a tradition of independent action that no joint enterprise was possible. " The gentlemen of Marseilles," wrote
Colbert, " only want small boats so that each man may have
his own."

The public also feared the covetousness of the Administration, whose new and often excessive zeal for economic
expansion seemed suspicious. Almost everywhere " subscriptions to the East India Company were regarded as a
disguised tax. The judges and financial officers who had
been forced to contribute proclaimed that it was a snare to
catch the nobles and others who were exempt from ordinary
taxation, and that in the end, when no one was expecting
it, the king would seize everything as he had seized the
revenues of the Hôtel de Ville. The shares of one thousand
francs were payable in thirds, and it was very difficult to
obtain the second and third payments." Four years after
the company was founded only five million francs out of
fifteen had been paid up. It was in vain that Colbert issued
fictitious dividends of ten per cent., for these fraudulent
proceedings could not go on very long.

But even supposing that the company was more or less
launched, its business was badly conducted. Its headquarters were established at Paris, which is not a sea-port,
nor were its directors sailors. Bureaucrats and bureaucratic
formalities were uselessly multiplied, while influence gave
important posts to utterly inexperienced officials. These
men were not content to go gently at first, but indulged in
luxuries before they had made any profit. Moreover, they
used their monopoly to reduce the number of ships and
voyages to a minimum and to raise the price of their imports
and exports. They ended by losing their customers and
killing the trade which they were supposed to develop.

The failure of the companies was due also to other and
deeper causes which affected all French maritime enterprises,
whether they were individual or collective, official or private.
The French as a whole were no more a seafaring nation than
they are to-day. The merchants of the sea-ports, unless they
were foreigners, were rather manufacturers or salesmen than
shipowners. On many occasions under Henry IV and

Mazarin they protested against the edicts which aimed at reserving the greater part of French trade for French ships, and which certainly resulted in raising freights. Colbert himself was ready to subordinate the interests of the mercantile marine to the export of manufactured goods. He would not allow the merchants of Marseilles to sell in Spain part of the cargoes they brought from the Levant. Their business was to export to the Levant as much cloth as possible from Languedoc.

Moreover, private individuals did not willingly risk their money in overseas trade. " Small fortunes were gradually absorbed by taxes or by the continual creation of new offices and salaries. The peaceful bourgeois was quite ready to buy an office which would give him an income and a social position, but his habits of economy and prudence kept him from risky investments.''[1] Louis XIV was not interested in commerce, and France, by virtue of her political formation, turned to the continent rather than to the sea. " From the tenth century, when Paris became the capital of a kingdom whose frontiers were limited by the Somme and the Meuse, the French kings were obliged to spend their time always pushing back, to east and to north, a frontier which was too close, and their subjects became habituated to land warfare. . . . France turned her back on the sea, and it was not in Colbert's power to make her face the ocean again. As to making her face both ways at once, experience showed him that her resources were insufficient.''[2] At the end of the seventeenth century and for the greater part of the eighteenth, while the flower of the nation's strength was devoted to continental politics, France was as powerless to protect her fishing fleets and her merchant ships as to defend her colonies.

This does not mean that the sailors of France did not hold at various periods an honourable position in the world. In the first half of the sixteenth century they surpassed the English and Dutch and disputed the first place with the Spanish and Portuguese. In Louis XII's reign they began to exploit the Newfoundland fisheries and opened permanent relations with West Africa and Brazil. Nearly every year

[1] Lavisse, *Histoire de France*, vol. vi[2], p. 424, and viii[1], pp. 270-271.
[2] Lavisse, *op. cit.*, vol. vii[1], p. 263.

French ships disembarked Brazilian " savages " at Rouen or Dieppe. After the Capitulations were signed French ships took the place of the Venetian and Genoese galleys in carrying French linen and cloth to North Africa and the Levant.

At the beginning of the personal rule of Louis XIV the situation was reversed. For more than a century, in spite of the efforts of Henry IV and Richelieu, the nation, overwhelmed by internal troubles, seemed to have lost all sense of its destiny as a sea-power. " The Canadian fur trade went not to Rouen or La Rochelle, but to London and Amsterdam. The only French slave-market, Senegal, was selling no slaves. The French flag was rarely seen at Martinique or Guadeloupe, while two hundred Dutch ships called there. Provence only sent thirty ships to the *Échelles*,[1] for her coasts were blockaded by the pirate fleets of Algiers, Tunis and Tripoli, and every night from watch-towers built at intervals along the coast beacons gave warning of the presence of the corsairs."[2]

Ten years later Colbert's energy put new life into the French mercantile marine. " The East India Company had been obliged to buy its first ships in Holland, but in 1671 seventy ships were built in France for various companies. The Company of the North failed, but private ships freighted in French ports made many voyages to the Baltic."[3] The West India Company did nothing, but nevertheless five hundred vessels flying the royal flag sailed each year to the Antilles. The moribund company sold licences to all independent French shipowners who asked for them, and gradually these individuals came to control the trade. In 1682 the East India Company opened the coasts of India to all French merchants on condition that they used the Company's ships and sold in the Company's shops, and under this regime of semi-freedom trade increased rapidly. The Senegal and Guinea Companies carried on a fairly successful trade in slaves, transporting about two thousand a year across the Atlantic. Along the coasts of France and England

[1] Ports in the Mediterranean which were under Turkish rule but which were open to the merchants of Europe: Constantinople, Salonica, Smyrna, Aleppo, Alexandria, etc.—M. R.

[2] Lavisse, *Histoire de France*, vol. vii[1], pp. 234 and 245.

[3] *Ibid.*, p. 253.

French sailors fished for herrings, sardines and mackerel, and the boldest of them penetrated as far as the Polar Seas in pursuit of whales.

But towards 1685 a change took place, for merchantmen no longer had the protection of the royal navy. The Levant trade fell mainly into the hands of the English, while the West Indian trade died out. In the very middle of the war Dutch ships, flying the Danish or Swedish flag, entered French ports and usurped even the coast trade which was reserved by law for French ships. " There was no building in spite of the bounties. Shipowners were not allowed to enlist regular sailors whom the king reserved for himself. Captains, forced to complete their crew as best they could, took adventurers, sick men or foreigners."[1]

But even this decline was not final. The East India Company alone, reconstituted by Law and saved from the Bank disaster, employed a hundred large vessels. In a quarter of a century (1715-1740) the number of ships engaged in foreign commerce rose from 300 to 1,800. If to these we add the vessels of all sizes used in the coast trade and in coastal and deep-sea fishing, the combined total amounted (about 1730) to more than five thousand ships manned by over forty thousand men. This growth was severely checked by the War of the Austrian Succession and by the Seven Years' War, but after 1764 renewed activity was apparent in the shipyards, while for several years the export of grain was useful in providing shipowners with heavy freights. This progress seems to have continued until the Revolution, so that at the close of the Ancien Régime the national flag was flying on at least a quarter of the ships which entered French ports.[2]

Either by the exertions of French shipowners or by the agency of their competitors, three-quarters of the foreign trade of France was carried by sea.[3] The great centres of trade were almost all situated on the French coast or within reach of it. There also were established free markets for goods to be re-exported. These were not a regular part of

[1] Lavisse, *Histoire de France*, vol. viii[1], p. 203.
[2] On the eve of the Great War the proportion was no bigger than this.
[3] To-day the proportion is two-thirds.

the country's commerce, but they interested Colbert and held an important place in the sum total of national activity.

In the middle of the seventeenth century Dieppe was one of the most flourishing ports of Northern France. Calais, which had been so long united to England, drew such prosperity as it possessed from the contraband trade with England[1] and from the Channel passenger traffic which it shared with Boulogne. Dieppe, on the contrary, during and after the sixteenth century, was in the first rank, not simply an active fishing-port[2] as it is to-day, supplying the capital with fish. Then its commercial relations extended beyond Spain and Portugal to both shores of the Southern Atlantic. "The tenacity of the Norman character, the seafaring and conquering temper which the people had inherited from their ancestors,"[3] in addition to plenty of money, gave its captains a marked superiority over those of other maritime provinces. Unfortunately the town was half ruined by the bombardment of 1694.[4]

The prosperity of the port of Rouen, on the other hand, grew without interruption. In the sixteenth century its trade already extended from Italy to Finland, and its merchants were trying to establish relations with the East Indies. At the end of the seventeenth century they had pushed as far as China, La Plata, Chili and Peru. But its future was insecure, for in spite of all works undertaken to keep the passage in the estuary clear of sand, the channel was not deep enough. Havre, founded in 1517 to take the place of Harfleur, which was choked with mud, was primarily a naval arsenal. Colbert constructed there wet and dry docks, magazines and smithies. A regular service united it with Lisbon and Cadiz. In the eighteenth century two new docks were begun, and East and West Indian traffic at once increased.

St. Malo was the chief centre for the export of Breton cloth to Spain and the headquarters of the Newfoundland and Iceland fishermen. On their return from the northern seas

---

[1] In the time of Henry IV Calais was also the centre of a contraband trade between Spain and Holland. *Cf.* Fagniez, *op. cit.*, p. 291.

[2] Like Boulogne.

[3] Pigeonneau, *op. cit.*, vol. ii, p. 442.

[4] Saint-Valery-sur-Somme carried on an equally active trade, thanks to the waterway which connected it with Amiens.

the St. Malo fishermen sold their cod not only at Bordeaux and Bayonne, but at Bilbao and even at Marseilles, where they exchanged them for the produce of the Levant. In spite of repeated bombardments, war, far from ruining them, made them more prosperous, for it was from this stronghold that the boldest and cleverest pirates in the kingdom ravaged the seas.

Nantes was the rival of St. Malo in the cod fisheries, and was the centre of the import trade in timber and metals from England and the northern countries; its trade with the West Indies soon became the main source of its prosperity. At the end of the seventeenth century it was faced with ruin, for the silting up of the mouth of the Loire forced ships of more than 300 tons to stop at Paimbœuf and transfer their cargo into barges. But these difficulties were overcome and the development of the West Indian sugar plantations assured the fortunes of shipowners on the Quai de la Fosse.

On the coasts of Aunis and Saintonge, Brouage, silted up and blocked by the ships sunk there by the Protestants in 1586, was now a dead town, but La Rochelle, in spite of the horrors of the terrible siege, continued to prosper (whatever may have been said to the contrary) through the export of salt, wines and spirits, for it was the only direct and free outlet for the *cinq grosses fermes*[1]—to wit, the whole of Central France. Although for a time the channel leading to the docks was neglected and allowed to silt up, in the eighteenth century it took a considerable share in the American trade. The loss of Canada dealt it a severe blow, but it was still flourishing at the time of the Revolution.

Bordeaux, about 1650, was La Rochelle on a larger scale. Although it was a market for prunes from Agen, woad from Toulouse, cereals from Languedoc, and raisins from the Landes, wine was the basis of its commercial prosperity. Breton ships came here to complete their cargoes of wine for the north and brought with them cod to be dried and re-exported to Catholic Spain. But a great change was coming, for at the same time that the opening of the Canal des Deux Mers made communication with Marseilles easier, the old city

[1] Five administrative districts organised by Colbert for the collection of taxes.—M. R.

found a new fortune in the American trade and especially in the slave trade. In the first quarter of the eighteenth century its trade doubled, and it reached its highest point at the time of the American War of Independence, when more than five hundred ships thronged the harbour. It became the centre of the trade with San Domingo, which represented two-thirds of the total trade of the French West Indies. Its population numbered a hundred thousand, at least twice as many as it had been eighty years before.

Although Bayonne, in spite of its privileges, and St. Jean-de-Luz, in spite of its hardy race of fishermen, fell into decay, France acquired Dunkirk (1662), which soon roused the jealousy and regrets of England. It was not only a big fishing port, but the meeting-place of merchants from all over Europe, who were attracted by its favourable position and its privileges, for Dunkirk and Rouen were the only ports on the western coasts which had the right to import the produce of the Levant direct, without passing through Marseilles, on payment of a duty of twenty per cent., and in 1704 Dunkirk also obtained the right to share in the American trade. Like St. Malo, it was a stronghold of bold corsairs who could make profit even out of war. But the Treaty of Utrecht condemned it to stagnation if not to extinction. In 1666, soon after the acquisition of Dunkirk, Lorient (l'Orient) and Port-Louis were created to serve as the headquarters of the ships of the India Company, and for more than a century they were the chief French *entrepôts* for the produce of Eastern Asia.

On the Mediterranean, Marseilles was almost the only large port. Narbonne and Aigues-Mortes were no longer of any consequence. Cette, created at the end of the Canal du Midi, had only a local importance as the outlet for the wines and spirits and occasionally for the corn of Lower Languedoc. The old Phocian city, on the other hand, had seen a great future unrolled before it on the day when Provence was united to France. In the sixteenth century it was indisputably the chief port in the kingdom and in the Mediterranean, and had supplanted Genoa, Leghorn and Venice in trade with Barbary and the Levant. After that its power declined. Mazarin abandoned it to the attacks of the pirates, while Colbert took from it the right of free trade

which had made it one of the great common *entrepôts*
between North and South. This was not finally given back
to it until the beginning of the next century; but then it was
attacked by the terrible plague of 1720. Thereafter it never
reconquered its supremacy either in Barbary—in spite of the
brilliant successes of the African Company, founded in 1741—
or in the Levant. It only began to prosper again when it left
its natural province and began to dispute with its flourishing
rivals on the mouths of the Loire and the Garonne for a share
in the American trade, while at the same time beginning to
take its place as the food market of Central Europe.

Among the cities of the interior, if we except Paris, which
was more especially a great interprovincial market, two
alone, Lille and Lyons, are worth mention in this rapid
survey of the great markets of foreign trade. In the seventeenth century the big manufacturers of Lille acted in concert
with those of Rouen to organise a service of direct export of
their cloth to Spain. From the time of the Renaissance the
merchants of Lyons had known how to make use of the
situation of their city, which stood at the junction of the
Rhone and the Saône, and was, moreover, near the Alps.
They had opened regular communications by way of Mont
Genèvre and the Little St. Bernard with the Milanese, who
sent them silks and arms, and with the Swiss of St. Gall and
Zürich, who supplied them with cheese and horses. They
also traded with Germany and Holland, with England
through London, Exeter or Plymouth, with Spain through
Genoa, the Col du Perthus or St. Jean de Luz, and with the
Levant through Marseilles. Their great fairs, created by
Charles VII and doubled in number by Louis XI, were
something like international exhibitions of the whole West.

§ 2. Internal Trade.

Predominance of the river routes; slow development of a system of
    roads; tolls—Letter post; coaches and barges, stage-coaches;
    carriage of goods—Decline of the fairs, organisation of markets—
    Nationalisation of the coinage; banks; variations in the rate of
    interest; new commercial legislation.

Just as the greater part of France's foreign trade was
carried on by sea, so internal trade chiefly used the waterways. Not only were the Seine and the Saône easily

navigable, but the Loire provided a valuable route into Central France, while the Rhone and the Garonne were not impossible, and some of the chief tributaries of these big rivers were accessible to moderate sized and small boats. Moreover, the watersheds separating their basins were so low and narrow that the plan of joining them by canals was conceived.

As early as Henry II's reign Adam de Craponne, inspired by the bold ideas of Leonardo da Vinci, suggested a plan to join up all the rivers in France. The development of the engineer's art already made it possible to glimpse the realisation of this vast scheme, for the first locks built in France date from 1575. Henry IV began by joining the middle Loire to the Loing. The Briare Canal, which was to serve as a model to Europe, opened a much cheaper route between the capital and the markets of Nantes and Lyons (via Roanne), and work was begun on the future Burgundy Canal. In the same vigorous reign the use of the smaller rivers was not overlooked. The Vesle was made navigable below Rheims, the Vienne below Châtellerault, the Cher below St. Amand, and the Eure and the Ourcq were also opened to trade. The great project of the Canal des Deux Mers was realised under Colbert (1681). The opening of this magnificent waterway, nearly 300 kilometres in length, cost two hundred million livres,[1] but the cost of transport throughout Languedoc was reduced by three-quarters. The Picardy Canal, planned by Richelieu, and finally executed by the financier Crozat from 1728 to 1738, united the Oise and the Somme and prepared the opening of a great inland waterway between Paris and Flanders.[2]

Unfortunately many of the rivers were the victims of the neglect of concessionaires or of the carelessness of the authorities, and numbers of mill-dams and fishermen's stockades, as well as the blocking of the tow-paths made the passage of boats almost impossible. It is true that from the middle of the sixteenth century the primitive but convenient method of rafting was developed under the encouragement of royal ordinances, and by this means great

[1] The livre is an obsolete coin about equal in value to the franc. —M. R.

[2] The Central Canal was not finished till 1793.

stretches of forest were exploited and timber travelled cheaply from the heights of Morvan to the capital.

This activity of river traffic resulted partly from the lack of roadways. At the time of the Renaissance three-quarters even of the royal roads had returned to a state of nature. The most important roads were only paved for a few miles, and then often relapsed into field tracks, continually encroached on by the farmers through whose land they ran. This neglect grew worse and worse until the day when Sully took the new title of " Chief Road Surveyor of France." The roads which came directly under his administration improved rapidly. He ordered that they should be widened, repaired, and straightened, and everywhere rebuilt broken bridges. Soon the royal Treasury devoted a million livres a year, a vast sum at that time, to road-mending. Where the upkeep of roads was the duty of different lords, Colbert forced them to do their duty by threatening to confiscate their tolls. Richelieu and Colbert, who were both obliged to find money for great wars, and moreover believed that the traffic of barges laden with goods was much more important than that of coaches and carriages, did not carry on this great work so brilliantly begun. It was not undertaken again until the Controller-General Orry regularised the royal right of forced labour (*corvée*) and made it general (1738). In this way he obtained from the beginning a supply of labour double that which he could have hired with the resources of the Treasury. Although the amount of work done by these forced labourers was sometimes small, still, under the direction of clever engineers,[1] an excellent road system was made. Even public relief works served the interests of commerce. Soon 40,000 kilometres of highway, most of which was paved or metalled, excited the admiration of the foreigner. But the secondary and the cross-country roads remained in so bad a condition as to render them almost unserviceable, and this shortage of local connecting roads was all the more troublesome because the makers of the great roads, in their desire to shorten the distance between two great cities, often ignored the existence of the smaller trade centres.

But the finest roads in the world are useless unless

[1] L'École des Ponts et Chaussées was founded in 1767.

travellers are safe from aggression and unhindered by
barriers. One after another Louis XI, Louis XII, Henry IV
and Richelieu were obliged to issue rigorous decrees to protect travellers from being pillaged by soldiers and attacked
by robbers.[1] The nobles were no less dangerous to the
freedom of trade, and they 'were more difficult to deal with.
The tolls which they collected on the pretext, usually false,
that they were used for the protection and maintenance of the
roads, formed a burdensome tax which hindered the development of trade. For three hundred years the government
strove to abolish these tolls. In the sixteenth century the
kings suppressed a number of illicit tolls which checked
navigation on the chief rivers, and invited merchants to
band themselves together in societies in order to inform
against the illegal exactions of the nobles whose lands lay
along the banks. Some of the tolls were founded on more or
less authentic titles, however, and if the Treasury could not
afford to buy them up, Colbert tried at least to reduce them
and to concentrate them at certain points. He succeeded on
the Seine, but left his successors to carry out the task as well
as they could on the other rivers. In the seventeenth century
there were forty tolls on the Rhone from the Savoy frontier
to Arles. "Coming down the Loire a bale of merchandise
which ought to have paid 10 écus[2] actually paid 30 or 40, for
the sailors were obliged to make presents to every toll-
collector if they wanted to avoid long halts."[3] To these
semi-feudal obstacles were added those which resulted from
monopolies such as that of the Parisian Hanse on the Seine,
which was suppressed by Colbert, or that of the *gribaniers*
or bargees of the Somme, which lasted until the Revolution.

It must be admitted that the kings themselves did not
hesitate to restrict freedom of trade if they thought it would
be to their profit. The States General of 1484 and 1614 in
vain demanded the abolition or diminution of the internal
Customs duties (*douanes*). Colbert only succeeded in freeing the *cinq grosses fermes*, within which henceforth no royal
transport taxes were collected, though they remained along

---

[1] The beginning of the eighteenth century witnessed the exploits of
the famous brigands Cartouche and Mandrin.

[2] An écu or crown is an obsolete coin worth about six francs.—M. R.

[3] Lavisse, *Histoire de France*, vol. viii[1], p. 209.

the frontiers of the neighbouring provinces. Moreover, many special payments were levied on special articles. Wool, for example, could only circulate freely after 1758, cattle after 1783, and it was only after the latter date that the inter-provincial grain trade escaped from the discretionary control of the intendants.

Nevertheless, the administration and the whole of society organised themselves in order to make the best use of the new means of communication. In the Middle Ages pilgrims, the Universities and certain merchant corporations had under-taken the transport of letters. Louis XI in 1464 instituted the first regular service of posts; every four leagues[1] on the high-ways the couriers of the king or the pope found good horses always ready to carry them at a gallop over the next stage. But in 1576, under the pretext of lightening the task of the University couriers, in reality in order to break up the privilege of a hostile body, Henry III instituted in each town " two royal messengers charged with carrying legal and other official documents " on behalf of poor pleaders. The post was thus opened to the public. In 1627 Richelieu issued a general list of charges. Two couriers set out from Paris every week for Lyons, Dijon, Bordeaux and Toulouse.[2] In each of these towns offices were set up for the reception and delivery of letters, not to mention seven offices set up to deal with foreign letters. These distances were generally covered at the rate of four leagues an hour in summer and an hour and a half in winter. Until the middle of the seventeenth century the letters were simply put in a case which the postilion carried on his saddle. Later they used two-wheeled mail-carts covered with tarred canvas. In 1672 the transport of letters became a State privilege, and it was farmed at 1,200,000 livres. In forty years the rent doubled, and in 1786 it was ten times as large.

But at no time were letters sufficient for the needs of trade, and it was necessary to establish rapid means of

[1] A league is equivalent to about four kilometres.—M. R.

[2] During the minority of Louis XIV, in 1653, a private person ob-tained the right of placing letter boxes in the streets of Paris and of distributing the letters. A label attached to each letter stated that the price of delivery, fixed at one sou, had been paid, and showed the day, month and year. But this innovation was not followed up.

transport for the merchants themselves. Francis I had already authorised his postmasters to hire horses to private individuals. To travel as quickly as the courier all a man had to do was to pay and to be as good a horseman as the postilion. Before the end of the century "coaches set out and arrived at a fixed day and charged a fixed fare, thus assuring to simple travellers a great economy of money and trouble."[1] But they covered only about thirteen leagues a day, and as they did not travel at night the journey from Paris to Orleans took two whole days. Moreover, they were open carriages which could only be closed when necessary with leather curtains. Drawn by four horses, they only contained eight places, and the baggage was piled in two wicker baskets fastened on behind. About 1650 they gave way to *carrosses* enclosed by wooden panels. This improvement in comfort was soon followed by an increase in speed. But at the end of Louis XIV's reign, travelling by a coach, " it took more days to go from one place to another than it takes hours to-day travelling by express."[2]

Barges were more comfortable but much slower. The first barges, which were called *corbillats* and made two voyages a week, had been established in Henry IV's reign between Paris and Corbeil at first, and later as far as Melun and Sens. They were towed on the return voyage. In the eighteenth century while the Paris-Lyons *diligence*, which was running almost daily by that time, took six days to do the journey, the barge took nine or twelve, according to the season. The *turgotines*, which were lighter and better built, and which were exempt from all tolls and Customs, and sometimes travelled even by night, made the journey more quickly, so that the passengers complained that they did not give them time even to go to Mass. In the *turgotines* the journey from Paris to Angers took two and a half days.

Light merchandise naturally profited by the increasing facilities offered to the traveller. The courier took charge of small packets, and the *diligence* service was supplemented by a similarly organised goods service. For heavy goods Henry IV organised a system of carriage along the high-roads and of haulage along the waterways, which Richelieu

[1] Pigeonneau, *Commerce de la France*, vol. ii, p. 402.
[2] Levasseur, *Histoire du Commerce*, vol. i, pp. 315-319.

incorporated in the *cinq grosses fermes*. At first all transport business was free and uncontrolled, but soon there appeared private companies which won a practical monopoly and sometimes, by raising the price of·transport, hindered traffic instead of encouraging it. In the seventeenth century the too heavily laden carts covered only seven or eight leagues a day and took four days to go from Paris to Orleans, though it must be admitted that the hills were steep and the roads muddy.

We must now see which were the chief meeting-places of merchants and merchandise travelling by land or water, by boat, horse or vehicle.

In the Middle Ages, when roads were even worse and much less secure, merchants travelled only at fixed seasons and in caravans to the traditional fairs. In the sixteenth century some of these great periodical fairs still existed. In Northern France the Rouen Fair still prospered, though the Fairs of Champagne had died out and those of Burgundy had declined. In Paris the Fair of St. Laurence, which had hitherto been held in a field, was in 1661 installed in an enclosure provided with stalls and shaded by trees. This fair lasted for two months. In the south the Fairs of Nîmes and, above all, of Beaucaire preserved all their splendour until the middle of the seventeenth century. The latter only lasted for three days, but merchants came to them not only from all over France, but from Switzerland, Germany, all the Mediterranean countries, and even from Persia. Colbert thought it worth while to send a squadron to protect the ships which were going there.

But in proportion as daily communication grew easier these great annual or quarterly meetings became unnecessary. Now that supplies reached the capital almost daily the old privileges still enjoyed by the Fair of St. Denis no longer sufficed to preserve its importance in the economic life of Paris, and the new Fair of St. Germain-des-Prés owed its animation rather to the popular amusements provided than to the commercial transactions concluded there. The four Lyons fairs, each lasting twenty days, had flourished in the sixteenth century, but were no longer important except as marking periods when the commercial activity of the city redoubled in response to certain temporary advantages. By the end of Louis XIV's reign the decline of purely commercial fairs was universal. Great merchants sold their goods through their agents, who were established in every big city; their stock-in-trade had become too big to move from place to place. At fairs only articles inferior in quality to those in ordinary shops were sold. " These fairs rarely lasted as long as the law allowed them. Even in backward provinces like Lower Brittany they were shortened by common consent of buyers and sellers."[1] Only agricultural fairs, especially cattle or horse fairs, like that at Guitray, near Caen, escaped the general decadence, and have indeed lasted to our own day.

In reality the chief cities in the kingdom (apart altogether from Paris, which as early as the sixteenth century numbered 400,000 inhabitants) fulfilled the function of huge permanent fairs. Foreign trade reacted on internal trade, and Lyons and Nantes became great interprovincial markets. In the central provinces Colbert created for a time free markets with the object of giving articles intended for export easier access to the ports. Orleans in the north and Toulouse in the south formed natural stations between the markets of the interior and the general distributing centres. The smaller towns became agricultural markets; after 1709 the government put into force again the old regulations which ordered that all grain from the surrounding district should be sold in the town market on a fixed day once a week. In the seventeenth century two great markets were organised just outside Paris for butchers' beasts; one was at Poissy for cattle from Normandy, the other at Sceaux for cattle from Beauce.

Unfortunately the intervention of the government in the sale of provisions was not dictated solely by the desire to regulate the public food supply, but also by fiscal interests. This concentration of commodities facilitated the collection of the innumerable taxes and offered a convenient field for the work of the innumerable searchers, weighers, gaugers, measurers, aulnagers, markers, controllers, essayers and so on,[2] offices which had almost always been created as a

[1] D'Avenel, *Paysans et ouvriers*, p. 339.

[2] At the end of the seventeenth century the number of these officials in Paris alone exceeded 2,000.

financial expedient and which hindered trade while pretending to help it. Sometimes the government itself monopolised the sale of certain articles. Such was the case with tobacco in Colbert's time, and soon afterwards with the retail trade in spirits, with the result that the consumption of both these articles was reduced. Moreover, municipal regulations were very burdensome and injured trade in some articles. At the corn market in Paris, for instance, official porters met the carts, would not allow the carters to unload them themselves, and demanded high wages. When the corn arrived at its destination it was the turn of the purchaser to be assailed by women who set up as brokers and extorted commissions. Then, on the pretext of helping to fill the sacks, the *ramasseurs* or gleaners of the streets arrived, and took care to spill some of the grain for their own benefit. So many expensive intermediaries did not make business any easier.

If means of communication and markets are the essential organs of commerce, measures and means of exchange are equally indispensable instruments. Progress in the development of weights and measures between the fifteenth and the eighteenth century was slight. One after another Louis XI,[1] Francis I and Henry II tried to obtain uniformity, but failed to break down the resistance of the nobles and of the force of custom. Three centuries of absolutism were not enough to force France to adopt the standards of the central government.

On the other hand the unification of the coinage had been in progress since the time of St Louis, and when the modern period began only royal money was being coined. But a good deal of foreign money, often considerably debased, was still in circulation. In 1636 there were thirty-eight different types of coinage in circulation, and Louis XIV could not postpone the work of purification. The advantage of having only one coinage would be small, however, if its value were not invariable. But during the Religious Wars the distressed monarchy had more than once had recourse to debasing the coinage, hoping to obtain at least a temporary benefit. In the critical years at the end of Louis XIV's reign the same expedient was resorted to, to the injury of trade. The value

[1] "He would have liked," said Commines, "everyone in his kingdom to obey the same laws and use the same weights and measures."

of money was only finally fixed in 1726, and this time the monarchy was faithful to its promise.

For three-quarters of a century now it had ceased to be easy for dishonest people to clip the coinage. When minted coins were substituted for the old hammered coinage, it was possible to make the crowns and louis so round and to cut them so neatly that all attempts to tamper with them were very obvious. A dependable paper currency would have been of great assistance to trade, but the issue of the first state notes in the last years of Louis XIV's reign was no more than an expedient to relieve the poverty of the Treasury. Their use gave rise to many abuses, and the edicts which attempted to make their circulation compulsory did not save them from discredit. A like fate overtook Law's bank-notes, which, however, did protect their holders from sudden monetary changes. Thus the imprudence of the government delayed the introduction of paper money for a century.[1] Merchants did indeed possess means of reducing to a minimum the transport of money, which, moreover, was made easier by the development of the postal system. Bills of exchange and transferred balances—in a word, " paper " payments—were used daily by great merchants even before the sixteenth century.

To complete this sketch of the material conditions under which trade developed we must trace the organisation and vicissitudes of credit. Even during the Middle Ages there were in France foreign banks kept by Jews, Cahorsins or Lombards, who continued their operations for several centuries. Then French banks were founded at Lyons (1543), at Toulouse (1549) and at Rouen (1566). After 1579 the government forced foreign bankers to be naturalised, and the French bankers themselves had to be licensed and to deposit a security. During the first half of the sixteenth century the rate of discount fixed for merchants or the interest paid to money-lenders averaged about eight per cent. It was at this common rate that the king issued his first loan in 1522. Then during the civil wars capital was scarce and some of it went abroad, with the result that money was dear and its price rose to ten or twelve per cent.

[1] For French colonial coinage, see Nogaro and Oualid, *L'évolution du commerce, du crédit et des transports depuis cent cinquante ans*, pp. 59-61.

When order was restored and trade revived, the government could put into effect the right which it claimed of regulating the rate of interest. In 1600 Henry IV, by enforcing an old edict of Charles IX which had remained a dead letter, lowered the rate from $8\frac{1}{3}$ to $6\frac{1}{4}$ per cent. It fell to 5 per cent. in the course of the seventeenth century. Law wished to reduce it to 3, but after his failure the legal rate of 5 per cent. remained in force until the Revolution, and roughly corresponded with that generally used by merchants. Many public loans and the disorder of the financial administration prevented it from falling to the same level in France as in the other great commercial powers. It was occasionally lower in Paris, where there was plenty of loose capital, but it was often higher in small towns and country districts. " To check the abuses of usury " during Fleury's ministry, national pawnshops (*monts de piété*) were set up in the principal towns. Their chief business was to lend money on securities and business effects. Turgot did a still greater service to merchants, especially to those of Paris, by creating in 1776 a private discount office (*caisse d'escompte*) under state control, which discounted all bills of exchange at the maximum rate of 4 per cent.

To deal with commercial lawsuits a new department was created on the model of the municipal tribunals of Central Europe. The first consular judges had been installed at Lyons and Toulouse in 1549, and the edict of Moulins, issued in 1566 at the instigation of Michel de l'Hospital, made the institution general. It had the triple advantage over ordinary jurisdiction of being free, simple and rapid. It is true that these special magistrates more than once gave proof of favouring big merchants at the expense of the small, but nevertheless they had the great merit of working out a practical system of law which the great edict of March, 1673 (the *Code Marchand*) did little more than confirm and much of which is still in force to-day. On one important point, however, the history of commercial law went through abrupt changes. The edict of Moulins, which had been issued soon after a series of sensational failures, and was, moreover, still inspired by the spirit of the commercial law of the gilds, condemned bankrupts to death. In actual fact the courts

had been content to condemn them to an *amende honorable*
or to the pillory, or, as a maximum penalty, to the galleys
for life. But Henry IV insisted on the letter of the law. He
even forbade compositions lest they should leave a loophole
for fraudulent collusion. In future any banker who feared
that he would have to stop payment had no thought but to
escape from a ruthless punishment by flight. The originators
of the *Code Savary* were the first to understand that by
moderating the rigour of the law in cases of honest failure it
was often possible to minimise the grave consequences of
their insolvency.

§ 3. The New Business Aristocracy.

Draper-mercers—Foreign and Jewish financiers; French financiers—
Participation of the nobles—Collective enterprises—Relations of
the new aristocracy with the old nobility and with the government.

The extension of international relations, the relative
unification of the national market, the development of roads
and of other means of communication and the organisation
of credit—all these facts are intimately connected, and can
be summed up in one formula—the advent of modern commerce on a big scale.

This does not mean that the small traders who had been
almost without rivals in the previous centuries disappeared.
Small towns and even certain parts of the big cities were still
full of small shops which sold " a little of everything," like
the village shops of to-day. Until the end of the eighteenth
century, moreover, the new high-roads, and still more the
cross-roads, were travelled by pedlars, sometimes riding a
horse or mule or ass or, more rarely, driving a cart. They
took their packs from hamlet to hamlet, from farm to farm
and did so good a trade as to provoke the complaints of their
competitors established in towns. They were not ephemeral
survivals of the past destined to disappear completely, but
bore witness to a normal persistence of economic categories
which social evolution tended to subordinate rather than to
destroy.

The dominant and characteristic fact of this evolution
was the emergence of a special class of rich merchants. Even
in the gild organisation the differentiation of manufacturers

and merchants had been marked.[1] The draper-mercers, for example, could sell all sorts of articles in competition with the artisans of their town, but could not make any. They formed the first of those famous Parisian corporations which were called the Six Companies (*Six Corps*), but precisely on account of the extension of their business they had loosened, if not broken, the bonds of a narrowly municipal régime. Throughout the kingdom they formed a huge association of *chevaliers*, and their "king," who did not definitely disappear until 1597, exercised almost royal rights, going so far as to issue masters' certificates in the name of the society. Immediately below them came the grocers, who were authorised to sell, in addition to their own special goods, vinegar, spirits, coffee and seeds in competition with vinegar-makers, coffee-house keepers and seed merchants. But, as was natural, it was outside this arbitrary and rather antiquated framework that the new class grew up.

How did this class amass the wealth which it employed in its multifarious operations? The early capitalists who were the first members of the new aristocracy of commerce were usually foreigners, who had made their fortunes abroad or after immigration to France. At Lyons in the sixteenth century most of the great merchants and bankers were Italians, especially from Genoa, Milan, Lucca and Florence. At Bordeaux, besides Italians, there were Spanish or Portuguese Jews, the former expelled by the government, while the latter " had good reasons for leaving their country. They all opened warehouses and shops for the benefit of their fellow-countrymen and sometimes only stayed in France until they had made their fortunes."[2] First under Catherine

---

[1] The interests of both classes were already quite distinct if not opposed. During the minority of Louis XIV, for example, Superintendant Bailleul ordered 130 of the richest merchants of the Six Companies to purchase 700,000 livres of stock which he had just created. The small merchant-manufacturers were undisturbed by this measure, which did not attack them directly; but the rich merchants, in order to make them support their claims, refused to give them orders. In the end the government gave way and substituted a tax on merchandise for the forced loan. It was paid by the consumers, or by the industrial and commercial classes combined. *Cf.* Levasseur, *Classes ouvrières*, vol. ii, p. 199.

[2] Fagniez, *Économie sociale sous Henri IV*, p. 290.

de Medici, then under Marie, Italian financiers began to set
up in Paris itself. This was the period of the Gondi and the
famous Zamet. After the promulgation of the Edict of
Nantes there was a new invasion, this time of the Huguenots, while Dutch and Germans disputed with the Italians
for the first place in the commerce of Lyons and established
themselves in the chief ports.

The Frenchmen's turn came at last. Henry IV had
treated foreign merchants generously and had given them
naturalisation certificates and many smaller favours without
exacting reciprocal privileges from neighbouring governments. Richelieu, however, insisted that they should pay
the same duties as Frenchmen. Moreover, sales and purchases on behalf of aliens could henceforth only be effected
through French agents, born of a French father, and French
merchants were forbidden to lend their name and trade-
mark to foreigners so that they might enjoy the privileges
of the town. French Protestants did not let slip this chance,
and since public offices and the liberal professions were soon
closed to them they sought an outlet for their activity in
business. In the middle of the seventeenth century the
brothers Hogguer were to all intents and purposes the
bankers of the royal exchequer, while Samuel Bernard and
Crozat were among the richest financiers in Europe. In
certain cities, such as Bordeaux, the foreign colony continued
to direct trade until the eighteenth century. But there is
no doubt that during the last two hundred years of the
monarchy most of the men who made large fortunes were
Frenchmen from the lower ranks of society. Among the
parvenus of Richelieu's time Macé Bertrand, who was worth
four million livres, was the son of a peasant; Le Ragois, who
had an income of sixty thousand livres, began life as a small
trader; Catelan, who gave his daughter a dowry of six
hundred thousand livres, was the son of an old clothesman;
Picard, who bought the marquisate of Dampierre, had begun
as a simple shoemaker.

These enormous accumulations of capital, which were as
much an object of wonder to contemporaries as the millions
of some Americans are to us, were derived from various
sources. Many had been won in purely individual commercial enterprises. Even more powerful than Jacques Cœur

before him, Jean Ango, the famous shipowner of Dieppe, had drawn such huge profits from his trade along the Atlantic coasts that he had taken explorers into his service and had been able with his own fleet to blockade the port of Lisbon and dictate terms to the King of Portugal (1530). The new developments of maritime trade offered such scope that from the beginning the nobles had been allowed to take part in it. Louis XI, Henry IV, Richelieu and Colbert in turn declared that they could in this way make money without dishonour. In the seventeenth century a certain Bouhier de Beaumarchais made thousands with his six ships in trade with America and the Indies. But the middle classes showed most enterprise and daring in overseas trade. Lalande Magon of St. Malo, in the very midst of the War of the League of Augsburg, sent two frigates armed with cannon to carry cargoes from Columbia to Buenos Ayres and Carthagena, and the terrible War of the Spanish Succession did not prevent him from carrying on a trade in gold and silver with Chili and Peru. Le Gendre, the famous merchant of Rouen, possessed a fortune valued at five or six million livres. At Bordeaux in the eighteenth century were formed regular dynasties of merchants, such as the Gradis, the Nayracs, the Bonnaffés, and, indeed, everyone in this great city took part in the American trade, and ordinary artisans and even servants with no capital threw themselves into colonial speculation.[1]

Internal trade also gave rise to powerful houses. " For one rich wholesale merchant who could be found in the reign of King Louis XI," wrote Claude Seyssel, the panegyrist of Louis XII, " you may find to-day more than fifty." In every big town agents, usually unattached to any company, acted as middlemen for the manufacturers. And although the nobles were not allowed to take a personal share in this apparently more vulgar business, they did not consider it improper to invest their money in trade. In the seventeenth century " most people of quality, lawyers and others, entrusted their money to wholesale merchants so as to make a profit out of it. The merchants sold their goods to retailers on twelve or fifteen months' credit, charging 10 per cent. interest, and making 3 or 4 per cent. profit."[2] In 1721 the

[1] See Carré in Lavisse, *Histoire de France*, vol. viii², p. 109.
[2] Savary, quoted by Levasseur, *Histoire du Commerce*, vol. i, p. 380.

Duc de la Force even ventured to open a shop for colonial produce, although he had not been received as a grocer. At that time most of the big merchants of Paris occupied whole houses, many of them regular mansions, which they often owned themselves. Some were interested in improving their shops, and the *Petit Dunkerque*, situated near the Pont-Neuf, " a rare shop for the sale of French and foreign merchandise and of all the latest products of the arts," may be regarded as the ancestor of our modern stores.

Both in the overseas trade and in more restricted operations collective enterprises multiplied side by side with individual enterprises. We have already spoken of the association of the merchants of Rouen, which was formed in the sixteenth century to trade with the New World. A century later at St. Malo, Danican and Magon formed societies for trade with China and the Indies. At Lyons, Paris and Lille rich merchants formed associations to extend their business. Outside these private associations larger professional societies were formed; they had nothing in common with the old gilds except that they proposed to defend analogous interests. In the sixteenth century, for example, the merchants who traded along the Loire united in a sort of syndicate to see that the river was kept in order and to obtain the suppression of arbitrary tolls. Moreover, there were the semi-official companies. The East India Company of 1664 was already organised as a joint-stock company in which the liability of each shareholder was limited by the amount of his share. In the organisation of the West India Company, founded by Law, the shareholders took the initiative out of the hands of the government, and nominated their own directors in a general assembly. Moreover, it was the first company in France to institute bill-broking. The army and navy contractors and the state corn merchants also formed big associations, half public, half private.

But it was the financiers, strictly so called, who amassed the biggest fortunes.[1] Many of them only managed private banks, but in some centres their business reached a formid-

[1] But very often until the end of the seventeenth century the same men were both financiers and merchants. See Savary, quoted by Levasseur, *Histoire du Commerce*, vol. i, p. 308, and Sagnac in Lavisse, *Histoire de France*, vol. viii[1], pp. 251-252.

able amount. For example, at Lyons after each of the four big fairs, large payments in silver and still more in paper were effected. A clearing-house was set up, and accounts to the amount of twenty million crowns were balanced without the disbursement of more than a hundred thousand. The town fixed the rate of exchange for the chief cities in Europe, and thus we find established there capitalists like the Anissons and the Hogguer brothers. Less important were the brokers who confined themselves to negotiating the bills and collecting the debts of the great merchants. On the other hand, the farmers-general played an important part in the state. They advanced to the government the proceeds of the indirect taxes, which they collected, and this gave them such a privileged position that the Treasury, in moments of stress, was obliged to turn to them to raise a loan. To the high rate of interest which they regularly charged were added the profits of stock-jobbing, that short-cut to wealth inaugurated with such a flourish in the time of the " System."

Here, then, was a new aristocracy which had grown up side by side with the old, and whose claims had to be recognised, willingly or not, by modern society. Their manner of living alone showed that the members of this class had raised themselves far above the ranks of the common people. " Often educated at college with the sons of magistrates and gentlemen, the seventeenth-century trader was no longer distinguished from the noble by his style of living. He was no longer a merchant; he was the head of a house, a great speculator, who had offices like a minister of state, who had correspondents at Cadiz, London, Frankfort, Hamburg, Amsterdam and Venice. He conducted business in his private office or at the Bourse (Stock Exchange) and left his clerks to do the selling."[1] In Richelieu's time the Catelans and Tabourets surpassed the greatest nobles in luxury, while in the eighteenth century the great merchants of Bordeaux adorned the town with their princely mansions. Some of them played the part of Mæcenas, as, for instance, Montauron, to whom Corneille dedicated *Cinna*, and Voltaire declared that " the manners of polite society have reached the very shops." Among the last farmers-general more than

---

[1] Pigeonneau, *op. cit.*, vol. ii, p. 456.

one made himself famous for his wit or his generosity. It is enough to recall the names of Helvétius and Lavoisier.

There was, moreover, nothing easier than for a rich merchant to enter a noble family, for there was no lack of ruined gentlemen ready to marry their heirs to the daughters of the rich middle class. If the ambitious "shopkeeper" wanted to ennoble his own name, he could buy for his son the office of recorder or procurator or receiver of taxes, or better still, if his means allowed it, a commission in the army, the office of counsellor of state, or a seat in the Parlement. If he wished in his old age to bear a title himself, he had only to buy an estate carrying seigniorial rights. Provided that his business were big enough, honours might even come to him without his seeking or paying for them. Louis XI, Francis I and Charles IX had only ennobled individuals, but Richelieu gave titles of nobility for life to any commoner who for five years had owned ships of two or three hundred tons, and allowed all rich wholesale merchants to take the rank of nobles. Towards 1760 the point had almost been reached when full nobility might be conferred on all great merchants.

At all events, they were allowed a place in the councils of the nation. It was not enough that members of the *Six Corps* should have the privilege of being consuls or aldermen. Henry IV set up a permanent Trade Commission, which Colbert transformed into a Council. Deputies chosen by the eighteen principal markets of the kingdom provided the majority of its members. They formed a body truly representative of national commerce. Their views were often listened to, and the king chose from among them delegates charged with the duty of discussing the economic clauses of great treaties. In the provinces the merchants had already had their Bourses since 1563, and after 1700 they had their Chambers of Commerce, which served as a nucleus for their organisation.

Two obstacles, however, hindered the triumphal progress of the commercial class. One was the survival of aristocratic prejudices which dominated, as it were unconsciously, the new aristocracy of trade. As soon as he had made his fortune the business man wanted nothing so much as to abandon trade, and to live like a lord—that is to say, do nothing. He disdainfully consented to take part in the affairs of his town, but he would have thought it beneath him to pursue his own business at the same time. As to the capital which he had amassed, he withdrew it from trade and after one or two generations it was all tied up in useless expenses, in sumptuous mansions and in stately châteaux surrounded by huge uncultivated parks.

The other obstacle was the result of the arbitrary character of the administration. The same government which honoured commerce in general and which sometimes flattered financiers, did not hesitate if a merchant dared to leave the country without permission to seize his goods and those of his relations who remained in France. Moreover, when there was danger that the high price of bread might cause riots, the government treated all grain merchants as suspects, forcing them to open their granaries, to supply markets at whatever cost to themselves, and to sell their reserves at a low price. In fact, when public safety seemed to demand it the government did not hesitate to apply rigorous measures against the merchant class. Only under the régime of liberty and equality which resulted from the Revolution did the commercial class come to the full enjoyment of its rights and the full consciousness of its dignity—at the risk of pushing the former to excess and abusing the latter.

II.—INDUSTRY

§ 1. The Evolution of the Gilds.

Extension and apparent consolidation of the gilds; attempts to widen their scope—Weakening of the system; workmen who worked at home, workmen who followed the court, and workmen of the Louvre; sale of master's certificates—Weight of royal taxation; imminent bankruptcy.

The period which we are studying saw at the same time the perpetuation of the industrial organisation of the Middle Ages and the development of new forms of production. Let us see first how it was that the old organisation was able to survive the transformation from an urban to a national economy.

From the reign of Louis XI to that of Louis XV the number of gilds in the kingdom never ceased to grow. The

reason that the absolute monarchy apparently favoured the
extension of a system which was in origin exclusively
municipal was that since the check of the communal
movement the towns had ceased to be offensive to the
government, which in any case had taken precautions to
suppress in them any desire for independence. Moreover, in
the sixteenth century it had contrived to replace the elected
magistrates of the most important gilds by its own officials.
Thus in multiplying the craft gilds the government ran into
no danger, but was even able to turn them to its own profit.

Louis XI was one of the first to realise that the new
masters created by the government would be additional
allies in his struggle against feudalism. Moreover, in the
interests of the good order of the kingdom, it was useful that
the gild system should be generally applied so that when it
was a question of safeguarding public interests, assuring
social tranquillity, or protecting or supervising labour, the
king's policy could be more uniformly and effectively applied.
For this reason the great ordinance of 1581, confirmed and
extended in 1597, ordered every artisan who had a shop in
towns or boroughs where gilds were not officially organised to
take the master's oath. Thus, says an historian,[1] " national
labour was enlisted and organised under the eye and hand of
the king." But what Henry III and Henry IV had decreed,
only Louis XIV was strong enough to put into execution. In
contrast to the earlier edicts, that of 1673, which renewed
them, was very strictly applied. In 1672 there were only
sixty gilds in Paris; in 1673 there were eighty-three; in 1691
a hundred and twenty-nine. Moreover, the system spread to
many towns where the royal authority would not have been
obeyed a century earlier.

It goes without saying that the crown had reserved the
right of drawing up the statutes of the gilds. Colbert had
taken care to remove this power from the lord chief justices
in 1668. The gilds were altogether freed from the feudal
magistrates in 1669; lawsuits were to be submitted either to
the jurisdiction of mayors and aldermen, which would be
cheaper, quicker and more docile to the wishes of the
administration, or were to be directly settled by the royal
courts. Until the day when they were for the first time

---

[1] Pigeonneau, *Histoire du Commerce*, vol. ii., pp. 227-229.

abolished along with the absolutism to which their fate was closely bound, these old gilds seemed almost to grow stronger. Those famous fraternities which the Church and the Parlements of the sixteenth century had agreed in condemning, and which the last Valois kings had tried to suppress, were openly reconstituted. After the defeat of the League, however, they had given up all political ambition and had ceased from turbulent manifestations, so that they no longer disturbed the government and indeed seemed to bolster up the still impressive frontage of a decaying edifice.

Another consideration which had inspired this royal policy for three hundred years was that the gilds on the whole were rich and might relieve the growing expenses of the Treasury. Louis XI tried to get a share of the profits of masters' fees and of the fines inflicted by *jurés*. The edict of 1581 ordered that before taking the oath every master must pay to the receiver of royal taxes a sum which in big towns might amount to thirty crowns. These fiscal clauses in the edict were the only ones which were strictly enforced and were reproduced to the letter in the edict of 1597. The edict of 1673 in addition forced all existing gilds to pay a fine to obtain confirmation of their privileges, and since the war with the Dutch was very expensive the fines had to be paid at once. Similarly the momentary hostility shown in the sixteenth century by the kings to the fraternities was not solely dictated by the desire to maintain order. It was the age of secularisation, and the kings would have liked to confiscate their goods. In any case, a threat of general suppression enabled them to raise money by selling dispensations.

While attempting to make the gild system universal the government also tried to correct certain restrictions which were manifestly incompatible with the new unity of the monarchy. It tried to enlarge, at any rate, the framework of urban economic organisation. The topography of many towns had altered materially, and the members of certain gilds had been obliged to leave the districts to which they had been originally confined in order to follow the movement of their customers. By doing this they cut themselves off from their associations which made a strong distinction between the city and the suburbs. The edict of 1581 specifically ordained that suburban masters of three years' experience should rank equally with the city masters. In 1610, by way of compromise, this privilege was restricted to two masters a year, chosen by jurymen. But the edict of 1673 officially incorporated all suburban masters in the city gilds. The Administration wished to put an end to the incessant frauds and interminable lawsuits provoked by a distinction which it was as difficult to carry out in practice as to justify in theory. But it took six years to accomplish this petty revolution.

A bolder step in connection with the unification of the kingdom was to open a permanent means of communication between the host of jealously exclusive societies formed by the local industrial groups. In 1581 it was decreed that an artisan who was received as a master in Paris might practise his trade throughout the kingdom. Moreover, in towns where there was a Parlement masters should exercise the same privilege wherever the court had jurisdiction, and so on in the case of the lower courts. But a hundred years later, even after the publication of the ordinance of 1673, Parisian masters experienced almost insurmountable difficulties when they attempted to set up in the provinces. Similarly the great edicts of the end of the sixteenth century had in vain proclaimed that an apprenticeship served in any town should be valid throughout the country; for a long time the recruiting of journeymen remained exclusively municipal. The decree of 1755, which reiterated this reform and ordered its enforcement, had to except from the number of towns whose gilds were open to " foreigners " the four great industrial centres of Paris, Lyons, Rouen and Lille. Thus the obstinate resistance of the corporations succeeded in reducing the effects of this modest liberalism.

It was with difficulty that the government had succeeded in breaking a barrier of another kind by authorising every artisan to be received into two gilds of the same kind. The number of apprentices that a master could employ had always been very limited. In the sixteenth century there had been a good deal of latitude allowed in the number of journeymen, but in the eighteenth century the regulations were again made much stricter in certain gilds. Some gilds only allowed one journeyman to a workshop, while others forbade masters to hire more than one shop, so as to prevent them from taking more than their share of a very restricted clientèle.

The royal power was really useful, however, when, instead of attempting to transform the internal organisation of a superannuated system, it encouraged all enterprises which by their very origin were outside it. It must be remembered that during the Middle Ages the towns which had gilds were only a minority. Notably in the great cities of Southern France there existed only trade fraternities which prevented any monopoly. Lyons until the middle of the sixteenth century had only three organised crafts—the goldsmiths, the barber-surgeons and the locksmiths. In the small towns and villages associations of artisans were on the whole unknown, and the three great edicts of 1581, 1597 and 1673 did not succeed in establishing them there. Even in many of the gild towns the free trades continued to outnumber the organised crafts.

Moreover, since the fifteenth century there had been a steady increase in the number of *chambrelans*, artisans who worked in their own homes. They had never been apprenticed, they would never be journeymen or masters, but thanks to the forbearance of the Administration they entered into more and more active competition with the regular masters. Kings even found it convenient to have in their service free artisans who followed the court; their number was raised from 160 under Francis I to over 400 under Henry IV. Most of them by this time worked for the public as well as for the king and his suite. They had simply bought at a good price the right to work as they liked and to sell their products where it suited them. These were new and dangerous rivals of the gilds. Another class of independent workmen was to be found in the workmen of the Louvre (*ouvriers du Louvre*) whom Henry IV installed in his own palace in the great " Galerie du Bord de l'Eau." Not only were these privileged workmen personally freed from the numerous formalities and restrictions of the gilds, but they also had the right of taking two apprentices, one of whom might become a master every five years without a masterpiece and in any part of the kingdom. After the creation of the West India Company the government wished to encourage the emigration of artisans to the Antilles, and it therefore declared that those who had practised their craft for eight years in the Antilles should *ipso facto* become masters, and on their return to France might establish themselves where they liked.[1]

The only thing that remained for the government to do was to make masters itself, and even this it did not fail to do. Sometimes it was the means of supporting a charitable institution. Thus artisans who taught their trade gratuitously to children in foundling hospitals were made masters by way of recompense. But more often it was an expedient to fill the Treasury or to satisfy the greed of the princes of the blood. For the royal *lettres de maîtrise* or masters' certificates were for sale, and they had only to be cheaper than the authentic certificates in order to find purchasers. But the gilds and municipalites revenged themselves for this abuse of power by piling obstacles and taxes on the unfortunate purchasers, so that many certificates remained on the market. The government, to whom the growth of the gilds was at bottom not very important, contented itself with forcing the established masters to buy up *en bloc* all the discredited certificates. Louis XI had inaugurated this practice, and recourse was had to it again during the reign of Louis XV.

But it seems that the government had at one time a definite intention of intervening in the recruiting of masters. By the edict of 1581 it reserved to itself the right of nominating regularly three masters in every craft and of dispensing in their case with the masterpiece. The *lettres de maîtrise* issued in 1767 are interesting not only because the government allowed all foreigners, consequently even Jews, to buy them, but also because the edict which established them stated that on this occasion the *Six Corps* would not be allowed to buy them up.

While their field of action was thus being restricted and their autonomy threatened, the gilds were weakening in another way as well, for they were growing poorer. Not only might they be called upon at any moment to buy up blocks of *lettres de maîtrise*, but the government in times of crisis created ridiculous and insupportable offices at random for the sole purpose of extorting money from industry by

[1] Levasseur, *Histoire du Commerce*, vol. i, pp. 367-370.

indirect means. Richelieu created one after another the hereditary offices of *contrôleurs-marqueurs-visiteurs* of linen (1627), *prudhommes visiteurs* of leathers (1629), *contrôleurs* of paper (1633) and of cloths and dyes (1639). During the minority of Louis XIV the gilds were so heavily taxed that they took an active part in the rising of the Fronde. In the last period of the reign charges of all sorts weighed so heavily on them that they were almost destroyed. "In 1691 the government declared that it was going to replace all gild officials, *jurés* and *syndics*, by agents of its own. In order to avoid this misfortune the gilds at once had to pay 300,000 livres. In 1694 the government decided to appoint auditors and examiners to control gild accounts, and a new sacrifice of 400,000 livres was necessary to obtain their suppression. In 1711 the government went so far as to forbid them to receive new masters."[1] Then they were forced to borrow large sums of money and had great difficulty in paying the interest on their debts. Moreover, it became difficult to recruit new masters. Liquidation was ordered, and they could not meet their claims. Offices, the redemption of which was henceforth obligatory, multiplied, while the creation of new masters by the government progressively reduced the profits of the old. It may be said that at the end of the eighteenth century the gild system, like the absolutism of which it was very largely the victim, was reduced to bankruptcy.

§ 2. Encouragement of Large Scale Industry.

Reasons of the monarchy—Immunities, reliefs and monopolies granted to manufacturers; State manufactures—The recruiting of labour: foreign artisans, peasants—Control of the supply of raw materials and of the sale of manufactured goods; protective duties and bounties on export.

Large scale industry, like the large scale trade of which it was the offspring, developed naturally outside an organisation which was worn out and soon to be cast aside. It was in vain that the government towards the end of the seventeenth century tried to force the workmen and masters of the

[1] Georges Renard, *Syndicats, trade-unions et corporations*, p. 118 *et seq.*

woollen industry to group themselves into sworn corporations round the factories. The gild system was incompatible
with the double concentration of capital and labour which
was the essence of the new manufactures. Very often,
indeed, these new manufactures were so novel in character
that no one thought of forcing them into the traditional
framework.

In the first half of the seventeenth century especially the
monarchy had two reasons for encouraging these new establishments, for they not only contributed to enrich the state,
but to keep it peaceful. Henry IV considered them " an
easy and pleasant means of purging the kingdom of all the
vices bred by idleness." Is not work, says a contemporary,[1]
" the curb of civil wars " ? Richelieu expressed the same idea
more harshly.[2] Colbert would have France share his own
passion for work. " I hereby give permission for manufacturers of woollen stockings to set up factories at Clermont
and Blesle as the inhabitants of these towns desire," he
wrote to the intendant of Riom. " Perhaps," adds M.
Lavisse, " the people did indeed desire them, but it is not
certain. The minister easily imagined that what he wanted
did exist. Gradually the whole kingdom was thus ' taken in
hand.' "[3]

It may be asked whether there was a sufficient supply of
capital available in the country and whether the necessary
groupings formed spontaneously. The gilds, in the exercise
of their various crafts and by their excessive sumptuary
expenditure, absorbed a good deal of capital. Rich individuals were not inclined to place their money in uncertain
enterprises when public stock, private loans and offices which
could be bought offered them safer and more honourable if
not more profitable investments. By nature " the French are
not a people greedy of gain. Money matters have never been
their greatest interest."[4] Therefore Colbert judged it necessary that the royal pleasure should be shown. He invited
the nobles to invest their money in the new enterprises and
even to take a personal part in them, guaranteeing them

[1] Montchrestien.
[2] " The people is a mule which is spoiled by idleness."
[3] *Histoire de France*, vol. vii[1], p. 221.
[4] Lavisse, *Histoire de France*, vol. vii[1], p. 263.

against any loss of dignity. He tried " to give *rentiers* a distaste for *rentes* " by pointing out the scorn, the hatred almost, with which he viewed their idle investments, and by threatening to reduce their revenues. In the case of officials and " farmers " who were more directly dependent on the ministry, he was still more urgent. But he only half succeeded. The rich merchants held back, and many financiers even desired the failure of enterprises which they had been forced to enter against their will, in the success of which they did not believe, and for which they feared they would be forced incessantly to make new sacrifices. The minister therefore had to employ other means. He was obliged indirectly to involve the public finances, and in order to attract and retain private capital he had to organise a whole system of privileges.

Louis XI had already promised exemption from taxation to all those who were engaged in mining, whether they were Frenchmen or foreigners, or even the subjects of kings with whom France was at war. Henry IV promised the same immunity to the first big manufacturers of linen and silks. The clerks and artisans in the royal factories created by Colbert were released from all contributions, the aliens who worked there could become naturalised without payment of fees, and the goods produced were freed from all taxes and tolls. " These great factories bore the king's escutcheon over their chief entrances. They were small vassal states of the king, depending only on him."[1] All employees enjoyed the privilege of being judged by the Master of Requests. The director was often ennobled; if need be, he and his family were even allowed to practise the reformed religion. It was only when Colbert had gone that religious intolerance outweighed economic interest. The Huguenots, to whom public office had become almost inaccessible, had naturally divided their energies between trade and industry. The Revocation of the Edict of Nantes robbed the kingdom of a considerable amount of its industrial capital.

A more important advantage was that the new manufacture was invested with a more or less complete monopoly, granted either to an individual or a company. Henry II granted one for ten years to an Italian who brought to

[1] Lavisse, *op. cit.*, p. 220.

France the secret of the making of Venetian glass and mirrors. In his reign several inventors received not only the right to exploit their process without being first received as masters, but also the exclusive right to use it for a certain number of years. The first industrial associations formed in Henry IV's reign received a temporary monopoly within a fixed area. To make up for the inertia or ill-will of private individuals, Colbert was obliged to organise regular manufacturing companies. To stimulate the zeal of shareholders he granted them exclusive privileges of varying extent and duration, twenty years for the glass manufacturer established in 1665, nine years for the French point lace company. The monopoly of these two companies extended over the whole kingdom; that of the Van Robais only for ten leagues round Amiens.

After Colbert's time the government preferred to grant privileges of sale either to particular manufactures or to strictly private companies. It was then especially that "limited and unlimited liability companies and particularly joint-stock companies began to drain into business part of the wealth usually employed in purchasing *rentes* and offices." Thus freer combinations tended to replace the rigid organisation of the old corporations. "The merchant from his counting-house and the magistrate from his chair of office could both participate in industrial progress."[1] Even great nobles could take part in it, and from the time of Henry IV they patronised and supplied the capital for various enterprises.[2]

The example of the government in hastening this development with money and good-will was by no means useless. Henry IV had furnished the first manufacturers of linen and cloth of gold with a part of their preliminary capital and had given pensions to the directors. Under Colbert the textile industries alone received eight million livres in the shape of unredeemable advances, subsidies, pensions and bounties on production, in addition to the big orders given by the state with the sole object of advertising their commodities. Colbert also persuaded certain towns such as Lille to provide them with premises, and certain provincial Estates such as those

---

[1] Sagnac in Lavisse, *Histoire de France*, vol. viii[1], p. 230.
[2] See Fagniez, *Économie Sociale*, p. 41.

of Languedoc and Burgundy to subsidise the young industries. " It is true that the sums given in aid to manufactures
were small in comparison with the amounts spent on ships,
and became insignificant in war-time. Louis XIV disdained
commonplace economic problems, and thought only of glory
and magnificence."[1]

But if Louvois maliciously allowed some of Colbert's
creations to fall into decay, he himself created or supported
similar establishments by the same means. His successors
founded still more of them either to introduce new industries
into the kingdom or simply to satisfy favourites. To the end
the monarchy persevered in giving help and encouragement
to capitalist industries. In 1727 part of the revenue of the
import duties collected on American merchandise was appropriated to the *Caisse du Commerce* and formed an ever-
increasing resource.

Finally on occasion the king himself set up as a manufacturer. Richelieu founded the royal printing-press, which
he installed in the Louvre. In 1667 the manufacture of
Gobelins tapestries became a state establishment, the
property of the king, exploited for his profit, and entirely
occupied with furnishing his palaces. In the middle of the
seventeenth century the manufacture of Sèvres porcelain
was founded on the same model. In Louis XVI's reign the
princes of the blood figured as captains of industry. " The
Comte de Provence patronised the earthenware manufacture ;
the Comte d'Artois had a chemical works installed by his
treasurer at Javel; the Duc d'Orléans set up glass-works at
Villers-Cotterets "; while the greatest of the nobles eagerly
followed so eminent an example. " The Ségurs, the Mont-
morencys and the La Vieuvilles were shareholders in the
glass-making company. Choiseul after his disgrace busied
himself with a steel-works. The Dukes of Humières, Aumont
and Charost took up mining concessions."[2]

The development of large scale industry demands both an
abundance of capital and a good supply of labour, for the
labour is just as important as the capital. At first there was
a shortage of qualified labour. Clever workmen, overseers and
even engineers were needed to manufacture the new articles

---

[1] Lavisse, *op. cit.*, pp. 225 and 263.
[2] Sagnac in Lavisse, *Histoire de France*, vol. ix, pp. 219-220.

and apply the new and unfamiliar processes, and since they could not be found in France they had to be brought from abroad. Louis XI promised perpetual exemption from taxation to any silk-workers from Greece or Italy who established themselves in his kingdom. Colbert used every means possible to bribe and attract Swedish miners and founders, Venetian glass-workers and Dutch cloth-makers, who were held capable of making fine cloth " with two-thirds of the wool " used by the French and of getting through more work in a day than they did in a week.

It goes without saying that once the new class of skilled labour had been formed, all emigration or desertion was strictly forbidden. The government went so far as to imprison artisans whom it had formerly enticed into France with gold, or foreigners who tried to engage the best French workmen. Deserters were stopped at the frontier, or dragged back by force from the foreign town in which they had taken refuge, if the fortunes of war chanced to put it in French hands. In the middle of the eighteenth century during crises of unemployment the weavers of Lyons were still kept under observation in their houses.

To secure a supply of local labour in the big factories Colbert granted the workmen various rewards and bounties for regular work, and even exemptions from the *taille* when several members of one family were at work in the factory. Moreover, the manufacturer received the exclusive right of recruiting in a certain district, or else the mayors and intendants did the work of recruiting officers, and both were not above making use of violence. From the first children or paupers in charitable institutions had been used, and some almshouses had become regular factories. Colbert asked the monks to give their alms half in bread and half in wool, on condition that their almsmen should bring back the wool in the form of stockings.

Finally recourse was had to the peasants. After 1762 textile manufacturers were authorised to set up their looms in country districts, where they found plenty of men who were out of work or anxious to supplement their incomes by extra work. Moreover, the tax of one-twentieth on industry was shortly suppressed in the villages. For the success of industry as well as for the defence of the kingdom an increase in population was thus necessary. Colbert had not failed to encourage this by granting exemption from taxation to young couples and big families.

All these measures which increased the supply of labour at the same time made it cheaper. The rural artisans in particular furnished an increasing supply of cheap labour. The Administration was, moreover, attempting to keep down the price of food. When in 1664 a new tax was put on the export of corn it was with the idea, among other things, of preventing an increase in the cost of the labourer's food. At the same time the government was trying to make industrial labour more intensive, with the result that in 1666 the number of holidays was reduced from 103 to 92.

This policy of universal industrialisation naturally met with some opposition. " France could supply her needs very easily from her natural resources, and she refused to over-work. Nowhere did anyone work as hard as Colbert would have wished. Everywhere the workers wasted a little time at the inn. What was the good, they said, of undertaking fresh work when they had enough to live on and pay their taxes ? Moreover, who knew if taxes would not be at once increased so that the Treasury and not they would profit by their extra work ?"[1] The results of Colbert's great and indefatigable efforts did not show themselves until after his death, and then were almost immediately endangered by the Revolution, which decimated the new industrial class. But the following century was to see it reconstituted on a far larger scale.

Once manufactures were established and their staffs collected the government set itself to facilitate the supply of the necessary raw materials and the sale of their products. As we have already shown, the government did not hesitate to interfere with the natural current of trade in order to attain these two objects. If the raw materials were to be found in France they were kept there, if necessary by force. For example, the export of wool was forbidden with re-doubled penalties under Richelieu. If, on the other hand, the raw materials came from abroad, not only were they given free passage across the frontier, but they were freed from all tolls on the road.

[1] Lavisse, *op. cit.*, pp. 225 and 263.

When the new product was ready for sale the least that could be done for it was to reserve for it not only all government orders, but the whole home market. Sometimes similar articles from abroad were burdened with protective import duties, sometimes their importation was absolutely forbidden. Francis I prohibited the import of cloth of gold and silver, Richelieu that of fine cloth, Colbert that of lace, his successors at the beginning of the eighteenth century that of printed calico. The prevention of the import of silks from Avignon resulted in all the industry of that town being transferred to Nîmes. In the hope that French industry might compete with foreigners in distant markets, further sacrifices were made. The export of industrial products was encouraged by special bounties, such as were granted on cloth exported from Languedoc to the Levantine ports known as the *Echelles*.

§ 3. Sketch of Industrial Development.

Coarse linen and fine cloth; Gobelins tapestries and Aubusson carpets; silks and laces; cotton; printed calico—Mineral industries: potteries, glassworks—Paper-making—Ironmongery and the heavy metal industry—Slow development of the mining industry—Domestic industries, urban and rural—Beginning of geographical concentration.

The chief industry which medieval France bequeathed to modern France was the linen industry. Whether hempen or flaxen, the linen produced was generally coarse, but for everyday use was unsurpassed in Europe, and the weaving industry was so well established in Normandy, Brittany and Champagne that even the Religious Wars were unable seriously to disturb it. From the sixteenth century, however, St. Quentin and Louviers had manufactured fine linens, and Henry IV deliberately set out to enable French manufacturers to compete with the Dutch in the Spanish market. But towards the end of the seventeenth century this new and flourishing branch of the industry found its development checked by the competition of Irish cottons and cambric, the reputation of which had originally been founded by a group of French refugees established at Belfast. Thus on the eve of the Revolution the manufacture of coarse linens such as the peasants wore alone preserved its prosperity.

More continuous progress was made by another traditional industry, the cloth industry. In the time of Francis I and Henry II, Rouen, Amiens and Nîmes were already famous for the manufactures of fine cloths and serges. But the decisive advance was made by Colbert.[1] It was one of his agents who discovered Van Robais and installed him at Abbéville. It was he who helped to establish at Caen a great factory for the manufacture of fine cloth capable of exporting its products to England. It was he who reorganised the old cloth industry in Languedoc so that it was able to conquer the markets of the Levant. And although it used chiefly foreign wools, notably from Castile, this semi-luxury trade was strong enough to survive even the crisis caused by the exodus of the Protestants. At the close of the Ancien Régime France was the leading country for coarse linen and fine cloths.

At the time of the Renaissance fine tapestries were still the monopoly of Flanders and Italy. The first French factory of this kind, which was to serve as a model to all others, was founded by Francis I at Fontainebleau, under the direction of Primaticcio, one of the chief decorators of the palace. But the civil wars struck the new industry a heavy blow, and only one small establishment in Paris survived them. Henry IV, however, put new life into the industry. He enlisted some Flemish in his service and with their help, on the banks of the Bièvre, in the house of those celebrated dyers, the Gobelins, he set up an establishment which was to be finally organised by Colbert. In the Louvre itself Colbert installed the manufacture of Eastern carpets. At the same time near Aubusson there existed country workshops for carpet-making, the origin of which may have gone back as far as the Saracen invasions. But these country artisans only made coarse tapestries and sold their products at the neighbouring fairs until Colbert raised the level of their industry. Throughout the next century French tapestry and carpets enjoyed a prosperity which was only threatened towards the end of that period by the growing fashion for Persian tapestry and painted wall-papers.

[1] The first " royal factory " for cloth had been established at Sedan in 1646, and continued to prosper after the expiration of its privileges, which came to an end in 1666.

The silk industry also became important at the beginning of the modern period. In the last years of the fourteenth century exiles from Lucca seem to have tried to set up this manufacture in Lyons. Louis XI took up the project again, but as he met with small welcome from the merchants of that city it was at Tours that he finally installed his trial manufacture, which by 1546 was employing no less than 8,000 looms. Meanwhile the new industry had taken root at Nîmes, and even at Lyons with the help of Genoese exiles, and under the liberal rule of the consulate it had developed spontaneously. In the latter city before the Wars of Religion the manufacture of silks and velvets, in addition to that of cloth of gold and silver, gave employment to more than 12,000 workmen. The factories created and financed by Henry IV, at Nantes for the manufacture of Bolognese crape, at Troyes for the manufacture of satins, and in Paris itself for spinning and weaving, had a very short life, but soon the manufacture of silk and worsted stockings flourished at Dourdan, at the Château de Madrid[1] and later at Nîmes. In the seventeenth century, helped by luxurious fashions in dress, the silk industry spread throughout the region round Lyons, even in the districts of St. Chamond and St. Etienne, where the peasants spent their winter leisure in weaving ribbons. Neither the silkworm nurseries of the Rhone Valley nor those in Italy and Spain were enough to supply this new demand. Lyons had to get part of its raw materials from the Levant via Marseilles, and Tours from China via St. Malo. In spite of the competition of refugee Huguenots in England, Holland, Brandenburg and Switzerland, and although the changes of fashion favoured Eastern silks or Indian muslins, this precious industry remained one of the most active in the country. Until the Revolution men wore coats, waistcoats and breeches of silk and often of brocaded silk.

The lace industry was earlier in origin, but its success was not so lasting. Under Henry IV the lace-makers of Senlis bade fair to rival their Flemish rivals. Later the French Point Lace Company, which for a time employed 5,000 workwomen, by putting Norman, Bourbon and Velay lace through a special process, obtained work superior to the finest white

[1] At the gates of Paris.

Venetian lace.[1] But the fashions of the European courts, on which this industry depended when it had ceased to receive state aid, changed in the following century, and lace was no longer *à la mode*. Nevertheless, in the eighteenth century Valenciennes still employed three or four thousand workwomen.

The cotton industry was the newest of the textile industries. In the Middle Ages a small quantity of cotton had been imported from the Levant via Marseilles, but only for use in making candle wicks. In the sixteenth century some fustian manufacturers had contrived to weave a cotton woof upon a warp of flaxen thread, but pure cotton cloths, such as damasked linen, were a luxury product, and the little that was used came from Italy, Germany or England. Cotton cloths and cotton stockings did not become important until about 1680. The spread of these new articles was checked by the government, which, not content with burning whole cargoes of real Indian calicoes, forbade manufacturers to " paint or print any flowers or other figures on any fabric made of cotton." Even in the first half of the eighteenth century the so-called *Siamoises* or Siam Cottons, handkerchiefs, aprons and striped or checked curtains, the warp at least of which was of silk or flax, were barely tolerated. In 1759, however, thanks partly to the example of Madame de Pompadour, the prohibition was removed. Then began the prosperity of Rouen goods—that is to say, of pure cotton cloth dyed with the famous Adrianople red. Oberkampf founded at Jouy-en-Josas[2] his celebrated cotton factory, where he spun and wove the cotton which he afterwards covered with his own designs. The development of spinning began soon after 1762, when a statute was passed dealing with the question of rural industries. Henceforth French thread took the place of the inferior thread which it had been necessary to import from India or Asia Minor. Cotton goods were soon in great demand not only for ladies' garments, but for house furnishings and hangings, while the factories at Rouen, Amiens and Troyes exported increasing quantities to the French and Spanish colonies.

[1] At Rheims a privileged factory was directed by one of Colbert's nieces, who was a nun in the convent of Sainte-Claire.

[2] In the valley of the Bièvre near Paris.

The chemical or mineral industries developed largely to satisfy the needs of the textile industries. This is obvious in the case of dye-works. Soap-works were set up at Amiens and Abbéville for the purpose of cleansing the wool. But they developed chiefly at Marseilles, where it was easy to obtain Provencal and Spanish olive oil and the soda obtained by burning the Mediterranean kelp. The pottery industry was naturally very old, and as early as the sixteenth century the potters of Rouen and Nevers had produced artistic work. In the time of Louis XIV French potters imitated Dutch porcelains, which were in their turn inspired by Chinese jars. Towards the end of the reign the sumptuary laws which restricted the use of silver dishes caused a great development of artistic pottery in Provence. In the eighteenth century the industry spread into the country districts, but when English competition, favoured by a plentiful supply of coal, increased, French manufacturers at first could scarcely contend with it. On the other hand, Sèvres china had a European reputation, and the discovery of beds of porcelain clay at St. Yrieix (1768) was the beginning of new prosperity for Limoges, a city famous of old for its enamellers.

In fine sand and sodium carbonate France possessed the chief raw materials necessary for glass-making. For a long time workshops for the manufacture of bottles, vases and window glass had been installed in the neighbourhood of the forests which fed their furnaces, chiefly in the Argonne, Lower Normandy and Lorraine. These common articles had been sold even in the Low Countries. In the eighteenth century, revived by the well-advised adoption of processes used in Bohemia, the industry continued to develop until it was attacked by the formidable competition of British glass-makers, who profited momentarily by the economy which they were able to effect by the use of coal. Meanwhile, France had robbed Italy of her monopoly of fine glass-making. The first glass-cutting works had been installed in the kingdom by a native of Bologna in the reign of Francis I. A little later the Gonzagues, Italians by birth, had introduced the industry into Nivernais. The works at Baccarat did not win their reputation until Lorraine became definitely French in the brilliant reign of Stanislas Leczinski. To Henry III belongs the honour of having founded the first factory for Venetian glass, but the glass-workers of Murano had preserved the secret of making mirrors, and it was Colbert who succeeded in winning it from them. The famous gallery at Versailles is a witness to the triumph of his efforts, while the productions of the factories at Tourlaville (in the Cotentin), St. Gobain and Dombes for a long time defied foreign competition.

There was yet another industry in which France had rapidly reached the first rank. From the beginning of the sixteenth century the paper-makers of Lyons had been famous far and wide. Soon, at the instigation of Olivier de Serres, rag paper-works were set up in Languedoc and Dauphiné, while later the manufacture was concentrated in towns like Troyes and Angoulême, where there was an abundance of pure water. After the Revocation of the Edict of Nantes the loss of the best workmen deprived the kingdom of the superiority which their skill had won for her. But even within the limits of the home markets the progress of education assured the industry of an easy market, which was enlarged at the end of the eighteenth century by the new fashion for wall-papers.

As was natural, the extension of the metallurgical industry came much later. The first blast furnaces were not built till about 1550. The iron industry was at first localised in wooded regions, where the mineral was easily extracted, such as the Bocage and Perche districts, and also round Autun and Semur, where Roman mineral workings were revived. But iron was at this time so scarce and so costly that the heavy metal trade was practically limited to the manufacture of weapons. At the end of the century France possessed thirteen cannon foundries, and hardly anything else worthy of notice, save the manufacture of scythes, established in Dauphiné in Henry IV's reign. The ironmongery trade, on the other hand, developed rapidly. In Richelieu's time cheap goods from Forez and Limousin rivalled those of Germany, and were exported to Spain and the Spanish Indies, while Laigle[1] had already specialised in the manufacture of pins. In Colbert's time the tin-plate industry, of which Bohemia had hitherto had the monopoly, was introduced into the

[1] In the Département de l'Orne.

Forest of Conches,[1] and a little later the cutlery trade was set up in Périgord and Berri. To supply the armies of the "Great Monarch," St. Etienne, Châtellerault, Charleville and Bayonne manufactured side-arms; Grenoble, thanks to the Allevard mines, forged both anchors and sword blades; Soissons and Franche-Comté made artillery. But it was especially in the newly conquered Hainault that the heavy metal industry was established. There twenty-four blast furnaces, fifty forges and six foundries, in addition to nail factories, were at one time all working at once, and employing three or four thousand workmen. In the eighteenth century forges were established in Lorraine, and naval cannon foundries at Ruelle and Indret.[2] Later William Wilkinson, the brother of the English "Iron King," and de Wendel, a forge-master of Hayange, united in founding at Creusot the first big metallurgical works in Europe (1785). But until the Revolution France remained dependent on Sweden and England for her supplies of raw and cast iron. As to steel, in the seventeenth century there was only one works at Metz, but in the reign of Louis XVI the steel-works of Lorraine, Alsace and Nantes, and especially the royal works at Amboise, brought about a reduction in the ancient import of English and German steel.

The French heavy metal industry suffered from the double disadvantage that the soil of France was poor both in easily worked ores and in fuel. Forges in Hainault and on the Meuse, for example, had to get their raw material from Belgium. In the time of Henry IV copper was discovered in the Pyrenees and tin in Gévaudan. But the working of these ores was no more successful than that of the auriferous sands of the Ariège or the gold and silver mines in the Lyons district.[3] The consumption of timber and the disappearance of the forests gave rise to alarm as early as Henry III's reign. About 1715 many intendants, fearing the total destruction of the forests, proposed to restrict the number of forges. Moreover, all the other indus-

---

[1] In the Département de l'Eure.

[2] Near Angoulême and on the Lower Loire.

[3] The success of the communal working of iron ores on the Upper Ariège and of the "Catalan" forges should, however, be noted. The latter were used quite recently.

tries suffered more or less seriously from this lack of fuel. It was not that France had no coal-mines at all, but they had scarcely begun to be worked. The attempts made during the reign of Henry II at Brassac[1] and St. Etienne had been unsuccessful, and France still relied on English coal, which had been imported regularly since 1520. A contractor who, in 1643, proposed to undertake the exploitation of the Brioude Basin only counted on employing about thirty workmen in each mine. In Colbert's time the most productive mines were those of Hainault, Forez, Bourbon, Alais and Saumur. The Hainault mines were scattered over a district of fourteen leagues, but were not active enough to enable the local forges to dispense with coal from Mons and Charleroi. The Forez mines were constantly being flooded, but their coal was sold at Lyons, where it was used for heating public buildings, and even in Paris. The Saumur mines competed with English imports in supplying the Loire towns. Under Louis XV, Artois still used foreign coal. It was only in the second half of the century that the famous Anzin mines, by reducing the price of coal by three-quarters, finally triumphed over Belgian competition and alone supplied five provinces. In Louis XVI's reign several mines, which had been among the richest, were abandoned soon after work had begun, the concessionaires being often ruined by over-production and a shortage of markets. In 1789 French coal-mines did not produce a hundredth part of what they produce to-day. Indeed, it may be said that the chief mining industry of old France was the salt industry. Salt was produced partly in the mines of Franche-Comté and Lorraine, but chiefly in the salt-pits of Aunis and Saintonge, which exported considerable quantities to all the northern countries, even as far as Eastern Germany and Muscovy.

The industrial development, which we have just sketched, was essentially the work of rich capitalists. But it must not be forgotten that even in the towns industry on a small scale was still indisputably preponderant, whether inside or outside the gilds. In proportion to their size towns contained more shops than they do to-day. In Paris during the Regency there were fifteen bakers to every ten thousand inhabitants, whereas to-day there are only seven. The same

---

[1] Near Brioude in Auvergne.

difference was seen in the provinces. Orleans, though it only numbered half as many inhabitants, had quite as many bakers as at present, and moreover many people still baked their own bread.[1] Among the trades connected with food, only one, of quite recent growth, assumed the proportions of a manufacture. This was sugar refining, which was established in the Atlantic ports, notably at Nantes, and in the towns on the lower and middle reaches of the Loire, Angers, Saumur and Orleans. In the second half of the eighteenth century there first began to appear improved methods of grinding, which increased the yield of flour by a sixth.[2] Among the industries which we have called mineral, although glass- and china-making had expanded into big factories, common pottery and tile- and brick-making still faithfully preserved the characteristics of old-fashioned industry, and the same is, of course, true of rope-making and the manufacture of sabots.

The gild regulations contributed in large measure to maintain small workshops. At Lyons, Paris and Tours the silk-workers' gild allowed each master to have only one shop and one apprentice. In the seventeenth century the single apprentice was equally the rule for the *sayette*-makers of Amiens; and two only were generally allowed to the makers of woollen goods. It is worth noting also that among the new industries several—and those the most characteristically national—were art industries which do not admit of manufacture on a large scale. The cabinet-maker, the enameller, and the goldsmith never need a very big establishment.

In the villages and in most of the smaller towns industry was carried on on a very small scale indeed, much as it still is to-day. The shoeing-smiths and millers were somewhat distinguished by their more elaborate plant from the rank and file of wheelwrights, locksmiths, coopers and masons, but all alike cultivated their piece of land in addition to following their trade. On the other hand, in many provinces, such as Brittany, Picardy, Normandy and Champagne, the peasants occupied their leisure and supplemented their wages by weaving. In Gévaudan each peasant had his loom, and everyone, even children four years old, worked to produce

[1] See d'Avenel, *Paysans et ouvriers*, p. 111.
[2] See Weulersse, *Mouvement physiocratique*, vol. ii, pp. 577-579.

7

coarse serges which sold for six sous an ell. In the Jura
clock-making was the chief by-industry. Everywhere women
spun for their families or for a manufacturer. Their spindle
was always in their hands.[1]

Already, however, industries were tending to become
localised and to concentrate in districts where geographical
conditions were favourable and where their raw materials
were easily obtainable. Thus the silk industry developed
chiefly in the provinces, where mulberry plantations had
been successful—that is to say, in Lower Languedoc, in
Upper Provence and in all the lower valley of the Rhone.
Lyons owed the prosperity of its chief industry mainly to the
double proximity of French and Italian silkworm farms,
which also made the fortune of Nîmes and Montpellier. The
decline of mulberry cultivation in the basin of the Loire, on
the other hand, caused the decline of the silk industry of
Tours, which in the sixteenth century had employed 40,000
people. Flax weaving developed chiefly in the districts
which grew it, in Flanders, Picardy, Brittany and Béarn.
The Pays de Caux and the Dauphiné produced the hemp
which they manufactured. Champagne, Picardy and Upper
Languedoc had been great sheep-grazing districts even before
the cloth industry settled there. The prosperity of the
Flemish woollen industry was explained as much by the
proximity of the Spanish Netherlands, whence came raw
material of excellent quality, as by the old local industrial
traditions. The Rouen district became a centre of the textile
industry because it could easily get supplies of wool, and
later of cotton, by sea. The proximity of markets must also
be considered; the relations early established with the Levant
contributed in no small measure to the progress of the cloth
industry in Languedoc, Provence and Dauphiné. Again, the
industrial growth of a town or a district might depend on
certain facilities of communication or an abundance of capital
and labour. Lyons, as we have seen, was a continuous fair
and international market, where all businesses and all ideas
flourished. Marseilles not only possessed local industries
such as shipbuilding and soap-making, but the manufactures
of hats, hosiery and printed cotton were also set up there, by

[1] See Babeau, *Vie rurale dans l'ancienne France*, pp. 146-148.

reason of the financial and commercial advantages which
every industry was sure of finding there.

It was, perhaps, in the cloth industry that this geographical concentration was most marked. In the course of
the seventeenth century there gradually disappeared " the
serges of Nantes and Malestroit, the cloths of Nîmes and
St. Omer, the *étames*, *revêches*, *bourracans* and *cordillats* of
Vendôme, Valence, St. Lô and a thousand other little towns
whose reputation vanished with their prosperity, and left
hardly a trace save in their archives. In those days competition between these towns was as keen as that between neighbouring countries is to-day."[1] Who remembers how Niort
specialised in the making of beaver, deerskin and chamois
gloves and of belts for cavaliers ? Nevertheless, in 1789 this
kingdom of 25,000,000 inhabitants still had very few big
manufacturing cities. Although Paris, which was the largest,
already numbered 600,000 inhabitants, Lyons, which came
second, had only 100,000, while Bordeaux scarcely reached
this figure, and Marseilles, Rouen, Nantes and Lille, which
came next, hardly attained half that number.

§ 4. Technical Changes.

The double obstacle of gild and state control—Beginnings of division
of labour—Applied science, the new machinery.

The growth of industrial activity and the development of
manufactures on a grand scale naturally brought about many
technical changes. But before examining them we must
briefly indicate the obstacles which they had to meet. These
were of two kinds, the one connected with gild regulations,
the other with state control.

The organised crafts showed themselves blindly hostile to
all new processes. Thus the button-makers in 1695 forbade
the making of buttons by machinery. The process was still
used secretly, but " the corporation refused to alter its rules
and to allow its members to use it, fearing that the new
process might diminish its profits by making and selling at a
cheaper price an article of which it claimed to have the
monopoly."[2] Metal button-makers protested against the

[1] D'Avenel, *Paysans et ouvriers*, p. 293.
[2] Levasseur, *Classes ouvrières*, vol. ii, p. 412.

manufacture of buttons covered with cloth. The plumbers carried on an heroic struggle against two Academies, the Parlement and the government, to prevent the introduction of a new method of producing lead, the superiority of which had been recognised in England for thirty years.[1] Although from the end of the sixteenth century artisans had been allowed to become members of two related crafts, thus making certain useful combinations possible, the test of the masterpiece was organised in such a way as to oppose all progress in the division of labour. Thus " the future hatter was given a pound of wool and other raw materials, and had to produce a finished hat, dyed and trimmed with velvet. He had to do everything himself, from fulling the wool to placing the feathers in position. This variety of processes could probably have been performed far more economically if divided between different workmen."[2] Mention must be made of the interminable lawsuits between the crafts, which multiplied as the breach between old and new methods widened and which absorbed uselessly a considerable amount of capital. The very laws which confined certain crafts to a traditional quarter of the city hindered the improvement of methods.

But in the sixteenth, and especially in the seventeenth century, industry came under another authority, that of the royal Administration. Its intervention was to a certain extent justified by the desire to maintain the fame of national manufactures and to safeguard the interests of the consumers, but it was too often inspired by an instinctive dislike for all individual enterprise and for all novelty. " In Colbert's ministry thirty-eight regulations and one hundred and fifty edicts were issued. In 1669 the government fixed the length and quality of cloths. Four months were given in which to break up the old looms and reconstruct them in accordance with the prescribed dimensions."[3] The use of iron cards was forbidden, as it was considered that they spoiled the appearance of the cloth. Stretching the cloth was also prohibited, although it was sometimes a necessity. To carry out these regulations a whole army of inspectors was necessary.

[1] Levasseur, *Classes ouvrières*, vol. ii, p. 505.
[2] *Ibid.*, p. 403.
[3] Lavisse, *Histoire de France*, vol. vii[1], pp. 224-225.

Colbert meant to choose them from among the upper merchant class, but he actually chose " official pedants who thought they knew something about it. These officers went into every town. In towns where the workers were organised in gilds, they saw that they were in good order. In towns where labour was unorganised they assembled the master-workers and made them elect wardens or jurors to be responsible for the regulation of work.'' Every piece of cloth had to bear the quadruple stamp of the weaver, the dyer, the manufacturer and the wardens. Goods sent into a town were to be unloaded at the town hall to be inspected there. The wardens were to have the right of entry everywhere, even (at least in theory) into the houses of the country weavers.

To punish delinquents it was not enough simply to confiscate the defective materials; they were exposed to public view; for a second offence the manufacturer was publicly admonished; for a third he was put in the pillory for two hours. An unfortunate cloth merchant might be the innocent victim of the natural shrinkage of his woollen goods. The artisans of Auvergne suffered innumerable confiscations before they were authorised, by special favour, to make their bunting a third instead of half an ell wide. The public welcomed demi-beavers—that is to say, hats made of wool and fur mixed; but this industry was forbidden under heavy penalties, since it might injure the Canadian fur trade, and until the end of the century the public had to choose between all-beaver and all-wool hats and nothing else.

Colbert, however, had tolerated certain breaches of the regulations, and his minute and anxious supervision was practically confined to the cloth industry. At his death the regulations increased in number and severity, and their application was made more general. New clauses were incessantly added to the old laws, and new decrees were issued to check innovations. Although the stocking-loom was finally permitted, its use was confined to fine goods and allowed in only eighteen towns. The intendants themselves issued decrees for their own provinces. M. de Basville in Languedoc fixed the minimum and maximum weight of blankets. Louvois everywhere increased the number of inspectors; he ordered the name and address of the workman responsible for each piece of cloth to be worked into the cloth itself ; the searchers went so far as to stop people in the streets if necessary, and exercised their right of domiciliary visits. Industry then was permanently at loggerheads with the government and had no resource save in passive resistance or fraud. The workmen fled from the shop when the inspectors were signalled.

During the first half of the eighteenth century the government succeeded in surrounding industry with a network of legislative restrictions, sometimes wise, often foolish and always annoying, which gradually hardened into immobility. Everything was fixed, down to the size of the " leaf " and " quill "[1] to be used, and the number of threads. It was forbidden to mix wools of different quality in one piece of cloth ; it was insisted that scissors going to the Levant should be tempered, although they were only destined for snuffing candles. In accordance with the tradition of the Middle Ages, advertisement was forbidden, especially the distribution of prospectuses, on the pretext that an honest workman " need use no artifice to entice purchasers."[2] The number of inspectors steadily increased. Many of them obtained the position by influence and were incompetent; some exploited the ever-increasing severity of the regulations and exercised an odious and venal tyranny over those subjected to them. Moreover, although the privileges granted to certain enterprises had the advantage of freeing the direct beneficiaries from the common servitude, at the same time they invested them with monopolies which checked all initiative on the part of their competitors.

But in spite of everything the material conditions of production improved. The increased size of the workshops, itself the consequence of a wider market, almost necessarily resulted in a certain division of labour. Doubtless at the beginning of the eighteenth century many of the royal factories, in spite of their vast premises surrounded by high walls, were still no more than a collection of workmen each working in his own room. But for some time the successive phases of manufacture had begun to be divided. For instance, in the seventeenth century " the Van Robais factory, which employed nearly 1,700 workmen, contained special

---

[1] Tools used in weaving.

[2] Levasseur, *Classes ouvrières*, vol. ii, p. 507.

departments for wheelwrights' work, cutlery, washing, dyeing and warping. Weaving itself was shared between several
classes of workmen whose work was quite distinct, such as
weavers, burlers, tuckers, pressers, winders, rowers and
embroiderers (the last four being usually women)."[1] For
fear lest the artisans should discover the secret of this ingenious series of operations, they were strictly forbidden to
go from one workshop to another. When in each of these
departments the process is split up again into various stages
and divided between different workmen, each man's work
will become so simple that a machine can do it, and the day
of modern machinery will be at hand.

It was indeed at the end of the seventeenth century that
French science left the realm of abstractions and turned
towards concrete nature. Natural history came much nearer
to the living reality, and chemistry was born. Scholars did
not disdain to take part in industry; Buffon constructed
improved blast furnaces at Montbard. Learned men and
even gentlemen of fashion were interested in experimental
science, and the Encyclopædia, edited by Diderot, directed
the attention and even the admiration of the public towards
the work of the artisans. Henry IV had already conceived the
idea of installing a museum of arts and crafts at the Louvre.
In the eighteenth century, besides the Royal School of Arts
and the School of Mines, which date from the reign of
Louis XVI, industrial classes were started at the Collège de
France and the Jardin du Roi. The Academy of Science
awarded prizes to inventors, while the government pensioned
them and provided them with money for their experiments.
In nine years Vaucanson seems to have received 180,000
livres for this purpose. Finally the example of a neighbouring state was to hasten the progress of discoveries and their
application; after the Seven Years' War the imitation of
England spread to the realm of industrial technique.

The early inventions were chiefly of machines which, like
the innumerable and eternal mills for flour, oil, paper,
sugar and even iron, drew their motive power from
running water regulated by man. At first they were chiefly
used in the textile industries. The stocking-frame, so important at a time when long hose were a part of men's

[1] Levasseur, p. 386.

as well as of women's dress, had already been introduced into Normandy from England in Henry IV's reign. But it was only under Mazarin in 1656 that it was adopted throughout the kingdom. Towards the end of the century the button loom began to be used secretly. The first half of Louis XV's reign saw the creation of various machines for fulling wool, folding cloth, cutting threads, and finally Vaucanson's famous machines for winding and throwing silk (1744).

In Louis XVI's reign the use of the flying shuttle in cloth-weaving was still generally unknown. Cloth manufacturers were only just beginning to replace teasels by metal carding machines and to stop shearing with *forces*, a sort of enormous scissors which were so heavy and slow that their use exhausted the workmen; but it was then that the Irishman, Holker, set up at the same time an improved woollen spinning-mill at Aumale and the first factory for making cloth by machinery at Rouen. In the cotton industry the use of English carding machines was introduced about 1750, while twenty years later, thanks again to Holker, the jenny, capable of working as many as forty-eight spindles, also crossed the Channel. It was used at Amiens in making velvet, and gradually its use was extended, without, however, entirely ousting the old spinning-wheel. With the financial help of the state some Englishmen, the Milnes, installed at the Château de la Muette cylindrical machines for carding and winding cotton, which could do twenty-four times as much work as a good carder and a good spinner together. Arkwright's spinning machine, which worked a hundred spindles, was for some time ignored by manufacturers, and it was only in 1784, in Calonne's ministry, that an Amiens cotton spinner obtained permission to set up the first of them. At about the same time also the ribbon industry in the country districts round St. Etienne and St. Chamond was revolutionised by the introduction of Zurich looms.

The new machinery was introduced into many other industries. In 1763 the paper-makers of Angoumois, Gâtinais and Auvergne adopted the superior machinery of their English and Dutch rivals, and soon afterwards the Montgolfiers set up at Annonay improved cylinders for

tearing up rags and refining the pulp. The invention of
the minting mill for making coins dated from Henry II,
but the old hammer did not altogether go out of use until
Louis XIV's reign. The first tilt-hammers for cutting and
drawing iron and copper wire were installed on the River
Essonne in the time of Henry IV; in the eighteenth century
rolled lead was gradually substituted for cast lead. Mining
machinery, however, was still very primitive.

Chemical processes were becoming more numerous, more
complex and more powerful. France possessed in Réaumur
one of the originators of scientific metallurgy, but she had to
obtain the secrets of manufacture from England. In 1769
the de Wendels, the great Lorraine forge-masters, for the
first time successfully used coke instead of charcoal for
casting, and in 1776 it was introduced into the Montbard
forges. In the seventeenth century the painting industry
had benefited by a new method of making white lead, and
indigo and cochineal had replaced woad in dyeing fabrics.
The candle and the taper, which had taken the place of
greasy oil lights, were themselves superseded by modern
lamps with a circular plaited wick, the flame of which was
made clear by a double current of air through a glass
chimney. After 1672 glass was cast instead of blown.
Bernard Palissy discovered white enamel, which was to form
the basis of all others. The Sèvres factory, having created
the delicate biscuit-ware, went on to produce a new and
excellent hard porcelain in imitation of Saxon ware. As it
grew the industrial population, both inside and outside the
gilds, began to break up into classes.

§ 5. Industrial Classes.

A. *The Industrial Hierarchy.*—Journeymen for life; masters, *jeunes,
modernes et anciens:* the *Six Corps*, master-merchants and master-
craftsmen—Great manufacturers.

Originally it had been intended that every workman
should pass through the journeyman stage, and that stage
was only a temporary one. But from the fifteenth century
onwards the masters began to close their ranks. The execution of a masterpiece, which was formerly demanded in only
a few crafts, became general, and the standard was raised.

The preparation of this work, for which the candidate had to procure the finest materials at his own expense, became more and more costly and sometimes lasted more than a year. At the same time entrance fees were raised, without prejudice to the presents it was usual to make to the judges.

This would have been unimportant if those judges had been impartial. But they did not hesitate to reject and to break the work of a clever artisan who did not manage to please them. All they cared for beyond their own interests were those of their sons and sons-in-law. For these presumptive successors the examination was reduced to a mere formality, a trifling test which only lasted twenty-four hours. Some gilds even decided to diminish the number of masters officially and to suspend all new creations for a certain time. Others claimed the absolute right of excluding any candidate even before examination. In the sixteenth century the butchers of Paris, Poitiers and several other towns passed decrees making their masterships hereditary.

Only the favourites of fortune could reach the ranks of this bourgeois aristocracy. If a man did not spare money he might succeed in obtaining from the grateful gild an exemption from the masterpiece, or a master's certificate, or by his magnificence and generosity he might conciliate the terrible examiners. But many journeymen could not undertake such expenses, and many were so impoverished by them that they could not afford to profit by their dearly bought title. In vain the Edict of 1581 stipulated that in every craft the making of the masterpiece should not take more than three months, that there should be appeal from the sentence of the *jurés* to a jury of masters chosen by the royal judge, and that no one should become a master until he had executed his masterpiece. More and more the mastership tended to become hereditary, and the number of those who were journeymen for life continually increased. They were called *valets* or servants or workmen, and were the ancestors of the humble wage-earners of to-day.

In certain crafts degrees of rank were marked even among the masters. A distinction was made between the *jeunes* who had been masters less than ten years, the *modernes* who had passed that stage but had not yet done duty as wardens, and the *anciens* who had already filled this office. These last

alone enjoyed the full privileges of the gild and formed the
majority in the assembly. During their time of office the
jurés were not only free from domiciliary visits and confiscations, but had all the gild funds under their control, and,
like the landed nobility, collected taxes for their own profit.
Their abuses were all the more serious in that these lucrative
offices tended to become hereditary in a few families.

The gilds themselves were far from being equal in dignity
or wealth. Not content with confirming the *Six Corps* in the
precedence they enjoyed on ceremonial occasions, Francis I
formed their wardens into a sort of upper council of Parisian
industry,[1] and until the eighteenth century these great crafts,
in which commerce was already becoming more important
than industry, showed by the splendour of their " patriotic
gifts " the greatness of their position. In those industries
where a big working capital was necessary the master-
merchants separated from the master-manufacturers. Thus
in the sixteenth century the drapers or clothiers formed a
special body of masters, while the master-weavers, fullers
and shearmen, whom they provided with raw materials and
whose products they sold, were now little more than their
employees. At Toulouse, at about the same time, there was
a clear distinction between the merchants who ordered the
silk to be made and those who actually made it, and the
master-printers soon fell into economic dependence on
the master-booksellers.[2] In the eighteenth century the
master-merchants of the Grand Fabrique de Lyon—that is
to say, the great traders in cloth of gold and silver—finally
obtained a recognition of their superiority to the manufacturers, whom they called disdainfully master-craftsmen.
The latter numbered more than 5,000, but the merchants,
though there were only 400 of them, had a capital of
60,000,000 francs.

In two crafts at least the masters gave up all pretence of
work and enjoyed a big revenue while leaving the exercise of

---

[1] See Renard, *Syndicats, trade-unions et corporations*, p. 113.

[2] Together booksellers, printers and type-founders formed the
Booksellers' Gild. They were almost entirely freed from the control of
the University after 1686, they were distinguished from the mechanical
crafts, exempt from the taxes which burdened the other gilds and enjoyed
the same privileges as the professors and students. See Levasseur,
Classes ouvrières, vol. ii, p. 484.

their profession to others. One of these was the *Grande Boucherie de Paris*, in which the master-butchers, after their office had been for some generations hereditary, finally let out their stalls to plain journeymen who, under the perpetual menace of summary eviction, paid them heavy rents. In the same way most of the porters at the Corn Market did nothing but draw the revenue of their office, leaving the work to be done by casual labourers.[1]

Doubtless these were extreme cases, and many masters behaved in very different fashion. In the towns, very often even in the cities, many of them did the work of ordinary craftsmen, working without journeyman or apprentice on materials supplied by their clients. Such were the tailors and cobblers. But we are familiar to-day with these medieval survivals, or rather with these elementary and eternal forms of petty industry. Moreover, many masters had but one journeyman or one apprentice. As late as the middle of the eighteenth century the twenty-six master-weavers of Orleans employed only fifty workmen; in the whole kingdom and even in Paris at that time (which after all is very near to our own) there were hardly more than twice as many workmen as masters. It is clear, however, that the early stages of industrial concentration tended to diminish the number of masters and to increase the number of workmen. At Troyes in 1701 there were ten master-printers employing ten journeymen; in 1764 there were only three masters employing thirty workmen; in Paris in 1755 the average of working printers was twenty to each establishment.

Was there less inequality in the ever-growing industrial world outside the gilds? If we consider the chief southern districts where the gild system had been of late growth, we see that the professional fraternities were there distinguished, among other things, by the absence of any distinct masters' grade.[2] But threatened on the one side by the organised craft gilds and on the other by the big new enterprises, the future held little hope for these old institutions. Moreover, when the protection of the masters changed to oppression many workmen doubtless tried to escape from it by setting up little workshops in their own homes. They were their

[1] See Levasseur, *Classes ouvrières*, vol. ii, pp. 106-108 and 370.
[2] See Claudio Jannet, *Grandes époques*, p. 260.

own masters, but even if the government defended them against the tricks and persecution of the wardens of the gilds, these *chambrelands*, as they were called, could not possibly compete with the new manufactures.

In the seventeenth century a new class of free workmen was growing up in the country districts. But if they remained independent the country weavers could not long compete with the factories in either the quality or the cheapness of their wares, and if they agreed to take their raw material from some big manufacturer and sell him the produce of their labour, they were nothing but wage-earners working at home. Thus the distinctions and divisions inherent in industrialism, which were already, as we have seen, widening or breaking up the gild framework, gradually invaded domains where the gilds had died out or had never existed.

At first sight the new industrialism seemed very simple. On the one side there were the few who had sufficient capital to buy machinery and fit up large workshops; on the other side were the many who possessed only their hands. As early as Henry IV's reign a linen factory of 350 looms was built at St. Sever, near Rouen. The silk stocking factory founded at the Château de Madrid in 1656 cost 300,000 livres to establish; the tin-plate factory, founded about the same time at Beaumont in the Forest of Conches, 50,000 livres more; the sugar refineries at Cette in the next century, 450,000 livres. Buffon alone, and without having to pay for the land, spent 300,000 livres on building his blast furnaces at Montbard. Mirabeau gives an account of the work of the Company of the Anzin Mines in exploiting their concession.[1] Twenty-two years were spent in excavating before the seam, which was situated at a depth of 300 feet, was reached; a vein of water had to be crossed, and over thirty shafts, some of them 900 and even 1,200 feet deep, were sunk and timbered. All this cost about 12,000,000 francs, while the network of galleries and the machinery cost another 8,000,000. Taking everything into account, this might well be the story of one of our huge modern enterprises.

The staff of these new establishments sometimes equalled the population of a small town. At the end of the seven-

[1] Speech of March 21, 1791.

teenth century the cloth manufacture at Saptes in Languedoc employed 600 workmen. About 1715 Van Robais had 1,500 men working for him in one factory at Abbéville, while at Lille the manufacturer Arnoult van der Cruissen employed as many as 3,000. In the eighteenth century the muslin manufacture at Puy-en-Velay constantly employed 1,200 workers; the silk and cotton manufacture at Limoges, 1,800; the "royal" hosiery works at Orleans, 800 in the town and 1,500 in the country. In Louis XVI's reign an ordinary manufacturer of wall-papers, like Réveillon, employed 400 workmen; an ironware manufacturer like the Englishman Alcock, 500; while the Anzin mines provided employment for 4,000 people.

The employment of capital and labour on such a large scale served to build up huge fortunes comparable to those of the great merchants, and hardly surpassed even by those of the financiers. The employment of rural labour in particular assured great profits to the manufacturers of Rouen, Lille and Lyons. Towards the middle of the eighteenth century it was stated that "the fifty chief manufacturers of Paris and Lyons were worth several millions of francs."[1] The succeeding generations of this industrial aristocracy grew in wealth; the Van Robais and the Montgolfiers were surpassed by the Perriers, the Réveillons and the Oberkampfs. These parvenus, born of the people, built themselves castles and lived like lords, and the king, not content with giving them medals or the Order of St. Michael, sometimes even conferred nobility on them. They transacted business with the intendants and corresponded with ministers, and the government often had to bow to their wishes. "In 1724 the king wished to buy arms at St. Etienne, but the armourers told him that they could not supply him because Perrin and Poinat of Lyons had bought up all the iron."[2]

But there was no more equality between these new "masters" of industry than there had been between the old. Not all of them succeeded, and among those who did prosper there were many who had only been able to enlarge their business by seeking sleeping partners among the merchants

[1] Goudard, *Intérêts de la France mal entendus*, 1756, vol. ii, p. 41.
[2] Germain Martin, *Grande industrie sous Louis XV*, p. 229.

or the financiers or even the nobles. Many, again, were forced to pay for the monopoly which enriched them; the gentleman with influence at court, who had obtained the privilege, only sold it to the actual manufacturer on condition that he shared in the profits. Moreover, the great manufacturers had created beneath them a series of directors, inspectors and controllers who stood between them and the nameless crowd of ordinary workmen, hired wage-earners, who formed the other pole of the system and on whom everything depended. Let us turn now to consider the conditions of their existence.

B. *Condition of the Wage-earners.*—The question of apprenticeship— Factory discipline—Competition of female and rural labour— Government attitude uncertain—Vicissitudes of the working classes.

We must now see how the wage-earners were affected by the changes which we have been describing—the evolution of the gild system, the development of industrialism, changes in the coinage and in the size of the population, not to mention the intervention of the government, which sometimes tended to modify these natural movements.

The same period which saw the widening of the gulf between masters and journeymen saw, too, the strengthening of regulations intended to keep the latter in subjection. The licence inherent in times of civil war only interrupted the steady process of subjection for a short time, and at the beginning of the seventeenth century it was taken up again with the assistance of the government and accomplished with the utmost rigour. The journeymen were no more than serfs of the gild and were strictly forbidden to work anywhere except in their masters' shops. The tardy adoption of the gild system by the Lyons consulate was only a measure of defence on the part of the masters. Election to the rank of warden or magistrate, as to that of master, was every day more narrowly controlled, and if a dispute arose between employers and employees the gild or municipal court showed itself less and less impartial. If anyone in its jurisdiction attempted to appeal to a civil court, a severe boycott checked such an attempt at independence. The rate of wages was fixed by custom, and the regulations forbade any master to offer more to entice workmen from another master. Municipal or royal ordinances often fixed a maximum wage.

While all gild regulations that were favourable to the masters were maintained or even readjusted, those which had hitherto protected the journeymen were relaxed. Such was the case with the regulation limiting the number of apprentices.[1] In the sixteenth century the Lyons printers took advantage of a strike to engage a larger number of apprentices than of regular workmen. The Paris printers for a time refused to hire any journeymen at all. The position of the men taken on as substitutes was very bad. They were paid practically nothing; the journeymen hated them, beat them unmercifully on occasion, and subjected them to worse molestation still if they continued to act as passive instruments of the masters' cupidity. In the printing trade the practice persisted of employing alongside the workmen who had served their apprenticeship a number of these outsiders, who were paid much less and were dangerous competitors. The medieval regulations forbade night-work, but from the sixteenth century onwards there were increasingly numerous breaches of this rule. The masters studied their own interests, the government those of the public, but no one protected the workers.

Gradually in spite of everything the bonds of the system were loosened. At the end of the seventeenth century the journeymen, who no longer lived in their master's house, would leave him without warning to go from place to place as they chose. But on the other hand masters could dismiss their men without notice, and workmen were engaged for short terms, sometimes even by the day. It was the beginning of a new order, but the people were freed from the traditional bonds only to fall under others. Would their position be any better in the new manufactures?

The position of labour in the new industrialism was, at first at any rate, almost as stable as it had been in the gilds. Contracts between master and man recognised a double obligation. The length of notice to be given before ending an engagement varied from twenty-four hours to a fortnight and even a month, according to the place and the trade. In paper-making it was six months, while weavers always had

---

[1] In 1770 the Chamber of Commerce demanded its total suppression.

to finish the work they had begun. In some royal manufactures the workmen contracted for a long term. At the end of the eighteenth century the Royal Glass Company of France engaged its staff for four years.

But, naturally enough, discipline was very strict in these vast workshops. If a man were a quarter of an hour late for work he might lose a third of his day's wages. The fine for a day's absence in the cloth of gold factory at St. Maur was three livres. From the first miners were subject to even stricter regulations, which the character of their work necessitated. In the lead, tin and copper mines at Beaujolais, as early as the fifteenth century, the workmen had to assemble in their gangs at the appointed time, take their candles and go down to the workings together. Anyone who was late lost his whole day. No one was allowed to leave work before the proper time, and thus work was continued day and night.[1]

In all workshops swearing, threatening, joking, talking and walking about were forbidden. Outside, when the workman was not completely interned in the factory grounds, he had to behave steadily, to be in his house by ten o'clock in summer and eight o'clock in winter, and he was not allowed to go outside a radius of one league without permission. When improved methods of lighting were discovered the manufacturers took advantage of them to increase the length of the working day, and when they realised that their prosperity depended on the poverty and docility of their employees they set themselves to increase both. " It is very important," wrote one of them in the eighteenth century, " to keep the workmen under the continual necessity of working, and never to forget that the low price of labour is not only directly advantageous to the manufacturer, but is indirectly so by making the workman more industrious, more regular in his habits and more submissive."[2]

The pressure of a twofold competition usually forced the workman to submit to the terms of the large employers. The first, more often a threat than an actuality, was that of female labour. There had always been a number of free workwomen, and certain crafts, such as fine linen-making,

---

[1] Georges Renard, *Cours d'histoire du travail professé au Conservatoire des arts et métiers.*

[2] Quoted by P. Brisson, *Histoire du travail*, p. 219.

embroidery, lace-making, and, originally, the silk industry, had even been reserved for women. Naturally, since their wages, in industry as in agriculture, were a third or even a half lower than those of men, the wages of the workmen would be bound to fall when once women entered into competition with them. This was certainly one of the motives which inspired the master-tailors of Paris when, in 1675, they protested against the foundation of a gild of dressmakers. In any case, it was the general opinion in the eighteenth century that the Grande Fabrique de Lyon would not have survived if the cheap labour of the women cord-makers had not been available. In this laborious work were employed five or six thousand young girls, brought from the country at the age of ten or eleven. When they reached the age of twenty many were promoted to be "readers" or warpers.[1] After 1768, when it became lawful to employ them as weavers, some manufacturers employed only workwomen. "It is sad," cried the strikers in 1744, "to see us on the streets without work, while girls are employed at the loom."[2]

The other and more serious source of competition was rural labour. It was dangerous enough when it was unorganised, because it was so cheap. In Gévaudan in the seventeenth century a spinner was content with two sous a day, and a weaver with eight. But it became much more dangerous when it was systematically exploited by the manufacturers, and this happened in several provinces in the eighteenth century. The various classes of urban workers, members of gilds, and workers in city manufactures, clamoured in vain against the common enemy. In vain the weavers of Lille protested against the decree which the Roubaix weavers received with pleasure.[3] In vain the workmen and masters at Amiens were for once united. The new legislation only recognised an accomplished fact, or yielded in advance to an irresistible evolution.

Divers other social phenomena influenced the condition of the workers. Except during the short period when the religious wars and the invasions made labour scarce, the

[1] See Levasseur, *Classes ouvrières*, vol. ii, p. 798.

[2] Quoted by Germain Martin, *Grande industrie sous Louis XV*, p. 330. Silk manufacturers also were already employing child labour.

[3] The decree of 1762. See below.

growth of the population was very unfavourable to them, since it tended to increase both the price of food and the supply of labour. Moreover, in the sixteenth century the masters did not fail to make a profit out of the change in the value of money by selling their goods at a high price, but they checked as far as they could the corresponding rise in wages. To the last, changes in the value of money always resulted in a loss to the wage-earner. In March, 1724, a recoinage made the livre equal in weight to a franc, although in the preceding year it had only equalled 63 centimes. On this occasion an official circular ordered a decrease in the nominal price of goods, but no effective drop was perceptible in raw materials or in food. In many places, however, at Paris, Rouen and in Dauphiné, the masters attempted to reduce wages.

The attitude of the government to the working classes was undecided and contradictory. On the one hand it seemed to be inspired by distrust of the workers and showed a brutal tyranny towards them. On two occasions when a general rise in prices took place, in 1572 and in 1577, the government tried to keep wages at the old nominal rates, which resulted in a very real loss for the workmen. This example was later followed only too often by the municipal authorities. Thus the jurats of Bordeaux in 1695 fixed the daily rate of pay at ten sous in the Graves[1] and eight sous in the Entre-deux-mers[1] and forbade the workmen to ask for more or individual masters to give more. In the sixteenth century the government was occupied with the question of the unemployed, but its only solution was to force them to work in the public workshops under pain of prison or the galleys (1534). We have already seen that skilled workmen—and even some manufacturers—were not allowed to leave the kingdom. In Calonne's ministry (1783-1787), as in Colbert's, this rule was strictly enforced. Those who were suspected of even contemplating desertion were watched and spied upon, and many people were imprisoned in the Bastille for no other reason.

In the eighteenth century the bonds that bound the workman to his master were breaking, and for that very reason a great effort was made to strengthen them. The

[1] Districts near Bordeaux.—M. R.

decree of 1749 ordered every workman, in cases where a definite term had not been agreed upon, to remain in his situation until he had finished his work. He must give eight days' notice before leaving and must not leave without a leaving certificate from his master, under pain of being fined or even dragged back to his old master by the police.[1] The workman could only dispense with his master's permission in a case of *force majeure*; and then he had to obtain the authorisation of the police. Moreover, masters were expressly forbidden to engage workmen who did not show their leaving certificates. In 1781 this system of successive certificates was replaced by the institution of a permanent certificate book, in which were entered all the debts which the workman had contracted to his late master, and these had to be paid off by his new master. Everything possible was done to bind the workman to the workshop.

It would, however, be false to represent the government's attitude to the worker as purely hostile. Although it opposed a rise in wages, it also took steps to check the rise in the cost of living. It may be that one of the reasons which prevented Colbert from allowing free trade in corn was the fear that the workman's bread might grow dearer.[2] He hoped, moreover, to obtain a rise in wages by the creation of new industries. "A large number of factories in one place would perhaps force the masters to pay higher wages," he said. The "heads of a single factory would no longer be masters of the workmen."[3] In the same way Trudaine de Montigny was glad that there was "free competition between the masters who bought labour and the workmen who sold it." The great minister of Louis XIV, by reserving jurisdiction over cases arising from conditions of work to the mayors and aldermen, had assured the workers of cheap and speedy if not impartial justice. It was no fault of his that certain

[1] "No similar obligations are exacted from the master, and this destroys the equality which should exist between two free men." Letter from Trudaine to Montyon, 1766. A decree of the early eighteenth century instituting a system of mutual notice was not really enforced except in the printing trade.

[2] In the Middle Ages industrial towns had always followed the policy of keeping down the price of food, with the assent of the big manufacturers.

[3] Quoted by Lavisse, *Histoire de France*, vol. viii[1], p. 330.

workmen, small masters, if not ordinary artisans, became
aldermen as well as the gentlemen and officials who had
knowledge of industry.

In some cases the government set itself to procure
employment for the workmen.   More than once the
intendants in the provinces or the lieutenant-general of
police in Paris intervened in the interests of public order to
force masters to provide work for their men.   Thus in 1708
d'Argenson summoned the masters and wardens of the
Merchant Hosiers who had closed their workshops, and persuaded them to reopen them.   One of the masters who was
less accommodating than the others was sent to the Châtelet.[1]
From 1740 *ateliers de charité* were regularly established,[2]
where the unemployed of both sexes and any age might
present themselves and earn enough to ward off starvation.
" Anyone in want has the right to come," wrote Controller-
General Terray.   In 1789 the Treasury spent nearly 2,000,000
livres on this work, without counting the contributions from
the towns.   It was this labour which was chiefly employed in
Louis XVI's reign in constructing an excellent road system.
Sometimes the government opposed the introduction of some
technical improvement on the grounds that it would throw a
whole class of workers out of employment.   Thus in 1684 the
use of the loom in making cotton stockings was forbidden,
for fear that the hand knitters should lose their livelihood.

It is difficult to be precise about the actual effects of these
various influences on the lot of the worker.   The length of
the working day seems to have fluctuated round about
fourteen hours, with a break of one or two hours for meals,
but it must be remembered that the number of working days
in a year was not more than 250.   Real wages, calculated in
relation to the cost of living, which is the only way of
discovering the real standard of comfort among the workers,
fell sharply in the second half of the sixteenth century.   From

[1] See Sagnac, in Lavisse, *Histoire de France*, vol. viii[1], p. 275.
[2] Already in the time of the League under Henry IV, and at the end
of Louis XIV's reign, recourse had been had from time to time to this
means of combating poverty.   Moreover, the free towns of Germany
had even in the Middle Ages " kept a store of work in reserve to support
the poor without the help of the Treasury."—Machiavelli's *Prince*,
chap. x.

1560 to 1580 the price of food increased fourfold, while wages
were only doubled. The drop in real wages lasted until the
last years of Louis XIV's reign, when the workers profited by
the relative depopulation of the kingdom. This rise, lasting
until about 1750, was at once followed by a new fall, which
was caused by the rapid growth of the population, and which
grew worse and worse until the Revolution. One fact is
certain; in the last twenty-five years of the monarchy the
rise in the nominal rate of wages was less than the rise in the
price of necessities, so that the position of the workers was
rather less favourable at the end than at the beginning of
our period.

C. *Conflicts between Masters and Men.*—Trade unions—Strikes—Prohibition of workmen's associations; riots.

As the gap between masters and men grew wider,
quarrels were inevitable and became more numerous as
time went on.

Doubtless in small businesses, where the masters continued
to live on terms of familiarity with a small number of
workmen, and where there was no marked difference in their
positions, a good understanding still existed between them.
Moreover, the journeymen sometimes found themselves
momentarily united with their masters against a common
enemy. Thus in the sixteenth century the working printers
joined with their masters to oppose the claims of the master-
booksellers; and thus, after the strike in the Grande Fabrique
at Lyons in 1744, the journeymen supported the master
manufacturers against the master merchants. Again, when
some of the gilds decided to allow only one journeyman to
a shop and to stop night-work, they possibly did so with a
view to raising the price of labour.

But in general, and especially in large scale industries,
it may be said that the workmen tried to organise
themselves apart from and against the masters. The
fraternities of the Middle Ages usually contained both
masters and men, whether they belonged to the sworn gilds
or to the unincorporated crafts. But in the sixteenth century,
although the men still paid their contributions (which were
sometimes stopped out of their wages), the masters, who had
sole control of the common purse, used it to reserve the

advantages of the association for themselves. The help they gave to the sick or unfortunate was scarcely ever given to an ordinary workman. For a time, and especially in the south, the men tried either to win a share in the management of the fraternities or to found new ones for themselves alone. But they soon began to rally round the journeymen's unions, which remained obstinately alive in spite of all prohibitions.

In 1655 the Sorbonne thought it necessary to pronounce a solemn condemnation against the efforts of the *Compagnons du Devoir*, a proof that they were multiplying. These mysterious societies possessed even at this time funds for mutual help. They set themselves to gain new members and sometimes held armed meetings. In the eighteenth century this form of trade unionism, or *compagnonnage*, developed in proportion as the gulf between masters and men became wider and as the working classes became more numerous and were concentrated in particular towns and in big factories. The small local groups were formed into two huge societies, the *Gavots* and the *Dévorants*, to which twenty-nine trades were affiliated, and each of which had its special ceremonies and signs. Moreover, when the recruitment of labour ceased to be exclusively municipal, many workmen made the so-called *Tour du France*, travelling about from place to place all over the country, and this new custom finally detached them from the old gild system and at the same time created a new solidarity of labour throughout the kingdom. At Dijon at the end of the seventeenth century the workmen came from all over France and were known by the name of their native province—Languedoc, Breton, Picard and so forth. They were quite prepared to seek work elsewhere if the masters did not treat them properly.

Each of the big workmen's associations had in every important town an inn kept by a married couple (*le Père et la Mère*), where journeymen who were bachelors could lodge cheaply. Even when unemployed they were lodged and fed on condition that they paid back the advances made to them later on, when they could. Needless to say, the sick were cared for and the poorest were helped on their way. But the chief business of the society was to find employment for its members. The administration of each section included, besides a *rôteur* or registrar who kept a list of all workmen who passed through the town, a *capitaine placeur* or employment officer, who kept in touch with his colleagues in other towns and did his best to get better wages for his comrades. Unfortunately the two associations did not work together and there was constant rivalry between them, as well as trouble with the workmen who belonged to neither. Moreover, there were inequalities even among the journeymen. They were divided into three classes—the *reçus*, the *finis* and the *initiés*, forming a sort of hierarchy, and beneath them were the probationers, whom they sometimes treated as servants. The *Renards*, for example, were given the most unpleasant work to do and sometimes acted as domestic servants to the journeymen.[1]

Thanks to their associations, the workmen were in a position to begin, if not to carry on, the struggle against their employers for better conditions of work. Their strongest weapon was the strike. In 1539 the journeymen printers of Lyons, who were very numerous and were organised in a fraternity, declared a *tric*—that is to say, a general stoppage of work. Their demands were for better food, more freedom in their work and a limitation in the number of apprentices. They did not hesitate to threaten the journeymen and apprentices who remained at work, and even attacked the masters and the police. But at the same time they tried to arouse the government's sympathy for their cause. "The booksellers and printers," they said, "have always, by every indirect method and crafty trick, sought to oppress the journeymen and use them as serfs, though the journeymen daily win for their masters great and honourable riches by their sweat and marvellous industry and even by their blood. Yet even if they survive the extreme fatigue of their laborious work, old age holds nothing for them, burdened with wife and children, save poverty, gout and other ills." After four months' strike the quarrel still dragged on, but it was not definitely settled until years later, and then by a compromise.[2]

A few weeks later the journeymen printers of Paris followed the example of their comrades at Lyons. Their chief grievance was the excessive number of apprentices.

[1] See Levasseur, *Classes ouvrières*, vol. ii, pp. 814-828.
[2] See H. Hauser, *Ouvriers du temps passé*, pp. 177 *et seq.*

The strike was not accompanied by violence and seems to have been a failure. At the same period the journeymen bakers of Paris were in a state of constant disturbance. Strong in their complete solidarity, free from all engagements, they did not hesitate to celebrate their festivals on any day of the week they liked, and demanded a rise of wages on any and every occasion. The recalcitrant master was boycotted. Sometimes when there was a dispute the workmen in several bakeries ceased work by common consent and marched through the town armed with sticks, daggers and swords, threatening the masters and even the journeymen who had not espoused their cause.[1]

From the middle of the seventeenth century journeymen seemed to feel that they were the disinherited class, while the masters saw in them their future enemies.[2] About 1681 the struggle between the masters and the linen-weavers of Normandy became so acute that about 4,500 of the latter, all good Catholics, emigrated to England. In the last years of the reign of Louis XIV social agitation increased, whether because the rise in prices increased the discomfort of the workers, or because they were encouraged by the depopulation, which was then becoming noticeable, to take a bolder tone. At Darnétal the journeymen cloth-workers excluded from the workshops anyone who did not belong to their society. In 1697 three or four thousand of them struck because certain masters had employed foreign workmen; they forced the masters to close down the factories and refused to return to work for a month. The journeymen farriers of the Maubert quarter of Paris rioted outside their masters' houses to obtain a rise in wages. In the hatters' and in several other gilds, if a master refused to employ an incapable journeyman, all the others at once left the shop, it was put on the black list, and woe to the journeyman who did not accept the decree of the community. According to Boisguillebert, sometimes " seven or eight hundred workmen in a single industry would suddenly and in a moment absent themselves, leaving all their work unfinished, because the masters wanted to decrease their day's wage by a sou . . .

[1] See Levasseur, *Classes ouvrières*, vol. ii, p. 118; and for further details see Hauser, *Les compagnonnages de Dijon.* 1907.

[2] Lavisse, *Histoire de France*, vol. vii¹, p. 327.

and wealthy merchants would go bankrupt simply because for two or three years they had been unable to find anyone to do their work, though they had plenty of it. . . .''[1]

In 1724 some of the Parisian hosiers ceased work to force the masters to reconsider an unjustifiable reduction in wages. They organised a strike fund, to which some of those who remained at work contributed. Under pretext of hearing Mass, they assembled in a body at the door of St. Paul's Church and vigorously converted those who had been ignorant of their movement. At Lyons in 1779 the silk-workers of the Grande Fabrique joined with the hatters in demanding a rise in wages, which they obtained for the moment at the price of a riot. In this industry certain classes of workers such as the shearmen and teaselers, who worked in groups, were notorious for violence, while others, such as the weavers, who were usually scattered about the country-side, were very easy to manage.

Although the policy of the government towards the wage-earners, considered as an unfortunate and defenceless class of subjects, was to a certain extent protective, it showed nothing but harshness towards the workers when they were half organised and beginning to assert their rights with violence. The Edict of Villers-Cotterets in 1539 forbade all association for industrial purposes. Thus masters' organisations as well as the men's were forbidden, but the masters only formed unions for the purpose of protesting against some act of the public authority, as when, in 1574, the master bakers and pastrycooks of Rouen joined together to escape the payment of the mill tolls collected by the town. Workmen's coalitions, on the other hand, were usually directed against the masters, and it must be noted that they had already been forbidden to journeymen in incorporated crafts by the gild statutes. The prohibition of all fraternities, assemblies and coalitions of craftsmen was renewed in 1572.

In strikes the attitude of the government was invariably hostile to the workmen. The judgment given by the Seneschal of Lyons in 1539 was against the striking printers on all essential points. Under pain of fine and banishment they were not to strike again, nor could more than five of them meet together at one time, and no work once begun

---

[1] Quoted by Levasseur, *Classes ouvrières*, vol. ii, pp. 389-393.

must be interrupted. It was not until some years later
(1573) that they succeeded, as a result of the weariness of
authorities and masters alike, in obtaining the reduction of
the number of apprentices to two to a working press. The
Parisian printers did not win even this partial advantage.
Francis I declared it would be an " extortion " and an
" exaction."

In the seventeenth century edicts against trade unionism
were multiplied, though with little effect. But when a strike
broke out the workers, by the very fact that they had
combined to cease work, had put themselves in the wrong;
and how could the Conseil du Roi or the Parlement show
indulgence to law-breakers, who were, moreover, accused by
the masters of ruining trade and the country? The government was in any case much more disposed to further the
interests of the industrial capitalists. By exacting a duty of
800 livres for the right to manufacture cloth of gold, the
edict of 1744, which was to cause serious trouble,
strengthened the manufacturing aristocracy, for it deprived
the master-craftsmen of all hope of ever rising above their
petty industry and small profits.

When it was realised that the workman's new mobility
gave him a chance of escaping from the watchfulness of the
authorities, still more severe regulations were made. The
edict of 1749 ordered any person who came to work in a
town to register his name at the registry office on arrival. In
1777 each workman was obliged to have a *cartouche*, a card
showing his identity and all his changes of employment. In
the same way, as the solidarity of the workers progressed,
the government redoubled its efforts to break it. Wage-
earners were forbidden to subscribe to illicit societies; not
more than four of them could meet together, even under
pretext of a social fraternity; they were not to intrigue
together to find work for each other or to leave it. The
penalty was imprisonment.[1] The edict of May 9th, 1761,
definitely suppressed all unauthorised fraternities.

Since authority took part in industrial conflicts it was
inevitable that the class against which it intervened should
sometimes turn against it. At Lyons at the beginning of the
sixteenth century famine roused the artisans, the *popolo*

---

[1] Edict of 1749, corroborated by Letters Patent in 1781.

minuto, against the municipal administration which served only too well the interests of the *popolo grasso*. One fine day in the year 1529 placards at the cross-roads summoned the people to the Place des Cordeliers, and at the sound of the tocsin 2,000 rioters, 200 women among them, began to plunder the houses of the consuls and the merchants. When the royal fiscal policy weighed too heavily on industry the workers rose in protest, with the consent and even the support of the masters. At Rouen in 1634 the establishment of a controller's office at the tanners' hall gave rise to considerable disturbances. In 1639 the institution of a controller of cloths and dyes brought about the revolt of the *Va-nu-pieds*. The Parisian market-women took part in the troubles of the Fronde. At Lyons when Colbert tried to impose his new textile regulations the workmen took the opportunity to rise. The women lace-makers of Auvergne, angry because they had been forced to give up their old methods for new ones pleasing to the minister, revenged themselves on the foreign women who came to teach them the new methods. The Alençon lace-makers did not confine themselves to leaving the factory, but mobbed the director as well. In Normandy the prolonged periods of unemployment at the end of the century produced revolts on several occasions. At Orleans in February, 1709, the creation of a stamp duty on stockings, which could only have resulted in reducing the sale of these articles, incited the manufacturers to close their workshops, whereupon 400 carders and other workmen went to the intendant and " spoke to him very seditiously and said that they would return the next day three thousand strong."[1] Despairing of ever being able to recoup themselves for the dues which were henceforth to encumber their humble industry, even the country artisans rebelled.

Thus was developed among the working classes that habit of insubordination which showed itself on every disturbance of the social order. At the time of Law's system the workmen took advantage of the confusion caused in prices by the issue of notes and by the edicts which changed the intrinsic value of the livre, to plot together to leave their masters or force them to pay extraordinary wages. The

[1] Quoted by Sagnac in Lavisse, *Histoire de France*, vol. viii[1], pp. 275-276.

famous edict of 1744 provoked a regular rising at Lyons. United with the master-craftsmen, the journeymen forced the municipality to capitulate, and it was several months before the wealthy bourgeoisie, backed by all the power of the crown, succeeded in again obtaining control over the town. But then the rising was ruthlessly crushed; one workman was executed, and two others sent to the galleys for life.

III.—AGRICULTURE

§ 1. The Sale of Produce.

Exportation of agricultural produce—Internal regulation of the grain trade—Development of the market.

The development of agriculture, like that of industry, depends on commerce—that is to say, on the growth of markets. We have already shown that agricultural exports were subject to various restrictions. Those on raw materials were inspired by a desire to protect national industries, while those on essential foodstuffs aimed at securing the national food supply. In the course of the three centuries we are studying the first class tended to disappear. Thus the export of wool became free from duty in 1716 and from all control in 1758, while the export of hemp was allowed after 1719. But the removal of control from the food trade was a much more difficult process. Although the export of cattle was allowed to a certain extent after 1763, corn still remained under control.

The rise in prices caused in the sixteenth century by the monetary revolution encouraged the government to set itself up as supreme arbiter of food supplies (1577) and to forbid the export of corn and even of wine. After the peace of Vervins, Henry IV waived both these prohibitions, but the first was re-established by Richelieu and often renewed by Colbert. Not that Colbert was, as some people have pretended, the systematic foe of agriculture. He was undoubtedly more interested in industry and in overseas trade, and gave these more attention. But he was also interested in the question of agricultural markets. He made what we call direct purchases of corn, wine, spirits, salted provisions and cattle from the producers. He even thought of protecting certain products of French soil against foreign competition. But, frightened by the terrible famine of the winter 1663-4, and convinced that the kingdom could scarcely feed its own people, he never allowed the free export of corn, and henceforth issued only provisional permissions for a short time and on payment of very high duties. The famines at the end of Louis XIV's reign determined the administration to enforce this system of prohibition, though it was totally suspended on occasion to allow the farmers to make some money with which to pay their taxes.

It was only towards the middle of the eighteenth century that this fear of famine began to be treated reasonably.[1] It was now realised that the remedies used only aggravated the evil, and that the farmers had no interest in procuring good harvests when they knew that abundance would only result in a big drop in price. In 1764 a succession of good harvests had indeed reduced prices almost to vanishing point. Free export was therefore once more allowed, subject only to the payment of moderate duties and the obligation to use French shipping. But for fear of an excessive rise in prices this outlet was soon closed, and it was not until the eve of the Revolution (1787) that there was any question of reopening it.

Indeed, the encouragement of the government would not have been enough to give France a large export trade in grains. Although French exporters had a big average surplus at their disposal and there were excellent markets in Holland, Sweden, Spain, Portugal and some parts of Germany, they had to meet the competition of Poland, Denmark and England. As to wines and spirits, which the government did not try to confine to the kingdom, though the abuses of the fiscal system did indirectly check their export, these articles, though beyond the reach of foreign competition, suffered cruelly from foreign reprisals; France taxed the manufactured imports of her rivals, who retaliated by taxing her most valuable commodities.

The resources offered by the home market to agricultural produce were naturally increased by the improvement of the means of transport. But the upkeep of natural waterways, which were particularly suitable for the transport of heavy

---

[1] Lavisse, *Histoire de France*, vol. vii[1], pp. 214-217.

and cumbrous merchandise, was very unsatisfactory, and the system of country roads hardly began to develop until after 1770, when the institution of unemployment relief works by the state made a supply of labour available. Moreover, freedom of trade did not develop as quickly as did means of communication. Wines were stopped at every stage on their journey for the collection of tolls, while the passage of grain bristled with barriers of all sorts. It was not enough to multiply tolls and provincial Customs duties to hinder its transport; the fear that the district would be short of food led the authorities to renew the old feudal or municipal regulations in order to keep it in the district where it was produced.

The seventeenth century showed itself even less liberal than the sixteenth on this point. To secure the food supply of the ever-growing capital an old fifteenth-century edict was revived, and its already rigorous provisions were made even more stringent. All grain for sale within a radius of ten leagues round Paris had to be brought to the Corn Market. The provinces themselves, under the guidance of their intendant or Parlement, jealously forbade all trade. "Everything here is bursting with corn," wrote Mme. de Sévigné from Brittany, " and I have not a *sol*. I am dying of hunger in the midst of plenty." The indispensable permits arrived too late; after 1699 traffic was officially forbidden, especially traffic by barges, which lent itself to smuggling. The harm such a system did to the farmers was very serious. In bad years they reaped very little, and the high prices which they obtained then did not compensate them for what they had lost in times of low prices. The rise in price only profited the favoured merchants who had obtained the exclusive right of importing corn from abroad, in which case there often followed a disastrous glut which forced the peasants, driven by necessity, to sell their corn at any price.

Moreover, the markets were subject to regulations drawn up in the decrees of 1693 and 1709, and all these tended to reduce the husbandman's profit to a minimum and sometimes to less than nothing. He was forbidden to do business with merchants except in the open market and towards the end of the day when the townsfolk had been served. In case of shortage he was forced to supply the market, and if he did not bring the required quantity of grain of his own free will his granary was broken open by force. If his produce found no buyer at the price he wanted to get for it, the government refused to let him take it away and if necessary fixed a much lower price for it. The farmer was thus the slave of the market.

Even if these restrictions had been set aside, the conditions of the trade in cereals would still have been the most unfavourable imaginable for the producer. In the sixteenth century the formation of any *entrepôt* of any size had been prohibited, and in 1661 the Parlement of Paris declared any society of corn merchants illegal. Thus in Colbert's time the food supply of Paris was in the hands of small merchants who were equally incapable of preventing crises of over-production in the districts whence they drew their supplies and of famine in the city. From 1699 this profession was closed to anyone who had not been duly authorised, registered and sworn in. It was a sort of semi-official monopoly created in the interests of a small class of people, and as usual the farmers bore the expense. If the government forced the merchants to sell cheaply, they recompensed themselves by making the farmers sell for next to nothing.

The official monopoly of purchase attracted public notice at last, when in the middle of the eighteenth century public granaries were instituted. Instead of being protected like industry, national agriculture was sacrificed. Instead of defending it against foreign competition, as soon as corn prices went up the government granted bounties to importers or sold its own stocks at a loss. The meat trade was subject to regulations which were ruinous to the breeder. In many provinces the butchers were invested with a virtual monopoly of sale and consequently of purchase. All the cattle destined for consumption in Paris could only be sold through the agency of the office of Poissy, which charged the exorbitant rate of 6 per cent. on its operations, and preserved its monopoly until the end of the Ancien Régime.

Both public opinion and the government finally realised that this policy, well intentioned as it might be, revolved in a vicious circle. It was not by overtaxing the farmers that the abundance on which cheap food really depended could be realised. It was not by opposing the establishment of private warehouses that the inequalities of harvests could best be repaired. Nor would the isolation of the provinces assure the equable distribution of grain through the kingdom. Free circulation of food supplies between the provinces had been allowed in practice during the sixteenth century and the beginning of the seventeenth. Louis XII had realised its advantages (1502), and Henry IV had maintained it. It was solemnly proclaimed in 1763, confirmed in 1774, and the principle was no longer contested. But, without mentioning general obstacles, such as tolls, which still remained, the special regulations concerning markets and corn merchants, as well as the public granaries, were only abolished for a very short time.

The position of other agricultural products showed a more marked improvement. Turgot suppressed tolls on wine, with the exception of the duty paid on entering a town. The cattle trade, freed from all restrictions and taxes, profited largely by the new transport facilities, and breeders all over the country began to compete with those of the Ile-de-France in supplying the capital.

But there were several other causes, more important than these half reforms, which contributed to the revival of French agriculture. The first was the development of industry. Some of the most famous manufactures, devoted to articles of luxury, certainly obtained their raw material chiefly from abroad. In the eighteenth century France did not produce a quarter of the silk and wool needed by her industry. But big manufactures of articles in general use were springing up, especially in the country districts, and these used chiefly local produce. The general standard of life of the people, moreover, tended to improve in the second half of the century, helped, doubtless, by the growth of industrialism and the re-establishment of peace. In any case, the population grew more rapidly than it had done for 200 years, increasing by 4,000,000 in thirty years (1760-1790). This unexpected increase, which redoubled the government's anxiety about the food supply so that many measures were passed contrary to the interests of agriculture, at the same time offered agriculture an unforeseen resource.

How far in effect were the conditions of this vast branch

8

of national activity changed? The nominal rise in the price of foodstuffs in the sixteenth century was followed, from about 1670 until the middle of the next century, by a profound depreciation which reached its lowest point in the slump of the years 1760-1764, and which was all the more disastrous because other goods had advanced in price. But after the latter date, by the combined effect of the various circumstances we have noted, the price of agricultural produce not only tended to equalise itself from year to year and from place to place, but also rose rapidly and continuously throughout the country. The revenue from land rose at the same time; within twenty-five years it had risen by a third and in some provinces had doubled.

The improved conditions of sale were not the only cause of this remarkable change, to which improved methods of working the land had also contributed. But the latter improvement, which was inevitably costly, could and would never have been undertaken if the farmer had not been sure of getting a better price for his produce.

§ 2. Conditions of Production.

Burdens of agriculture: feudal and ecclesiastical exactions; royal impositions; communal servitude; lack of capital—Slow disappearance of these burdens: exemptions given for draining and clearing land; movement in favour of agriculture in the second half of the eighteenth century: influx of capital—Respective merits of *métayage* and *fermage*—Big farmers and smallholders—Recruitment of labour.

To profit by the increased size of the market, agriculture, like industry, needed capital. But for a long time money was not available for the land because agriculture was burdened with heavy charges and privileged competition.

In the first place the land was subject to feudal and ecclesiastical exactions, of which the most burdensome was the *mainmorte*.[1] The peasant had no heart to cultivate his land if his inheritance ran the risk of returning to the lord of the manor by escheat. Nor would anyone want to purchase land on so precarious a tenure. The right of *lods et ventes*

---

[1] The *mainmorte* was a right of succession in virtue of which the lord inherits the property of the serf who dies without children living in community with him. It meant that the serf could not alienate his holding.—M. R.

(duty paid to the lord of the manor on the sale of any land there), which was often as high as 12 per cent. of the selling price, prevented the tenants from improving their holdings. The prevalence of *domaine congéable* (land held at the lord's pleasure), from which a man might be evicted at any moment even if his family had held the land time out of mind, did not encourage the tenants to make any effort to increase the value of the land. The right of *franc-fief*, which was the appropriation of a year's revenue every twenty years and at every change of proprietor, prevented commoners from buying nobles' land. The *retrait lignager*[1] caused these newly sold lands to remain practically masterless for a year. As to the tithe, it was very burdensome because it was levied on the gross produce, without taking into account the cost of production. On poor land it sometimes had to be paid out of capital, and thus it hindered their cultivation.

Passing to the royal taxes—for agriculture had to bear the expense of two superimposed social organisations—we find that the most ruinous was the personal *taille*. This tax was supposed to be collected from the cultivator's profits, but it often sapped all his resources, for the assessment was arbitrary, not only as between man and man, but as between parish and parish. It seemed to be established for the express purpose of discouraging the peasant from trying to improve his land and stock. This variation, which opened the door to all abuses, was all the more dangerous because the tax was paid by the cultivators and not by the proprietors, and the excellent principle that agricultural implements and plough animals were not distrainable was more often violated than respected. Henry IV had in vain ordered that it should be applied even in cases of debts to the state (1595). The agents of the government for their own convenience were not slow to seize from an insolvent peasant the cattle without which he must inevitably be ruined.

In addition to these burdens on their land, the peasants were subject to various personal burdens. It was from them that the militia was chiefly recruited, and they alone were

[1] Legal action by which the heir of the seller could reclaim the sold land after a certain interval and without having to pay for it. Thus noble families were protected against the extravagance of any holder of the estates.—M. R.

subject to the *corvée* (forced labour on the roads) which became a regular institution after 1738. In parishes along the high-road all men from sixteen to sixty years of age were in theory required to work, but heads of families as a favour might be replaced by their wives and daughters. Each one had to present himself at the appointed place with his tools, his oxen or horses, and his food. The work might last from eight to forty days at the pleasure of the intendant.

The hunting and game rights of the king and of the nobles formed another of the farmer's burdens. Henry IV had, indeed, forbidden the nobles to go through growing corn or through vines before the vintage. But an edict of Louis XIV had ordered commoners to leave a breach in all their enclosures for the passage of the nobles' carriages, and had particularly forbidden them to hunt even on their own land. The nobles hunted less and less, with the result that game swarmed, but the farmers were not allowed to protect the crops from their ravages. In the eighteenth century, especially in the district round Paris, royal game preserves were extended and all the neighbouring land was lost to cultivation. The kingdom was turning into a private park. The corn could not be cut when it was ripe lest the partridges' nests should be disturbed.

Moreover, agriculture was no freer than it is to-day from other financial burdens. Many of the farms were burdened with ground-rents which represented the interest on usurious loans which could not be paid off. And if such land were divided endless litigation ensued, for the purchasers of the various lots were indefinitely liable for the payment of arrears.[1] On the other hand, agriculture was then still bound by fetters it has now shaken off, the fetters imposed by tradition in the interests of the com-munity. In many provinces " a meadow could not be en-closed, at any rate completely, because for eight and a half months in the year all the inhabitants had to have access to it. The same was true also of all pastures on the waste-lands, plough-lands after the harvest, assarts and fallow fields.

[1] Another source of litigation: " When the tenant on a long lease or in perpetuity sold some land, the buyer had an obligation not only towards the tenant but also towards the original owner." See Lavisse, *Histoire de France*, vol. vii[1], p. 334.

Ploughing could not be done every year in every field, because intensive cultivation would not have allowed time for the grass to grow on the plough-lands between the summer reaping and the autumn sowing." Often two neighbouring parishes would agree to let their flocks wander freely over the waste pasture of both parishes (*droit de parcours*).

Much more might be said of the burdens of all kinds which, by making the peasant's life one long torment, reacted on the productivity of his labour. And, naturally enough, this constant persecution of agriculture resulted in deflecting from it capital which could find other safer and more profitable investments. Rich men preferred to invest their money first in offices, stocks or financial affairs, and later in retail trade, overseas and colonial trade, and the new large scale industry. The big profits made by these enterprises and the frequent issues of public loans kept the rate of interest so high that the farmer could not afford to borrow, even if the money-lenders had not been frightened by the doubtful character of the securities offered.

Since the Concordat of 1516 many ecclesiastical estates which had fallen into the hands of absentee owners had been deserted. Henry IV in vain exhorted the nobles to follow the example of Sully and Olivier de Serres and live the ample and active life of country gentlemen on their estates. But the policy of attracting the most important nobles to the court, initiated by Francis I, and renewed by Louis XIV, had succeeded too well. The other nobles became soldiers, financiers or magistrates and knew their estates very little better. They had, moreover, obtained the right of using their money in any branch of economic activity, but they were still forbidden to farm out their lands unless they belonged to the crown, the Church or the princes of the blood. The rich bourgeois also took good care not to leave their peaceful life in the free towns to go and farm their property. For, once established in the dull country, they became ordinary commoners and were loaded with the innumerable burdens, vexations and servitudes which we have just attempted to describe.

A slow, uncertain and intermittent progress did, however, take place during the 300 years of absolute monarchy. Although seigniorial rights decreased very little and even, on the eve of the Revolution, showed a tendency to increase, the government on several occasions tried to help agriculture. Charles VIII, Louis XII, Henry IV and Colbert succeeded in momentarily lightening the weight of the *taille*. In 1768 the total amount of this tax was fixed once and for all, though unfortunately only for the whole country, without any details of distribution, and Turgot abolished the regulation which made the chief men of each parish collectively responsible for the payment of the parish's assessment. The suppression of the tax of a twentieth on industry in the country districts also afforded some relief. In the second half of the eighteenth century the government avoided as far as possible taking the peasant from his work, even for the construction of roads or helping with military transport. Some intendants allowed the peasants to commute their service for money, and although the general abolition of the *corvée*, proclaimed for a moment by Turgot, was not maintained, at any rate this policy of commutation was assured. It was also applied to the militia; voluntary recruiting, helped by the subscriptions of those who preferred not to enlist, was gradually substituted for the blind chance of enlistment by lot.

The encroachments of the community on private property were also restrained. The right of enclosure, which had existed for some time in certain provinces such as Brittany, was extended to Béarn, Franche-Comté, Lorraine, Champagne, Roussillon and some parts of Burgundy (1768-1770); while the *parcours* at least was suppressed in Alsace, Dauphiné, Languedoc, Hainault, Flanders and Bourbonnais. Louis XI had already prepared the way for private ownership of the commons by fixing the rules governing their division between the lord of the manor and the tenants. From 1770 to 1789 a great number of decrees authorised their division between all those who had a share in them. This development of private property naturally favoured the progress of agriculture, for the peasant would put new energy into cultivating the land from which he would henceforth receive all the profit.

Moreover, it must not be forgotten that except during the civil wars and times of invasion and great distress there was relative security in the countryside. For a time, during the reign of Henry IV, the "Father of the People," peace had seemed so secure that the peasants' weapons "grew rusty, and men made caldrons of the morions and old corselets." Henry IV was also vigorous in suppressing vagabondage, and although in the eighteenth century it was still a menace which the government did not know how to check, it was never so destructive of property as the depredations of the soldiers had once been.

On two occasions—at the beginning of the seventeenth century and in the second half of the eighteenth—the government even gave positive encouragement to agriculture. Henry IV, who every day after dinner had Olivier de Serres' work read to him for half an hour, took care not to neglect such a source of riches. When he established postal stages in the small towns scattered along the high-roads, he meant to furnish not only travellers but also farmers with good horses. He dreamed of nothing less than draining all the marshes in the kingdom, and in order to realise this grandiose project he called in the help of a Dutch contractor, Bradley, on whom he conferred for seventy-five years the title of master of the dykes, and with whom the proprietors were to come to an arrangement; and he declared in advance that all drained land and all workmen who took part in the work should be exempt from the *taille*. Thus all the swampy district of Bas-Médoc, which is still called Little Flanders, was reclaimed, and the work was so successful that it served as an example for others. A century and a half later (1764) the government went back to this fruitful policy and granted exemption from all royal taxes and even from tithes for twenty years to all newly drained lands. Great stretches of land were still uncultivated waste, and this problem also was taken in hand; proprietors were encouraged to reclaim it, and those who did so were promised complete exemption from taxes for fifteen years (1766).

There was, indeed, at this time a powerful movement of opinion in favour of agriculture. The indolent Louis XV instituted experiments in drying grain at his own expense. The future Louis XVI, like the Emperor of China, put his hand to the plough, and when he became king he wore a potato flower in his buttonhole and wrote a memorandum on the destruction of rabbits. In 1760 a Committee of Agriculture was formed; it was a consultative body and acted as a research and information bureau. In the provincial assemblies created by Necker the Tiers-Etat of the country districts obtained representation equal to that of the urban Tiers-Etat. Indeed, it had been proposed to create an order of peasants, such as existed in Sweden, and the idea was destined to reappear in the so-called *cahiers* or lists of grievances drawn up in 1789. Burdened with debt as it was, the state found means in 1784 to distribute 3,000,000 francs to help the farmers who were victims of the floods, and in the year preceding the opening of the Estates-General a great royal agricultural prize was instituted, and was to be presented to the winner by the king in person. The Estates of Brittany and Languedoc vied in generosity with the central administration. Public sympathy and private initiative led the way for these administrative measures and supported them. In the ten years from 1760 to 1770 there was an outbreak of enthusiasm for country life. Rousseau preached the return to Nature, Thomson's *Seasons* and the *Georgics* of Virgil were translated; poets sang of gardens, even of kitchen gardens; Greuze turned the sensibility of the age towards the charms and virtues of *la vie champêtre*. Agricultural societies were formed everywhere and competed with intendants and rich men in their zeal to reward and stimulate the new energy of the farmers. Soon the first agricultural committees were organised in Paris, and even in the middle of the agitation provoked by the financial and political crisis a lottery was arranged to help the unfortunate peasants.

The land at last began to receive some of the capital it needed. Many abbeys expended considerable sums on the improvement of their properties. Many of the nobles, and particularly the Breton nobles, spent at least a few months every year on their country estates, and some of the greatest of them devoted their leisure and their money to the development of agriculture. Some of them founded regular centres for the study of agriculture, as did the Marquis de Turbilly in Anjou, the Duc de Béthune-Charost in Berri, the Duc de Choiseul at Chanteloup, the Duc de la Rochefoucauld at Liancourt, M. de Montyon in Brie and Lavoisier in Blésois.

The lesser proprietors, nobles and commoners, learnt the lesson taught by the great landowners. For a long time the bourgeois had only bought "noble" lands in a spirit of ostentation—for this was the only way which the sumptuary laws had left them of showing their wealth—and they had not farmed the lands any better than had the ruined nobles from whom they purchased them. But in the second half of the eighteenth century the possession of landed property seemed to them not only a guarantee against the fall of *rentes* and the risks of speculation, but as itself a profitable investment. A sign of this new interest was that from 1760 onwards various financial companies were formed to undertake the work of reclamation. On the other hand, the small proprietors and peasant farmers, who had not enough capital to improve the yield of their land, profited by the reduction in the rate of interest, which gradually fell to 5 per cent., as well as by the reform of the mortgage system in 1673. Moreover, stores of grain (*monts frumentaires*) were established by the generosity of private individuals, and from these seed was advanced at moderate interest to the farmers, to be repaid in kind after the harvest. Thus it was not only the progress of rural industries which brought money into the countryside.[1]

We must now consider what was the best method of applying capital to the land, and what was the most advantageous system of landholding from the point of view of agriculture.

During the last three centuries of the Middle Ages the predominant system of landholding tended to place the effective ownership of the land in the hands of the cultivator. In return for an annual rent fixed once and for all he was in effect assured of perpetual possession. He could leave his land to his heirs, or rent or sell it, provided that the new owner fulfilled the conditions insisted on by the nominal proprietor in the original agreement. But in the sixteenth century, when land was becoming less plentiful and its value

[1] Even Law's system had given unforeseen help to poverty-stricken agriculture. Some landowners had profited by the high price of land, which resulted from the fall in the value of money, to pay off big debts by selling a small piece of their property. Others, a little later, profited by the depreciation of notes to pay their creditors cheaply. And even among the fortunate speculators who had bought land to consolidate their new fortune, there were some who thought of making their estates more profitable by spending on them some of the money they had amassed.

was increasing, the duration of land leases was progressively reduced to a very small period of years. The nominal proprietor would no longer consent to abandon for an indefinite time the eventual increment of his property. Henceforth, instead of an invariable quit-rent, the cultivator had to pay a rent, the amount of which was discussed and altered at each renewal of the contract. Usually, for lack of other resources, he paid it in kind, by handing over to the proprietor a fixed proportion—a half, for example—of every harvest. Thus he became a *métayer* (farmer who pays his rent in produce). If, however, he could afford to pay in money, he could obtain, for the duration of his lease, an agreement fixing the amount of his rent independently of the variations in harvests. Such a man was known as a *fermier* (farmer).

It is interesting to consider whether *fermage* or *métayage* was more favourable to good agriculture. The *métayer* was usually poor. Since he had no money at his disposal, it may be presumed that his tools were of the simplest kind, and the heavy charges imposed on him by the revaluation of his land made him still poorer. Often the proprietor had to supply him with all his seed and stock, but since the proprietor was often an absentee living at court or in town, he could not give help when it was most needed. Naturally the unfortunate cultivator, thus ill-equipped, worked with little enthusiasm. Used as he was to poverty, he felt no desire to struggle for comfort. To save trouble, he cultivated the least remunerative crops, or wore out the cattle which did not belong to him by using them for cartage work for which he was paid. Moreover, he knew that custom obliged his landlord to support him, for a time at least, if his incapacity or misfortunes reduced him to absolute starvation. In short, "it is as impossible for one of these unfortunates to be a good farmer as it is for a convict to be a good admiral."[1]

The situation of the *fermier* was quite different. He was well equipped with the necessary implements, and had numerous cattle. He had money in reserve to provide against natural accidents or variations in prices, while if he succeeded in improving the yield of his land all the profit

[1] Mirabeau, *Ami des hommes*. See G. Weulersse, *Mouvement physiocratique*, vol. i, p. 334.

was his, at any rate until the end of the lease. Thus his interest lay in cultivating his land well. If the landlord neglected to carry out indispensable repairs, he could to a certain extent do them himself, while on the other hand he offered excellent security to the landlord who was disposed to provide him with new means of improved farming. But *fermage* would only produce good results given two conditions. First, the lease must be long enough to allow the farmer to reap the fruit of the sacrifices he had made, and secondly, the farm must be big enough. From 150 to 200 hectares,[1] for example, was the average size recommended by the Physiocrats. In this way a great saving was realised in buildings and in labour, for one shepherd could look after a big flock just as easily as a little one.

But in the sixteenth century *fermage* was still an exception and was only practised by the great ecclesiastical landowners who themselves directed the exploitation of their estates. In Henry IV's time the system began to develop in Normandy. It was already established in Flanders and Artois when those two provinces were added to France. The natural richness of the soil and the market facilities favoured its extension in Picardy, the Ile-de-France, Maine and Anjou. But by the middle of the eighteenth century it had only been adopted on about a fifth of the arable land in the kingdom, and *métayage* still maintained an almost exclusive predominance in the central and southern provinces. Even in the north the *fermiers* suffered from the effects of the continued depreciation in the price of cereals. For example, in the Soissons district many of the rich cultivators had been replaced by *haricotiers*, poor peasants, who, having no cattle, could not manure the soil or plough it properly.

But in the ensuing years agriculture on a grand scale began to spread. Where there were numbers of small farms "consolidation" took place, and the big farms which, since the seventeenth century had swept away so many cottages on the plains of Beauce and Brie, became common in all the northern and western provinces within reach of the capital. In some provinces estates had been so divided up among the heirs and the various shares were so entangled that each cultivator spent most of his time in getting from one part of

---

[1] A hectare equals about 2½ acres.

his farm to the other. It was essential that such estates should be consolidated, and an edict of 1770 with this object encouraged the amicable exchange of strips of land.

The abbots of the great monastic orders had usually remained faithful to their traditional custom of granting their *fermiers* leases for life and even of allowing each farm to be held perpetually in the same family. But an unfortunate edict of 1693, which established new rights of control over notarial deeds, aggravated the tendency in lay estates to shorten the term of leases. Throughout most of France the custom spread of not leasing land for more than nine years, because a longer lease was regarded as a temporary alienation and was then subject to many royal taxes in addition to the *lods et ventes*. The decrees of 1762 and 1775, however, extended the limit of exemption from registration duties to twenty-seven years.

Thus what may be called capitalist agriculture was developed. But this does not mean that other methods of improving the soil were doomed to disappear. If big or moderate sized farms were more suitable for the cultivation of grain, small farms were better fitted for flax or hemp or poultry farming. And there were many crops which needed even less land. Vine-growing and market-gardening, for example, needed for success little more than manual labour and devoted attention to tiny plots of ground.

Although increased capital was the essential factor in agricultural progress, it would have been of little use if the wealthy proprietors had not been able to procure the necessary labour easily. It is unquestionable that, at any rate at certain periods, excessive distress had resulted in heavy mortality in the country districts, especially among children, and some places were almost depopulated. Moreover, from the seventeenth century onwards there was a distinct migratory movement from the country to the towns. The chance of escaping from the militia, the development of domestic service, the number of posts available in the fiscal administration, the help given by municipal relief works, the misery of rural life and the relatively high salaries promised by industrial prosperity—all these things lured the peasants to the city.

Even in the agricultural districts, moreover, industry

sometimes robbed agriculture of the necessary labour. Sometimes a huge factory drained the surrounding district of its labour, and sometimes domestic manufactures installed in the cottages themselves distracted the villagers from the land. Even in 1665 the Estates of Burgundy were anxious about the effects of the extension of manufactures on husbandry and vine-growing. An edict of 1723 ordered that throughout Normandy, with the exception of the city of Rouen and the town of Darnétal, all weaving of flax or cotton cloths must cease from July 1st until September 15th. In 1724 the intendant of Provence had fears that agriculture would be neglected for silk-weaving, while at the end of the century Arthur Young attributed the desolation of the country districts of Brittany partly to the development of the cloth manufacture.

Landowners complained not only that agricultural labourers were scarce, but also—with self-interested bitterness—that they were disinclined to work. Labourers might be seen mounted on their asses begging from hamlet to hamlet rather than trying to get work. In the end the habit of indigence sometimes destroyed all taste for work in the most wretched of the countryfolk. But we know also that from 1760 onwards the population of the kingdom was increasing rapidly. In the country districts especially it was stated that " the population was infinite," that there were " hosts of children " and that marriages and births were the daily events of the countryside. The disappearance of some of the small farmers was balanced by the multiplication of very small peasant-proprietors, who were willing to work on the big estates in order to supplement the too slender resources provided by the intensive cultivation of their scrap of land.

§ 3. Development of Production and Technical Progress.

Restriction of rights of common pasture; beginning of the division of common lands; government regulation of cultivation—New scientific agriculture: Olivier de Serres, Duhamel du Monceau—Animal and mineral manure; biennial and triennial rotation of crops; machinery—Principal new crops: the mulberry, crops for fodder; the potato — Silviculture and horticulture; improved yield of cereals; extensive breeding; improvement of the breeds of cattle and sheep; breeding studs.

The extension of the market and the growth of agricultural capital naturally brought about an increase in total production and an improvement in methods of cultivation. But this double progress was checked by certain obstacles which must now be described more fully.

The common pasture rights over meadows and open fields were not only a restriction of private property calculated to discourage landowners and capitalists, but were also a very wasteful method of farming the land. They were considered indispensable to the keeping and breeding of cattle, and this opinion was so firmly rooted in men's minds that in the sixteenth century it was declared illegal even to plough a field which had once been a meadow. In Henry IV's reign the common enjoyment of pastures remained a principle which no one dared to infringe, not even the king.[1] Even in 1788 it was seriously questioned whether the clearing of the pastures would not compromise the existence of the flocks.

But in reality free pasturage could only breed thin and sickly cattle, and the *parcours* was doubly harmful in tiring the animals to no purpose and spreading disease. The often premature opening of the meadows on June 24th and their late closing on March 25th hindered the growth of the grass and forced the grazier to mow too soon. Indeed, the common pasture robbed the cattle of more food than it produced for them, and, moreover, it hindered the development of all kinds of artificial grass crops which would have enabled the nation's flocks and herds to be doubled or trebled in size. In the end the government saw its mistake. We have already described the measures taken in the second half of the eighteenth century to restrict this wasteful system. Under

[1] See d'Avenel, *Paysans et ouvriers*, pp. 60-64.

Louis XVI a tribunal forbade all private persons to possess cattle unless they had first shown that they possessed sufficient pasture. This was a complete reversal of the old order.

Wastefulness reached its height on the commons. The proprietors, or rather all those who could claim to have common rights, put forth their best efforts to maintain the existence of what was often nothing more than a mass of brambles and heather. In 1625 the parishes round Chinon protested against the clearing of 365 acres of so-called woodland which was to be converted into meadow. They said that " they would have no more thorns to heat their ovens." Where the commons were under grass the grass was never given time to grow, for each man wanted to forestall the others, and so it was nibbled and trampled down as soon as it began to show. The economists of the eighteenth century were not wrong in declaring that this " common ownership is one long devastation and brigandage."[1] From 1750 onwards, therefore, these common lands began to be divided. But long before this time the government had been obliged to regulate the rights of use and pasturage which the communities enjoyed in the forests. In some parishes where, a hundred and twenty years earlier, everyone had the right to cut wood for his own use and *for sale*, an edict of 1551 stipulated that " neither the lord nor the inhabitants may cut except for their own use and for making their own tools." In several places pasturage was forbidden from October 1st until March 15th.[2]

Other barriers also stood in the way of agricultural progress. It is difficult for us to realise the childishness, not of the routine, but of the superstitions of peasants 300 years ago. In 1662 one town in Provence asked the Archbishop of Arles for permission to exorcise the caterpillars and other insects which were ruining the white oaks. In 1737, again, a commune asked for an exorcism against the lice which were devouring the millet; elsewhere cattle which ate vegetables were excommunicated. Even the upper classes showed themselves very unenlightened as to their true interests. We know already that at one time the nobles did not hesitate to

[1] See *Mouvement physiocratique*, vol. i, p. 412.
[2] See d'Avenel, *op. cit.*, p. 43.

let the game eat their crops or to ravage them themselves while hunting. The feudal right of *champart*, and the ground-rents paid in kind, prevented the cultivator from ever varying his crops. When at last the government intervened to secure the country's grain supply its actions were not always happily inspired. Obsessed by the fear of famine, Colbert declared war on vine-growing. In 1731 it was expressly forbidden to plant any new vines, and for thirty years the intendants, their zeal stimulated by private interests, executed this edict with severity. Henry IV had tried to forbid the sowing of buckwheat; had he been obeyed, the kingdom would have lost its only resource in bad years. The government professed a religious respect for wheat, and went so far as to forbid the reaping of oats until after the wheat had been harvested.

Nevertheless, the scientific study of agriculture was spreading. The first step was the republication of Jehan de Brie's old treatise, which dated back to 1522. Then Charles Estienne, the printer, drawing on ancient sources, composed his book *Des rustiques travaux*, based on Roman agricultural writers, and soon followed by the *Prædium rusticum*, which was translated into French by his son-in-law, the physician Liébaut, and became the popular handbook known as the *Maison Rustique*. In 1563, under the enigmatic title of *Recette véritable par laquelle tous les hommes de France peuvent apprendre à multiplier et à augmenter leurs richesses*, Bernard Palissy published an excellent treatise on agriculture. Finally in 1600 appeared the *Théâtre d'agriculture et mesnage des champs*, by Olivier de Serres. The success of this book was so rapid that in three-quarters of a century twenty editions were published. Colbert, whose untiring energy embraced everything, occupied as he was with his manufactures, tried to institute a public service of agricultural information and statistics.

But it was only in the eighteenth century, when public opinion began to move in its favour, that agriculture, like commerce and industry, became the concern of the state. In 1750 Duhamel du Monceau published the first volume of his famous *Treatise*, introducing British agricultural methods to France. In the same year appeared the *Almanach du Bon Jardinier*, in which celebrated botanists like the brothers

Jussieu collaborated. Ten years later agricultural societies began to popularise the new principles. The attempt made by Colbert to create an agricultural administrative service was revived and resulted in 1785 in the constitution of a practically autonomous committee, of which Lavoisier and the physiocrat Dupont de Nemours were members. It kept up an active correspondence with the intendants and issued instructions to all the farmers in the kingdom. In 1764 and 1765 were organised the veterinary schools at Lyons and Alfort, which were the first in Europe. In 1771 a model farm was founded at Anel, near Compiègne, and for a time received state aid from the minister Bertin.

The most elementary chapter of the new agricultural theory was that which trught the uses of manure. At the beginning of the seventeenth century there were still some provinces, such as Provence, where, either from policy or from indifference, its use seemed to be unknown. From that time, however, the idea was generally accepted that the cattle must be given plenty of litter so that it could be spread over the fields afterwards. But manure was scarce because the herds were usually allowed to wander about, and the practice of penning them was almost unknown. The abundance of stable manure, even when supplemented by the dung from the dove-cote, did not compensate for the lack of cattle dung. Even a man of genius like Bernard Palissy only guessed at the principle of fertilising the soil with the ammoniac salts contained in animal droppings.

Only the most elementary use was made of mineral manures. For example, if a farmer wished to take a crop from the same field in two successive years, he burned the stubble on the field after the first harvest, a process known as *brûlis* or *écobuage*. The use of cinders of various kinds was also known in some provinces, such as Maine, in the sixteenth century. But for a long time the farmers used chiefly marl or lime, and Palissy composed a treatise on this subject. Sometimes *compost*, or mud dredged from the rivers, was used. On the Atlantic coasts they used *tangue*—that is to say, calcareous sand produced by the crumbling of shells; and an edict of 1618 declared that it could be taken away from the shore freely in spite of the claims of the nobles. The value of sea-weed and kelp was no longer overlooked. They were employed so much, indeed, that in 1731 it was necessary to regulate their use in order to check a wastage which threatened not only the fertility of the coast-lands, but also the breeding of fish and the soda industry. But it was only towards the middle of the eighteenth century that Réaumur[1] established the first principles of agricultural chemistry in France, and that the practice of mixing manures and dosing the soil scientifically, which had long been done in England, began to be introduced into French agriculture.

At the time of the Renaissance most of the land was only cultivated one year in three. The fallow was the pivot of this old system of agriculture, and it was thought that the land needed two years' rest to one year's use. Indeed, the scarcity of manure made this long respite almost indispensable, and it was the only thing which kept the soil fresh. The absence of any systematic weeding also made it necessary, in order to assure the periodical extermination of weeds after each manuring. If anyone wanted to break loose from this custom, which was held as an article of faith, communal pressure prevented him from taking any initiative. It was all very well for Bodin to protest against the idea " that the earth lost its vigour as it grew old," but his protest was founded only on vague optimism.

The mistake of traditional agriculture lay in the lack of variety of the crops, which feudal custom had fixed whenever the lord took his rent in kind. Olivier de Serres was one of the first to distinguish between the plants which exhausted the soil and those which did not. He established the fact, for example, that beans revived the soil after wheat had been grown in it.[2] But even in 1760 a biennial rotation of crops was still in force (one year in two was fallow). The Physiocrats tried to universalise the triennial rotation of wheat, oats or other small grain, and fallow; while for the best land they wished to apply a four-year rotation or even the perpetual rotation adopted in some parts of England and in France in the Caux district. By Louis XVI's reign there was much less fallow.

To obtain a better yield from the land it was not enough

---

[1] In his *Mémoire sur la nature des terres.* 1730.
[2] See Renard and Dulac, *L'évolution industrielle et agricole depuis cent cinquante ans*, p. 331.

to fertilise it and arrange the crops better. The soil also needed a far more thorough ploughing. Towards the middle of the eighteenth century, especially in the south, the old wooden ploughs without wheels were still in use. The poorest of the peasants traced their furrows with a simple implement of curved wood, which was not always even furnished with an iron point or blade, and which could be drawn by two donkeys. It was a century and a half after Olivier de Serres had shown the necessity for deep ploughing that the first ploughs worthy of the name were made with coulters and big wheels, and they only came into general use after the Revolution. The harrow and the roller had long been used, and towards the end of the Ancien Régime clod-crushers were introduced in Languedoc. The sowing-machine, which was an economy both of seed and labour, had scarcely begun to be used. Only the sickle was used in reaping the harvest, for the use of the scythe, which made it possible to cut the stubble level with the ground, was forbidden,[1] and it was only used in meadows. Corn was threshed entirely by flails, and winnowing-fans were very rare. Usually the grain was put into an osier basket and shaken in the wind, as is still done in the Far East.

Other agricultural equipment was scarcely less primitive on the small farms. Metal was still so dear in the seventeenth century that almost all shovels and spades were made of wood, and only a few were iron tipped. Since these were very heavy, they had to be made narrow in order to be manageable, and this lengthened any work. The carts could carry very little, since the bodies rested on wooden axles. Methods of dealing with animal pests were naturally very rough, but in 1767 we find the ministry ordering a gratuitous distribution of sulphur bellows destined for the destruction of mice. Irrigation had been practised for a long time, at any rate in the Mediterranean region; the Canal of Craponne dates from 1548. At the same period Bernard Palissy elaborated the theory of artesian wells. In the eighteenth century the Parlement of Paris favoured agricultural hydraulic undertakings by granting them the profits of the process of expropriation.

[1] In order that the field might be used as common pasture after the harvest.

More remarkable than the improvement of agricultural equipment was the increased variety of the crops raised. The beetroot, brought from Italy to Provence, became common in kitchen gardens; it was then regarded simply as a nourishing vegetable. By a curious coincidence the sugar-cane was also tried in Provence in Henry IV's reign. Two new cereals, buckwheat and maize or Indian corn, both from the Levant,[1] were introduced at the same time, the one in the north and west and the other in the south. But both were regarded only as poor crops. Hop-growing developed only near the German and Flemish frontiers, notably in Picardy. The collection of dye plants was enriched by madder and woad. The first, brought from Flanders to Southern France, prospered, thanks to the public encouragement given it, first under Colbert and later in the second half of the eighteenth century. The second for a time made the fortunes of the Lauraguais and the Toulouse district, but was soon deserted in favour of indigo.[2] In vain Colbert and his successors declared the use of woad obligatory in dyeing cloths; the development of trade with the Indies dealt it a fatal blow. Another new crop which suffered from outside competition was tobacco. It would have done well in Languedoc and Guyenne, but was checked at the outset by the regulations destined to protect the West Indian planters, and by the monopoly of purchase invested in the *Ferme Générale*.[3]

But the most important acquisitions were the mulberry, fodder plants and the potato. The mulberry dates back to Louis XI, who had already tried to acclimatise this tree with its precious foliage on the French side of the Alps. At the end of the sixteenth century it had spread through Provence, Languedoc and Dauphiné. Henry IV caused it to be systematically planted in the four districts of Tours, Orleans, Paris and Lyons, while Sully introduced it into his own province of Poitou. At the Château de Madrid, at Fontainebleau, and even at the Tuileries silkworm nurseries and silk-

[1] Maize originally came, as we have shown, from Central America, but it only reached Western Europe through a station on the Levant.

[2] Note also, as an exclusively exotic product, the dye given by the cochineal, an aphis which breeds on American cactuses.

[3] In 1687 the collection of all indirect taxes was placed in the hands of a single company, the *Ferme Générale*.—M. R.

spinning and weaving workshops were established. Agents, who were supplied from the royal establishments, were commissioned to sell mulberry seed and silkworms' eggs cheaply, and to divide them among the parishes; moreover, the monasteries were to set up nurseries from which the parish priests were to distribute plants, and finally experts were to go round the country both to teach the people and to buy cheaply the silk produced. But since no bounty was given to breeders, many people thought the new enterprise too expensive and only undertook it very unwillingly. Moreover, the climate was not uniformly favourable to it, and although the efforts of the government were crowned with success in the dry regions of the lower Valley of the Rhone and on the shores of the Mediterranean, they failed almost entirely in the basins of the Seine and the Loire. Within narrower limits and in districts with a suitable climate Colbert took up again the work begun by Henry IV and abandoned after him, and henceforth the government was always interested in this industry.

The introduction of fodder crops was still more important. Charles Estienne, Liébaut and later Olivier de Serres had pointed out the advantages which they offered both for cattle-breeding and for the improvement of the soil. But little notice was taken of their advice, and at the end of the seventeenth century fodder crops were still almost unknown in France. We know that custom was opposed to their development. The owner of land sown with sainfoin had to obtain a warrant to drive off the cattle which his neighbours turned on to his land at the ordinary time of " common of, shack." But from 1750 onwards the regulations of village farming did often include lucerne and other grass crops among the land to which access was forbidden all the year round, and thus even the aftermath was saved. Following the example given by the English farmers, the Physiocrats demanded that as much land should be devoted to grass crops as to grain. They were to form a third part of the new triennial rotation, and the official authorisations to enclose, which were successively granted to the different provinces, enlarged the domain where this programme could be followed. Notably in Brittany, Franche-Comté, the Nivernais and Limousin (thanks to Turgot) clover and lucerne

became common. In Louis XVI's reign the turnip, dear
to Townshend, was successfully introduced into Auvergne.
Next to the Procureur-général La Chalotais, the Vicomtesse
du Pont, sister of the Duchesse de Liancourt, was celebrated
for her lucerne, to which she devoted no less than 125 hectares
on her land near Ermenonville. In 1786 the Agricultural
Society of Paris awarded its highest prize to Gilbert's great
memoir on fodder crops. But taking the kingdom as a whole
the progress of the new grass crops was very slow. In some
provinces, like Languedoc, they failed completely, while in
Gascony lucerne was only used for litter.

The potato, as is well known, was brought from North
America at the end of the sixteenth century and soon spread
over England, Holland, Flanders and even Italy. In France
Turgot popularised it in Limousin. But almost everywhere
it was thought to be dangerous to man and was only cultivated for cattle food, for which it was very useful. Moreover, potatoes and Norfolk turnips were the first weeded
crops for which the hoe was used, and which could consequently be sown immediately after the field had been
manured, without any fear of an outbreak of weeds. But
the potato would not have become important in France
so rapidly had not Parmentier, in the celebrated treatise
published by Bertin in 1778, demonstrated that it was fit for
human consumption, while Louis XVI himself, at Bertin's
instigation, proved to all classes of society that it furnished
the most varied and most economical food.[1]

The old branches of national agriculture, which still
remained the most important, also benefited from the
progress of science. The forest, against which in the early
Middle Ages the cultivator had waged fierce war, had been
later considered as an inexhaustible resource, and the owners
wasted it as much as the users. In the sixteenth century the
growth of the population, the extension of agriculture and
even the development of furniture led to those widespread
fellings which disquieted Palissy and made Ronsard weep.
To supply the growing demands of their luxury the lords did

[1] Two other vegetables, the Jerusalem artichoke and the tomato,
also came from America, as well as turkey-breeding, introduced from
Mexico by the Jesuits. Erckmann-Chatrian, in the *Histoire d'un
paysan*, have described the resistance made to the use of the potato.

not hesitate to resort to premature felling. Soon forges and glass-works ate up whole districts. The consequences of this thoughtless disafforestation were so serious that they soon provoked governmental interference; in 1595 the vice-legate forbade the inhabitants of Comtat-Venaissin " to thin the woods or make any clearing on the mountains because of the great damage it does to the low country." The celebrated *Ordonnance des Eaux et Forêts* of 1669 specified that no clearing of wood should be done without permission, and established special regulations for steeply sloping districts. Colbert was not thinking merely of preserving the plains from the dangers of torrents. He intended that the kingdom should furnish him with an abundant supply of the materials necessary to build his fleets. But his excellent regulations soon ceased to be observed, and at the end of the reign the danger was becoming so acute that the exploitation of the Canadian forests was already being discussed. The zeal for clearing which was shown in the agricultural districts from 1760 onwards entailed further irreparable damage in Velay, Vivarais, the Cevennes and Dauphiné.

The danger was so obvious that it gave rise to the first attempts at reafforestation, while those forests which remained were much more carefully looked after. The system of regular fellings, introduced on the crown lands by Henry IV, and made general by Colbert, was gradually adopted on all lands, both communal and private. Foreign trees were common in parks towards the end of the eighteenth century, and were useful alike in horticulture and in forestry. In the seventeenth century, thanks to La Quintinie, the management of orchards and of vegetable and flower gardens improved. But the new processes employed in the gardens of the king and the great lords or in the intendants' nursery gardens had still to be made known to ordinary country-folk. This great work was begun by Moreau de la Rochette, who distributed gratis to farmers slips of improved fruit-trees and opened for foundling children the first school of horticulture.

The old textile crops seem to have been concentrated chiefly in the north-western provinces. In the eighteenth century, however, flax spread into Brittany and hemp into Berri. In 1786 exemption from taxation for twenty years was granted on all clearings made with the object of growing flax or hemp. On the other hand, geographical concentration is undoubtedly the most striking characteristic in the history of the vine during this period. At the beginning of the sixteenth century the vine was cultivated throughout almost the whole of France, even where the climate was least suitable, as in Normandy, Picardy and Artois. In fact, it may be said that the difficulty of communication forced each district to produce its own wine. But soon the progress of commerce made it possible for the respective merits and demerits of the different provinces to be taken into account. In Henry IV's time vine-growing had already disappeared from the damp shores of the Channel, and was developing on the sunny slopes of Burgundy. In the seventeenth century the vineyards of Champagne became famous; in the eighteenth, those of Médoc; thus wild and unhealthy wastes became the richest lands in the kingdom. In short, vine-growing developed to such an extent that the government feared it would cause a decrease in the amount of corn-land, and attempted to restrict it. Wine benefited both in quality and quantity by this local specialisation. Although vine-growing needed neither a large amount of capital nor elaborate equipment, and although the processes of making wine had even at the end of the Middle Ages reached a high pitch of perfection, there was an immense difference between real wine, which was more in demand every day, and the bitter verjuice which had once contented most of the population.

Most of the improvements in the technique of agriculture were aimed at improving cereals. The yield of corn-lands was eventually increased. At first most cornfields had only yielded about four times the amount of the seed sown on them—about 6 hectolitres[1] to the hectare—only a third of the present average crop. But towards the end of the eighteenth century the yield had doubled, even on naturally mediocre land. This improvement, however, was only possible as the result of a corresponding development in stock-farming, and this fact explains why it was so slow.

In the sixteenth century the cultivation of cereals, threatened on one side by the progress of vine-growing[2] and

---

[1] A hectolitre equals rather more than two bushels.
[2] The royal officers were ordered to see that vines nowhere occupied more than a third of the available land.

stimulated on the other by the growth of the population, had encroached largely on the pasture-land. The old proverb which says " He who changes his cornfield into meadow increases his wealth by half " was forgotten. For nearly 250 years, except for a short and brilliant period during Colbert's ministry, people ignored the advice of Olivier de Serres, who had said that " pasture is the firm foundation of all agriculture," and during this time the nation's flocks diminished rather than increased. The famine of 1709 had forced the peasants to kill their few remaining cattle, and this disaster had been repaired very slowly. In 1713 live-stock leases (*baux à cheptel*) were made easier, and this made it possible for the bourgeois, as it were, to lend the farmers the cattle they needed. A decree of 1746 inaugurated governmental legislation concerning the diseases of cattle, which was definitely organised under Turgot. We have noticed the foundation of veterinary schools, and the crowning point of this work of regeneration was the freeing of the cattle trade. But breeders still followed the old extensive system which entailed a waste both of manure and of land, for the beasts were allowed to wander over vast stretches of pasture carefully preserved for their use. The progress of corn-growing, both in acreage and in yield, depended ultimately on the success of intensive breeding.

Fodder crops were an essential factor in producing good breeds, but the first necessity was to improve the methods of cross-breeding. Underfed and breeding haphazard, the half-wild animals that wandered over the pastures were often mere skin and bone. " An ox offered with great pomp by the town of Moulins to Charles V was regarded as a phenomenon because it weighed about a thousand kilos. Such animals are a common sight to-day at the country shows, and cattle weighing half as much again go every month to the slaughter-house at Villette. This explains why at that time tallow was as scarce as hide was abundant."[1] It was only at the beginning of the seventeenth century that anyone thought of introducing Dutch cows (*flandrines*) into Normandy, Poitou and Charente. These cows were big and lanky, their calves could be separated from them after a very short time and they gave milk all the year round. Colbert

[1] D'Avenel, *Paysans et ouvriers*, pp. 188-189.

provided the breeders with Swiss bulls, and in the eighteenth century German bulls were also imported. Later, when venison grew scarce and butcher's meat was more in demand, breeders tried to produce fat animals. In Louis XVI's reign bullocks destined for killing already weighed much more than they had done in Henry IV's reign.

The same progress took place, though more slowly, in sheep-breeding. As early as Colbert's time experiments were made in cross-breeding with Flemish, English and Spanish rams, but they were not successful until the following century, when in 1764 Daubenton made his decisive tests. Since what the breeders wanted was abundance and fineness of wool rather than an increased weight of meat, they used Castilian rather than English breeds. In 1763 the Marquis de Barbançois had succeeded in establishing a Spanish flock on his estate at Berri. Turgot bought 200 merinos, and Louis XVI at last obtained from the Court of Madrid the celebrated flock which was installed at the Bergerie de Rambouillet (1786). Champagne became the chief sheep-breeding province with over a million and a half of sheep.

The horse, noble hero of the battlefield, had for a long time been the object of great care. Colbert, however, decided to control breeding-studs. Until that time remount depôts had been scattered about by chance on gentlemen's estates, but they were now placed under the direction of a royal equerry. The enterprise was not successful everywhere, and failed altogether in Languedoc, for example. It was especially hampered by the decree of 1718, which reserved to the nobles the right of possessing royal stallions and tried to forbid all breeding except by them. The number of horses declined, and in spite of the development of breeding in Brittany and the creation of the breeding-stud at Pompadour and of twelve new depôts, the farmers, who had little use for blood horses, complained that they were badly provided. On the other hand, Spanish donkeys had been successfully introduced (1710), and mules were already prospering in Gascony and Poitou.

In fine, by the combined effect of the extension of markets, of an increased supply of capital and of technical improvements, French agriculture made marked progress. The area under cultivation and the yield per hectare were both increased. But this development had not been continuous. It had been interrupted by two periods of stagnation and even of retrogression. The end of the fifteenth century and the first half of the sixteenth formed the first period of prosperity. If we can believe Claude Seyssel, who sings its praises, a third of the kingdom was brought under cultivation between the years 1480 and 1510. It is certain that there was a regular outburst of cultivation which attacked even the great forests and the banks of navigable rivers, and against which it was necessary for the government to take measures (1528). "Even on the burning plateau and rocky plains of Provence, which modern agriculture neglects, Vaudois colonists settled and twenty towns and villages arose."[1] Again, in 1565 Bodin testified to the flourishing state of national agriculture. Everywhere rents and the selling price of land were rising to figures hitherto unknown.

Then came the crisis of the Religious Wars. Progress was only resumed at the beginning of the seventeenth century and lasted until about 1675. During this period the price of land went up again, although the price of corn fell—a sure sign of a better yield. The great wars at the end of Louis XIV's reign and the fall in the price of corn, which lasted until the middle of the eighteenth century, caused much of the land to fall out of cultivation. In the Mantes district, within reach of the capital, a quarter of the land was waste in 1715. About 1750 half Brittany was waste-land, as well as great tracts in Poitou, Limousin and Bourbonnais. But in the last forty years of the monarchy everything was changed. In Brittany alone 25,000 hectares were cleared between 1764 and 1769. On the latter date the extent of the clearings throughout the kingdom amounted to 200,000 hectares; in 1780, in spite of interminable and ruinous disputes on the part of the landowners and nobles, it passed 300,000. And we have already shown how rapidly ground-rents were increasing at the same time.

[1] Doniol, *Histoire des classes rurales*, pp. 278-279.

§ 4. Social Classes in the Country.

The noble landowner and the small peasant proprietor—Condition of
the *fermier* and the *métayer*—Day labourers: slow disappearance
of serfdom; variations in real wages; restriction of common rights:
misery of the agricultural proletariat towards the end of the Ancien
Régime.

We have now to consider the respective condition of the
different classes who shared the land and the work of the
land, and to see how landed property and agricultural profits
were distributed.

The great "noble" properties grew steadily smaller. The
Italian wars and later the religious struggles decimated the
nobles, just as the Crusades had thinned the ranks of the
feudal barons, and the luxury of the court ruined them.
Henry IV tried in vain to build up again a strong country
nobility who would serve as intermediary between the king
and the country-folk. Men of quality, at any rate the richest
of them, continued to run into debt and to pay their debts
by selling their land. This process grew more marked
throughout the seventeenth century and was not checked
until the end of the eighteenth. But it must be noted that
in 1789 the nobles still possessed a fifth of the land, though
not of the cultivated land, while the lands of the clergy, the
increase of which had had to be limited, were at least as great
in extent and of much greater value.

Francis I's wish to absorb the nobility into the court
was realised at the same time as Louis XI's dream of the
" gradual expropriation of the noble by the bourgeois."[1]
Who should buy the land put up for sale by the impoverished
nobles, if not the men enriched by commerce and industry ?
Even between 1520 and 1570 a considerable part of the land
of the nobility had passed into the hands of commoners, and
this great movement of transfer continued uninterrupted
until the end of the monarchy.

Below the great noble or bourgeois landowners stretched
the class of peasant-proprietors or semi-proprietors. Of
these the former held the old allodial lands (*alleux*),[2] which
had survived in great numbers in Berri, Champagne and a

---

[1] Pigeonneau, *Histoire du commerce*, vol. ii, pp. 267-270.

[2] Lands held by hereditary right, though certain dues had to be paid
to the lord.—M. R.

few other provinces, while the latter held all the land which had been granted to villeins for a very long and practically indefinite term. Like the lease in perpetuity (*censive* or *bail perpetuel*) properly so called, the *locataireries* of Languedoc, the *albergements* of Bugey, Dauphiné and Savoy, certain forms of *domaine congéable* in Brittany and the *bail à comptant* in use among vine-growers, conferred on the tenant most of the rights of ownership.[1] The burden of rents payable in kind was progressively reduced from the sixteenth century onwards by the fall in the value of money, and at the same time the law was doing its best to relieve the land of the other seigniorial rights which weighed on it. Moreover, the peasant who lived on the produce of his land and had no need to buy anything, only benefited by a rise in the price of food. The humble dwellers in the countryside were fortunately placed at that time. "Instead of the wretched cabins built of mud, wood or stones, and covered with thatch and reeds, good stone houses with tiled roofs began to be built. The use of linen spread. Sabots and shoes of leather replaced the sandals of the Middle Ages. Though the peasant still ate little meat, his bread was less coarse, and in the vine-growing districts he drank good wine instead of being content with sour stuff made from the refuse of the vintage."[2]

But we know, too, that on the one hand the relative scarcity of cultivable lands and their increased value, and on the other hand the growth of the population and their increased needs, had incited the real owners of the soil to adopt new methods. They had defended their rights and cared for their own interests more assiduously; and the practice of granting short leases had led to the formation of another class, the simple tenant farmers, whose position we must now examine.

It was estimated that about 1680 the land held by the peasants either in *censive*[3] or in *alleu* amounted to about a fifth of the kingdom.[4] This class of little proprietors or

[1] Old local systems of land tenure, all of which involved the payment of rent to the lord.—M. R.

[2] Pigeonneau, *op. cit.*, vol. ii, pp. 35-36.

[3] Land held on payment of *cens* or rent.—M. R.

[4] See Lavisse, *Histoire de France*, vol. vii[1], pp. 335-340.

semi-proprietors formed even then the majority of the rural population, and it increased in the next century. Farmers, artisans and even labourers bought their scraps of land, and in 1760 it may be estimated that the villagers owned about a quarter of the agricultural land, a proportion which increased in the following years. But most of these peasant-proprietors owned minute pieces of land, and " dwarf properties " were especially the case in vine-growing. This *morcellement* was accentuated by the incessant division of inheritances, for it was exceptional for any family to hand down its estate undivided. In Brie, in Henry IV's reign, when a noble wanted to make a park of thirty hectares, he had to buy up 200 plots of land. In Flanders estates of moderate size could only be made by consolidating forty or fifty small holdings.[1]

This dispersion of property into a multitude of tiny holdings was not without great drawbacks to the well-being of the country-folk. "Divisions are the ruin of the village farmers," wrote Guy Coquille. "A proprietor who has nothing to do," said Arthur Young sadly, "will pick up a stone from one place in order to put it down in another, and will walk ten miles to sell an egg." But the advantages of association were not entirely unknown to the members of this humble rural democracy. In Picardy and Champagne, for example, they clubbed together to buy a plough. Another method of co-operation was seen when the smith, the wheelwright, the harness-maker, the ploughman, the mason and the thatcher, each of whom owned a scrap of ground, had it ploughed by the farmers for whom they worked, and as they did not spare their own labour they succeeded in making an income out of the smallest scrap of land.[2]

The great landowners who did not farm their lands themselves rented them either to *métayers* or to *fermiers*. The latter, who were fewer in number, naturally occupied a higher rank in the rural hierarchy. In the seventeenth century the most prosperous of them already formed a sort of agricultural bourgeoisie. They were most numerous in districts where the *taille* was assessed on real estate, for there it was less burdensome. But even in districts where the *taille* was personal they contrived, where their landlords were powerful

[1] See Babeau, *Vie rurale dans l'ancienne France*, p. 130.
[2] See Weulersse, *Mouvement physiocratique*, vol. ii, p. 316.

enough to protect them, to get off lightly or even to be exempted in the assessment. These village " cocks of the walk," of whom Colbert often talked, had " fine farmhouses, surrounded by moats, flanked by towers, with the family arms over the door. They possessed charters in which their lands and buildings were inscribed, and plans whereon the houses, roads and trees were painted in bright colours. Even the humbler houses covered with thatch were very pleasant. The hall was fine enough, with its corner cupboards, its brick fireplace and its dressers covered with shining pewter."[1] In Champagne many of the farmers had fifteen or twenty horses in their stables, and more than twenty cows in their byre. In Burgundy there were men who had got half the land of the village into their hands and sometimes had it cultivated for them by *métayers*. In Brie some of them, " more comfortable and better off than the nobles," lived like gentlemen and sent their children to the towns, where they bought offices which ennobled them.[2]

But in contrast to these rich farmers there were many who were less well off than their labourers. In the second part of Louis XIV's reign the fall in the price of grain, the increase of taxation, the frequent passage of troops, the excessive requisitions and forced labour for the army, in addition to the oppression of governors, nobles and collectors of rent and the *gabelle*—all these assailed the prosperity even of the wealthiest. Many succumbed to the attack. Only four years after the death of Colbert an official memorandum stated that " once the husbandmen of Maine and the Orleans district had all that was necessary for working their farms. To-day there remain only poor *métayers* who have nothing."[3]

The condition of the *métayers* was often miserable, scarcely better than that of the labourers. They ate only buckwheat, and in many provinces, according to Dupont de Nemours, " they had on an average only 28 livres a head to spend on food and clothing for the whole year." They were " literally only half alive." Their rough plough without wheels forced them to plough " doubled up like animals "; they had only donkeys to draw it, and some of them even yoked their half-naked wives along with them. The un-

---

[1] Lavisse, *ibid.*   [2] See Babeau, *op. cit.*, pp. 149-150.
[3] Quoted by Levasseur, *Classes ouvrières*, vol. ii, pp. 350-351.

reasonableness and suspicion of the landowners and the oppression of government agents reduced these wretches to "a sort of slavery."[1] Even the lot of the *fermiers*, who survived the crisis, was very precarious. To discharge the expenses caused by the wars, great landowners, with the exception of a few abbots, tried to increase their revenues by imposing excessive increases of rent, which they called premiums (*pots-de-vin*).[2] Then the cultivator, unable to fulfil his engagements, was pursued by the bailiffs and police set on him by his master, while at the same time he fell under the summary jurisdiction of the inspectors of the *corvée*.

Soon the noble grew tired of these long proceedings and made an agreement with a business man, who, on payment of a commission, guaranteed him the exact payment of the sums due to him. In the seventeenth century non-resident abbots set this bad example, and one can guess the fate of the farmers left to the mercy of unscrupulous agents. In the first half of the eighteenth century, when absenteeism became almost the rule, the owners of big estates formed the habit of entrusting them to a farmer-general, or even to a contracting company, who sublet them in lots and had them farmed as they liked. Thus the land had to support two masters instead of one, in addition to the workers, and these agricultural contractors not only exhausted the land, but often established a reign of terror in the countryside.

The needy gentleman who lived in retirement on his modest family estate was often no kinder, while the new bourgeois landowners were often enough exacting *parvenus*, greedy for financial profit, who had still less sympathy with the struggles of the cultivators. Was it not the Tiers-Etat which demanded in 1614 that beds and agricultural tools should be seized "in default of dues, rents and services" owing to the landlord?[3] Finally the *fermier*, succumbing under the burden, had no longer the possibility, always open to the old *tenancier à cens*, of escaping his debts by flight.

But towards 1760 the evil became so serious and so

---

[1] See *Mouvement physiocratique*, vol. i, pp. 485-492, and vol. ii, p. 448.

[2] *Ibid.*, vol. i, p. 452.

[3] See d'Avenel, *Paysans et ouvriers*, p. 355, and *Fortune privée*, pp. 223, 242; in *Mouvement physiocratique*, vol. i, pp. 440-442, and vol. ii, p. 190.

threatening for the future of agriculture that protests were raised against the abuses of the farmers-general, the impoverishment of the real farmers and the misery of the *métayers*. The Physiocrats demanded that the growth of a class of big capitalist farmers should be encouraged by assuring them, not only wealth, but the dignity which was their due. Those cultivators who " had to be continually on horseback to keep in touch with the whole of their estates " were true bourgeois, the natural equals of the great manufacturers and merchants. England showed France how they must be honoured, and in the end at the meetings of the Agricultural Society of Paris the farmer, the Maréchal de France, the prince, the minister and the magistrate all sat together in the order chance ordained.[1] Moreover, it is certain that during the last twenty-five years of the Ancien Régime *fermiers* and *métayers* shared in the profits which the increase and better sale of produce won for agriculture. In 1774 Moheau declared that he found in the country districts fewer mud houses and more men who wore woollen clothes and drank wine.

Below them were the day labourers who neither owned nor rented land and possessed only their labour. Usually they, like the industrial workers, enjoyed complete freedom of person and of movement. Serfdom, however, had not entirely disappeared. From the sixteenth century it was only a memory in Normandy, and only a few traces of it remained in Languedoc, but it continued to exist in Nivernais, Bourbonnais, Auvergne, Champagne and especially in Burgundy and in provinces annexed to the crown, such as Franche-Comté; and there were whole communities of serfs on the estates of the Church. The wish expressed by the States-General in 1614 that " all lords, lay or ecclesiastical, should be obliged to free their serfs in return for an indemnity " had no effect. Necker could only pronounce the complete suppression of the *mainmorte* and personal serfdom on crown lands (1779). He could not even enforce the principle of redemption on private estates, where it was estimated that there were still a million and a half serfs.

Undoubtedly the condition of the serfs had improved. " The master's right to follow and reclaim his serf was

[1] See *Mouvement physiocratique*, vol. ii, p. 156.

almost everywhere abolished. The serf could free himself by giving up his servile land and part of his movable goods to the lord. As his rent was fixed by custom, he could hoard up a little money. Indeed, he was sometimes less miserable than the free labourer."[1] Nevertheless, in Louis XVI's reign "the serf could not make a will nor, without the lord's permission, could he marry out of the estate or out of his rank. His children could inherit from him only if they lived with him continuously, and if he had no direct heirs his possessions fell to the lord."[2]

Freed from serfdom the agricultural worker was merely a wage-earner whose condition varied according to the supply of labour and the demand for it. In the second half of the fifteenth century his wages had been relatively very high. In the sixteenth century, as a result of the depreciation of money and the growth in population, his real wages diminished by about one-third.[3] Only after the Religious Wars, when agriculture was prosperous, did the labourers benefit momentarily by the reduction in their number. In spite of the regulation of 1601 and others like it, which tried to impose a maximum rate of rural wages at least in the provostship of Paris, wages did rise until the time of Richelieu. Then they fell again until the end of the first and glorious period of Louis XIV's reign. The depopulation resulting from the wars checked this fall, and in the period 1685-1715 agricultural labourers were paid on an average 8 or 9 sous a day. But this slight increase in their wages, together with the low cost of living, was balanced by heavier taxation and the increase of unemployment, which diminished the normal number—already reduced to about 180 a year—of working days.

During the Regency and the ministry of Fleury a slight rise was noticeable, analogous to that which had marked the reign of Henry IV and the minority of Louis XIII. But from the middle of the century onwards, although nominal wages usually remained stationary, real wages fell rapidly by reason of the high price of food, which itself resulted from the growth of the population. Contrary to the statements of

[1] Lavisse, *Histoire de France*, vol. vii¹, p. 334.
[2] Carré in Lavisse, *Histoire de France*, vol. ix, p. 255.
[3] See d'Avenel, *Paysans et ouvriers*, pp. 28-29 and 65-67.

landowners and rich farmers, who complained that they were short of labour, the progress of the population in reality surpassed that of agriculture, and labourers had to take low wages in spite of the increased cost of living.

The rural proletariat did not even manage to keep the resources offered by common pasture rights. In most districts an immemorial custom allowed the landless labourer to pasture a cow and a few sheep on the free land. But in the sixteenth century the right of grazing cattle on the fields was reserved to landowners or wealthy farmers. Similarly in the forests manifold rights of pasture, pannage, underwood and so forth allowed the tanner to gather bark, the baker copsewood, the potter charcoal and all the inhabitants of the parish wood for their own use. With the consent of the king (1515 and 1518) the nobles tried to reduce these traditional rights to such an extent that the complaints of the wronged commoners even reached the Estates-General of 1576 and 1579. The government of Henry IV and Sully checked this progressive dispossession of the country-folk. Certain forest rights were re-established, and certain communities which had alienated their rights were allowed to repurchase them. The people interested defended their rights vigorously, and the law favoured them. " The Bishop of Montpellier was forbidden to appropriate pasture-lands even if they could be brought under cultivation." In other places where the appropriation had already taken place, the judges decided " that experts should examine whether, outside the land newly converted into pasture, there was enough land left to feed the cattle."[1]

But soon the heavy taxes, which the Thirty Years' War caused to be imposed on the parishes, forced a number of them to sell their rights, and in certain districts of Provence this forced abandonment led to a general exodus of the cultivators. A century later the courts, inspired by the interests of silviculture or of more intensive agriculture, were inclined decidedly to the restriction of common rights. " But lately," wrote a Norman curé in 1774, " our poor had the right to cut a faggot of wood in the forest. Henceforth even that is forbidden them."[2] At the same time the heaths and

[1] See d'Avenel, *op. cit.*, pp. 45-47 and 60-64.
[2] *Ibid.*, pp. 53-60.

marshes, of which it had been said that "Nature made them expressly for the common use of the inhabitants of the country," continued to decrease in extent. Henry IV himself had given the signal for numerous clearings, and the enterprises of Bradley had roused the anger of the inhabitants of the river banks who were deprived of the fishing by which they lived. The clearings made in the second half of the eighteenth century aroused still more active protests. The rich took possession of the best of the waste-land and exploiting companies went so far as to despoil the peasants of the land which belonged to them, but which they were too poor to cultivate, when they could not show their title-deeds. The loss of the common rights which they had enjoyed for centuries was enough to make the existence of the poorer country-folk very precarious, and their condition was made worse because, in the words of a contemporary, " the wealthy farmers could dispose of the workmen's day with still more tyranny " now that they were deprived of all direct participation in the products of the soil.[1]

The parallel transformation which took place in the commons had the same result. Louis XI had already allowed the lords to take a third on condition that they abandoned all claim to the rest. These *triage* arrangements had given rise to the abuses which the famous *Ordonnance des Eaux et Forêts* of 1667 tried to remedy. It stated that the lord had a right to this partial confiscation only when the original concession of the land to the inhabitants had been free, and on condition that the two-thirds remaining should be sufficient for the use of the parish. But usually the lord's claims were successful.

Moreover, during the religious wars many communities found themselves forced to alienate their collective domain, and the expenses of the Thirty Years' War and the Fronde caused further alienations. To prevent this waste of the patrimony of future generations Colbert took the step of forbidding alienations (1667 and 1669). But in spite of this the rich contrived to reap the fruits of communal property. In Picardy, Normandy and Brittany the number of cattle a man was allowed to pasture on the common was propor-

---

[1] *Mouvement physiocratique*, vol. ii, pp. 451-452.

tionate to the extent of his lands. In Artois landless labourers had no right of pasturage on the parish meadows.

In many places, however, custom fixed a uniform total for the cattle which each inhabitant might graze, and it is certain that " the suffering part of humanity," as they were called in an edict of the eighteenth century, made most of their living by this.[1] But this common use was too directly contrary to the interests of intensive agriculture to pass without strong protests. From 1750 onwards in the districts of Auch and Pau the commons began to be divided. The government once more intervened to defend as far as possible the interests of the poorer people. It decided (1769) that the lands to be shared should be divided into equal parts between all the families, that the lots should be indivisible, inalienable, unseizable, hereditary in the direct line only, and that no inhabitant should hold more than one lot. In spite of everything, " in many places the great landowners took more than their share. In Champagne, Bourbonnais, Franche-Comté, Lorraine, Barrois and Béarn the waste-lands ceased to be common property only to become the property of one man."[2]

In fact, only two ways remained by which the agricultural workers might escape from the position of hired labourers pure and simple. They could either become owners of a scrap of land which they worked themselves, a method employed by the most fortunate of them, or they might try to supplement their resources by domestic industry. For a long time, in certain mountain districts, the peasants had occupied the enforced leisure of the long hard winters in making small articles of wood or metal. In the seventeenth century, and still more in the eighteenth, the textile industry spread in the country districts. The domestic loom no longer worked only to supply the family needs, but also to execute the orders of the manufacturer in the neighbouring town. It may be that this competition of rural labour made the position of urban labour worse, but the spread of industry in the villages at least enabled the labourers to obtain better conditions from the landowners and wealthy farmers. The complaints of the latter on this point are very significant.

But on the whole the agricultural proletariat led a

[1] See *Mouvement physiocratique*, vol. ii, pp. 456-458 and 573.
[2] See Carré in Lavisse, *Histoire de France*, vol. ix, pp. 214-215.

miserable existence. Their usual food was " bread made of rye with the bran left in, black and heavy as lead. Even children ate this bread, so that a girl four years old had a stomach as big as a pregnant woman's."[1] Often they were reduced to bread made of acorns and roots. Moreover, they were periodically decimated by famines. " The winter of 1663-1664, for example, was terrible. A missionary who passed through Maine, Touraine and Blésois reported that in one village of 200 people, 180 of them had no bread. Another counted in the town of Châteauroux alone nearly 200 orphans whose parents had died of hunger. In Beauce the poorest farmers had abandoned everything, and all their servants had become beggars. You might see hordes of poor people along the hedges and thickets gathering wild fruits for food. There was no refuge for them but death."[2] In the latter part of the reign these horrors became more frequent. Everyone knows the terrible picture drawn by La Bruyère. In the following century famines were certainly less frequent and less severe. But towards 1750 the wretched condition of the labourer was shown in the poorness of his clothes, and his position, as we know, certainly did not improve until the end of the Ancien Régime.

The misery of the poor country-folk was so profound that they rarely took part in any revolutionary movement. The rising of the district between Douarnenez and Concarneau in 1675 seems to have been the work of the peasant farmers rather than of the labourers, as is shown by the programme of the insurgents. " The fourteen parishes declare themselves united for the liberty of the province. They wish to abolish the *champart* and *corvées*, which are contrary to Breton freedom. The daughters of nobles shall be allowed to marry commoners. The curés shall be paid wages and shall no longer claim tithes or stipend. Justice shall be administered by capable men chosen by the inhabitants. Hunting shall be forbidden from March 1st until the middle of September. Dove-cotes shall be destroyed. A man shall have his corn ground where he likes." The revolt of the Carhaix district, a little later, seems to present the same character. We know from Mme. de Sévigné's letters how cruelly it was suppressed.

[1] See *Mouvement physiocratique*, vol. ii, p. 448.
[2] Lavisse, *Histoire de France*, vol. vii¹, pp. 214-217.

The troops, billeted on the peasants, committed the most horrible crimes, even skewering children on the spit.[1] In the eighteenth century the peasants' anger turned chiefly against feudal exactions, and hatred was keenest where serfdom existed. It was in those districts that the first châteaux were burnt. But everywhere landless labourers and peasant farmers looked with envy at the broad domains of the Church and the nobles.

BIBLIOGRAPHY

AVENEL (d'): *Paysans et ouvriers depuis 700 ans.*
　La fortune privée à travers sept siècles (2nd ed., 1904).

BABEAU: *La vie rurale dans l'ancienne France* (1883).

BRISSON, P.: *Histoire du travail et des travailleurs* (1906).

LAVISSE: *Histoire de France, des origines à 1789.*
　Vol. vi², *Henri IV et Louis XIII* (Mariéjol).
　Vol. vii¹, *Louis XIV (1re partie), Colbert* (Lavisse).
　Vol. viii¹, *Louis XIV, Fin du règne* (Sagnac).
　Vol. viii², *Louis XV* (Carré).
　Vol. ix, *Louis XVI* (Carré).

LEVASSEUR: *Histoire des classes ouvrières en France*, 1789. 2 vols., (2nd ed., 1900-1). *Histoire du commerce de la France*, 2 vols. (1911-12).

MAUGIUN: *Études historiques sur l'administration de l'agriculture en France*, 2 vols. (1876-7).

PIGEONNEAU: *Histoire du commerce de la France*, 2 vols. (1885-9).

RAMBAUD: *Histoire de la civilisation française*, 2 vols. (1887).

HAUSER, H.: *Ouvriers du temps passé* (XVIᵉ siècle) (1899).

FAGNIEZ: *L'économie sociale de la France sous Henri IV* (1897).

MARTIN, GERMAIN: *La grande industrie sous le règne de Louis XIV* (1899).

WEULERSSE: *Le mouvement physiocratique en France* (de 1756 à 1770) 2 vols. (1910).

BALLOT C.: "La révolution technique et les débuts de la grande exploitation dans la métallurgie française." *Revue d'histoire économique et sociale*, 1912, No. 1.

SCHMIDT, CH.: "Les débuts de l'industrie du coton en France." *Revue d'histoire économique et sociale*, 1913, No. 3.

---

[1] Lavisse, *Histoire de France*, vol. vii¹, pp. 352-355.

CHAPTER V

ITALY

In contrast to the countries we have hitherto studied, Italy did not form one state; she was, in the famous epigram, only a " geographical expression." Not only did the numerous political units of which she was composed fail to unite themselves even in the loose bonds of a federation, but they were divided by fierce rivalries, which even in the sixteenth century sometimes ended in bloodshed. A sort of peace was at this period imposed by foreign intervention alone, for it was inevitable that a country so divided against itself should serve as a battlefield for the strong centralised monarchies which surrounded it, and that so rich and fair a domain should become their disputed prey. No power, however, succeeded in conquering the whole peninsula, and the Spanish influence, which was almost without rival for a century and a half,[1] was later counterbalanced by that of Austria.[2] It is therefore within the narrow limits of each little state that we must follow the thread of economic and social evolution. But we must be prepared to notice, during this series of rapid sketches, whether there were not wider factors shaping these diverse destinies to the same end.

§ 1. Venice.

Commercial decadence—Brilliant but shortlived prosperity of art industries—General decline of economic activity.

We must begin with Venice, for the proud Queen of the Adriatic was unquestionably the chief power in Italy at the end of the fifteenth century. Two hundred thousand inhabitants were crowded together on what was surely the strangest site on which was ever formed so large a com-

[1] The last part of the sixteenth century and the whole of the seventeenth.

[2] From 1713 to 1738 Austria was mistress of Naples, and she occupied Milan throughout the century.

munity. This semi-aquatic republic had succeeded in
extending her mainland possessions from the frontiers of the
Milanese to those of Austrian Carniola. She was installed on
the opposite peninsula of Istria, and on the Dalmatian coasts
on the flank of the kingdom of Hungary. The fall of Constantinople had resulted in her losing the isles of the Archipelago, but she still kept several stations on the shores of the
Peloponnesus. She had just inherited the great island of
Cyprus (1489), and she kept Crete.

Venice had founded her wealth and power chiefly on the
precious trade with the Eastern Mediterranean, and at first
this did not seem to be seriously threatened. The progress
of the Mussulman invasion was almost compensated for by
the exclusion of Genoese competition. Moreover, in 1454
the Venetians had been clever enough to obtain important
privileges from Mahomet II himself. A thousand workmen
worked in their dockyard, and thirty thousand sailors
manned their fleet of three thousand ships. But the Turkish
powers hindered the passage of caravans from Asia, and
Venice herself abused her monopoly by putting up the price
of spices. Then the Portuguese, determined to reach these
Indies which seemed every day farther off, sought and found
a new and much cheaper route. In vain did the Venetians
launch the fleets of the Sultan of Egypt to help their Arab
friends and to chase these unexpected invaders from the
Indian Ocean. In vain did they dream of cutting the
Isthmus of Suez, which was all that separated them from
the enchanted ocean. Centuries passed before this route
across the Red Sea was opened, and never again did it lead
to the port of the Lido.

The Ottoman Empire grew rapidly, however, and Venice
sacrificed everything to dispute every foot of the Eastern
Mediterranean where she had reigned so long undisputed.
She lost Cyprus in 1570, Crete in 1669, and her last possessions in Morea in 1719. The sultans never forgot what her
heroic defence had cost them, with the result that although
all her powerful rivals, France, Holland and England,
obtained concessions from the Turk, Venice was refused
everything. The destruction of her commercial supremacy
was completed by Spanish and Barbary pirates, who fired
her ships within sight of the lagoons where they feared to

venture. Meanwhile other enemies, less cruel but no less dangerous, came from the Atlantic. Dutch and English vessels, more cheaply fitted out, competed victoriously with Venetian shipowners even in their own waters.

Deprived of her commercial activity, Venice might at least have served as an international market for the nations who had supplanted her and have made a small but certain profit from their success. But this was not to be. When she had been supreme in trade her merchant aristocracy had been able without risk to put heavy duties on all goods passing through the port, and this they blindly continued to do. Moreover, on the false pretext that their fleets protected the Adriatic against the corsairs, they levied new duties, which were made more burdensome by the corruption of the officials who collected them. International shipping turned from this inhospitable port all the more readily because the neighbouring towns of Ancona and Trieste offered wide privileges. Venice ceased to be the market and provisioning centre even of Lombardy, with which her water communication was so easy. Merchandise for the plains of the Po now came more cheaply from the fair at Sinigaglia or even across the Apennines by Leghorn. The transalpine trade was kept up only on one route, from Primolano and Pontebba in the direction of Carinthia. The republic was reduced to exporting simply its own products and importing articles for its own consumption. But the Customs duties interfered even with this necessary commerce, and an active contraband trade grew up, in which even the first families in the state took part without shame and which robbed the Treasury of much of this unlucky source of revenue.

The government itself grew more and more corrupt and allowed private interests to outweigh the general good. Government was concentrated in the hands of a few powerful families. Distrustful, suspicious, and relying on informers, they presented a perfect type of oligarchy. The people, deprived of all initiative, lost all interest in public affairs and knew only the name of liberty.

Moreover, natural conditions, which had hitherto protected Venice, seemed now to condemn her to isolation. While ships of all nations increased in size, her lagoons were silting up. " Big ships," wrote Montesquieu in 1728, " can-

not approach within four leagues. Even at that distance
they are often obliged to wait for the rising tide, so seriously
is the port of the Lido blocked by the sand from the canals."[1]
The government promised privileges to shipowners, master-
mariners and sailors; they encouraged insurance companies;
they executed useful naval works at Spalato in Dalmatia and
Durazzo in Albania, and on the banks of the lagoons they
built the *murazzi*.[2] But these efforts had no effect against
the powerful causes of decadence which were at work.
Neither did the commercial treaties which the government
made with Sardinia, Portugal, Denmark and Russia serve
them better. They had to give up the idea of enriching
themselves by trade. But Venice had amassed so much
capital that she had the means to sustain her splendour for
some time in financial business and in certain industries.

She remained, in fact, one of the chief financial centres
of Europe, and her citizens played an important part in the
financial administration of several European kingdoms. A
state bank was founded in 1586. But Venetian bankers were
no more famous than the Genoese. Where Venice excelled
all other Italian cities was in the methodical application of
art to industry. She conceived and carried out the idea of
infusing a whole people with the artistic superiority of the
few, and of drawing from it not only glory but profit.
Although the artist and the artisan still remained distinct in
the workshops, they worked in close collaboration. " Great
artists entered the humble workshops of the woodcarver, the
blacksmith, the stonecutter, the carpenter and the gold or
silver smith, to advise them and help them to attain perfection in their crafts."[3] The artisans in their turn supplied
suggestions and executive ability to their teachers; the dyers
and weavers contributed to the education of the painters. In
fact, the whole town was for those who were fortunate
enough to live there a marvellous and perpetual school of
decoration. The government itself took pains to encourage

---

[1] See Kovalevski, *Fin d'une aristocratie*, pp. 42-52.
[2] Enormous walls built of blocks of Istrian marble, 33 feet high,
and from 40 to 50 feet wide, rising perpendicularly from the lagoons and
falling down towards the sea in a series of terraces. Two people could
walk abreast on the top of them.
[3] Molmenti, *Venice, Golden Age*, vol. i, p. 122.

this new development and did not even hesitate, when occasion offered, to open the narrow gates of the city to foreign workmen.

For some time, moreover, several luxury trades had been established there. Even in the fifteenth century the gilded bronzes, magnificent examples of which were given to Soliman the Magnificent by the Venetian nobles, had acquired a brilliant reputation, and Brescia was famed for the making of bronze weapons, especially arquebuses. On the banks of the Rialto delicate inlaid work of coloured wood and charming furniture inlaid with ivory or cornelian were made. Artists from Faenza and Urbino had brought with them the process of majolica, and Dutch workmen had introduced the art of tapestry. The manufacture of silk goods was very successful there; at one time 4,000 workmen were employed making velvet, satin, taffetas and cloths of gold and silver, and although a decline set in at the beginning of the sixteenth century, Venice kept her superiority in silk embroidery and silk lace. Woollen caps were exported to the Levant and Barbary, and 20,000 workmen were making fine cloth for export to the West. In the service of these two great textile industries the art of dyeing was constantly making advances. In the sixteenth century was discovered the famous "Venetian red," which has stood the test of imitation and of time. The preservation of such secrets was, in the city of Tintoretto, an affair of state. Long established and very strict regulations forbade the unlicensed use of any chemical product and fixed the season during which dyes might be prepared. For drying vast spaces were reserved and ingenious contrivances fixed to the fronts of the houses.

New industries also developed, designed to please the mind or the senses. It is scarcely necessary to remind the reader of the beautiful books published by the Aldis, who had the honour of substituting the *octavo* for the unwieldy *formats* of their predecessors. In the workshops of Murano glass was successfully made without mould, model or compasses, with a tube and a lamp. According to his fancy the workman, with the help of a simple spatula, blew from the liquid mass he held suspended at the end of his tube fragile bowls, cups and flowers, which, as they cooled, took on a variety of delicate shades. In 1606 a means was discovered of colouring crystal without losing its transparency and of cutting it with facets like diamonds. A little later they succeeded in producing panes of clear glass which finally replaced the dark bottle-glass in windows, and in casting sheets of glass which would seem small to us, but which then were unusually large (1680). In the middle of the sixteenth century Venice was enriched by another speciality; needle lace and bobbin lace were both invented by her, and other nations long envied this subtle skill which enabled Venetians to grow rich by their fingers and almost without raw material. Finally, Venice inherited the industry of Cordova, and scattered in seventy workshops clever workmen, who formed a branch of the painters' gild, made wonderful articles of repoussé leather.

Gradually, however, this splendour disappeared. Here, too, competition arose on all sides. English drapers learnt to do without Venetian dyes. French or Flemish point became more popular than Venetian lace. Lyons silks were unrivalled. Although the secrets of the city had been published outside in spite of stern prohibitions and punishments, Venice remained closed against the progress accomplished by the foreigner. In Bohemia at the end of the seventeenth century the manufacture of glass was transformed by the application of certain chemical and mechanical processes. A Venetian artisan, returned from Prague, in vain revealed the new methods to his countrymen; the Murano workshops disdained to adopt them. The gilds, no longer animated by high artistic ideals, had become the homes of routine and were powerless to adapt themselves to large scale production. The rich patricians might have invested their money in the new manufactures, but they preferred to put it into estates, parks and villas. The increasing burden of taxation on internal trade ended by crushing industry. A momentary recovery took place in the eighteenth century in the mainland towns. Large breaches had to be made in the monopoly of the gilds of the metropolis in order that the cloth trade might regain a measure of prosperity at Verona, Padua and Schio, where water-power could be used. The rope-makers who used hemp from Bologna, the linen manufacturers of Friuli who used flax from Lithuania, the *camelotti* or shoddy manufacturers, who wove cloth for the Turks of Angora wool and called it camels' hair—these, too, took on a new activity which the jealousy of the mother-city had hitherto repressed, and which, in fact, precipitated her decline.

It is clear enough that in the eighteenth century this beautiful city, floating like a water-lily on the lagoons, was a centre of pleasure rather than of work. It was a town of joy, of serenades and masquerades, of gondolas and bar-carolles, of picturesque and theatrical festivals, the rendez-vous of kings in exile and foreigners in search of amusement. The people lived partly on the wealth of the visitors, and the old commercial and financial aristocracy lived on the remains of their former fortunes. Meanwhile the small trading and industrial classes had both remained for 300 years imprisoned in the gild system, from which the solvent influences of a free capitalism had been carefully barred. In the silk industry, for example, the merchants had been forbidden to become manufacturers themselves or to hire looms to the artisans, and the traditional limitation of the numbers of apprentices and looms had been strictly maintained. The big manufacturers had talked in vain of the growth of the market and the necessity for competing with Bologna, Ferrara and Trent. The small masters carried the day. As their trade decreased the heads of the gilds tried to restrict their monopoly to a still smaller number of members.[1] Naturally this was not the way to improve their position. Even the local market, which they had thought was their own, escaped them in the end, for fashion was stronger than prohibitions. Only the gilds which supplied the city's food remained masters of their reduced clientèle and imposed their own prices.

In spite of vain attempts at general reform (in 1577 and 1630), almost all the crafts of Venice remained rigorously closed. United in the same spirit of angry exclusiveness, journeymen and masters were so blind as to procure the expulsion of the Grisons, who, taking advantage of the treaties, had succeeded in entering some of the smaller crafts (1766). This was in odd contrast to the free cosmopolitanism of the bold merchants of the best period in Venetian history. In the end neither masters nor men benefited by this exces-

[1] See Broglio d'Ajano, *Die Venetianischen Seiden-Weberzünfte*, pp. 40-59.

sive protectionism, and although a careless gaiety still reigned in the streets of Venice, the comfort of all classes of the population had decreased.

As to agriculture, the Venetian government had never thought it an object of primary importance. The city itself, which, with its narrow suburbs, had at first formed the entire body of the republic, and which always remained the centre of the empire, could never have more than kitchen or flower gardens—and those " gardens of the sea," the lagoons. But 30,000 people lived on the produce of these amazingly rich gardens and fisheries. In the mainland possessions of Venice the value of the soil varied according to the province.[1] In Friuli the numerous survivals of feudalism, the extent of the common lands, and the numbers of enclaves had favoured sheep-breeding at the expense of regular agriculture. In Trevisa, on the other hand, and in the district round Este, many patricians had estates, and this gave rise to a more intensive system of farming. Cremasco grew an abundance of corn, hemp and silk, Istria produced wine and olive oil. Almost everywhere since the fourteenth century serfdom had been replaced by long leases, but the peasants, who had now become semi-proprietors, lacked the capital necessary to improve their holdings. There were very few *fermiers*, but there were hundreds of needy *métayers* who practised the biennial rotation of crops and extensive breeding on the waste-lands, and almost ignored the resources of fodder crops and artificial grasses. Moreover, wide stretches of land were Church property. The Venetians, on the plea that they were the bulwark of Europe against the infidels, had obtained the suppression of a few convents from Pope Alexander VII (1656), and had forbidden congregations to acquire land without state authority. But these efforts had failed to check the continuous growth of ecclesiastical property. It was only after 1770 that, following the example of other Italian states, the Venetians were able to free these lands from a pious and sterile sequestration.

Strong in her 140,000 inhabitants and governing nearly 3,000,000 subjects, Venice, towards the end of the eighteenth century, could still figure as a power. She went down, like the sun on her lagoons, in a blaze of purple and gold. But

[1] See Kovalevski, *op. cit.*, pp. 72-95.

the refined or corrupt indolence of her nobles and the idleness of her people had undermined her economic activities as well as her warlike spirit. Only the façade of the splendid building remained, and a puff of wind was enough to destroy it. The Treaty of Campio-Formio (1797) wiped out the republic, like another Poland, from the map of Europe.

§ 2. Genoa.

Political decadence; international market; the Bank of St. George.

Its very existence was a problem for the little republic which was narrowly confined between the Apennines and the sea and whose glorious past offered such a remarkable contrast with the size of its territory. The Genoese succeeded in maintaining their independence to the very end of the period we are studying. Although Louis XI had united them to Milan, and Louis XII had conquered them when he conquered that duchy, Spanish support enabled them to win freedom again (1528) and to withstand the covetousness of the Duke of Savoy and the pretensions of France. Two hundred years later the Austrians imposed a ruinous capitulation on them (1746), but they still remained autonomous until they fell under the domination of Napoleon (1805), and later of their neighbour Piedmont (1815).

We must now see what had been the form of government during this difficult period. In 1506, when the city rose against the French, merchants and artisans joined together against the nobles, who were supported by the foreigner, and these two classes shared the government. But when in the following year Louis XII crushed the popular party and restored the patrician authority, the rich bourgeoisie, the *popolo grasso*, hastened to abandon the *populo minuto* of the artisans and to join the nobles. Thus the revolution of 1528 assured national independence, but also the triumph of the two rich classes. Henceforth all those who owned property enjoyed political rights, but the small folk could never see their names on the golden book of the city, unless they had rendered some exceptional service to the state. Inequalities of birth were effaced by wealth. It was, indeed, the beginning of modern times.

Nearly all the members of this bourgeois aristocracy, who

henceforth held all power, owed their wealth and their more or less recent fame to maritime commerce, which was the only fruitful field of enterprise open to the republic. But the victorious competition of the Venetians, and later the advance of the Turks, narrowed this field. By 1560 Genoa had lost all her possessions in the Levant, even Chio, and her trade was limited to Egypt, and since the Bosphorus was closed she no longer received the corn of South Russia, which now travelled by Dantzig to Amsterdam. Ocean trade, in which she had been one of the first to engage and which had been made possible by the route discovered by one of her own sailors, had long been shut to her by more powerful and conveniently situated states. She still, however, preserved relations with North Africa, and her settlement in Corsica was favourable to her coastal trade in the Tyrrhenian Sea. During the sixteenth century she made a profit out of her naval resources by hiring the powerful squadrons commanded by Andrea Doria to Francis I or Charles V, and many of her captains made fortunes out of their prize-ships. Nevertheless, the port would have declined had not the government put new life into it by granting privileges to foreign traffic (1595). Dutch, English and French ships used the harbour freely, and in spite of the competition of Leghorn and of the Corsican revolt, which lasted from 1726 till 1768, draining her finances and finally depriving her of a useful base, Genoa remained the chief market on the Italian coast. Her port was not the outlet of a vast hinterland, nor was her own flag the most common one along her quays, but she was a great international market, the rival of Marseilles.

At the meeting-place of so many merchants there was naturally a remarkable concentration and a brisk movement of capital. Genoese banks could have flourished on their exchange and brokerage business alone. But many Genoese, whose fortunes had been made in the old heroic days and only partly invested in land, still had capital available for vast financial operations. The old patricians, who were the richest, had for a long time been official money-lenders to the government, which had gradually been forced to mortgage most of the resources of the state to them. In the fifteenth century, for the purpose of keeping their common debtor solvent, the creditors of the city had united to form a permanent commission of control. This was the famous Bank of St. George. In 1453, in order to make sure of a sound security, the *Casa di San-Giorgio* claimed the government of Corsica, and in 1539, in the first days of the plutocratic oligarchy, it took over the administration of the public debt. Thus it controlled all the finances of Genoa.

So strong an organisation, which united the advantages of private security and public power, was capable of extending its action beyond the frontiers of the state which supported its fortune. In 1528 the King of Spain, who had to make payments to Placenza, the Low Countries and Besançon, applied to the bank to manage the affair. To support his imperial policy he needed great sums of money, and the bank advanced the necessary amount. It is true that the Spanish monarchy proved incapable of meeting its engagements. Its bankruptcy in 1627, which was not the first, provoked so serious a crisis in Genoa that the government, to avoid worse evils, decreed a general *moratorium*. But Genoa had obtained so many commercial privileges in the various states of the Spanish monarchy, and up to the very eve of the bankruptcy had controlled so much of the revenue, that the failure of the debtor left the creditor still in a strong position. The Genoese had become the first bankers of the Mediterranean, and the *Casa* prospered continuously until the day when, forced to pay the enormous war indemnity imposed by Austria, it had to suspend payment for the first time in its existence. Its resources were, it is true, still large, for besides enormous properties in land its annual cash income amounted to more than £500,000. But the national disaster gave it a fatal blow.

While the Genoese patricians were thus attracted chiefly to financial business, the new nobility and the rich middle class preferred to devote themselves to internal trade and industry. Beside the old cloth industry, the silk manufacture developed from the end of the fifteenth century, and, in addition to gold and silver work and shipbuilding, formed one of the chief branches of manufacturing activity in Genoa, while its commodities were among the chief exports. It was naturally encouraged and supported by the prohibition of foreign silks, but in spite of this it declined rapidly. For this merchant people, who so generously gave to foreigners the freedom of their port, put heavy export duties on their own products, and silks were no exception to this blind fiscal policy. Moreover, in spite of the merchants' protests, the gilds remained rigorously closed against foreign workmen. The consequence was that this industry was unable to organise itself on a big scale or to revive as it ought to have done, and thus lost its only chance of competing with the silk manufacture of Lyons.

To sum up, at the end of the eighteenth century, although Genoa was no longer that "*merveille de richesse*" which enchanted Louis XII, she had maintained and even increased the number of her inhabitants. In the town itself there were about a hundred thousand, and in the whole republic over half a million. Luxury, if not art, was widespread. But the condition of the poorer classes had been precarious enough during this period of semi-prosperity. The Bank of St. George, the financial organ of the oligarchy, opposed any redemption of the public debt, and thus perpetuated the heavy indirect taxation which crushed the mass of consumers. When it created markets, when it constructed the "free port" at its own expense, and when it subsidised the short-lived India Company (1653), it only gave back to the state some of the money which it had taken and distributed among the creditors. The democratic revolution of 1797 did well to abolish its usurious privileges. The dominant plutocracy oppressed the people still further by manipulating the food supply. The authorities who supplied the town with salt, corn, meat, oil and wine sold these articles at enormous profits and kept prices so high that most of the working class could hardly buy them. The result was that the mass of the people were so poor and in such misery that the whole organisation of society was affected, and the rich were obliged to organise charitable institutions (1539) and to increase private generosity in order that they might enjoy their wealth in peace.

§ 3. Tuscany.

The Medici and the house of Lorraine; the free port of Leghorn; slow
decline of the *arti*; revival of agriculture.

At the end of the fifteenth century Florence was a republic
only in name. By the power of money Cosmo dei Medici
(1434-1468) had established a dynasty there, and his successors, Piero, Lorenzo and Juliano, had ruled as masters.
The short-lived theocracy of Savonarola (1494-1498) only
delayed the final triumph of this ambitious family. In 1513
they again seized the power, and in 1532, when the city
succumbed to the coalition of the Emperor and the Pope,
Alessandro dei Medici was proclaimed hereditary duke. At
the price of their liberty the Florentines were at least to
know the advantages of peace. Pisa, after the capitulation of
1509, had definitely submitted, and later Sienna did the same,
and in the end these sovereign cities were reconciled under
the domination of the same princes within a united Tuscany.
Happier than the rest, this region of Italy ceased to be a
battle-ground for foreign armies. It remains to be seen
whether this long period of peaceful absolutism was favourable to the economic activity of the country. In any case,
it must be noted that towards the middle of the eighteenth
century Tuscany had the good fortune to undergo a change
of masters. After 1737 the house of Lorraine succeeded and
substituted for the oppressive routine of the Medici a boldly
reforming and almost revolutionary policy.

A rich state can keep its financial power for some time
even when it is declining. Throughout the Middle Ages so
much wealth had accumulated in the city that banking had
naturally become a fundamental activity, and remained so
even when industrial production was becoming exhausted.
It was, indeed, a family of bankers who had conquered
supreme power. Although under the domination of Lorenzo
the Magnificent there still existed thirty banks in Florence,
as early as the time of Cosimo so much financial business had
become concentrated in the hands of the Medici that they
had been able not only to buy up a great part of the land of
the republic, but also to act as bankers to popes and kings.
A great future had then seemed to open to Florentine
financial enterprises, but unfortunately absolutism has its

dangers even when exercised by a financier. Lorenzo had so confused his own business with state business that when he had involved his private fortune in unfortunate speculations it was the state which went bankrupt to save its " prince "; the interest on the public debt was reduced, dowries deposited in the *monti* were confiscated, even the coinage was debased. The credit of Florence never recovered, and foreign banks, often founded by Florentines or in imitation of them, killed the Florentine banking business by their competition.

Nor did the establishment of a strong and stable power at once turn to the advantage of internal trade. For a long time the Medici reserved to themselves the most profitable monopolies, such as that of corn, and until 1737 there were Customs duties even between town and town. For a long time, moreover, private individuals were forbidden to buy anything in order to sell it again, and had to use the expensive agency of official brokers; and it was with difficulty that the shopkeepers obtained permission to keep their doors open during the fifty holidays which had been added to the fifty-two Sundays. Tuscany was, indeed, given a mercantile marine, but it was entirely in the hands of the duke. Mediterranean trade had already been attacked by the Turkish invasion and the discovery of the ocean route, and the trade of the Italian cities had suffered from the gradual closing of the great national markets; but in spite of all this the dukes levied heavy taxes on imports and exports. It was only under the Lorraine dynasty that this fiscal policy was wisely moderated. Commercial treaties were renewed, prohibitions were almost entirely abolished and protective duties lowered. In the seventeenth century, however, Leghorn, which had been bought by the republic, was declared a free port. In order to people the town, adventurers had been summoned from all the neighbouring cities. These formed a population which, though rather mixed and turbulent, was full of initiative and had made of this free territory one of the most flourishing places in the Western Mediterranean. Dutch, English and French ships regularly called there, it was an excellent base for operations against the corsairs, and it was the bankers of Leghorn, together with those of Genoa and Lyons, who fixed the rate of exchange in Mediterranean countries.

The prosperity of this free port did not, however, guarantee the industrial activity of the country on whose shores it was situated. The Medici, and the moneyed aristocracy who had triumphed with them, were disdainful of most manufacturing enterprises. They distrusted the workmen, and the workmen themselves, ill-treated and underpaid, had gradually lost their zest for work. At the end of the fifteenth century the *arte della lana* (cloth-workers' gild) still numbered 200 workshops. But production had already been affected by strikes, and an irresistible exodus of workmen, German, Brabançon and native, and later even of some of the masters, hastened the progress of the foreign competition which this weak organisation could not resist. Soon raw material was lacking as well as customers, and when finally England forbade the export of wool the gild received its death-blow.

The prosperity of the *arte della seta* (silk-workers' gild), which was of later growth, lasted longer. The industry was helped by the increase of luxury, and its raw material was assured by the development of mulberry plantations and silkworm nurseries all over Italy. Fugitives from Venice betrayed the secrets of its great rival, and the gold and silver brocades of Florence were sold throughout Europe. But Tours and Lyons soon began to dispute this lucrative monopoly. Moreover, here, too, Florentine labour became so scarce that the masters were reduced to filling their deserted workshops with workmen from Lucca. Tuscan pottery, on the other hand, enjoyed a certain prosperity. The manufacture founded by Francisco dei Medici at Cafaggiolo (1581) carried on the traditions of Majorca, and produced the first porcelain made in Western Europe. The factory set up rather later by the Marchese Ginori also had a brilliant success. And lastly the iron-mines on the Isle of Elba had begun to be more actively worked.

Setting aside these last two industries, together with printing, introduced from Germany, which the double censorship of Church and state was soon to drive into freer countries, and tapestry, which had been introduced from Flanders and which a state factory was trying to naturalise on Florentine soil, it was the gilds which continued to regulate Florentine labour. They were scarcely favourable for increased production. There were very few of them which did not try to discourage inventors, and most of them insisted on the strict maintenance of a meticulous and antiquated technique of work. It is not they but the government which must be credited with having founded some big factories and the first professional schools.[1] The gilds spent their energies on empty quarrels. No one was allowed to exercise two crafts, silk merchants were forbidden to sell linen or woollen stuffs, the pork butcher was not allowed to encroach on the ordinary butcher by selling fresh pork, and the second-hand clothes dealer was not allowed to sell new clothes. The struggle between the gilds of Florence and those of the subject cities was very bitter, until finally the artisans of Sienna, Pistoia and Arezzo gained the same right to work as was enjoyed by the Florentines. Longer still was the conflict between the towns and their suburbs. It was only in 1738 that the humble villagers of the duchy were allowed to enter the noble profession of cloth-making without formal registration. Attacked by numerous competitors, bending under the weight of taxes and of the sumptuary expenses which they could not reduce, even finding difficulty in collecting the subscriptions of their members, the old *arti* went to their ruin.

We must, however, distinguish between the two types of *arti* which in the course of economic evolution had become separate from and even opposed to each other. In the fifteenth century every pretext had been used to reduce the *Arti Minori* to powerlessness and poverty. In the provision trade a more or less sincere care for the public food supply and a real desire to keep down the price of the workers' food led to the fixing of low prices. Small shopkeepers were forbidden to set up their stalls in the street, wool-beaters to disturb the silence of the night, innkeepers to open their houses near churches. In some of these small crafts all formalities of entrance were officially abolished, and they were all left at the mercy of domestic competition. The coming of the Medici marked their fall. By arbitrary grouping their numbers were reduced from fourteen to five, and later to two, and these organisations were henceforth only administrative bodies void of all social reality.

[1] In 1563 Cosimo founded a school of design, anticipating by two hundred years the " Leopoldine " schools (1778).

The position of the *Arti Maggiori* was very different. Doubtless they had lost all political influence, their professional jurisdiction was restricted, their accounts were controlled, and the grand duke sometimes interfered even in the appointment of masters. Gradually, however, the masters became an hereditary caste, and in these little aristocracies authority was vested in the hands of officers appointed by his serene highness. These narrow oligarchies obtained from the duke all the powers necessary to keep the workers in the perpetual submission which was henceforth their lot. Under pain of a fine, a workman was forbidden to leave his master without paying his debts, and masters were forbidden to hire workmen so indebted. Under pain of a public flogging, a workman was forbidden to leave his workshop without finishing his work, and no one must be hired without a certificate (1595 to 1602). The government only intervened on behalf of the workers when the masters seriously abused their advantages, as, for instance, when they half starved the workers in order to economise. Only a few of the big manufacturers understood that the best way of keeping their workmen was to make them comfortable, and they founded friendly societies for their staffs. The gilds, however, still performed pious works and administered charitable institutions. It was their boast that they fulfilled these humane duties to the end, although their economic functions were over. In 1770, anticipating the reform which Turgot tried to effect in France, the Grand Duke Leopold I, at the suggestion of his counsellors Pompeo Neri and Tavanti, abolished all entry fees into the gilds, instituted freedom of trade and of industry, and suppressed the old commercial tribunals. This was, in effect, to put an end to the gild régime.

Strangely enough, the decline of industry in Florence brought about the recovery of Tuscan agriculture. In pursuit of their fortunes the city merchants had not scrupled to exhaust the country districts, and had impoverished and depopulated them by their oppressive exploitation. The dukes were wiser. They prohibited the indiscriminate disafforestation of the mountain districts, ordered plantations of olives, mulberries and vines (in Chianti), and began to drain the Valley of Chiana. But for 200 years their efforts bore no fruit, because they were opposed by institutions which the dukes dared not reform. The policy of food control was applied throughout the duchy and was enough to discourage agriculture. The state proclaimed itself sole purchaser of corn, oil and wine. It bóught them at whatever price it liked, for it could always bring prices down by allowing foreign competition, and since it had to sell at a moderate price in order to secure public tranquillity, it necessarily bought at a low price. The cultivator, therefore, was sure never to gain and often to lose on the transaction. Certain blundering taxes like that on salt, which in the Sienna district made stock-farming impossible, the heaviness of feudal dues and the extension of mortmain lands were still further obstacles to the re-establishment of rural prosperity. Some of the peasants were reduced to seeking a living else-where, in the city workshops or even in begging. The rest continued to vegetate in the position of *métayers* on holdings which were almost hereditary.

Only towards the middle of the eighteenth century was there any decisive improvement. The city patricians returned to the land at last and brought with them the two things which it most needed—capital and knowledge. Not only was a botanical garden made in Florence, but in 1753 the society of the *Georgofili* was founded, " a real agricul-tural academy, whose head was the leading ecclesiastic and whose members were the leading nobles of Tuscany."[1] This prepared the way for the triumph of the new agriculture. Bolder rulers pursued on a much larger scale the drainage schemes so feebly begun, and even attacked the salt-marshes. More important still, by secularising a number of eccle-siastical estates and by restricting the use of trusts and entails, they strove to give a greater fluidity to landed property, and at the same time they freed it from seigniorial and communal bonds by restricting hunting and fishing rights and abolishing common pasture rights. The culti-vators benefited by an important reduction in their rents, for the proportion of their harvest which they had to give to the lord was reduced from a half to a third ; and the simplification and equalisation of taxes also turned to their

[1] See *Mouvement physiocratique en France*, vol. i, p. 36, and *Histoire du travail à Florence*, Renard, vol. ii.

advantage. Proprietors and *métayers* alike profited by the
disappearance of state monopolies and by the freedom
granted to the home and even to the foreign trade in provisions (1767).[1] A new era seemed to be opening for Tuscan
agriculture.[2]

§ 4. The Papal States.

There is little to say about the Papal States from our
point of view. Yet they were vast in extent and had the
advantage of stretching from sea to sea. Their central
position and the priestly character of their ruler sheltered
them from invasion for more than 200 years. Nor did they
lack natural resources, for they could supply Venice and
Genoa with corn, and the Legations produced an abundance
of flax and hemp.

But Rome no longer attracted a stream of gold and
pilgrims from the whole of the Christian world. She had
lost the homage and the offerings of Northern Europe.
Nevertheless, after the Catholic restoration, of which the
Council of Trent was the most powerful agent, the Papacy
still benefited by the money which came from the regions
which remained faithful to the Holy See. This formed the
most certain part of the Papal income, and there was nothing
to prevent the profitable investment of such capital in banking business. From his own dominions the Pope could at any
rate rely upon Customs dues, which served as a security
when he borrowed money. Thus art-loving Popes like
Leo X, and ambitious and energetic Popes like Julius II
and Sixtus V, transformed the Eternal City, adorning it with
fine monuments, and giving it splendid aqueducts and beautiful fountains, while they successfully cleared their territory
of the bandits who infested it, and even tried to extend its
boundaries at the expense of neighbouring states. The only
thing which none of them thought of doing was to increase
the value of the land. At the end of the eighteenth century
it could be said that the administration of the Catholic Cross
was no better than that of the Turkish Crescent.

Even at the beginning of the sixteenth century the *Agro*

[1] The regulation of the food trade was definitely abolished in 1775.
[2] But in 1757 the agricultural production of Tuscany was hardly
equal to a third of her industrial production.

Romano was almost depopulated. The temptation for the great landowners to increase the number of their sheep was too strong to resist, and the government trusted to foreign supplies to make up the deficit of corn.[1] There was no systematic eviction, but by the natural interplay of causes analogous to those which, towards the end of the old republic, had led to the extension of *latifundia*, sheep-farming again expelled agriculture. The district round Rome began to take on that gloomy deserted aspect which even to-day strikes the traveller with astonishment and dismay. Of what use, then, was the great enterprise of draining the Pontine marshes, to which all the Popes, from Leo X and Sixtus V to Pius V, had devoted themselves? Throughout all the states of the church the policy of food control, which was followed invariably until 1802, would alone have been enough to discourage the efforts of the cultivators. The food ministry bought officially, at a price fixed by itself, all the corn which it needed, and people who stood well with the ministry were often enriched by a private licence to export. The ministry taxed even meat and bought all the oil on the market at a low price, selling it again at any price it chose.

There was no industrial middle class except at Bologna. There were not even any flourishing artistic industries except at Faenza and Urbino, where the old *faïences* and potteries, ornamented with mythological designs, still remained famous. And outside the Fair of Sinigaglia, which in the eighteenth century succeeded in attracting a thin stream of the Venetian trade, there was no organised internal trade. Pius VI[2] only with difficulty succeeded in suppressing internal Customs duties.

It seemed as though foreign trade, too, must necessarily succumb beneath the double burden of an oppressive fiscal system and ecclesiastical intolerance. But the Papacy moderated both its religious pretensions and its financial claims in favour of the one good port which it possessed. Paul III (1533-1550), the restorer of the Inquisition and founder of the Congregation of the Index, authorised his subjects of Ancona to trade with all the infidels of the East, Turks and Greeks alike. In the following century liberty of

[1] See Claudio Jannet, *Grandes époques de l'histoire économique*, p. 302.
[2] 1775-1800.

conscience was guaranteed to all Dutch and English sailors staying there, so that the town should lose none of its prosperity. Finally, in 1732 all export duties were abolished, and from that day free Ancona began to surpass fallen Venice. Meanwhile, on the continental frontiers the most active trade was carried on by smugglers.

Thus the Papacy was both a parasite living on the foreigner and a government which paralysed its own subjects.

§ 5. The Kingdom of Naples.

General decadence of agriculture, commerce and industry; depopulation of Apulia; misery of Sicily—Attempts at reform under the Bourbon dynasty.

In this rapid sketch of the Italian states those which we have been considering succeeded, more or less, in maintaining their independence. Tuscany, indeed, did in the end fall to the House of Lorraine, which was closely related to that of Austria. But the kingdoms of Naples and Milan fell under the domination of Spain at the very beginning of modern times, and more than 300 years elapsed before these two countries, after several changes of masters, recovered their lost liberty in the bosom of a free Italy.

At the time of the Italian wars the kingdom of the Two Sicilies had already been governed for nearly 200 years by princes of the House of Aragon, and its conquest by Ferdinand the Catholic made South Italy an integral part of the Spanish Empire. After a short interval (1713-1735), when it passed from the Madrid Hapsburgs to the Viennese Hapsburgs, this vast territory fell again into the hands of the Spanish Bourbons.

The kingdom consisted partly of steep and barren mountain districts and partly of rich plains naturally fitted for agricultural development. Indeed, in the fifteenth century there were few provinces in Italy where cultivation was so intensive as in the immediate environs of Naples and in the rich *Terra di Lavoro*, which the Viceroy Peter of Toledo (1532-1553) succeeded in making healthy. On the other side of the Apennines, however, the Plains of Tavolieri, to the north of Foggia, suffered from an excessive extension of sheep-farming. From the end of the Roman Empire the major part of these fertile lands, fifty miles in length and from three to five miles wide, had been state property, and successive governments had always forbidden the occupants to devote more than a fifth of their farms to agriculture.[1] This extraordinary conduct on the part of a landowner is explained by the importance of the tolls collected when the sheep changed their pastures. These tolls amounted to 200,000 ducats a year, and when the kingdom was shared between Louis XII and Ferdinand of Aragon the division of this revenue was the first cause of quarrel between them.

To the inveterate abuses of the royal fiscal system were added those of feudal oppression. The barons were in agreement with the government on the question of encouraging sheep-farming. In 1467 they had obtained privileges like those of the Castilian *mesta*, and all Apulia was henceforth brought under the system of common pasture. Thus in the course of the sixteenth century the number of sheep increased from 600,000 to the almost incredible figure of 5,000,000.[2] Peasant proprietors, whose corn was henceforth eaten in the blade by the flocks, sold their land cheaply. *Métayers* and tenants were more or less brutally evicted. Uprooted from the land and reduced to the condition of a mere proletariat, they took refuge in the mountains to escape the valley scourge of malaria. There they settled in big villages, where their descendants remain to this day, and scraped a wretched living from the few days' labour which neighbouring farms still had to offer them. At the end of the eighteenth century, although their ranks had been thinned by the general depopulation, there was so much waste-land that they could only find work for four months in the year, and even in the height of the season there was such competition among them that their wages were rarely more than tenpence a day.[3]

Moreover, the nobles, who were for the most part of foreign origin, in order to keep themselves in luxury, did not hesitate to impose scandalous monopolies on rural trade, and these still further hampered the progress of agriculture and made life difficult for the country-folk. Profiting by the insecurity which reigned in the country as a result of their

[1] See Vidal de la Blache, *États et nations de l'Europe*, p. 523.
[2] See Jannet, *op. cit.*
[3] See Kovalevski, *op. cit.*, p. 85.

policy, the nobles forced merchants to buy expensive safe-conducts for every flock they took from market to market, at so much a head. On the roads they left only a small number of inns which they rented to tenants, who had to compensate themselves for their high rents and risks by charging high prices to their forced customers. Finally they bought up all the products of the country and all foreign imports, in order to buy the one at the lowest and to resell the other at the highest price possible. From the reign of Charles V onwards many of the peasants, exasperated by this ingenious system of extortions, preferred to flee to the mountains, where they led the freer and scarcely more precarious life of brigands.

The merchants of the towns were hardly more fortunate. Although they suffered only indirectly from feudal exactions, they were the easiest victims of royal taxation. Peter of Toledo saved them from the competition of the Jews, who thought to find a refuge in Naples when they were expelled from Spain, and he instituted *Monts-de-Piété* to lower the rate of interest. But this help was useless, and they could never prosper so long as all goods imported and exported were subject to exorbitant duties. Moreover, the coinage was constantly fluctuating. At any moment for any purpose—to help to pay the expenses of a war or to make a viceroy's fortune—the government might vary the real value of money. It is hardly surprising that in 1648 Masaniello, a simple fisherman, succeeded in raising the people of Naples in revolt.

Industry had found a wise protector in Ferdinand the Catholic. This king, one of the wisest Spain has ever known, set himself to encourage the silk industry. An adroit combination of tariffs protected it from foreign competition, workmen from Venice brought with them the secret of gold brocades, and half the population of Naples found lucrative employment in this industry. But the demands of taxation and arbitrary regulations soon interrupted this brilliant prosperity. The government wished to keep this source of wealth in the capital and forbade workmen to set up their workshops in the country (1647). Only the merchants and manufacturers " of the royal Customs of Naples " were allowed to buy the cocoons. A little later (1685) all technical improvements were absolutely forbidden. Cotton spinning and

weaving were in danger at the same time and for the same
reasons.   Genoese and Catalan merchants supplied the
kingdom, and were even given monopolies in return for
money.   The Neapolitan aristocracy made no protest, for
they had learnt from the Spanish aristocracy a supreme disdain for all that concerned manufacture or trade.

Sicily, which suffered from a harsher and if possible more
inept régime, presents an even gloomier picture of decay.
There, too, although the export of sulphur was to a certain
extent important, agriculture was the main resource, and
there, too, administrative blunders threatened to exhaust
it.   This island was fitted by its climate to furnish a large
part of the European supplies of sugar, cotton, rice and silk,
and in these exotic products only the southern provinces of
Spain had the same title to compete with the East.   But
mulberries spread all over Italy and a large part of France,
Lombardy was covered with rice-fields, and the West Indies
with plantations.   The ancient Trinacria might at least have
remained one of the granaries of the Mediterranean, but the
Spanish government controlled the corn trade, decided what
quantity should be exported, and fixed the prices.   Its
intentions may have been admirable, but the results were
disastrous.   The corn-lands gradually shrank in size, and in
some years the isle of plenty became the isle of famine, where
the wretched peasants rose in revolt, demanding bread.
Industry was of necessity even more feeble, for Sicily could
not compete with Tuscany, Venice, Catalonia or Liguria in
fine cloths or silk goods.   In good years she sent her corn to
them and they sent in return the products of their manufactures.

Nothing less than a change of dynasty was necessary to
shake this lethargy from the whole kingdom.   The Bourbons
were scarcely installed upon the throne of Naples than they
had the wisdom to entrust the government to a reforming
minister who, for the good of the country, was to remain
in power for forty-three years (1735-1777).   Tanucci first
attacked the privileges of the feudal nobility, both lay and
ecclesiastical, and abolished seigniorial jurisdiction at the
same time as the tithe.   Then, in order to increase both the
wealth and the population of the country, he declared war
on the monasteries, the refuge of idle celibates, and only

allowed ten ordinations to every thousand people. He encouraged trade by recalling the Jews. To revive agriculture he suppressed the food administration and raised the prohibition of corn cultivation in Apulia. He encouraged clearings and facilitated the flow of capital to the land by instituting the registration of mortgages. But he provoked much ill-will by his bold innovations, and his work did not survive him in its entirety. The kingdom had still to suffer many misfortunes under a succession of unworthy rulers.

§ 6. The Milanese.

Short life of luxury trades; introduction of new crops; disastrous influence of the Spanish administration—Work of recovery inaugurated by the Austrian administration which succeeded it.

The modern history of the Milanese may be summed up as nearly two hundred years of Spanish domination (1526-1713) and nearly a hundred years of Austrian domination (1713-1797); a long period of decadence followed by an attempt to recover from it.

In the domain of the Visconti and the Sforza, whence sprang the "Lombards," the great business men of the Middle Ages, so much money had been amassed that Milan ought to have remained one of the financial centres of Europe, in spite of incessant wars and foreign conquest. But the Spanish administration would have killed any prosperity, for its greed was insatiable. It was not Madrid itself that drained this wealth; the New World sufficed for its needs. But the military chest demanded by the necessities of Spanish policy in England had to be filled incessantly. Moreover, huge sums were necessary to support the mad luxury of the Milanese Court, and of the magistrates and Castilian ministers, of whom it was said: "In Sicily they nibble, in Naples they eat, but in Milan they devour." The perpetual distress of the Treasury justified all demands. Merchants were asked for loans, which were repaid if circumstances permitted. Private banks, in which individuals had thought it safe to deposit their money, were not safe from the claims of this imperious and needy despotism. And as a crowning scandal the state was officially proclaimed bankrupt in 1671. The nobility, either from pride or from prudence, had taken their money out of commerce and invested it in land, and entails and trusts immobilised most of the big fortunes unless they were dissipated by extravagance.

Until the end of the sixteenth century, however, the rate of interest remained low, and the spirit of enterprise still lived, at any rate among the middle classes, for industry still prospered. It was even encouraged by the prevailing luxury; at Milan there were manufactures of arms, of gold and silver wares and glass, while at Como there were manufactures of fine cloth, silks, and gold brocade. These exquisite and magnificent articles spread the renown of Milanese artisans throughout the West. The capital was the centre of a wealthy society which passed its time in perpetual fêtes, fencing, dancing and going to the opera. The young nobles of Europe went there to be initiated into the ways of polite society. The carnival of Milan rivalled that of Venice. There was a demand for the industrial arts; the stringed instrument-makers of Cremona, the Amati, the two Guamari and Stradivarius, were renowned throughout the neighbour-hood.

But soon these traditions of work were overcome by inertia. Men no longer wanted to work; they did not even trouble to make a living. Moreover, new competition made the struggle more difficult, for in the seventeenth century English cloths began to penetrate into Lombardy. The government seemed to delight in discouraging the last efforts of industry. Taxes of all sorts were redoubled, and an unfortunate tax on indigo sufficed to kill the dye-works. Within eight years, from 1616 to 1624, Milan lost 24,000 workmen, and the number of cloth workshops dropped from seventy to fifteen. In 1715 only five remained. This inertia, which spread to all industries, reacted so cruelly on the condition of the workers that the government tried to force the masters by heavy penalties to provide work for them as usual (1654). But this was useless when industry was dead.

The country was so rich in natural resources, and during the Middle Ages had been so well cultivated, that it had been justly called the "Garden of Europe." On the eve of the wars which were to rob Milan both of its independence and of its fertility the Sforza princes had almost finished their work of improvement on the rich alluvial plains, where only water

10

was lacking. The Martesana Canal, the plans of which are said to have been made by Leonardo da Vinci, had joined the plains round the capital to the Adda, as already the *Naviglio Grande* had joined them to Ticino, and, passing through the city itself, the *Naviglio Interno* linked together these two great arteries of irrigation and trade.[1] For some years it seemed as though all the revolutions which had taken place could but result in a greater variety of production in this favoured district. The green foliage of mulberry-trees imported from the Levant continued to spread its shade along the hill-slopes, while on the damp and fertile plains Indian corn (then called Turkish corn, for it was imported from America by way of the Levant) prospered. This cereal by its novelty escaped both the tithe and the demands of the feudal lord, for it was mentioned in no contract between landlord and tenant, whether the latter paid in money or in kind, and it therefore spread with astonishing rapidity. Everywhere it took the place of barley and other small grains and even encroached on the wheat-fields. Finally, rice, another crop of distant origin which had been carried from South to North Italy in the preceding century, spread rapidly over the flood-lands of Lower Milan.

But then exorbitant taxes chilled the ardour of cultivators and landowners. It was useless to labour and spend money when the total revenue of the land did not equal the amount of taxes imposed on it. Not only did direct taxation eat up agricultural capital before it could be applied to the land, but indirect taxes, and especially the strict regulation of the corn trade, robbed the farmer of all hope of obtaining a profitable market for his produce. All corn merchants were subject to an inquisition which ruined their business, and the export of grain was forbidden. In 1588, on the pretext of persuading the people to weave the product of their cocoons themselves, the export of raw silk was forbidden. The only result was to injure the silkworm nurseries. The government even went so far as to restrict cattle-breeding, lest it should put up the price of fodder destined for His Majesty's stables. It is not to be wondered at if fields once carefully tended fell back into the waste, if in many districts of this land, so blessed by Nature, there was a shortage of food, which the

---

[1] See Vidal de la Blache., *op. cit.*, p. 433.

bad repair in which the roads were kept often turned to famine. Small wonder, too, if lands that had been conquered from the floods were allowed to relapse.

This decadence ceased with the Spanish domination. But the country had to wait for the end of the great wars which devastated Lombardy until the middle of the eighteenth century, before it felt the effect of the reforms accomplished by its Austrian masters. It was then that the work of regeneration inaugurated by Count Firmiani[1] had full scope and all sources of life and wealth were revived. The foundation of a *Monte* for silk—that is to say, of a fund which allowed proprietors of silkworm nurseries to obtain advances on reasonable terms—spared them the ruinous necessity of selling their harvest in a hurry at a poor price. The coinage was restored and the thalers of Maria Theresa (1777) were accepted in all European markets and in the East as worth more than the old ducats. Industry revived, especially at Como. A new land survey led to the simplification of the financial system ; taxation was more equally distributed over the different classes of society, and the suppression of the system of farming the taxes put an end to many old abuses. The state found money to undertake the interrupted work of irrigation, and the peasants, already relieved by the equalisation of taxes, worked with a will to increase their harvests, now that there was nothing to check their sales. The old prosperity did not, indeed, entirely return, but it was a good sign that between 1749 and 1770 the population of the duchy increased by more than a quarter.[2]

§ 7. Piedmont.

Piedmont was only half Italian, for it was united to Savoy, and it has played a more important part in the diplomacy and wars of Europe than in economic history. It owed its political importance to its position as a gateway to the Alps, but the passes which it commanded were not great trade routes, and mountains covered the greater part of the state.

---

[1] He also has the honour of having created in Milan in 1768 a chair of political economy for Beccaria.

[2] It increased from 900,000 to 1,130,000.

Yet agriculture was its chief resource. Although, as in the rest of Italy, serfdom and entails hindered the division of land, it was nevertheless very much divided, at any rate on the plain and the lower mountain slopes, where most of the cultivators were also landowners. The Duke Emmanuel Philibert, having strengthened his absolutism, had emancipated the serfs (1561). Exactly 200 years later King Charles Emmanuel III authorised the commutation of feudal personal services, which in any case were not very heavy. Thus the country was well cultivated, covered with mulberry-trees and vines, which climbed the trees and were trained into arbours. On the other hand, industry was almost non-existent. The competition of Milan and France, both near neighbours, prevented the development of the silk industry, and silkworm breeders sold their raw silk to foreign agents, often at a low price. Only a little cloth of gold and silver was made. At the end of the seventeenth century there was not a single cloth factory in the kingdom, and Turin had 40,000 inhabitants when Montesquieu visited it in 1728 and called it " the most beautiful village in the world." The minute regulations issued to encourage the growth of manufactures seem rather to have checked them. Therefore there was no powerful bourgeoisie. Commoners could only make money in medicine or law, and when they had made their fortunes they hastened to buy titles.

To sum up, the monarchy of Sardinia was not the least prosperous state in the peninsula, nor were the mass of its people (who numbered 1,200,000 at the end of the seventeenth century) the least happy, but it was undoubtedly the most backward in economic development. The mineral wealth of the island which gave it its name remained almost untouched.

§ 8. Conclusion.

A general glance over the economic activity of Italy during modern times shows all the states involved in a common decadence. There were various causes for this important fact.

The first was, of course, the displacement of the centre of commerce. The Mediterranean, in which Italy held so favourable a position, ceased to be the principal theatre of the foreign trade of the West and the high-road of the traffic between Europe and Asia. All the Italian ports shared in this decline, and even the most important of them were henceforth no more than centres of local trade or ports of call. But the chief cause of Italy's profound and incurable weakness was her internal divisions. If she had been united she would not have suffered so cruelly from the effects of the maritime revolution, and would have kept the leading part at least in the Mediterranean trade, which was only relatively unimportant. But even on the distant shores of the Levant it was the ocean powers which triumphed over the obstacles raised by the Turkish conquest and took the first place from Italy.

These divisions were equally fatal to internal trade and reduced it to miserable retail transactions. Everywhere the roads were broken by bogs, harassed by tolls, and infested with brigands. The lack of political concentration was matched by a no less serious lack of economic concentration. In these small uncentralised states the old urban economy survived and there was no room for manufacture on a grand scale within the narrow organisation of the gilds, which here preserved an importance which they had lost elsewhere.

As a crowning misfortune, of all the foreign masters whom divided Italy was condemned to suffer, it was Spain, the harshest and most barren of all, who was finally successful. Moreover, Italian society itself seemed momentarily exhausted by its premature splendour in the last century. Landed capital was tied up in entails and mortmain, financial capital in the paltry operations of usury. There was little work, and there was no eagerness, except perhaps for pleasure, to balance the boredom of semi-idleness, whether in luxury or in poverty.

Finally, it must not be forgotten that in many places men had to struggle against the enmity of Nature itself. Torrential rivers broke their banks and brought marshes and fevers in their train, forced back the sea and made unhealthy deltas, silted up ports and ruined important cities such as Sybaris and Croton had once been. There were earthquakes and volcanoes, like Etna, which in 1669 wiped out Catana and destroyed 90,000 people. To meet these scourges, where it was possible to do so, incessant care and toil were necessary.

The neglect of necessary work by one generation made the
situation more and more difficult for succeeding generations,
and in many places civilisation, discouraged and powerless,
gave up the unequal struggle.

But in spite of poverty and depopulation the economic
genius of the race was not extinguished. Many lost children
of Italy, bankers and contractors, had made fortunes in other
lands; and even in their own country, thanks to the close
relations maintained between artisans and artists, two orders
of workers whom the course of modern economic development
has too often separated, the artistic industries long continued
to flourish. And even Italian agriculture, burdened as it was
with taxes and receiving little help, preserved the memory of
the supremacy it had once held. The jonquils and tuberoses,
of which the Bolognese horticulturists were so proud, paved
the way for the marvels of Dutch gardening. Throughout
the sixteenth century Italian villas served as models for the
nobles and princes of Northern Europe, and the agricultural
science of Lombardy and Tuscany, enriched by the observation of the ancients and by the lessons of long and careful
experience, was far in advance of the times. It was there in
1567 that the essential principle of the rotation of crops was
discovered. And at a time when the expansion of Russia to
the shores of the Black Sea was threatening Italian corn
producers with a new competitor, it was, so to speak, among
them or at their instigation that Vallerius, the famous
Swedish agronomist, published his great work, of which the
title alone is significant: *Agriculturæ fundamenta chemica*
(1775). Moreover, it was the very distress of Italian agriculture which gave rise to those valuable institutions, in which
financial speculation and assistance to the cultivators were
so well united, the *monti frumentarii*. From the seventeenth
century onwards the farmers were helped by these stocks of
grain, which were lent to the cultivator without any security
other than his personal bond, and which he repaid in kind,
both capital and interest, after the next harvest.

Italy lacked unity and strength indeed, but she preserved
her ingenious spirit and her beauty: her soft climate, the
charm of her old towns and her countryside, and the master-
pieces of her artists. In the middle of the eighteenth century
there appeared a new species, the tourist, who was of English

origin. From that time onwards Italy found, as it were, a new industry, and by degrees made a great deal of money out of foreigners who were attracted by the excavations at Pompeii and Herculaneum, which gave the signal for a new classical Renaissance. Modern Italy was destined to benefit widely by the monuments of her glorious past.

BIBLIOGRAPHY

CANTÙ: *Histoire des Italiens.* (1859-62.) Vols. vii and viii.

BROGLIO D'AJANO: *Die Venetianischen Seiden-Weberzünfte.* Stuttgart. (1893.)

KOVALEVSKI : *La fin d'une aristocratie.* (Turin, 1901.)

MOLMENTI : *Venice.* Translated by H. F. Brown. 3 vols. (London, 1907-1908.)

RENARD: *Histoire du Travail à Florence.* 2 vols. (Paris, 1913-1914.)

SIEVEKING: *Studio della Finanza genovese nel mediœvo e en particolare sulla Casa di S. Giorgio.* (Atti della Societa Ligure, vol. 35. 1906-1907.)

CHAPTER VI

SWITZERLAND

Development of cattle-breeding and of industry—City bourgeoisie and rural democracy—The *heimatlosen*.

SWITZERLAND at the beginning of modern times had already passed through her heroic age of political development. The Battles of Grandson and Morat had definitely won for this federation of little democracies and free imperial cities an independence which was to be finally acknowledged by the Treaties of Westphalia. But the age of economic development was just beginning. Safe in their neutrality, this energetic people turned their attention to the works of peace. The country was for the most part unfertile, but it stood at one of the cross-roads of Europe, and this central position enabled it to enter into close relations with many states and to act as intermediary between them. The valleys which lay between these rugged mountains were, moreover, very thickly populated, and the surplus population carried the influence of their little country across the frontiers.

The republic also offered a refuge to exiles and malcontents from neighbouring countries. An important place must be given to these refugees from France, England, Italy and Germany, the victims of religious intolerance or of political persecution, who came to Switzerland in search of the right to live in freedom, but brought with them in return their skill, their strength of character, their capital, and often some new industry such as tanning to Lausanne, clock-making to Geneva, and the ribbon manufacture to Basle.

It was, as we shall see, the progress of foreign relations which gradually transformed the economy of Switzerland.

As the Swiss nation grew it could not hope to live entirely on the produce of its own soil. The dampness and harshness of the climate forced farmers to give a far larger part of their land to breeding than to agriculture strictly so called. It was therefore natural that the Swiss should become exporters of cattle. Every year, indeed, saw an increase in the number of cattle which crossed the passes of the Alps or the Jura or simply went down the Rhine to the Fairs of Piedmont, Lombardy, Franche-Comté and Alsace. The lack of winter fodder alone made this trade necessary. The Swiss plateau was equally abundant in horses. It was from these peaceful pasture-lands that, at the beginning of every war, their powerful neighbours bought their remounts; and the service of carriages along the great international roads, like the Gothard, which crossed the country, always demanded a large number of draught animals. Moreover, a pastoral industry had grown up, of which the products were already famous. In the eighteenth century cheeses from Emmenthal and Gruyère were sent, not only to France and Italy, but even to the Levant and to Egypt.

But the scarcity of food production had to be balanced by the work of artisans and the resources of industrial exports. Berne manufactured cloth. St. Gall produced fabrics made of flax and hemp, and later muslins and embroideries, the immense success of which was not checked by French prohibitions. By way of the Rhine they reached Holland, and thence penetrated into every country. The leisure left by a pastoral or forest economy and the enforced inactivity of a long winter contributed to develop, in the heart of the mountains, industries which produced articles to pay for the corn bought in South Germany and Austria. And the more the industrial population grew, the more this traffic developed.

Basle, Zurich and Geneva thus became the natural markets between France, Germany and Italy, and financial business developed rapidly. In the sixteenth century Calvin's city was open to Frankfort Jews as well as to Italian business men. Two hundred years later the Genevese were called "the kings of credit," and the capital which they had invested in the public funds of France amounted to 10,000,000 francs. Indeed, the last financial minister under the old French monarchy was himself a Genevese banker, Necker. Fribourg itself profited by this financial expansion. Although internal trade, in spite of numerous tolls and duties, began to increase, and new roads were made on the model of the Hauenstein Road between Soleure and Basle, built at the time of the Renaissance, Switzerland owed her new prosperity chiefly to her international relations, the influence of which was felt throughout her economic life.

At the beginning of the modern era the exploitation of the iron-mines of Valais and the salt-mines of Bex had already begun, and there were several forges in the bishopric of Basle. But the textile industries were not very prosperous. Cloth-making was in a very feeble state at Berne, and the efforts of English refugees to re-establish it at Aarau and Zurich were unsuccessful. But in the sixteenth century some Italian artisans introduced silk weaving and dyeing on the banks of the Limmat, and later spinning was established at Schwytz, Glaris and Engelberg, while the manufacture of velvet brought wealth to Berne and Basle. Two centuries later, and almost in the same places, appeared the cotton industry, which at Zurich attained a high degree of perfection. Moreover, the Renaissance had brought about the growth of an entirely new industry in this land of freedom. Basle, where Erasmus went to die, became the capital of the printing world, and its presses, together with those of Geneva (" the Rome of Calvinism "), Lausanne and Yverdon, disputed with Holland the honour and profit of issuing books forbidden in France. An important paper-making works was established at Serrières, near Neuchâtel. A thousand feet higher, on the high plateau of the Jura, another industry, watch-making, had developed from winter idleness and the ingenuity of the mountain folk. As early as the sixteenth century watch-making had been introduced into Geneva by refugees from France or Italy, but the first watch made in the Valley of Locle and Chaux-de-Fonds dates from 1679. A century later the annual production of gold and silver watches in this distant canton rose to 40,000.

It is true that in spite of this high figure of production the industry was still entirely manual and domestic. Similarly the 40,000 persons engaged on embroidery at the end of the eighteenth century worked only with their hands and in their own homes. Nevertheless, the progress of the textile industries had led to the formation in the chief towns of big workshops, if not of big factories, and this implied a certain concentration of capital. The old gilds played a considerable part at the time of the Reformation, and they remained in possession of the town governments. They formed the skeleton of those increasingly narrow and exclusive bourgeois oligarchies which held in submission not only the bulk of the town population, but also the country people in the surrounding districts. At the beginning of the eighteenth century the country town of Winterthur began to manufacture linen and even silk, in addition to steel. Zurich at once forbade all places in the canton to manufacture silks or linen (except unbleached), and they were only to sell their products to merchants of Zurich. Gradually, however, breaches were made in the monopoly of these municipal aristocracies. In 1749 Basle allowed a limited number of tanners to set up outside the walls on payment of a duty to the urban masters.[1] To ward off the dangers of unemployment, lace-making was encouraged in the country districts, and a fund was created from the contributions of masters and men to relieve the unemployed. Soon weaving spread into the country districts of Emmenthal and Argovia; but many of these country weavers were no doubt working at the orders of members of the old gilds.

Swiss agriculture, as we have shown, was characterised by the predominance of stock-farming. This specialisation was imposed by natural conditions and was accentuated by the development of foreign commerce, so that in 1800, according to a contemporary opinion, " an epidemic among the cattle would have been a greater national misfortune than an epidemic among the people."[2] In the sixteenth century there was still a good deal of land under the plough, for arable land as well as pasture had profited by drainage schemes and by the division of the common lands. But from that time onwards many fields had been converted into meadows or sometimes into vineyards. Vine-growing spread round Schaffhausen and on the banks of Lake Leman and the Lake of Neuchâtel, and was constantly improving in these privileged districts where the climate was suitable.

It was only towards the middle of the eighteenth century that decisive progress was made in rural economy as a whole.

[1] See Vuillemin, *Histoire de la confédération suisse*, vol. ii, pp. 244-262.

[2] Quoted by Rappard, *L'agriculture suisse à la fin de l'Ancien Régime*, p. 39.

In Switzerland, as in England, this progress began with the return to Nature. Rousseau, though not the originator, was the most powerful agent of this movement, which so moved men's souls. His eloquent descriptions made them, for the first time, know and love the lakes, woods and meadows, the green retreats and paradises, and this middle region of the Alps, where the mountains become gentle turf-clad slopes. And this new-born love for the beauty of the country had a double economic effect.

In the first place, it attracted to the Alps many travellers, brilliant birds of passage who could not but leave some of their precious feathers in the hands of the innkeepers. Mountains had long inspired fear and a sort of sacred horror. Now they began to appear terribly beautiful, tragically splendid. They were explored, described and painted. They attracted a stream of curiosity, of sympathy and of visitors which was never to stop again, and which was for Switzerland a river of gold.

Moreover, the simple life and patriarchal customs suddenly became the fashion. *La Nouvelle Héloïse* was read again and again for the pictures which its author loved to give of the rustic pleasures of the vintage or hemp-cutting on a Vaudois farm. The Feast of the Vine-growers at Vevey, which had for ages been a little gild festival like hundreds of others, now took on an entirely new splendour.[1]

This interest in country life naturally had its effect on agriculture. Up till that time the new methods of ploughing used in Flanders had scarcely been adopted in the country. But with the foundation of the Natural Sciences Society at Zurich in 1747 and the Economic Society at Berne in 1759 a whole new science of agriculture developed. Better methods of forestry, of irrigation and of manuring were learnt. The use of mineral manures, such as marl or charred turf, became general, and town refuse was also used. This artificial fertilisation of the ground allowed the substitution of the triennial for the biennial rotation in many places. The introduction of clover and lucerne finally ousted the fallow year, for they secured the perpetual regeneration of the soil by a rotation

---

[1] See Renard, *L'influence de la Suisse romande sur la France* (Recueil inaugural de l'Université de Lausanne, 1892), and the official handbook of the feast of the vine-growers (1889 and 1905, *Notice historique*).

of appropriate crops, and at the same time provided new resources for intensive breeding. The introduction of the potato was a remedy for insufficient harvests. It was imported from Ireland in 1697 and spread quickly, especially during the second half of the eighteenth century, when scarcity of food, which became more marked as the population increased, made the government decide to encourage its cultivation near the towns by exempting it from tithes, a concession which was sometimes wrested from it by peasant revolts. It was, indeed, taxation which opposed the progress of agriculture, for while movable wealth enjoyed complete fiscal immunity, landed property was loaded with taxes, and the producer, always threatened with foreign competition, could not transfer to the consumer any part of the burden imposed on him.

We must examine the position of the country-folk rather more closely. Serfdom had finally disappeared. In the sixteenth century in certain districts, such as the bailiwicks of Thurgovia and Argovia and on the lands of the Abbey of St. Gall, families of peasants were still sold like cattle. But the influence of the Reformation, and the spread of humanitarian ideas, together with the hostility of the independent towns to feudal tyranny and the fact that impoverished nobles found it profitable to convert their hateful rights into money, set a term to this servitude. Even the forced labour services were made lighter.

Not only did the cultivators win personal freedom, but most of them gained the unquestioned ownership of the land they worked. Only that part of the country which lay between 500 and 1,000 feet up was dominated by big private landowners, who went in for intensive breeding. There the cheese industry was concentrated, and either the produce of the flocks was brought up in advance as a speculation by big exporters, or the village communities supported co-operative cheese-making establishments on their own account and sold their produce. Higher up the mountains the extensive system of breeding was followed, and here it was rare to find the Alpine pastures owned by the rich farmers of the plains. The mountain democracies had almost always kept them in undivided possession. Pastures which were covered with snow for seven or eight months in the year, and forests

which served the villages as ramparts against avalanches,
could only be exploited collectively, and thus it is that even
in our own times a relic of the system of communal property,
known as the *allmend*, still remains on the mountains. In
the lowest part of the agricultural zone, big and even
moderate sized estates were few, although their owners took
most of the profit of the common lands. The old landed
aristocracy had long been dispossessed by the towns, which
had shared the land among their inhabitants. The custom
of dividing estates equally among heirs had carried this
parcelling out of the land to extremes, and, in industrial
districts particularly, many holdings were not more than
three acres.

But these small proprietors bore very heavy burdens.
During the Thirty Years' War many of the inhabitants of
the devastated countries had fled to this peaceful refuge.
The sharp rise in the prices of provisions and land which
resulted from this influx had awakened in the peasants a
taste for luxury, and when the refugees had gone they had
been obliged to mortgage their lands in order to support
their new way of life. Later the necessity of improving their
equipment and the facilities offered by the low rate of interest
had led many of them to burden their land still more. On
the other hand, the city oligarchies, heirs of the old nobles,
levied many heavy taxes on them. In addition to the *lods*
which constituted a sort of tax on the transfer of land, they
made them pay a fixed rent, which represented either an
acknowledgment of the original concession of the land or a
payment for certain works of public utility, and also a proportional tithe, equivalent to a third or a quarter of their nett
produce, and this was levied on all kinds of produce indiscriminately.

Lastly, below the city bourgeoisie and these small rural
democracies there was a sort of proletariat, half urban and
half rural, half native and half foreign. Local egoism, excited
either by religious suspicions or by the pride of the wealthy
burghers, had divided the free and equal citizens of old
Switzerland into a number of classes, the lowest of which
had been reduced to extreme poverty. In the sixteenth
century it had been thought necessary to forbid the
marriages of these victims of municipal exclusiveness. Each

commune had been forced to feed its own poor, to keep them in their legal domiciles and to institute systems of official charity. When there was no other means of getting rid of the beggars who besieged their houses or wandered in bands about the roads and forests, the wealthy even organised hunting parties against these wretched *heimatlosen* (homeless ones). In the seventeenth century the disbanding of the armies after the Thirty Years' War led to the recrudescence of these two scourges, vagabondage and pauperism, and even at the end of the eighteenth century neither had completely disappeared. Battues were still organised against wanderers, and in 1768 it was found easy to recruit a company of these unfortunates, who were quite ready to leave their inhospitable fatherland for the distant solitudes of Sierra Morena. The custom of hiring out her most robust sons to foreign kings as mercenary soldiers had become established in Switzerland. The country was ripe for the changes brought about by the French Revolution.

BIBLIOGRAPHY

DAGUET: *Histoire de la confédération suisse,* vol. ii. 2 vols. (Geneva, 1879.)

VUILLEMIN: *Histoire de la confédération suisse,* vol. ii. 2 vols. (Lausanne, 1881.)

RAPPARD: *Le facteur économique dans l'avènement de la démocratie moderne en Suisse,* vol. i. (Geneva, 1912.)

CHAPTER VII

GERMANY AND AUSTRIA-HUNGARY

THE political evolution of Germany during our period passed through four phases.

It began with the end of a period of brilliant prosperity. Then, as a result of the religious wars, which were dominated first by questions of religion and later by questions of interest, a profound separation grew up between the North, where the Reformation triumphed, and the South, where the Rhine remained, according to a contemporary expression which might also be applied to the Danube, " the street of the priests." When peace was re-established by the Treaties of Westphalia in 1648, Germany was exhausted and divided. She was outwardly a splendid body, but in reality all her limbs were at variance, and she had, so to speak, two heads : Austria, which wore the imperial crown, and Prussia, which grew rapidly and soon became a kingdom full of military vigour and ambition.

For nearly a hundred years Germany was reduced to a secondary rank, subject to French influence and overrun by princelings who modelled themselves on Louis XIV. They built little reproductions of Versailles, tried to unify their territories, to increase their power at the expense of their subjects and their territory at the expense of their neighbours, took pleasure in parades and ostentatious ceremonial, and encouraged only luxury trades.

Things remained thus until the middle of the eighteenth century. But then liberal ideas, which had been born in England and popularised and taught by French philosophers, began to spread on the Continent and reached Germany. The wind of reform blew through Europe. The sovereigns did not dream of giving up their absolutism, but they showed a care for the prosperity of their states which did not always evaporate in words. It was the age of enlightened and benevolent despotism; that is to say, of social improvements imposed from above, by the prince and for his profit. The

most usual improvement was to diminish the privileges of
the Church, the extent of its lands and the number of its
convents. The princes also fought against medieval survivals, suppressed certain *corvées*, and tried to introduce,
if not more justice, at any rate more humanity into the
relations between nobles and peasants. They stimulated
economic development, regularised the financial system, dug
canals, made roads, cleared waste-land, instituted manufactures and encouraged trade and the education of the
upper classes. In this way in many places marked progress
took place. Frederick II in Prussia and Joseph II in Austria
represented this movement and worked with equal ardour to
increase their power, their revenues and the wealth of the
nation. The word " nation " can be used of that period, for
there was an awakening in the minds as well as in the energy
of the people. Germany was coming out of her long torpor.

§ 1. Germany from 1500 to 1648.

Short period of commercial and industrial prosperity; misery of the
workmen and the peasants—Devastation and depopulation of the
country during the Thirty Years' War.

At the end of the fifteenth century the persistence of
territorial separatism and the chronic weakness of the
central government had not prevented the German States
from becoming one of the most flourishing regions in
Europe. And for many years it seemed as though this
prosperity, which had been born in the midst of so many
feudal survivals, would only increase as the result of the
changes which were opening a new era in the West.

While the Hanseatic League continued to enjoy an uncontested supremacy in the north seas, German merchants
tightened the bonds which, thanks to the relative easiness of
the pass by the Splügen and the Brenner, connected them
with Venice, the great metropolis of the Mediterranean.
They took thither useful and precious metals, raw materials
such as leather, or manufactured goods, for their industry
was fairly well developed. They brought back spices, sugar,
fine glass and luxurious stuffs. The *Fondaco dei Tedeschi*
(German Warehouse) which they had created on the shores
of the Adriatic had, since its reconstruction in 1505, grown

into a large establishment. It contained warehouses and shops, a hostelry for travellers and private lodgings for the merchants, who sometimes numbered as many as a hundred. Numerous branches, founded at Strasbourg, Cologne, Lubeck, Nuremberg and Augsburg, fed the activity of the main establishment. As soon as the new route to the Indies had been discovered, merchants from the two last-named towns installed themselves at Lisbon, and German ships accompanied the great expedition directed by Francisco de Almeïda in 1505.[1] But only a few of the business houses which had flourished on the Italian trade found themselves able to take part in the trade of this new market. The journey through France and Spain was longer and more costly than that through the passes of the Central Alps. Only the great companies were rich enough to have their agents in the Portuguese capital, and they monopolised this profitable business. This gave them the practical control of the home market, and even necessities did not escape their monopoly. Big fortunes were made at the expense of the small traders, and speculations in banking, of which the Jews no longer held the monopoly, made them still larger. The failure of some of the banks only completed the ruin of the too trustful citizens who abandoned their modest fortunes to their care.

A similar development was taking place in industry. While the old cloth industry was spreading from the Low Countries along the Rhine Valley, a new industry, which got its raw material from distant lands, was beginning to grow up at the termini of the roads from Italy. At Augsburg, Nuremberg, Chemnitz and Leipzig the cotton of the Levant was spun and woven, sometimes mixed with native-grown flax. The increase of the manufacture of Saxon cotton goods, which were even exported to England, gave a similar impetus to the dyeing industry. Thus alongside the gilds, membership of which tended to become obligatory, which often formed federations with other towns, and which were useful in keeping up the standard of workmanship, there arose a new class of industrial enterprises, typified by the big cotton manufactures of the Fuggers at Augsburg.

---

[1] The Hamburg bankers bought the whole of Venezuela from Charles V, who was pressed for money. They did not, however, succeed in colonising it, and soon sold it back to Spain.

But whether one considers these big establishments or the humble crafts where production still preserved a semi-patriarchal character, the gulf between employers and employed grew steadily wider. In 1465 the journeymen edge-tool makers of Nuremberg left their masters, who did not feed them to their satisfaction, and took their craft into other cities. In 1503 the journeymen tailors of Wesel revolted, and were only appeased by the arbitration of the burgomaster. Almost everywhere the workmen were demanding a shorter working day and higher wages. Here as elsewhere they suffered from the monetary revolution and the monopoly enjoyed by the commercial companies aggravated the cruel effects of the increased price of necessities. It was not long before the urban proletariat united with the peasants to demand the abolition of debts and the reduction of the capital amassed by the great commercial companies, and to sketch in their programme the outline of a communist society.

The most unfortunate class was that of the peasants, and their condition was made more insecure by three facts. The first was the increasing influence of Roman law, which was founded on the idea of absolute and exclusive private property. The jurists furnished the nobles with excellent reasons for appropriating the common lands and for restricting the rights of the commoners, especially by forbidding them the right of hunting in the neighbouring forests. Secondly, the nobles, both lay and ecclesiastical, loaded the peasants with taxes and *corvées* in order to support their luxury. The bishops even claimed to levy the tithe not only on crops but on cattle. Lastly, the commercial companies used their financial power to lower the price of agricultural produce, which they nevertheless sold again to the towns-people at very dear rates. If to these be added the wide-spread disturbance of established ideas at the beginning of the sixteenth century, the desire for social justice, which was awakened by the study of the Bible, and the new ambitions which were arising everywhere, even in the lowest depths of society, one can understand the violence of the movement which in 1525 aroused the peasants of Suabia, Thuringia and Alsace against the nobles. Under their red and white flag they proclaimed themselves " brothers in God,'' attacked monasteries and castles, demanded hunting and fishing rights, the re-establishment of common lands, and the abolition of most of the *corvées*. This was a real social war, and for a moment it struck terror into the nobles, for the peasants had the support of several towns, particularly of Strasbourg. But it soon ended in the pitiless extermination of the rebels.

Six years earlier the Reformation had begun. For more than a century religious divisions were to transform the country into the scene of bitter struggles and soon into a battlefield for the foreigner, and at the same time were to rob the country of the fruits of its premature and short-lived prosperity.

Rivalries and wars interrupted the course of trade. Even in the intervals of comparative tranquillity the central government was powerless to provide the necessary transport facilities. The Diet could not even establish a uniform coinage in this divided and tottering empire. In 1520 and 1595 the emperors had instituted in favour of the family of Tour and Taxis an hereditary office of postmaster-general of the Holy Roman Empire and the Hapsburg States. But after a century's activity this important service, which the development of printing made still more necessary, began to decline. As the imperial power grew weaker, the area in which it worked grew smaller, and at the end of the eighteenth century it only applied to the Austrian states and the principalities of Southern and Central Germany.[1] In the midst of this disorganisation and anarchy some of the towns could scarcely continue their business. The fairs of the great Bavarian and Franconian cities, especially that of Leipzig, the Saxon metropolis, preserved their importance. The demands of Berlin secured for Hamburg a new traffic which partly compensated for the losses of her merchants in British and Scandinavian markets. But the commercial currents which kept up communication between Germany and the rest of Europe were intermittent and only supported a few urban centres.

Industry suffered still more. Only two towns kept up

[1] The family of Tour and Taxis retained this privilege until 1867, when they sold it for a sum of £1,500,000. They still kept the privilege of free postage for themselves, but they lost this soon because they used it indiscreetly.

their reputation : Augsburg for jewellery and gold and silver work, Nuremberg for toys, ironmongery, clock-making[1] and haberdashery. Big banks were founded there, at Augsburg in 1619 and at Nuremberg in 1621. But there was no protection of national manufactures; local interests were stronger than the good intentions of the Diet. It was in vain that England prohibited the import of German goods; Leipzig, which benefited by free trade, opposed the adoption of a tariff of reprisals, and Hamburg did not hesitate to conclude a private treaty with England. On the other hand, during these troubled times many of the old gilds had lost the secret of careful workmanship, which had justified their monopoly; but their leaders occupied themselves with increasing strictness in trying to keep out new masters. Moreover, the municipal oligarchies were no longer checked by any superior authority and made no attempt to fix wage rates in proportion to the cost of living. Naturally such a state of things produced unrest among the workmen. At the call of the Anabaptists of Zwickau, humble miners, tailors and shoemakers of Saxony rose in revolt to correct the social evils from which they suffered and which Christ had condemned. They demanded the abolition of debts and severe measures to check the accumulation of capital in the hands of a few men. But Luther himself disavowed their aspirations towards equality; he wished to free minds, not bodies, and to change beliefs but not society. After terrible battles and after the tragic Siege of Munster, this social and Biblical revolution was drowned in blood.

Agriculture undoubtedly benefited, at least in the Protestant states, by the suppression of tithes and the secularisation of Church lands. But the convoys of grain which left the German ports did not witness so much to the prosperity of agriculture as to the general depopulation of the country. Moreover, only big landowners in certain privileged districts could export grain, and even then the price was so low that they made very little profit. The lot of the peasants was never more wretched. Serfdom, the abolition of which had been demanded by the rebels of 1525, weighed still more heavily on most of the country people, while the free labourers had to watch their real wages continually diminish-

[1] See Dr. Fallet's researches on this subject.

ing as the price of living rose. Luther had said : " It is no
use joking with Mr. Everyman ; he must be driven violently
and corporeally to do his duty . . . the people must feel
the bridle." Instead of the old customs destroyed by the
insurgents, the nobles imposed new ones, more arbitrary and
more oppressive still. They even laid their hands on the
lands of the customary tenants in perpetuity, whose holdings
had been consecrated by agelong custom. The Bavarian Code
of 1618 treated these *de facto* proprietors simply as " pre-
carial " tenants unless they could produce legal title-deeds.
The law of Mecklenburg in 1606 stated that the peasants
were simply cultivators and should never be considered as
holding perpetual leases. In Holstein those who obstinately
tried to claim a right of ownership to land which had been in
their families for generations were evicted altogether.[1] It
was scarcely surprising that the mass of the people lived in
" wretched mud or wooden huts, thatched with straw and
built on the bare earth. They were clad in rough canvas
and had no food but rye bread, oatmeal porridge, peas or
lentils, and whey."[2]

In many districts, moreover, the Thirty Years' War swept
away both these wretched means of livelihood and the population who lived on them. When the towns themselves were
not spared by the soldiery of friend or foe,[3] there was no
hope for the people of the open country. It was not merely
that the war must support itself and that the smallest towns
had to feed hosts of soldiers who dragged their families about
with them, but these terrible guests took away everything
they could carry and destroyed the rest for amusement. A
retreating army would even set fire to ripe corn, in order to
check the pursuit of their enemies by starvation. Whole
regions of Germany were thus laid waste. Famine and plague
followed the armies. The banks of the Rhine were thick with
ruins, and in some places you might travel for twenty leagues
along its banks without finding a village or even a house. It
is estimated that a third of the villages of the Empire were
abandoned.

[1] *Cf.* Ashley, *Economic History*, vol. i, part ii, pp. 272 *et. seq.*
[2] *Cf.* Janssen, *L'Allemagne à la fin du Moyen-âge*, vol. ii, p. 606.
[3] There were dozens of ruined towns, Magdeburg, Wurtzburg,
Heidelberg, Speier and Mannheim among them.

§ 2. Chief German States from 1648 to the End of the Eighteenth Century : Prussia.

Agricultural colonisation and industrial development in Prussia—
Vicissitudes of Bavaria and Saxony.

When at last the religious wars came to an end in 1648 the Empire was only a shadow; the real power was vested in the principalities which had grown up within it and which henceforth were entirely independent. It is impossible to study all of these, and the most interesting was the artificial state formed by the group of scattered territories governed by the Elector of Brandenburg. These provinces, spread along the Baltic coast and the banks of the Rhine,[1] were not thickly populated, and indeed supported no more than half a million people, but the prince who had united them had already conceived the bold design of making them into a prosperous and powerful state.

After the Treaty of Westphalia the Great Elector[2] had all his work before him, for his domains were not favoured by Nature and had, moreover, been laid waste during the war. He and his successors had, in fact, to undertake the work of colonising their own state. The most urgent of the tasks imposed on them was the improvement of the soil. The Great Elector himself during his youth had seen the example set by the Dutch, the cleverest cultivators in Northern Europe, and his wife, the electoral princess, had been born in Holland, and collaborated actively in the policy of agricultural regeneration. Dutch engineers were employed to drain the marshes which extended along the flat shores of the sluggish rivers of Brandenburg and Prussia. One of the districts thus reclaimed for agriculture in the Valley of the Netze still bears the name of *Hollander Bruch*. A century later Frederick II had to undertake similar work along the Valley of the Oder, and thus the newly conquered Plain of Silesia and the district round Kustrin were made fertile.

---

[1] Duchy of Prussia, Electorate of Brandenburg, archbishopric of Magdeburg, duchy of Cleves, principality of Hohenzollern.

[2] The successors of the Great Elector (1640-1688) were Frederick I (1688-1713), who was the first to hold the title of King of Prussia; Frederick William I (1713-1740), the " Sergeant king "; and Frederick II, " the Great " (1740-1786), the conqueror of Silesia.

Model farms (*hollanderies*) were founded for the improvement of cattle-breeding. Soon a rigorous sanitary policy succeeded in preventing the ravages of murrain. To improve breeds stallions were brought from Dessau and rams from Spain. Thanks to the efforts of the Sergeant King, who was not merely a recruiter of giant grenadiers, butter-making made great progress, for he founded a special school of dairy farming, the pupils of which were generously endowed.

Meanwhile a greater variety of crops was cultivated. The wife of the Great Elector grew the first potatoes in Germany in her garden, and though their edible qualities were long ignored, large quantities of alcohol were extracted from them. Peasants were obliged to plant six oaks and six fruit-trees before they married. It was chiefly the French refugees who brought the arts of fruit cultivation and market and flower gardening to Moabit and Charlottenburg in the neighbourhood of Berlin. They also imported the tobacco plant and the mulberry, though the latter never flourished in that inclement climate. The Seven Years' War checked this progress for a time; Prussia emerged victorious but covered with ruins. It was estimated that 15,000 houses had been burnt; there were no more plough teams, and men had to draw their ploughs themselves. As Frederick II said himself, everything had to be begun all over again. He set to work courageously, and during the last twenty-three years of his reign he spent twenty-five million crowns on the encouragement of agriculture. Under his care hundreds of villages were rebuilt and 17,000 army horses were distributed throughout the country.

Soon agricultural production became more intensive than it had been before the war. Fallow land was reduced and English turnips and other fodder crops were tried, first on the royal domains and later on private estates, in order to enrich the poor soil of Brandenburg. " This year we have made 70,000 acres[1] of meadow," wrote the king to Voltaire; " these acres will feed 16,000 cows, whose manure will enrich our sandy soil."

At first there was a serious scarcity of men on the land, so the rulers set themselves to attract colonists from neighbour-

[1] The French acre (*arpent*) is equal to about an acre and a half (English).—M. R.

ing countries. The Sergeant King installed 20,000 fugitives
from the archbishopric of Salzburg in Prussia. His son
organised two permanent recruiting agencies to repair the
losses of the Seven Years' War (about half a million men);
one, at Frankfurt-on-the-Maine, was the centre for South
Germany; the other, at Hamburg, was specially charged with
the work of stopping emigrants who passed on their way to
America. When the recruiting sergeants did not bring in
enough men, although they were stimulated by bounties,
peasants were seized by main force from the Polish frontiers[1]
or along the borders of Bohemia and Saxony. In years of
scarcity stores of corn were distributed, and this quickly
attracted the miserable peasants who were dying of hunger
in neighbouring states. In this way Frederick II gained
300,000 workers.

He attracted capital to agriculture in a thousand ways.
He reduced the common pastures and encouraged the formation of big enclosed farms of the English type, where the
farmer could live like a *bourgeois*. He encouraged clearings
with promises of exemptions and rewards. To the poorest
peasants he distributed seed, ploughs and horses. He rebuilt
their ruined houses and even, if need be, founded new
villages himself or forced the big landowners to build them.
He advanced money without interest to needy squires. He
accepted as currency drafts on mortgages, which were
guaranteed by all the landowners in the district. Finally
he organised the first agricultural bank in Northern Europe
(1769).

The condition of the peasants hardly kept pace with the
improvement of agriculture. Under the Great Elector,
serfdom, which differed little from slavery, was extended,
and it became more difficult to win freedom. Even the so-
called free peasants were closely attached to the soil, and
their children were forced to undergo several years' domestic
service in the lord's house. The agreement of 1653 delivered
over the country-folk bound hand and foot to the nobles
of Brandenburg, who took the opportunity to increase the
amount of forced labour and even proceeded to brutal evic-

[1] In 1771, 7,000 young Polish girls were forced to marry Pomeranian
Grenadiers, and their parents were obliged to furnish several head of
cattle as a dowry.

tions, against which the government raised a very feeble protest.[1] But Frederick I and Frederick II interested themselves in the welfare of the peasants. It was not only for his military exploits that " Old Fritz " was popular. He allowed the peasants to appeal directly to him against the abuses of which they were victims. When a peasant arrived at Potsdam to present a petition, he was registered, received, heard and sent home with fair words if not with full satisfaction.[2] The burdens of serfdom were mitigated and it became easier to win freedom. Brutality on the part of the masters was punished by imprisonment. The government fixed the amount of dues and services owed by tenants to their lords, and even intervened to supervise the contracts which were drawn up between landowners and labourers. It also encouraged the division of large estates, but the landless labourers did not get any share in them, and the multiplication of enclosures and the division of the common land tended to make their existence more precarious.

Industrial development was more rapid. In 1648 Berlin had less than 6,000 inhabitants; at the death of Frederick the Great, a century and a half later, its population numbered 114,000. Outside the small urban crafts working for local consumption, the Hohenzollern states had only a few small cloth manufactures and breweries, which, however, had a certain reputation. It may with truth be said that it was the 20,000 Frenchmen exiled by the Revocation of the Edict of Nantes (1685) who brought industry on a large scale to Brandenburg. " Thanks to them," Frederick II wrote later, " Berlin had goldsmiths, jewellers, watchmakers and sculptors." Huguenots from Sedan or Languedoc created the cloth manufactures at Frankfurt-on-the-Oder and Königsberg, which were soon capable of clothing the whole army. French refugees founded the first manufacture of printed stuff, they introduced the stocking loom, they set up the first paper factory. They taught the Elector's subjects the arts of making candles, plate-glass and beaver hats. In

[1] The whole country population was submitted to barracks discipline. There were to be no marriages and no travelling, even in the interior of the country, without the permission of the military authorities.

[2] See Paganel, *Histoire de Frédéric le Grand*, vol. ii, p. 217, the conversation between Frederick II and the bailiff of Fehrbellin.

the metal trade, where skilled labour was not so important, their influence was not so strong, and the progress of this industry was therefore slower. In the seventeenth century the country only possessed a few cannon foundries and numerous iron-wire works. The Sergeant King brought artisans from Liège to work in his new arms factories at Spandau and Potsdam, but it was not until the reign of his successor that mining and heavy metallurgy became important. In the ten years following the peace of 1763, 264 manufactures sprang up, and Frederick II wrote to Voltaire on September 5th, 1777 : " I am returning from Silesia, with which I was well content. . . . We have sold to the foreigner five million crowns' worth of linen and one million two hundred thousand crowns' worth of cloth. A cobalt mine has been found in the mountains, and will supply the whole province. We are making vitriol as good as the foreigner's. One industrious fellow manufactures indigo like that which comes from the Indies. A much simpler process than that of Réaumur has been discovered for making iron into steel." At the same time the Berlin silk manufactures began to compete with those of Lyons, and the capital was provided with sugar refineries which enabled it to dispense with supplies from Hamburg.

The administration encouraged inventors by instituting courses in applied science. But from the very beginning a strictly protective policy was adopted towards industry. The export of raw materials, such as wool, was forbidden ; the home market was closed to the competition of industrial rivals ; exclusive privileges were awarded to private individuals who accepted both the help and the control of the state. Several royal factories were founded, such as the porcelain works at Berlin. The maxims which Colbert had put into practice long years ago in France were adopted wholesale, and Frederick II showed himself as strict as his father on this point. " I exclude as many articles as possible," he said, " because it is the only way of forcing my subjects to become their own manufacturers." Circumstances justified this apparently obsolete policy, and the outcome proved him right.

In one branch of the protectionist programme the kings of Prussia showed themselves supreme, and that was in

attracting foreign labour. All kinds of promises were made
to future French emigrants by the famous Edict of Potsdam
in 1684. Guides and money were provided for their journey.
On arrival they were given a free temporary lodging and a
site and materials to build a house suited to their needs.
They were granted exemption from taxation for ten years
and were freely enrolled as citizens or gildsmen. It is easy
to understand why exiles even from England or Switzerland
took refuge in hospitable Brandenburg. To these privileges
Frederick II added exemption from military service for two
generations, and advances of money. We must not, however, imagine that the success of manufactures had ruined
the old gilds. They defended their privileges victoriously
against the competition of rural industry, and for a long
time controlled a large part of the national production.
Their constitution scarcely changed at all, and the government only succeeded in making access to the jealously
guarded mastership a little easier.

The fact is that the new state was still living in semi-
isolation, although its population had increased tenfold. It
had not achieved so important a place in the field of international commerce as in the political world. The first big
commercial houses which opened continuous relations with
the foreigner had been founded by French Huguenots, and
it was the Jewish colony of Berlin, strongly supported by
Frederick II, which first began to make the capital a
financial centre; the German nobles were forbidden to take
any part in trade. Königsberg was linked to Pillau by a
canal, but, ice-bound as it was in the winter, it could never
become a great port, and it was not until 1720 that the kings
of Prussia acquired Stettin. The Great Elector had tried in
vain to found at Emden on the North Sea a company to
exploit the Guinea coast. Of all the commercial companies
begun by Frederick II, including the Maritime Insurance
Company and the Levant Company, none succeeded. Trade
was hindered during his reign by frequent variations in the
coinage. There is a tale that a peasant was refusing the
six-pfennig pieces offered him by a baker in exchange for
his corn, when the king happened to pass by. "Why don't
you take the money?" he said to the man. "Well, would
you take it?" was the answer, and Frederick had no

reply. His ideas of borrowing money from French financiers on the security of the taxes, and of starting a lottery on the Italian model, met with no greater success. Only in internal trade was decisive progress achieved. The Great Elector linked the Spree with the Oder, and Frederick II lengthened the chain from the Oder to the Vistula. Thus a valuable system of waterways was created, stretching from Breslau to Hamburg, and Berlin, which held the central position, could rival Leipzig as the chief market in Germany. From 1655 onwards a system of electoral posts, which replaced the Taxis posts, enabled a traveller to go from Berlin to Königsberg in four days, and gradually tolls were suppressed. In 1765 a national bank was founded for loan and discount business. It was subsidised by the government, but was secured against administrative interference, and was of great assistance to the slowly developing commercial class.

Prussia was already a great military state, but she had to wait another half century before becoming an economic power.

Among the other German states there are none whose development can be compared with that of the kingdom of Prussia. Bavaria, which might have played the same part in Southern Germany as Prussia played in the north, had been too often overrun by foreign armies. During the century and a half between the Thirty Years' War and the French Revolution she experienced barely forty years of comparative prosperity. The Elector Ferdinand Maria (1651-1679) was fully occupied in repairing the ruins with which his states were covered. After the War of the Austrian Succession, Maximilian III (1745-1777) had to do the same work again. Only then did agriculture, which was henceforth the principal resource of the state, begin to recover. A number of ecclesiastical estates were secularised, the position of the peasants was improved at least on state lands, vagabondage was suppressed and new methods of farming were tried. All these measures tended to increase the productivity of the state, which in 1789 numbered 2,000,000 inhabitants.

The history of the electorate of Saxony was even less brilliant. Wallenstein's troops and the Swedish armies had devastated the country, and in that terrible period it had lost half its inhabitants (a million and a half out of three millions). The mischievous custom of appanages doomed it to repeated divisions. Its dukes, moreover, were only anxious to imitate the splendour of Louis XIV and to create at Dresden a magnificent court like that of Versailles, and they did at least succeed in making their capital one of the chief artistic centres of Europe. In 1697 the election of Augustus II as king of Poland finally sealed the fate of the country. Not content with abandoning the religion of his people for that of his new subjects, he oppressed his Saxons in a thousand ways in order to sustain an unequal conflict against Charles XII of Sweden, and he even sold part of his electorate in order to support his precarious kingship. His only merit lay in the fact that he continued to adorn Dresden and that he used the discovery of the valuable seams of porcelain clay on his territory to found at Meissen (1709) the famous manufacture which was the first in Europe to produce hard porcelain and founded the fame of Saxon china. The Seven Years' War involved the unhappy country in disasters almost as serious as those which it suffered during the religious wars. Only the double possession of a fertile soil and of mineral wealth[1] enabled the state, ruined and indebted as it was, to recover towards the end of the century. The great trade of Leipzig, however, permanently diminished in importance, for since Breslau had become Prussian the commerce of Eastern Europe flowed towards Berlin rather than to the old Saxon market.

The princes of the smaller German states were even less conscientious in their dealings with their people. The Duke of Wurtemberg hired out 6,000 of his subjects to serve in the French armies during the Seven Years' War, and a little later the Duke of Hesse-Cassel sold more than 16,000 of his to the English, to go and be killed in America[2] while he built his château of Wilhelmshöhe with the price of their blood. All the princes undoubtedly took part in this " white slave trade," but they did not all deserve the cutting name of " merchants of men " which Schiller gave them. There

---

[1] In 1765 a mining-school was founded at Freiberg, which the teaching of Werner made famous.

[2] Instead of the King of England's own subjects, whose arms were too precious in industry.

were a few exceptions, such as the Duchess Amelia and Duke Charles Augustus of Saxe-Weimar, who were the protectors of Gœthe and Schiller, and made a deserted little town in a poor and dull country the literary capital of Germany, or the Margrave of Baden, who took a pride in applying the principles of the Physiocrats to his state. But in many of these princelings lived the cruel and narrow spirit of the old feudal knights. Such was the Duke of Zweibrugen, who amused himself by keeping a menagerie of wild men, whom this sinister hunter-prince (little better than a bandit chief) would watch as though they were rare animals.

The other centres of the economic life of Germany were to be found among the old cities of the Hanseatic League. Hamburg, which was situated at the head of a deep estuary and at the outlet of a network of waterways, in addition to being favourably situated for ocean trade, now finally outstripped Lübeck. In the eighteenth century it was not only, like Stettin, a port for Berlin. It was already the chief port of embarkation for emigrants to the New World, and as soon as the independence of the United States was assured its merchants opened profitable relations with the young republic.[1]

§ 3. The Austrian Monarchy during the Seventeenth and Eighteenth Centuries.

It is convenient to study Austria separately from Germany, for the treaties of Westphalia, while leaving the Hapsburgs in possession of the imperial title, had turned their ambitions away from a domain where their political authority was more than half overthrown and where even their territorial power was to be encroached on by the expansion of Prussia. Their efforts were more successful in the east, where, not content with repulsing the last assaults of the Turks, they reconquered from them the whole of Hungary. It is true that they had also inherited the Low Countries and that the arrangements for the succession in Spain and Poland established their power in North, South and Central Italy. But we have studied elsewhere, in their

---

[1] In 1779 the first insurance company for movables was established at Hamburg.

natural setting, these external possessions of the monarchy, and we shall here examine only those states which formed the body of the empire.

All these states were alike in that they were essentially agricultural and that the peasants were all serfs. But in Bohemia this system had been established at the end of a terrible war, and was therefore characterised by especial severity. After the Battle of White Mountain in 1627 the common law declared that " whoever could not prove that he had been freed belonged to the lord on whose land he was established, or on whose land he was born, if his parents were foreigners. The peasant existed only for the lord. When the lord wanted new land cleared and cultivated, he urged unmarried peasants to marry, in other cases he forbade marriage. If two runaway serfs belonging to different lords married and were recaptured, each of the masters took his own serf and the children were shared between them."[1]

The free peasants, weighed down by the burdens imposed on them, were scarcely more fortunate. And for a century and a half this terrible misery, the absolute physical and moral degradation of the Czech people, continued and increased. When the German nobles, who despised the people, ceased to live on their estates, they were delivered into the hands of stewards, who ruled by terror and violence. The peasants were forced to give six days' labour in a week, more than they had done formerly in a year. They were entirely incapable of paying the taxes demanded of them. Their food was a disgusting bread made of couch-grass and sawdust. If they fled they were overwhelmed with punishments; if they revolted they were savagely repressed. In the other provinces the condition of the peasantry was undoubtedly less appalling, but everywhere they had to perform heavy *corvées*, at least three days a week, and everywhere they were subject to the so-called justice of their lords. *Rustica gens, optima flens, pessima ridens*[2] was a current saying, a fit replica of the medieval *Poignez vilain, il vous oindra* (Treat the villein roughly and he will serve you well).[3]

[1] E. Denis, *La Bohême depuis la Montagne-Blanche*, vol. i, p. 336.

[2] The peasant is best when he cries and worst when he laughs.

[3] An institution peculiar to Austria must be mentioned here. In Croatia, in the region always threatened by the Turks, Prince Eugene had

Very few peasants escaped from this misery. At the end
of the eighteenth century there were only about twenty en-
franchisements a year throughout the whole of Moravia.
There was nothing to hope for from the generosity of the
masters, and it was only in the period of "Benevolent
Despotism" that the government decided to take general
measures. In Hungary, Maria Theresa succeeded in imposing on the magnates a decree which allowed the peasants to
move about and to bring up their children as they liked, and
gave them the right of appeal to the court of the *comitat*[1]
against their lords. In 1775 she issued the famous edict
limiting the amount of the *corvée* throughout the empire.
She left to her son Joseph II, the avowed disciple of the
Philosophers and the Physiocrats, the honour of bringing
about the triumph of "reason and humanity" and of earn-
ing the glorious title of "friend of the peasants." The edict
of 1781 conferred many advantages on these unfortunates.
They gained, above all, personal freedom, not only freedom
of movement such as the Hungarian peasants already
enjoyed, but liberty to marry as they pleased. Their
children were freed from the obligation of domestic service
in the lords' houses, and fines were abolished. Their ownership of the lands which they had cultivated for centuries was
recognised, in fact, on payment of a fixed rent, for from
henceforward tenants could be evicted only in clearly defined
circumstances and never without an indemnity. The only
questions which remained to be definitely settled were those
of *corvées* and *banalités*,[2] and Joseph II dealt with them by
abolishing both. At his death only the *corvées* were re-
established, and as, since the time of Maria Theresa, the
Treasury had realised that its interest lay in transferring
the heavier part of the land tax from the cultivator to the

---

organised the *Confins militaires* when he conquered it in 1699. Here the
inhabitants were theoretically soldiers from birth till death, and girls
could only inherit lands granted by the State if they became the wives of
soldiers. Even in peace time the peasants had to leave their fields and
go to guard the frontier one week in every three. They were bound to
the soil as well as to military service.

[1] An administrative subdivision of Hungary.—M. R.

[2] Obligatory use of something belonging to the lord, *e.g.*, mills.—
M. R.

proprietor, the peasant, free from the danger of increased taxation, was at last relatively well off. This social reformation was soon rewarded by a marked improvement in scientific agriculture.[1]

The long survival of feudalism was no more favourable to industry than to agriculture. The serf was bound to his master's lands and could not, even within those limits, follow a craft without his master's permission. Moreover, the *banalités* and innumerable monopolies enjoyed by the nobles in milling, distilling, brewing and many other manufactures prevented the growth of any independent establishment. The arbitrary regulations of urban gilds and the prohibitions which they passed against village workshops were further obstacles to the development of manufactures. Even the great industries which were made necessary by the increasing requirements of the nation, were for a long time the monopoly of a small circle of the aristocracy of the court. In the eighteenth century the Emperor Francis I himself set up as a government contractor. The great nobles followed his august example, and this privileged competition discouraged private enterprise.

At last in 1774 the gilds were reformed if not suppressed. Country industry was allowed to organise itself, and seven years later *banalités* were abolished. At the same time that the government removed these internal obstacles from the industrial field, they surrounded it with a high barrier to protect it from foreign competition. They levied high protective duties (as much as 60 per cent. on the value of the article), even on colonial products. They issued strict prohibitions against smuggling, and smuggled goods were burnt by the public executioner if they were discovered. If this was not enough, the new manufactures were heavily subsidised. Thus in the capital, of which it had been said not long before that " they can't make even a silk stocking there," glass and porcelain manufactures developed. But the great development took place chiefly in Bohemia. There the old glass and metallurgical industries revived as in the rest of the empire, but in addition the textile industries grew rapidly. Cloth-making spread throughout Moravia, and

---

[1] It was also the result of the secularisation of Church lands accomplished by the Emperor.

flaxen and hempen fabrics were exported from Bohemia even to America. These big manufactures were, indeed, often organised by foreigners, Swiss, French or English, but the whole nation reaped the benefits of their enterprise.

Internal trade developed concurrently with agriculture, industry and population. A service of imperial posts was arranged to facilitate transport, and the famous *Via Josephine*, crossing the mountains of Carniola from Karlstadt to Zeugg, opened a new access to the Adriatic. For a time it had seemed as though this great continental monarchy would even take part in oceanic trade. But the first East India Company founded by Charles VI had been very short-lived, and the second, founded by Joseph II at Trieste, was in its turn ruined by Anglo-Dutch hostility. These repeated efforts only achieved the establishment of a few factories scattered along the coasts of China, India or West Africa.

Austro-Hungarian commerce was more successful on a less ambitious scale and in a less distant field, the Black Sea. In order that merchants and their goods should have safe passage there, Charles VI established a fleet on the Danube, while the fleet of the Chambers and Companies of Commerce instituted by Maria Theresa had its headquarters at Kilia Nova and was specially intended for the supervision of this trade. Joseph II concluded a commercial treaty with Russia, and obtained from the Sultan freedom of navigation on the lower Danube, the Black Sea, the Sea of Marmora and even in the Dardanelles. Thus grain and hides from Hungary could easily reach Genoa and Marseilles. On the Adriatic, Fiume and Trieste were made first free towns and then free ports. Fiume was principally engaged in importing colonial produce, but Trieste carried on an active export trade by smuggling the products of Venetian Istria, and it became the centre of an important trade with the Levant, where Maria Theresa founded many consulates. Neapolitans, Greeks and Dutch all had factories there, and about 1776 it was estimated that 6,000 ships visited its quays every year. The Austrian merchant marine even visited the shores of the Western Mediterranean, where Joseph II had opened relations with the Barbary states.

Thus Austria, seeking for outlets to the sea, followed on the one hand the course of her great river, and on the other opened for herself a road to the Mediterranean through the Adriatic. She still possessed the Low Countries, but she was destined soon to lose them and thus to be pushed still more to the east, whither she was turning already.

BIBLIOGRAPHY

JANSSEN, G.: History of the German People at the Close of the Middle Ages, trans. M. A. Mitchell and A. M. Christie. (1896-1910.) Vols. i. and ii.

LAVISSE: *Études sur l'histoire de Prusse* (3rd edit. 1890).

PAGANEL: *Histoire de Frédéric le Grand.* 2 vols.

LEGER, L.: *Histoire de l'Autriche-Hongrie.* (1879.)

DENIS, E.: *La Bohême depuis la Montagne-Blanche.* 2 vols. (1903.) And the classic German works by Karl Bücher, Wagner, Sombart, Schmoller, etc.

CHAPTER VIII

THE SCANDINAVIAN STATES

THE Scandinavian states must rank among those which have been reduced by their small extent or feeble resources, by internal divisions or foreign wars, or by the slowness of their economic and social evolution, to playing only a secondary part in the history of labour. In 1448 the Union of Calmar, which had made Denmark, Norway and Sweden into one big monarchy, came to an end, and these states were never again all three united. We must therefore study their divergent and often antagonistic histories separately.

§ 1. Denmark.

Slavery of the peasant class; stagnation of industry and of maritime trade—Slow recovery towards the middle of the eighteenth century.

In the sixteenth century Denmark, weakened by the final loss of Northern Sweden, but still possessing the south of that country as well as Norway, might have become a leading European power but for internal anarchy. In 1523 the nobles, not content with having gained hereditary possession of their fiefs for themselves, declared the monarchy, on the contrary, to be merely elective. Thus they had the power of life and death on their estates, and the king was to be henceforth the docile nominee of these sovereign nobles. The Reformation was only another means of strengthening them, for they alone profited by the confiscation of Church lands, and the States General were no longer even summoned. The state engaged in unlucky wars against the Emperor and against Sweden, it lost all its provinces on the other shore of the Baltic, and twice ran the risk of partition. It was only when the monarchy was restored in 1660 that, under a government which was firmer and more careful of the country's interests, some measure of prosperity was regained.

Although it held the key of the Narrow Straits, Denmark

had always been essentially an agricultural country. But at
the end of the fifteenth century the condition of the mass of
the peasants had changed for the worse. Strict serfdom was
substituted for the old liberal relations between lords and
cultivators throughout the kingdom.[1] Now that the nobles
were completely free from royal authority, they imposed an
increasingly heavy yoke on the peasants. They enforced
their jurisdiction over them, and, on the pretext of making
them respect hunting rights, inflicted cruel punishments on
them. Many small proprietors fell, willy-nilly, into the ranks
of tenant farmers or labourers, both of whom were subject to
the *corvées*. The few free cultivators who remained were
crushed beneath the weight of feudal exactions. Gradually,
in spite of several unfortunate attempts at rebellion, this
harsh system spread throughout the country, for the great
families, having absorbed the Church lands, proceeded to
dismember the lands of the crown. Free from all anxiety
and from all control, the nobles led a life of luxury and
indolence. They had no taste for the fatigues of war and no
energy to look after their estates. The peasants were entirely
in their hands, but they took no interest in them unless the
impoverished government tried to get some money from them
or to impress them for military service. Then the nobles
intervened to assert their exclusive rights; theirs alone was
the revenue of the land, and they owned its people body and
soul. The people, on their side, resigned themselves to this
feudal servitude, thinking it better to have one master than
two. The nobility supplemented their resources by the
monopoly which they created in the chief branch of agricultural trade; only nobles or citizens were allowed to fatten
beasts for market. Thus the peasants were stifled by extreme
poverty, and waste-land increased to such an extent that in
Christian V's reign (1670-1699) the Danes had to buy the
butter and cheese for their army from Holland.

At the beginning of the next century it seemed as though
the peasants would recover a measure of prosperity. The
monarchy, which had already emancipated its own serfs, felt
itself strong enough to proclaim the general abolition of
serfdom (1699). The nobles could no longer sell their serfs
and were obliged to grant them their freedom in return for a

---

[1] See Boissonade, *Le Travail dans l'Europe du Moyen-âge.*

fixed payment. They were even forbidden to transfer one of their farmers from a cultivated holding to waste-land, and any serf who had lived for a certain time outside his master's domain could not be dragged back against his will. But Frederick IV tried to organise the peasants whom he had freed from this narrow feudal slavery into a vast militia for his own profit and for the defence of the realm (1701). Unfortunately he left to the nobles the right of choosing those who were to form part of this new army, and thus clumsily furnished the old masters with a new instrument of oppression, and laid a heavy burden upon those who had just been freed from the old servitude. Thus the enthusiasm created by the edicts of emancipation only lasted a few months. Moreover, considerations of public order, no less than the fierce demands of the nobles themselves, soon led the king to take back with one hand what he had given with the other and to re-establish the old serfdom in a new and scarcely less burdensome form. A decree of 1724, which was perhaps inspired by English legislation, enrolled all the peasants between the ages of fourteen and thirty-five, and appointed a fixed domicile for them during that period. This decree was executed throughout the country, so that even those fortunate districts where personal liberty had hitherto survived now shared this common slavery.

It seemed that the day of deliverance would never dawn. In 1730 the militia was abolished, but was re-established almost at once. The peasant was again forbidden to leave the land where he worked without a regular passport from his master. The master naturally almost always refused it, and there was nothing to prevent his heaping taxes and annoyances on the unfortunates who lived under his jurisdiction, bound to the land like convicts. Soon, under the pretext of military service, the period of fixed domicile began at fifteen or even at nine years and lasted until death. Meanwhile the sale of the crown lands continued. Speculators bought them up at a low price, and the crown furnished them with every facility for turning them into fine estates, which meant reducing the number of farms and even sometimes destroying whole villages. The country districts were depopulated, and then the landowners had to get their supply of labour from orphanages and workhouses.

After 1764, however, the first of the Bernstorffs set an example to the other nobles by abolishing the *corvée* on his lands and granting his farmers long leases. The great land-owners began to realise that these humane and just measures resulted in an increased revenue from the land. In 1771 another reforming minister, Struensee, tried to remedy the abuses of the *corvée* by legislation and set up a loan fund for farmers who wanted to buy their land. But it was not until 1780 that the second of the Bernstorffs finally abolished serfdom.

No agricultural progress had been possible under the idle and oppressive domination of the nobles. Even the import of foreign corn was prohibited, and this had both increased the cost of living for the poor and encouraged the cultivators to pursue the traditional routine, while the levy of the tithe in kind had discouraged the clearing of any but the best ground. Towards 1740, no doubt, the administration showed by its acts a desire to use the soil to better advantage. But more was needed for the recovery of national agriculture than the creation of a department of rural economy, or the intro-duction of the potato into Jutland (1759), or even the en-couragement given to the division of the common lands (1781). The wishes of the government and of agricultural theorists could only be realised by a population of free peasants.

Industry suffered no less severely than agriculture from the victory of the aristocracy. While the peasants lost their personal freedom, the citizens were despoiled of their economic privileges and their political rights. Members of the old families or noble German immigrants monopolised the most lucrative crafts, which became, as it were, industrial fiefs in their hands, at the expense of the urban gilds; and while the old industrial leaders were impoverished by this ruinous competition and arbitrary dispossession, the new leaders only brought a haughty negligence to the conduct of their business. Thus it was not until the first thirty years of the eighteenth century that modern industry was born in the kingdom.[1] First the government took care to raise barriers against the tide of foreign imports and to clear a field where

[1] In the seventeenth century there is nothing worth notice except the sugar refineries which resulted from the trade with the West Indies.

young industries might make their first attempts; it was forbidden to wear jewellery, lace and silk or woollen materials which had not been made in Denmark. By this means, and in spite of an active contraband trade, industry was born—or reborn—at Copenhagen. In 1740 nearly 7,000 persons, scattered in workshops of varying sizes, were working with their hands to supply the needs of the whole kingdom. Even in Norway, which had hitherto been regarded as a country of forests and fisheries, various industries developed. A Black Company was founded there to improve the manufacture of pitch, tar, lamp-black, powder, iron, sulphur, alum and vitriol.

In the reign of Frederick V (1746-65) and during the ministry of the first Bernstorff textile industries developed. The cloth manufacture at the Golden House employed as many as 1,400 workmen. The royal silk manufacture possessed over a hundred looms, and two hundred others were divided between fifteen private enterprises. The metallurgical industry was represented by a few foundries and arms factories.[1] This development was brilliant enough, but certainly somewhat forced. The government was not content with preventing foreign competition, but bribed foreign workmen to teach their secret processes, granted large subsidies, and created new monopolies—wiser than the old, indeed—at the very time that it was destroying the old ones.[2] But the time was at hand when much more freedom was not only possible but necessary. In 1761 the government forbade the creation of new gilds and reserved to itself the right of dispensing with the masterpiece when it thought fit. Before the end of the century the second Bernstorff (1773-1797) suppressed all industrial monopolies.

Internal trade had also been at a very low ebb for 200 years. It was controlled by a narrow oligarchy of native or German nobles who, through ignorance or disdain, misused their exclusive rights and reduced trade almost to nothing.

[1] Horseshoes were still brought from Sweden.
[2] In the same reign a Chair of Economics was endowed at the University of Copenhagen. It must also be noted that during the ministry of Struensee (1770-1772) the Moravians established themselves in Christianfeldt, which became one of the chief manufacturing centres in the kingdom.

Christian III, who died in 1559, had succeeded in establishing the uniformity of the coinage as well as of weights and measures, but the government had so often since then had recourse to debasement that his reform had little effect. About 1624 the active spirit of the Hanseatic League succeeded, in spite of the unsympathetic atmosphere of the time, in creating a postal system the administration of which was entrusted to the four most important commercial societies. But it was not until Charles VI's reign that a decisive symptom of commercial progress showed itself. This was the creation in 1736 of a bank for deposits, exchanges and loans. It was carefully guaranteed against governmental interference, and in a short time it caused the rate of interest to fall from 6 to 4 per cent. We must also note between 1777 and 1783 the construction of a canal between Kiel and the Eider. This made communication between the two sides of the peninsula almost as easy by the south as by the north.

In foreign trade Denmark had in the sixteenth century competed successfully with the Hanseatic League and had wrested from them the trade with Norway. But she had only finally succeeded in shaking off their domination by throwing open the Sound to their rivals, the Dutch. This was only changing one master for another. She tried in vain to free herself from this new domination, which was soon shared by the English, by making commercial treaties with France and Russia and creating privileged companies. Such were the Iceland Company (1602) which later controlled the trade with Nordland and Finmark, and the East India Company (1616) which founded the small factory of Tranquebar on the Coromandel coast. Moreover, the government acquired the Island of St. Thomas in the West Indies (1672) and encouraged whale-fishing off the Greenland coast. But in spite of all these efforts the mercantile marine did not develop. Even Copenhagen relied for its revenue on the tolls which it collected in the Narrows rather than on the commercial activity of its port. It was not until Charles VI made commerce, like agriculture, an affair of state that Denmark began to recover her maritime power. Then the East India Company extended its operations as far as China and roused the jealousy of the Dutch, while the West India Company bought the Isle of Sainte-Croix from France, and after the suppression of its monopoly in 1753 trade with the West Indies increased still more. The Iceland Company unfortunately kept its monopoly and used it to exhaust the resources of the island. But the kingdom now had 12,000 sailors, and in the reign of Frederick V Danish shipowners, profiting by the treaties made with Genoa, Naples, and the Barbary states, developed their carrying trade on a large scale. This enterprise was very successful, and the emancipation of the English colonies in North America opened a still wider field to it.

If we except the last half of the eighteenth century, the economic and social evolution of Denmark is characterised by a sort of arrested development, which is all the more remarkable because both in geographical conditions and in natural resources the kingdom is very like Holland. But it lacked an active middle class. This class, which was the necessary agent of progress, suffered first from the scorn of the aristocracy and then from the forced inertia to which it was condemned by an absolute government which had been too long powerless against the nobles. Thence resulted a long period of stagnation, which was shown in a slow but continuous process of depopulation.

§ 2. Norway.

Re-establishment of rural democracy—Dismissal of the Hanseatic League; development of the national mercantile marine.

It is somewhat difficult to give a separate account of the economic and social development of Norway, because throughout our period this country was an integral part of the kingdom of Denmark. But during the reign of Christian IV (1588-1648) the national spirit of the people awoke. It is true that its growth was checked almost at once by the wars which troubled North Europe during the second half of the seventeenth century, but the long period of peace which opened in 1720 allowed it to develop.

The history of Norwegian agriculture is particularly interesting from the social point of view. The peasants in this privileged country had never known serfdom or even villeinage. They had always enjoyed complete personal

liberty, and only in the southern province of Finmark had
they been forbidden to become landowners. Towards the
end of the Middle Ages, however, so marked a concentration
took place in land holding that many of the small proprietors
found themselves reduced to the condition of *métayers* or
tenant farmers, and most of the land was in the hands
of big landowners. But the traditions of the old rural
democracy did not entirely die out. The crown intervened
in favour of the people, and the edict of 1685, more efficacious
than any of its predecessors, limited the landlord's right to
collect rent from lands which he had leased or farmed out.
Moreover, it forced all landowners working more than one
farm to pay a double tax on the revenue of all the others.
By the time this legislation was repealed in 1799 the land of
Norway had returned for the most part to the hands of the
peasants, its ancient and rightful owners.

Norway, however, is a country in which three-quarters
of the soil is unsuitable for agriculture. Thus, though the
people were energetic and thinly scattered, they had to
import foreign corn to support life, and until 1788 they were
only allowed to get these indispensable supplies from Denmark. Timber was the only natural wealth of Norway. From
the sixteenth century onwards the forests were actively exploited. Oaks, pines and firs fell in millions beneath the
woodcutter's axe, and almost at once it was necessary to take
measures to save whole provinces from an irremediable devastation. For example, it was made illegal to set up any saw-
mill without permission, and in the eighteenth century it was
only in Finmark that wood could be cut freely.

The sea was a valuable supplement to the resources of the
soil, for it was fortunately warmed by currents, and the coast
was rich both in harbours and in breeding-grounds for fish.
The abundant supply of fish compensated for the scarcity of
meat in the people's food. But some means of preserving
fish had to be discovered before they could become an article
of export. For a long time they were simply dried, and at
the end of the fifteenth century Norwegian fishermen began
to use the salting process which the Dutchman Beuckel
invented in 1416 for herring. But it was not until the seventeenth century that they learnt from English merchants how
to salt cod.

At the beginning of modern times the little industry which the country possessed was concentrated at Bergen in the hands of the Hanseatic League.

Bergen,[1] an excellent port and a flourishing market, was built in the shape of a horseshoe. On one side the shore was skirted by the German colony, which was called the Bridge. On the other side was situated the Norwegian part of the city, which was called Overstrand. Between these two stretched a long street where the German artisans lived, for the colony was breaking into two divisions, the merchants and clerks who formed the aristocracy, and the artisans, who were organised in five gilds, of whom the shoemakers were the most important. They were rather despised and kept at arms' length by their wealthier countrymen, who, however, united with them against the natives.

The merchant quarter was divided into twenty-five courts (Court of the Bream, Court of the Mantle, etc.). Each was isolated and fortified, and guarded by mastiffs and watchmen. Each communicated by a bridge with the sea, and each contained, first of all, a huge building, on the ground floor of which were the warehouses and shops, and on the first floor the lodgings of the merchants. Then there was a big open space, and behind were cellars and store-rooms for the merchandise and a big common hall called the *schütting*. Here the members had their meals and kept warm in winter, the smoke from the fire finding its way out through a hole in the roof.

In these courts lived about 3,000 inhabitants, divided into "families." But they were all men or boys, clerks, sailors or apprentices; women were excluded as troublesome and indiscreet. These merchant-monks were condemned to forced celibacy. They were forbidden to marry the women of the country or to spend a night outside the courts where they were interned. But it must not be concluded that life was therefore exemplary in these commercial monasteries. The men who were shut up at night found compensations during the day in the Norwegian quarter, or they were rich and very popular with women.

The merchants who consented to this confinement under-

[1] Émile Worms, *Histoire commerciale de la Ligue Hanséatique*.   Paris, 1864.

took to trade for the benefit of the Hanseatic League for ten years. Since they were in the position of a garrison in a conquered country, they imposed severe tests to try the courage and strength of newcomers. For example, on a certain day a strange masquerade took place with great ceremony to the sound of wild music. When evening came everyone met in the *schütting* and a fire of grass and branches was kindled to give out a thick smoke. Then each novice in turn was hoisted and suspended in the opening whence the smoke escaped. He then had to answer certain questions, and was kept there until he was smoked like a ham, when he was lowered and well drenched with water. At other times they went in grotesque procession to cut fresh rods from the trees. Then, when everyone was assembled in the *schütting*, an old merchant made a speech in praise of order, fidelity and diligence, after which the apprentices were handed over to masked men, who flogged them with the rods to the sound of drums and cymbals. The ceremony, which scarcely ever passed without bloodshed and disorder, ended with a banquet at the expense of the newcomers.

Among the artisans an even more brutal game was played. The apprentice was forced to remain for a fixed time in a pit filled with filth and lime. If he tried to come out before his time, he was driven back with stones.

The Hanse merchants who led this strange existence were induced to do so by the enormous profits and privileges which they gained by it. They had the monopoly of trade for the whole of Norway. Any merchant who did not belong to the Hanse was forbidden to send more than two ships a year to Bergen, to land anywhere else or to sell his cargo except wholesale. In this way competition was eliminated, and if necessary intruders were massacred. The Hanse merchants, on the other hand, were exempt from all direct taxation, paid reduced Customs duties and were only subject to their own jurisdiction. The two following facts give some idea of their supremacy. The Norwegians were not allowed to buy fish until the German colony was provided for. Again, one day the Germans pursued one of their enemies, a Norwegian, and killed him in the heart of the convent where he had taken refuge, and the convent itself was burnt during the tumult. They were, however, defended against popular fury by the Archbishop of Drontheim, who urged the services which they rendered to the state. It was they who stimulated agriculture by opening markets for its produce, and encouraged trade by making money plentiful and preserving the country from pirates.

The Hanse merchants had established their domination partly, no doubt, by force of arms, but chiefly by force of money. They were lavish in their presents to the great lay and ecclesiastical nobles. Then when the town had been pillaged and burnt by pirates they had lent money to the inhabitants on good security and had sold on credit to retailers burdened with debt. The inevitable crash came, and the people, unable to pay, saw their goods and houses seized. It was then that the natives took refuge in the new quarter on the other side of the horseshoe, leaving their creditors comfortably installed in the old town, which had thus become the property of foreigners.

These details of the methods of the Hanse merchants explain the hatred in which they were held and the revolts which often broke out against them. As soon as a state felt itself strong enough to have a navy and some guns and to practise commerce and industry, it did its best to get rid of them. Norway's turn came in the sixteenth century.

When in 1559 these arrogant foreigners were expelled, their places were partly filled by others who were less arrogant and more pliable, and free associations took the place of the old closed gilds. The Norwegians of the port towns were fishermen, manufacturers and merchants in one. " Tailors," said a writer at the end of the sixteenth century, " go salmon fishing, and barbers sell beer." It was not until 1621 that regular and exclusive corporations, which were to last for 200 years, were organised again in the towns. The most characteristic industries of the country, however, still remained scattered about the forests. These were the small saw-mills and rough nail-making works which almost always made use of the water-power of the streams by means of rustic mills. Manufactures worthy of the name only appeared about 1700, a few paper-works, a few oil-mills and a few flour-mills. The large scale textile industries were only represented by prison workshops where coarse linen and woollen fabrics were made. It was the state, too, which established salt-works at Valloe in 1739 and bought the glass-works which had been made by the Black Company (1775). In 1646 important copper mines had been opened at Roeros and are still worked at the present time.

With a good coastline, plenty of timber, and a population of hardy fishermen, Norway was soon to become the centre of an active export trade and the possessor of an excellent mercantile marine. Not until they had overthrown the monopoly of the Hanse merchants, and after a century of continuous effort had profited at last by the disasters of the Thirty Years' War, did the Norwegians succeed in winning Bergen from German domination. But they still had to face the competition first of the Dutch, and later of the English and Scots. Thus, although the demand for Norwegian timber increased as shipbuilding developed in Europe, and although salt fish and copper ore provided increasingly plentiful freights, the export of which was not seriously checked either by Customs duties or by privileges granted to certain towns, the native shipowners still found their business slow in developing. But during the eighteenth century the number of their ships rose from 400 to more than 800, and henceforth most of the export trade was in their hands. Having thus become one of the chief naval powers of the north, Norway seized the opportunity of the American War of Independence to resist British pretensions. In 1781 she formed the League of Armed Neutrality with Sweden and Russia to vindicate the freedom of the seas.

The structure of the country is sufficient to explain why the development of internal communication was much less rapid.[1] At the end of the sixteenth century a postal service had been improvised by ordering the peasants who lived near the roads to furnish travellers with horses in return for a moderate payment fixed by law. But it was not until later that the transport of letters was regularly organised, and only in 1720 did the private monopoly give place to a public service. The first high-road made in the country was no older than 1630 and led simply from the banks of the Drammen to the mines at Kowsberg.

The population of this large but poor kingdom had more

---

[1] The same thing is true of England, q.v.

than doubled in 150 years, and a century ago it had reached the relatively high figure of 900,000 people, more than a third of the present total.

§ 3. Sweden.

National Independence: Gustavus Vasa—Brilliant industrial development: Jonas Alströmer—Reconstruction of rural democracy, consolidation of farms and agricultural improvements.

In Sweden each of the three centuries which we are studying presents very different characteristics. The sixteenth century was marked by the emancipation of the nation and the establishment of a strong monarchy. The triumphant revolt of Gustavus Vasa consecrated the independence of the new state, which now only had to extend to its natural frontiers by annexing the southern shore of the peninsula, and it also marked the foundation of a powerful dynasty. The new king, strong in the enthusiasm felt for him by the mass of his subjects, lacked only money, and had to borrow from the Hanse merchants at Lübeck in order to overthrow the Danish domination. But he found a means of paying off his debt and of filling his treasury as well. The Lutheran Reformation, which was adopted very quickly by his subjects, allowed him to secularise Church lands. Thus, possessed of 13,000 farms scattered throughout the country and of the hidden treasures of the monasteries, he was master of the state, and in 1544 the throne was declared hereditary in his family.

The following century saw the kingdom turned into an empire and the Baltic into a " Swedish lake." The rulers of Stockholm were not satisfied with the south of the Scandinavian peninsula and the eastern shore of the Narrows. Finland had belonged to Sweden for centuries, and now the Baltic provinces, Pomerania and the mouths of the Oder and the Weser fell one by one into Swedish hands. Russia, Poland, Denmark and even the Empire all suffered from this rapid expansion, which was sealed by the treaties of 1660, and of which Gustavus Adolphus and Charles X were the heroes. To Charles XI fell the task of completing the internal centralisation of the country. While the kings had thrown themselves heart and soul into European wars, the nobles had seized the opportunity to extend their domains and to usurp fiscal privileges. They dominated the Diet, imposed their will on the monarchy and established a heavy tyranny over the lower classes. By taking away the legislative power of the Diet in 1682 Charles XI instituted an absolutism which was readily accepted by the middle and lower classes for the sake of its wise economic administration and certain social reforms.

In the eighteenth century came the extraordinary adventure of Charles XII and the collapse of the fragile empire. Reduced almost to its original frontiers, the kingdom enjoyed peace at any rate. But the monarchical power had foundered in the storm, and the nobles, having defeated it, produced nothing but anarchy to take its place. It was now the turn of Sweden, made a still more tempting prey by her newly revealed wealth, to be threatened with dismemberment, and to ward off this imminent danger Gustavus III won back the essential privileges of the monarchy (1772). Soon, however, constitutional monarchy was not enough for him, and following in the steps of Charles XI he re-established absolutism (1789) in order to support the prosperity of the country and the interests of the people against the pretensions of the nobles. But he fell a victim to the hatred of the aristocracy.

Let us turn to inquire how the Swedish people lived and laboured during this brilliant and varied history, in which they showed themselves so valiant.

The chief natural wealth of this country, where the soil was poor and the climate severe, lay in mines and forests. Thus Gustavus Vasa, who was anxious to endow his new dynasty with the most indispensable instrument of power, had appropriated all the resources of the subsoil, and had, moreover, reduced the surface landlords to the position of usufructuaries. Nor did he leave these subterranean treasures undisturbed. He brought German miners to exploit the silver mines at Sola and the copper mines at Garpenberg, and he sent experts abroad to study foreign methods. From Germany also he brought founders and forgemen. And at the same time there sprang up numbers of big saw-mills worked by the power of the waterfalls.

But soon state mines and metallurgical enterprises began to flag, or if they were worked by companies invested with a public monopoly they only benefited the monopolists, who thought more of increasing their profits by putting up prices than of developing production.[1] The urban industries meanwhile were checked by two great obstacles which the Chancellor Oxenstierna mentions in his memoirs about 1640. On the one hand they were imprisoned in the rigid framework of a narrow gild system, which did everything to raise selling prices and to increase the profits of the masters of the gild, and nothing to increase production or improve quality. On the other hand, the towns were burdened with heavy taxes, and constantly called upon to provide billets and transport for the army. Their finances could not bear the burden, and industry suffered. A few manufactures had, indeed, been founded by foreigners, particularly by the Dutch, who had set up cloth manufactures which were soon large enough to clothe the whole army, breweries where the methods of Dantzig and England were used, a few glass-works, and even a sugar refinery (1650) and a tobacco factory (1660). But during the seventeenth century, and especially during the years 1631-1648 and 1654-1660, it may be said that war was the chief industry of Sweden. Sometimes, as, for instance, after the death of Gustavus Adolphus, the officers hired themselves and their soldiers to anyone who liked to engage them. Sometimes, as at the beginning of Charles XI's reign (1672-1697), it was the king himself who sold his alliance and the support of an army which was considered one of the best in Europe. It was only in the second half of his reign that administrative reforms became more important than great political designs.

Only after the extravagant exploits of Charles XII did the kingdom really enter on the path of economic progress. The honour of having created the first real textile factories and of having thus introduced the new large scale industry belongs to Jonas Alströmer. He had travelled much in England, and he had just completed a close inspection of the silk manufacture of Tours and the stocking manufacture of St. Germain when he learnt that he was to be prosecuted on the charge of having bribed some workmen (1723). He thereupon hastened back to Sweden, though not without

[1] The annual production of the foundries, however, reached 10,000 tons in the seventeenth century. In 1611 a latten metal manufacture was founded, and has lasted to the present day.

pausing on his way to examine the processes used in making fine cloth at Abbéville. Immediately on his return to Sweden he began to organise cotton and woollen manufactures. He had to get everything he needed from abroad, looms, dyes and skilled labour. Everything had to be smuggled, with great effort and danger. In the interests of his heroic enterprise he did not hesitate to expend enormous sums of money, and himself crossed the sea no less than twenty times. Within four years he triumphed over all these accumulated difficulties and over the additional obstacles which the jealousy or distrust of his countrymen had thrown in his path. In 1728 the king came to visit his establishments at Alingsos, and this ceremonial visit to an obscure town near Gothenborg which he had raised to the rank of an industrial metropolis, was proof of his success. There he had set up cotton-spinning mills, and factories for cloth, lace, ribbons, dyes and tanning, and at the death of its founder this small district employed 18,000 workers. Alströmer, marvellous organiser that he was, had also been interested in the older industries and had introduced the latest English improvements into the metal trade. It was then that the refined iron of Dannemora began to be famous.

The restoration of order at the end of the century and the succession of an enlightened sovereign naturally resulted in fresh progress. Although the ruin done in the Alingsos district by the recent disturbances was not entirely repaired, and although the suspension of the bounties granted to many of the manufactures by the royal bank shook their somewhat artificial prosperity, progress was apparent in other directions. The development of the silk stocking manufacture at Stockholm caused great uneasiness to the Lyons manufacturers,[1] and French diplomats tried alternate threats and promises of pardon in order to obtain the return of some clever Languedoc artisans, who were in their opinion responsible for the success of this unexpected competition. The order of Vasa was created to reward, among other public benefactors, those who exploited mines, and with the help of English workmen Sweden was soon able to produce and even to export steel. Henceforward the workmen

---

[1] In 1760 there were in the kingdom 69 silk manufactures, employing 2,500 workmen.

formed an essential element in the population. But fluctuations of the market or crises of unemployment might reduce some of them to beggary, and therefore, to prevent their causing disturbances or becoming a burden on the state, the government followed the example of England and opened workhouses (1773) where this unneeded labour might be used. All able-bodied paupers were no longer entitled to public charity, but, willy-nilly, had to earn enough to ward off starvation. Work became more continuous and more intense in all crafts, and twenty-two holidays were suppressed as useless.

When Sweden was united with or subject to Denmark all commerce belonged to the Hanse merchants, and without their pecuniary aid Gustavus Adolphus might not have been strong enough to establish national independence. But the new king had not freed his country from the political oppression of Denmark simply to leave it in economic subjection to a German league. He concluded commercial treaties with the Low Countries, England, Russia and France and drove out the expensive Hanse intermediaries. The national mercantile marine benefited by the opening of direct relations with foreign countries, and in 1559 there were already sixty-two ships engaged in foreign trade alone. The exports were almost exclusively raw materials, iron ore and pig-iron, copper, timber[1] and tar, or the products of the fisheries, such as oil, eels and dried salmon, or skins of animals trapped in the thick forests of the north. Imports consisted of manufactured articles and of agricultural produce from warmer climes. From Denmark came saltpetre and hops; from Germany, ironmongery and haberdashery; from the Low Countries, canvas, silks and spices; from England, cloth, zinc and lead; from France, salt, wines and spirits. On the other hand, the crown abused its power and hindered instead of helping commerce when it debased the coinage to meet its own pressing necessities. It would have been well, moreover, if the king had abolished some of the more obstructive features of the gild system, and had instituted some free fairs at any rate in the capital, and had not prolonged so unreasonably the existence of monopolies which discouraged

[1] Masts, yards, and beams shaped with the axe; also unbarked timber, which was bought by the wind-driven sawmills of Holland.

private initiative. But in spite of these obstacles Stockholm, which had become the sole and privileged market of the Northern Baltic, opened its first bank in 1656. Even before this time a postal system had been organised, at first by means of messengers who were expected to cover on an average three and a half miles an hour, and later by couriers on horseback (1646).

It was not until the eighteenth century that there was any fresh commercial development. Oxenstierna had suggested in his memoirs that shipping should be encouraged by granting bounties on cargoes exported in Swedish ships. Alströmer succeeded in instituting a protective policy, very like the British legislation to which it was directly opposed, for it was essential that Sweden's powerful neighbour should not monopolise shipping as she already controlled some of the mines.[1] Gustavus III completed this work of economic defence by granting exemption from personal taxation to all sailors in the service of native shipowners. Meanwhile commercial treaties had been renewed, notably with France, which in 1741 obtained the privileges of the most favoured nation in the port of Wismar. An East India Company had been founded, though, as a matter of fact, it had done very little.[2] Alströmer, who became its president, also founded a Levant Company, which profited by the re-establishment of friendly relations with the Dey of Algiers to carry the Swedish colours into the Mediterranean. He also persuaded the government to buy the Barima district south of the Orinoco, where he dreamt of founding a colony. In Gustavus III's reign the Greenland Society was formed for whale fishing. The activity of all the ports increased, and in the hope of making an important place of call on the Cattegat, Marstrand was declared a free port, and Gothenborg, not far away, became one of the chief outlets of the kingdom, as soon as a canal was made between the North Sea and the Baltic. The Chancellor Oxenstierna had already suggested that the great southern lakes should be used for this purpose, and between 1744 and 1751 the engineer Polhem

[1] This Swedish Navigation Act dates from 1724. In 1720 the national marine only numbered about 100 ships; ten years later it numbered 500.

[2] Founded in 1731, it at any rate existed until 1813.

constructed the famous Stockholm dam, fifty yards long and twelve wide, which remained in service until the middle of the last century. In the reign of a king who was a disciple of the Economists the restoration of the coinage and the re-establishment of credit contributed still further to this brilliant growth of commerce.

As regards agriculture, the general conditions of soil and of climate were too unfavourable for it to prosper greatly except in a few southern provinces. The restoration of the national monarchy, moreover, had not brought it only advantages. Undoubtedly the Reformation, which had followed so soon afterwards, had relieved the land of the burden of tithes and had brought a huge stretch of Church lands into the market. But Gustavus Vasa had claimed for the crown not only woods, rivers and lakes, but also all the coastal fisheries, all common lands and all uncultivated land. This extension of the domain of the state had in many districts reduced the inhabitants to the position of "precarious" tenants, and sometimes the despotic liberator intervened even in private estates to regulate the details of farming. He made better use of his power when he installed agricultural colonies in the northern forests and introduced Dutch cattle into the kingdom.

The soil of Sweden could not hope to receive much attention from peasants and nobles when they were winning the admiration of the world for their discipline and courage on German battlefields, and when the whole people was burdened with a crushing taxation. The most that can be said is that the incessant needs of the army encouraged horse-breeding. On the other hand, the nobles had forced the state to pay highly for their services. Especially during the reign of Christina (1632-1654) they had been given immense grants of crown lands, and this extension of large properties in the hands of the nobility was not favourable to agriculture. All the energy of Charles XI (1672-1697) was needed to effect the necessary restoration of the crown lands. While the nobles, thus despoiled of their too easily won domains, were obliged to enter the service of the state in order to live, most of the lands which they restored to the crown were sold to the peasants. Thus was reconstituted the strong rural democracy which had once been the mainstay of Swedish power and which to this day forms the chief element in Swedish society.

But until the middle of the eighteenth century peasant agriculture suffered from the excessive subdivision of holdings. The land of each village was divided into several parts, and each peasant possessed several holdings in each division, long strips often so narrow that the owner could not turn a cart round there without encroaching on his neighbour's land. Naturally it was impossible to enclose these strips, and thus all the peasants of the village were forced to sow and reap and send their cattle to pasture at the same time. It was an exaggerated form of the communal bondage of the open field system, which, indeed, existed in most of the countries of Europe. From 1749 to 1762 various measures were passed which insured that no farm should consist of more than nine separate lots, four of plough-land, four of pasture, and one of forest. Laws were passed to facilitate the exchange of strips, and by the end of the century this salutary work of consolidation was finished.

Meanwhile the indefatigable and universally active Alströmer drew fresh sources of wealth from a somewhat barren soil by the introduction of new crops. In 1723 he introduced the potato, which he brought from France, and which was soon covering great stretches of country round the factories at Alingsos. He even tried to naturalise a more delicate plant—tobacco—in those northern regions. The sight of some vicunas in the menagerie at Chantilly was enough to make him attempt to acclimatise them in his own country, and he successfully introduced Angora goats, then almost unknown in Europe, as well as English cattle and Spanish and Moroccan merinos. Thus Sweden ceased to be entirely dependent on the foreigner for the raw material of one of its young textile industries. Later, towards 1760, the passion for agricultural science, which was strong in most of Europe, spread to Sweden. An academy had already been created, with the chief object of studying the properties of the soil and of directing its cultivation. In 1775 Wallerius published his *Principles of Agricultural Chemistry*. All sorts of expensive and often ill-considered enterprises were undertaken, but at any rate the drill began to come into general use. On the very day of his coronation Gustavus III founded the

Order of Vasa, and in the first rank of those for whom the new honours were designed were placed those who by writing or experiment had rendered some service to agriculture. When, following Alströmer's example, he tried to naturalise the mulberry in Sweden, he was uselessly flying in the face of Nature, but if his audacity was here excessive, he also took innumerable wise measures to increase production. He allowed free trade in corn; he rented out the crown lands on more or less long leases to farmers who possessed both the will and the means to farm them to the best advantage; he granted generous help and exemptions to the small cultivators. About 1773, when famine and disease had decimated the rural population, he organised free distributions of corn in the provinces. Moreover, he freed the country of vagabonds, and granted exemption from all personal taxes to any peasant who had four children. On these peasant holdings, which were now consolidated and freed from the communal routine, the perpetual rotation of crops soon took the place of a triennial and even of a biennial fallowing. The soil of Sweden began to repay labour which had always been free and which now became more methodical and more fortunate.[1]

BIBLIOGRAPHY

ALLEN, C. F.: *Histoire du Danemark* (translated into French. Copenhagen, 1878). 2 vols.

La Suède. Son peuple et son histoire. Exposé historique et statistique publié par ordre du gouvernement. (Stockholm, 1900.)

GEFFROY: *Gustave III et la cour de France.* (Paris, 1867.)
Histoire des États scandinaves. (Paris, 1851.)

La Norvège : Ouvrage officiel publié à l'occasion de l'Exposition universelle de Paris. (Christiania, 1900.)

BOYESEN: *History of Norway.* (London, 1886.)

---

[1] From 1570 to 1775 the population of Sweden (reckoned within the modern boundaries) seems to have increased from 900,000 to 1,925,000.

CHAPTER IX

POLAND—RUSSIA

LEAVING out of account the Ottoman Empire, Eastern Europe at the beginning of modern times comprised only the two states of Poland and Russia, and the former was destined to dismemberment at the hands of the neighbouring powers of Central Europe and of the immense empire which stretched into Asia.

§ 1. Poland.

Institution of serfdom; decline of the middle classes; decay of commerce; economic and social anachronism.

In the sixteenth century the Polish monarchy was, after Muscovy, the largest state in Europe and belonged much more definitely than Muscovy to the domain of Western civilisation. With ill-defined frontiers, it was, indeed, obliged in the seventeenth century to cede some of its conquests, first to Sweden and later to Russia; but it was not these external defeats which brought about its ruin, which resulted rather from the vices of its political constitution. This unhappy country was destined to anarchy from the day when its monarchy became elective and the electoral assembly called in a foreign prince (1572), and more especially from the day when the Polish nobles obtained the mischievous right of *liberum veto*, which allowed the smallest minority—even one man—to annul the decisions of the majority (1652). Religious divisions between Roman Catholics, Protestants, Arians and Greek Catholics, and the military weakness of the kingdom, hastened its decline. But there was yet another germ of ruin in the economic and social organisation of the kingdom, and it is on this point that we must fix our attention.

In this essentially rural country the modern era opened with the institution of serfdom. The Statute of Piatrkov in 1496 bound the peasant to the soil. If he accepted this restriction of his liberty, at the price of heavy *corvées*, he might remain in enjoyment of the land he cultivated. But if he wished to emigrate he had to give up all he possessed to the lord, and in every family all the children but one were bound by the same conditions as the father. This new servitude grew continually heavier until the nobles, who by the *pacta conventa* of 1753 had become the real masters of the government, even claimed the right of pursuing runaway serfs on to their neighbours' lands, and proclaimed that the peasants were dependent entirely on the goodwill of their lords. Certainly they never reduced the peasants to the condition of slaves who could be bought and sold, and perhaps they treated them rather less harshly than the Muscovite masters were to do. Nevertheless, all hope of agricultural progress was lost, and the cultivator lived wretchedly on rye and milk, while the small supply of wheat which the great estates produced was exported for the lord's benefit. It was agriculture of a very poor type which gradually spread on the steppes of the Ukraine, pushing before it the semi-nomadic stock-breeding practised by the Cossacks, who often showed fierce resistance. The carelessness of the noble was matched by the indolence of the serf. Moreover, in the absence of all public control, no better use was made of the forests than of the soil.

The decline of the middle class was no less serious. This class, which developed in the thirteenth century, was of German origin, and for a long time, secure in its privileges, it had held itself aloof from the life of the nation. But at the very moment when the towns were beginning to be really Polish the nobles robbed them of all their rights. The same Statute of Piatrkov which enslaved the peasants attacked the prosperity of the townsfolk. They were forbidden to buy land, to make alcohol of grain and to sail on the Vistula. These were the monopolies of the nobles, who also reserved to themselves the right of presentation to ecclesiastical benefices and to the episcopate, and who finally monopolised labour, since only one of the sons of a peasant was allowed to work outside the estate.

Craftsmen might have found employment in supplying the luxurious needs of the nobles, but even this resource was denied them, for all import duties on foreign manufactures were abolished, and it was the fashion to prefer them to native products. Merchants at least might have profited by the import of these articles and the export of grain, but as a matter of fact this trade was mainly in the hands of Jewish colonies in the towns or of the German merchants at Dantzig, who formed so many little states within the state. Money went into the neighbouring countries. The gilds of Cracow, which had already suffered from the fall of Constantinople and the consequent alteration of trade routes to the north, lost all their trade. Warsaw, which had replaced. the older city as the political capital, was long before it became an economic centre. Moreover, no one was responsible for the upkeep of the roads. They were not the business of the lesser nobility, who had definitely fallen under the influence of the great Lithuanian nobles, nor of the magnates, who were entirely preoccupied with their family interests. Heavy carts with thick wooden wheels dragged their way along tracks which were frequently broken by bogs and swamps.

Thus at the end of the eighteenth century Poland, still wholly feudal, divided into hostile clans and with two profoundly unequal classes, was a political, social and economic anachronism. Its arsenals were empty, its fortifications were tumbling to bits, and its army was almost non-existent. Thus all that was needed for its destruction was that the neighbouring powers, strong in their modern organisation, should unite for a moment. Prussia, Russia and Austria partitioned the territories of this nation which was once so great. The Poles became one of the martyr-people of Europe, for national consciousness awoke at the very moment when they ceased to form a state.

§ 2. Russia.

Serfdom made universal and more severe; slow progress of agriculture—
Introduction of modern industry—Development of commercial relations with the West.

Since the Mongol invasions in the thirteenth century Russia, or rather Muscovy, seemed to belong to Asia rather than to Europe. But Ivan the Great (1462-1505) and his grandson Ivan the Terrible (1533-1584) had succeeded in driving back or defeating the Tartars and had turned their country's destiny towards the West. These early tsars laid the foundations of a strong monarchy by consolidating Russian territory, by uniting the republics of Novgorod and Tver to, Moscow, and by bringing the feudal nobles or *boyards* into subjection. In 1613 the succession of the Romanoffs, whose dynasty lasted to our own day and brought anarchy to an end for the time being, also brought Russia into closer contact with the Western nations which alone till then had really constituted Europe. But it was not until the reign of Peter the Great (1689-1725) that the Russian state, transformed on the model of other modern states, and having won access to the open seas, became really capable of receiving slowly but almost uninterruptedly the influences of Western civilisation. The brilliant and fantastic Catherine II (1762-1796) only continued the work of the founder of Petersburg.

Russia had always been what it was to remain almost to the present day—an empire of peasants—and from the sixteenth to the eighteenth century it became an empire of serfs. For a long time those who cultivated the land had been able to regard themselves as its real owners, in return for paying taxes to the tsar and performing the customary labour[1] for the lord or *boyard*. The community or *mir*, governed by the *starost* and the elders, was alone responsible for these various dues,[2] and the individuals who composed it had complete personal liberty. At the end of the fifteenth century serfdom only existed here and there, but in the reign of Ivan the Terrible the system of *coloni* became general.

To balance the feudal power of the great *boyards*, the tsar allied with the lesser nobles called *dvorianes*. It was they who had profited most by the monetary revolution which, between 1550 and 1575, had reduced the value of the rouble by two-thirds. They lived on their estates throughout the year and bought practically nothing from outside, so that the rise in the price of necessities could only increase their wealth, and they were able to give valuable help to

[1] Usually three days a week.

[2] In the greater part of Russia the *mir* did not receive the undivided ownership of the land cultivated by its members until rather later. See Waliszewski, *Ivan le Terrible*, pp. 22 *et seq*.

the founder of the autocracy. In return he sacrificed the peasants' freedom to them. Henceforth the cultivators were enrolled as part of the nobles' property and could no longer leave their masters to seek new ones.[1] In Theodore's reign (1584-1598), on the suggestion of Boris Goudounof, they were definitely forbidden to pass from one estate to another. They were *krepostnyi*—serfs bound to the soil.

This retrogressive development had been hastened by the misery which the unlimited increase of taxation[2] had caused in the country districts. The land had to bear almost the whole cost of the new government. Rather than sink under the burden, the peasants sought safety in flight, and in order to prevent the ruin of the *dvorianes*, who were the best servants of the state, and the collapse of the whole fiscal system, the government had to check the fugitives by force. Before Boris Goudounof a peasant could not be made to give up the land which he cultivated unless he was indebted to the lord for certain advances. In the last years of the sixteenth century, however, the lord was given an absolute *droit de suite*[3] over all the occupants of his domain. Free *métayers* (*polovniks*) still remained, bound only by an agreement for a fixed number of years. But gradually the landlords refused to sign any contract which was not perpetual. Even the *censitaires*[4] of Black Russia, who held their lands collectively, were crushed by taxation and were reduced to taking refuge with the neighbouring proprietors, who were " always ready to catch deserters in the trap of contractual serfdom."[5] Only a few succeeded in preserving an insecure freedom by becoming Cossacks or emigrating towards the new lands of Siberia. The mass of the peasants fell insensibly to the level of the *kholop*—that is to say, of slaves taken in war or bought in the market. Henceforth they were treated as movable property, as cattle. They were sold apart from the land, and the arbitrary power and cruelty of the masters could be exercised unchecked on these defenceless beings.

---

[1] *Cf.* Edmond Théry, *La transformation économique de la Russie*, p. 5. Paris, 1914.

[2] Whole populations were reduced to feeding on grass, roots and bark in summer, and on straw, dried and ground, in winter.

[3] Right of following runaway serfs wherever they might flee.—M. R.

[4] Tenants who held by a *cens* or money quit rent.—M. R.

[5] Waliszewski, *Le berceau d'une dynastie*, pp. 45-46.

Peter the Great tried in vain to improve their position. He ordered sales of serfs to be restricted to cases of absolute necessity, and he forbade the lords to divide members of one family among different estates. But this had little effect. Since the nobles had been made responsible for the payment of the tax on all people living on their land, they could force the tsar to give them complete control over all these " souls." Thus, although the tsar had not expressly intended it, the evil of serfdom spread to the entire body of peasants, and attacked even the small proprietors, some of whom were of noble origin. Serfdom followed the growth of the empire. As the Muscovite landowners established themselves on the Cossack lands, and as the Turkish peril disappeared, the free occupiers of those vast steppes suffered the universal degradation. Moreover, the enormous works undertaken by the ambitious sovereign entailed an insupportable amount of forced labour from the peasants in certain regions. Hundreds of thousands of them lost their lives in the building of Kronstadt and Petersburg and the construction of the Ladoga Canal.

In the eighteenth century there was no improvement; in fact, matters grew worse. The trade in serfs became an important branch of commerce which Anna Ivanovna tolerated by taxing it, and which Elizabeth officially recognised (1741). When in 1762 military service ceased to be obligatory for nobles, the peasants were enrolled in their stead, and many landowners opened what were practically markets of recruits. Others set themselves to breed these human cattle. They bought young or rough-looking serfs at a low price and fed them and trained them, and finally sold them at a large profit. The best looking of the girls, for instance, were sold into Turkish or Persian harems. As among primitive people wealth is reckoned by heads of cattle or sheep, so here wealth was reckoned by heads of serfs. Debts were paid with them, and they were staked at cards. In addition, these unfortunates had to bear the tripled and quadrupled weight of state taxes and feudal dues. When they attempted to procure any improvement in their lot the ukase of 1767 forbade them, on pain of the knout and of forced labour in the mines, to make any complaint against their masters, and it authorised the masters to deport recalcitrants without trial to Siberia.[1] And this cruel system was now applied to the Little Russians of the southern provinces as well as to the Big Russians of the centre. Even the crown serfs were sold with the lands they occupied and fell by thousands into the lowest depths of serfdom.[2] The results were wholesale desertions on the frontiers; bands of runaway serfs defied the police and took to brigandage; assassinations and attempts at rebellion multiplied. Finally the disappointment of the hopes raised by Catherine's reforming tendencies resulted in the rising of Pougatchef, in the Lower Volga country, which became a fierce Jacquerie (1769).

What agricultural progress could be compatible with this profound degradation of the peasantry?[3] They were so burdened by the exactions of royal agents that they even gave up the idea of working more in order to save a little money. The spread of serfdom would have entailed a hopeless decline of agriculture had not some enlightened sovereigns attempted to improve its material conditions.

The Tsar Alexis (1645-1678), father of Peter the Great, was particularly intent on developing the military power of Muscovy and on extending his territory westwards. But he also encouraged agricultural colonisation, and cleared enormous tracts of the waste-lands. But they were farmed extensively and only produced poor crops, such as rye, oats and buckwheat. Very little wheat was grown. Cattle breeding scarcely existed; there were no oxen except on a few big estates, and the few stud farms which had been established were not enough to improve the poor breeds of horses used in the country. There was no question of the scientific management of forests, and the first fruit gardens

[1] It goes without saying that deportation included work in the mines. In 1765 the knout replaced the cat-o'-nine-tails as the instrument of daily punishment. As many as 100 strokes might be given, the equivalent of 17,000 strokes with a rod. The wretches who were suffering from this torture were forced to return to their daily task by refusing them food.

[2] About a million serfs on the lands confiscated by the Church retained, however, a measure of freedom.

[3] When Diderot expressed astonishment at the filthiness of the peasants round St. Petersburg, Catherine is reported to have replied, " Why should they take care of a body which does not belong to them ?"

had only just begun to flourish on the imperial estates at Vladimir. Even the alienation of the crown lands did not always tend to improve agriculture, for the big landowners did not trouble to increase the revenue of lands which they hardly knew, and the small landowners succumbed beneath the weight of fiscal charges.

Peter boldly launched out in new directions. He tried to acclimatise the Hungarian vine on the banks of the Don, and the Persian vine on the shores of the Caspian. In the lower Valley of the Volga he planted the mulberry. But he was more successful when he introduced tobacco in the south and potatoes in the centre, when he forced the *popes*[1] to instruct their people in gardening, when he encouraged the crossing of native cattle and sheep with foreign ones, and when he introduced model breeding-studs (1712). It was by his orders that the peasants began to use the scythe instead of the sickle at the harvest, and were first taught how to use manure and to select seeds. Later the Tsarina Elizabeth created a land bank, which lowered the rate of interest from 15 to 6 per cent. for distressed landowners, and Catherine II populated the empty Ukraine with German colonists. On the Rhine, particularly in the Palatinate, and also in Moravia, " she established agents whose duty it was to furnish the emigrants with the means of making the long journey with their families, all piled into their big German carts drawn by four horses. On their arrival in Russia the controller of the colonies gave each family a house built of stone, a cow, a pair of oxen and a plough, together with a sum of money during the first year of settlement. . . . At the end of ten years the land, house and garden became the sole property of the colonists. The controller then made an account of everything which had been supplied to them, and they paid interest on it at 5 per cent. for fourteen years. They were exempt from military service for twenty-five years and were not even obliged to billet soldiers."[2]

Russian industry developed as slowly as agriculture. The manorial workshop, such as Western Europe had known five centuries earlier, was still one of the essential methods of industrial production. The *boyard's* household included all

[1] Greek priests in Russia.—M. R.
[2] *Souvenirs du Comte de Rochechouart*, pp. 90 *et seq*. Paris, 1889.

the workmen who were needed to supply the needs of the family, and each village, if not each peasant household, made everything necessary for its modest requirements. Thus urban labour was of little importance and very loosely organised. The towns, no less than the country, suffered from the troubles which marked the early years of the seventeenth century, "the shifts of a hard-pressed treasury and the excesses of a greedy and corrupt administration." Even Moscow lost a third of its inhabitants. Moreover, the townspeople were not specifically distinguished by law from the mass of the country-folk. The position of towns had been decided by strategic rather than by economic considerations, and when Alexis tried to make them into industrial centres he found it almost impossible to adapt them to any new purpose, so cramped was the space within their walls and so frequent the outbreaks of fire.

It was outside the towns that industrialism was born; either in their suburbs (*slobody*), where, however, there was no clear distinction between artisans and peasants, or in rural communities which here and there specialised in the production of some particular article; in one place leather goods, in another (for instance, round Nijni-Novgorod) the wooden boxes used to carry merchandise from the fair to Moscow. And naturally it was not in the old cities that the first manufactures on a large scale, either native or foreign, grew up. Most of them, indeed, were fixed by natural conditions in places distant from the towns. In the reign of Ivan the Terrible the iron, copper and rock-salt mines in the Kama and Ural districts made the fortune of the Strogonofs, one of the few great families who had survived the ruin of the old nobility, while the Province of Astrakhan took new life from the fisheries of the Lower Volga, the fleeces of still-born lambs and the salt-pits of the steppes. During the reign of Alexis a Dutchman began to extract iron in the Olonetz district, a Dane made forges not far from Tula, some Germans erected powder- and glass-works near Kaluga, and bell and cannon foundries at Moscow, while a Frenchman directed a glass-works on behalf of the tsar himself. But most of the establishments which were thus springing up on all sides remained completely foreign to the life of the nation. Although a few native workmen were employed, they were only unskilled labourers who learnt none of the secrets of manufacture. Moreover, the Muscovites distrusted these " Western sorcerers " quite as much as they admired them.

It was in the reign of Peter the Great that the modern economic spirit finally penetrated the Russian administration. This " barbarian of genius " tried to organise national industries, both small and large. At the same time as he created gilds of artisans and masters he also formed a superior professional class which could only be entered by a few artistic craftsmen, and the members of certain liberal professions, and wealthy merchants and manufacturers. Elizabeth completed his plan by opening the ranks of the *tchin*[1] to manufacturers. Foreigners were granted many privileges, the right of acquiring land, of practising their trade, of marrying a woman of the country and settling down there, or of leaving when they liked. They, indeed, formed the bulk of the new manufacturing middle class. In addition to the serf-craftsmen, who worked for their master's profit either in his own house or outside, there appeared a class of factory workers. They had been bought by the manufacturers and were now serfs of the factory as they had been serfs of the land. In their mud huts thatched with straw, or in their forest *isbas*, the peasants themselves learned to make shoes of bark (*lapti*) and coarse linen.

To encourage private enterprise the government had recourse to some of the classic expedients of Colbertism. It forbade the export of wool; it made the use of native cloth obligatory for all liveries; it granted numerous subsidies; it even founded and directed a number of workshops of its own. Peter the Great, however, had never wholly believed in state monopolies, and when his financial position allowed it he gave up these public factories to private individuals (1723). Catherine II remained faithful to this liberal policy, which was only too well justified by the two deep-rooted vices of imperial administration, the greediness of the nobles and the dishonesty of the officials. In any case, 200 factories were founded during the reign of Peter the Great, manufacturing woollen cloth, sail-cloth and chemical products. Frenchmen set up factories for stockings and carpets. The Englishman Humphry introduced improvements in the manufacture of

[1] The universal hierarchy of officials, instituted by Peter.

leather which were soon made obligatory on everyone, on pain of confiscation and the galleys.[1] Admiral Apraxine installed the manufacture of silk brocades, and a simple *moujik* succeeded in producing lacquer of a superior quality. The mining industry also continued to develop; landowners were forbidden, under pain of death, to conceal the presence of a mineral deposit on their estates, or to oppose its exploitation by a third person if they neglected to work it themselves. The foundries and forges which multiplied in the provinces of Moscow and Kazan made the fortune of the Demidofs.

Commerce slowly followed in the wake of industry. In the sixteenth century internal trade hardly extended farther than the district round each town, and those who engaged in it—Jews for the most part—were the serfs of the town they lived in, and were treated simply as *moujiks*. For traffic between the towns there were no roads worthy of the name, only a single paved causeway, and otherwise nothing but tracks and footpaths. Travellers had to depend in summer on waterways, and in winter on the frozen snow which everywhere gave easy passage to sledges. Moreover, all the roads most usually frequented were blocked by innumerable tolls and infested with robbers. Post relays could only be obtained by private individuals in winter, and the transport of their letters was not organised until 1665, and then only in two directions—towards Poland and Courland. The chief national market was a fair which was held at Mologa on the Upper Volga, and lasted four months. Trade was almost always carried out by means of barter, for the little money there was in the country was mainly foreign and was seized upon by the tsar. Buyers and sellers competed in dishonesty.

At the accession of Ivan IV, Muscovy had foreign relations only with Asia and the East. The fall of Constantinople had closed the approach to the Mediterranean, and Poland and Sweden barred the way to the Baltic. It was not until a century later (1553) that the English expedition under Chancellor established a precarious contact with the West through the White Sea. Soon afterwards a few Russian merchants began to appear in London and Antwerp, but for the most part it was the foreign merchants, Dutch or English, who invaded this new world. They went regularly to the

---

[1] It consisted of the substitution of tar for tallow in preparing the hides.

fair of Nijni-Novgorod, where the products of two continents were exchanged. From 1652 onwards these *gosti* or foreigners were established in a special quarter at Moscow, the famous suburb where the young Peter was to seek, not without some jeopardy to himself, his first lessons in Western civilisation. Sometimes, again, it was the tsar who, in the manner of the Pharaohs, seized the profit of trade for himself. For example, he received each year in the Kremlin the blue and black fox skins, the sables, beavers and ermines from Perm and Pechora, and from Siberia, which was becoming Russian territory,[1] together with the silks, tea, spices and pearls brought to him by caravans from Turkestan, Persia and Armenia. He forced the landowners to sell him cheaply wax, honey,[2] tallow, hemp, soda, tar and deerskins, and these he resold at a high price to Asiatic merchants or to English traders at Archangel. Moreover, he reserved to himself the exclusive right, or at least the first claim, to sell Western imports, such as cloth, lace, mirrors, ironmongery, wines and fruits.

Peter the Great realised that such a system was barbarous and opposed to the development of trade. On his accession he would willingly have abandoned all those regalian rights which tended to make the tsar the sole merchant of the kingdom. But financial necessity forced him to maintain and even to increase the commercial privileges of the crown. He did not hesitate to retail Hungarian wine, while his minister Menjikof leased the White Sea fisheries and sold cod-liver oil and otter skins. But as soon as the peace with Sweden was signed (1719) he abolished all these survivals of Asiatic despotism at one stroke. Henceforward all branches of trade were free, and Catherine II only made an exception in the case of corn. But the empire now stretched to the shores of the Baltic. On the shores of this open sea, which was almost entirely free from ice, Peter, at the cost of heroic efforts, founded his new capital, the first city in his empire which was not a mere collection of wooden houses round a fortified palace. In order to hasten the growth of Petersburg, he forcibly deflected thither the trade which used to go to

[1] In 1584 the Cossack Ermak reached the banks of the Irtish, and the colonisation of these newly discovered lands was begun by the Strogonofs.

[2] The province of Riazan was rich in bees.

Archangel, and undertook the work of joining the Volga and the Neva by a canal. Otherwise he did not trouble much about transport. The rivers and tracks would serve well enough, and he left to his successors the task of freeing them from the brigands who overran and the toll bars and Customs houses which beset them. But he was interested in the education and honesty of merchants. He sent the sons of wealthy traders to finish their education in England or Holland, and he waged a pitiless war against their old habits of fraud and dishonesty, the legacy of a long servitude. Fifty years later Catherine II could entrust the rich commercial class with the administration of the cities.

Foreign trade remained, it is true, chiefly in the hands of foreigners. Although they no longer enjoyed government favour, they still possessed two advantages over their Russian competitors—a better established fortune and a wider experience. Even in trade with the interior the Russians only acted as agents. Russia was still far from being self-sufficing, although she had entered the Concert of the West and was already accounted one of the chief military powers in Europe and the world. Her economic future was already foreshadowed, distant still, but magnificent.

BIBLIOGRAPHY

GRABIENSKI (Smolenski): *History of the Polish Nation.* (Cracow, 1906.) In Polish.

LUBOMIRSKI: *The Polish Peasantry from the Sixteenth to the Eighteenth Centuries.* (Warsaw, 1862.) In Polish.

ULANOWSKI: *The Polish Village in its Juridical Aspect.* (Cracow, 1894.) In Polish.

KORZON: *Histoire intérieure de la Pologne au XVIIIᵉ siècle.* (1896.)

POSNER: *Le Paysan polonais.* Conférence faite à l'École des Hautes-Études Sociales de Paris en mars, 1916 (published in the *Revue internationale de Sociologie*).

RAMBAUD: *Histoire de la Russie.* (1878.) English translation by L. B. Lang, 2 vols. (1879.)

HAUMANT: *La Russie au XVIIIᵉ siècle.*

WALISZEWSKI: *Ivan le Terrible.* (1904.) English translation by Lady M. Loyd. (1904.)

Le berceau d'une dynastie : les premiers Romanovs. (1909.)

Pierre le Grand. (1897.) English translation by Lady M. Loyd. (1897.)

Le roman d'une impératrice (Catherine II). (1893.) English translation by Lady M. Loyd, 2 vols. (1894.)

CONCLUSION

I.—CHIEF CHARACTERISTICS OF THE HISTORY OF LABOUR IN EUROPE FROM 1500-1800

§ 1. Medieval Survivals and their Gradual Disappearance.

LOOKING back over the three centuries we have just studied, we naturally see there many survivals of the preceding epoch. Medieval society on the whole had been characterised by the predominance of the warlike spirit over the mercantile or, more properly, the economic spirit. Force of arms had prevailed over wealth.

Yet was it not truly this spirit of adventure, this love of great deeds, finding so little scope in the new order and security of Europe, which, every bit as much as the desire to make their fortunes, led on the *Conquistadors*, the founders of the first colonial empire? The seas which their daring opened to the ships of all the world were the scene of innumerable and bloody struggles. Piracy was rife, and ships which ventured there sailed in squadrons. It is easy to understand why this heroic traffic was never forbidden to the nobility, even in France. On the Continent wars raged incessantly, no longer between castle and castle or province and province, but between state and state. They were now vast and costly enterprises, and if they encouraged certain branches of farming such as horse-breeding, and certain industries such as heavy metallurgy, and even such forms of maritime enterprise as privateering, they nevertheless exhausted the real sources of wealth, squandering men and money in pure waste. At times, for example, French shipowners could not find crews for their ships because the king had taken them all for his fleets.

Commercial rivalry between nations, even when it did not cause war, provoked cruel defensive measures. At Venice in the middle of the sixteenth century " any artisan who took a useful industry out of the country was stabbed," and Florence also decreed death to anyone who revealed the secrets of her industries to the foreigner. In Holland anyone who communicated the charts drawn up by her sea-captains to another nation was executed. Until 1825 English artisans were officially forbidden to leave the country; and the emperor-philosopher Joseph II had all smuggled goods burnt by the public executioner. By the Treaty of Westphalia the Dutch closed the Scheldt for nearly 200 years, " thus outrageously depriving the inhabitants of Antwerp of the advantages destined to them by God and Nature."[1] For fifty years the English obstinately insisted on the filling up of the port of Dunkirk, the loss of which they could not forget.

Gradually, however, more humane ideas crept into international relations. Already Louis XI had made treaties with two great commercial powers of the time, the Venetians and the Hanseatic League, assuring their merchants of protection at the French fairs even if France were at war with their countries. At the beginning of the sixteenth century Spain, and in Richelieu's time even Morocco, suppressed the right of wreckage on their shores. The *droit d'aubaine*[2] was gradually suppressed in all the countries of Europe. In France a decree of 1669 exempted the merchants of all nationalities from it, even if France were at war with their countries. In 1781 the Armed Neutrality drew up articles which as far as possible guaranteed the freedom of maritime commerce against the arbitrary claims of the belligerents.

Undoubtedly the old traditions of economic isolation were far from disappearing even when they no longer corresponded with the new conditions of commerce. Almost all states tried to preserve, as a most precious advantage, their self-sufficiency in the matter of food; almost all controlled the corn trade in a manner reminiscent of the old grain restrictions observed on manorial lands or in the territory of the urban republics; at the beginning of the eighteenth century the exportation of grain was still punishable by death in France. Even Colbert's industrial mercantilism allowed the reduction of trade with neighbouring countries to a minimum, for he claimed that while all countries must come to France

[1] *Cf.* Vidal de la Blache, *États et nations de l'Europe*, p. 29.
[2] The custom by which the estate of an unnaturalised foreigner lapsed to the crown at his death.—M. R.

for various things, she could dispense with all help from them.[1]   But until this prohibitive system was removed smuggling did increasingly efficacious service as a corrective to its excessive harshness.   Moreover, even open warfare did not entail a complete breach in the official commerce between kingdoms; throughout the seventeenth century Spain remained the best client of France.   Economic life as well as thought began to be European, and neither the conflicting ambitions of governments nor even the hatreds of the nations could destroy this new solidarity.

In the internal economic organisation of most of the nations some relics of feudalism survived.   It is scarcely necessary to recall the long survival of internal Customs dues and seigniorial privileges.   But some of these privileges, such as the right of the chase, were continually being extended in France, although the progress of civilisation made even their maintenance intolerable.   Moreover, when a money economy had long been established the continuance of rents and dues paid in kind was not only useless but burdensome, because it prevented the cultivator from ever varying his crops.   In the same way the refusal to allow the worker to leave the place where his work was, and the exaction of forced labour and boon days, were flagrantly contrary to all the principles of modern society.   Serfdom was, indeed, driven back throughout the West, but the institution of *corvées* for the maintenance of the public roads remained a startling anachronism. The spirit of the time demanded, on the contrary, that military service should become a free and well-paid profession, and the organisation of the militia, which was the prelude to universal compulsory service, has the appearance of a retrogressive movement.   Moreover, a dim reminiscence of the subordination of the individual, so strongly marked in the feudal system, appears in another form in the restrictions imposed by the trade unions on their members.

In the Middle Ages religion had acted as a counterpoise to the doctrine of force, and with it had been the dominating force in society.   At the dawn of the new era religious passions were far from being exhausted.   In the hearts of some of the men who led or organised the great transoceanic expeditions the desire to convert unknown and distant

[1] *Cf.* Levasseur, *Histoire du Commerce de la France*, vol. i, p. 420.

peoples to Catholicism, to the religion which already bore
the name of universal, mingled with more earthly motives.
Crusaders were to be found among the *Conquistadors*, sons
of the heroes of the Spanish or Portuguese *reconquista*.
Europe herself for more than a century was torn by conflicting heresies and devastated and drenched with blood by
religious wars. In contrast to the Renaissance, which marked
in the West the birth of a new and perhaps eternal youth,
the Reformation, which was on some sides the beginning of
spiritual and mental freedom, was a definite step back. The
pitiless rigour of Calvin was a harsh check upon the profound
aspirations of the modern mind.

Nevertheless, these two great movements, whose hostile
principles battled in the minds of sixteenth-century men,
were not long in achieving harmony, if only in order to adapt
themselves to the material necessities of the time. This
powerful reawakening of the religious spirit ended in the
partial secularisation not merely of Church property, but of
social life. Many monasteries were suppressed with their
property, and their charitable foundations and many holy-
days were abolished; all these lands and hours which once
were devoted either to the satisfaction of mystic idleness or
to the exercise of pious beggary were now absorbed by
earthly industry. Moreover, even more completely than its
originators had intended, the Protestant Reformation freed
the individual, and merely by forcing him to learn to read
precipitated and infinitely increased the immense results of
printing, and willingly or unwillingly joined the Renaissance
in preparing the way for the revolutions of science. The
very religious persecutions, ending as they did in the expulsion or the departure of heretic capitalists and workmen,
served to spread new industries. The Jewish emigrations
from Lisbon to Salonica and London and from Valentia to
Salonica and Tunis created strong commercial links between
all the distant shores of the European seas. Groups of
foreigners, Jews or Huguenots freed by religion or race
from common rules, played important parts in the financial
development of various countries, for the "most Christian"
and "most Catholic" kings and individuals were only too
ready to seek their help.

§ 2. The Development of National Economy.

National economy, the way for which had been prepared by the political revolution of the fifteenth century, developed continuously. Everywhere the work of internal unification went on as the natural consequence of the improving means of communication. Undoubtedly in many countries barriers still remained, not only barriers raised by Nature, which man's genius was as yet powerless to overcome, but also those which had arisen from old social combinations and which were destined sometimes to be removed only at the cost of a new revolution. But long before the modern state had achieved the maximum of unity compatible with natural conditions, it came into conflict with neighbouring states and raised against their rival industries an almost insurmountable barrier of protection. An interesting detail of this progressive nationalisation of commerce is furnished by the purification of the French coinage in the seventeenth century; the royal coinage became the national coinage and drove foreign money out of circulation, just as it had driven out seigniorial money before. The government even went so far as to disqualify foreign bankers, and manufacturers were always ready to welcome any measures taken to reserve the national market for them.

On the other hand, the state also included under its sovereignty and its protection vast colonial domains which were simply extensions of itself. The time of private conquests had passed. The royal police had driven adventure-seekers across the oceans, and they were no longer allowed to keep the fruits of their exploits for themselves. The economic control of the state, exercised in the interests of a more or less numerous class of citizens in the mother-country, soon fell heavily on these distant domains. In spite of the long weeks of the voyage which then separated them, the bond between the mother-country and the colony was never closer. Trade with the colonies was really more strictly regulated, if not more active, than trade with neighbouring states or even between the different provinces of a single kingdom.

§ 3. Progress of Capitalism.

In the framework of the nation the new economic ideal was realised in the shape of a system which can already be called capitalist in the modern sense of the word, for it rested on a more or less marked concentration of capital, which entailed corresponding changes in the organisation of industry and in the condition of the workers. Capital is, it is true, almost as old as labour or as mankind itself, and is traditionally defined as the product of former work, or wealth previously acquired, used for the execution of new work and the acquisition of new wealth. But what specially characterises the modern era is the steady and progressive tendency of capital in every country to accumulate in order to produce huge business enterprises.

The first in order of importance and of date were commercial enterprises. Commerce, which had hitherto been half confused with industry, now became distinct and took the lead. Then, by widening the markets, it caused a second concentration of capital of another sort and brought about the transformation of industry. Thus during this period, which might well be called the *mercantile* period, using the term in its original and wider sense, the word commerce served to describe all activity productive of wealth, and the first modern economic theories took the form of commercial theories.

The predominant form of commerce from the sixteenth century onwards was foreign commerce, and the most distant form of foreign commerce, maritime trade, in which the consumer is at the greatest possible distance from the producer. Take France, for example, washed by two seas, but also closely attached to the heart of the Continent. In the seventeenth century it was estimated that three-quarters of her foreign trade, in terms of value, were carried on by sea; to-day the proportion is not more than two-thirds.

This was certainly not because the sea routes were safest. In addition to natural risks, which were much greater, there were those which resulted from an almost perpetual and hardly disguised state of war. There was no effective police force such as the kings had organised on the Continent, and the ships were forced to sail in caravans, just as during the

Middle Ages merchants had been wont to travel to the fairs under the menace of the robber barons. But all these difficulties, far from discouraging distant trade, seem merely to have forced shipowners to arm their ships more heavily.

The reason was that maritime trade brought about a marvellous decrease in the cost of transport. Even to-day sea routes are cheaper than much shorter land routes, in spite of the multiplication and improvement of roads, the organisation of rivers and canals and the creation of railways. The steamer has not altogether replaced the sailing vessel, nor will it; and between our largest sailing ships and the sixteenth-century caravels the gap is not so big as between the waggon of those days and our goods train. We must notice, moreover, that though the sea might be infested with enemies it did not bristle with Customs barriers, and it alone was open to international traffic. Therefore we see this or that trade, which had hitherto used the Isthmus of Languedoc, or the Valleys of the Rhone, the Saône and the Rhone, leave these for the sea route through the Straits of Gibraltar. Thus, although Mediterranean trade had suffered a temporary decline, the ocean remained the only path to those Eastern regions, the products of which always fetched a good price. We have already explained how free trade could exist between the continents, when Europe itself was intersected by Customs barriers.

It must, however, be observed that the great sea powers henceforward possessed extensive territories. The day was past for the merchant republics, Venice, Genoa and the Hanseatic towns, whose whole dominions—including both metropolis and "factories"—covered only a few square leagues, and whose empire resided in their fleets; urban economy could not compete with powerful kingdoms. Even the sharp decline of Portugal and more gradual decay of Holland are largely explicable by the fact that they did not possess a large enough Continental base. It was a result of the universal protectionism. Commercial cities which did not control their hinterland always ran the risk of being short of outbound freight, and the big states were so anxious to develop their own mercantile marines that they hindered in every possible way the operations of the small states, which were reduced to the part of carriers.

It is obvious that increased facilities of transport resulted in many changes in the material of foreign trade. In the early Middle Ages only luxuries and semi-luxuries circulated, articles which took up little space and weighed very little, yet were very valuable. But now articles in general demand, often heavy and cumbrous, could pass from sea to sea without being burdened by excessive transport charges. From the New World, for instance, at first only precious metals and rarities were exported, but before the end of the eighteenth century North American corn was competing with English corn in England, and American iron also appeared on the European market. With still more reason, the raw materials and numerous manufactured products of that continent, which was so easily accessible to the sea on all sides, gave rise to an intense and continuous stream of imports.[1]

Though less startling and less rapid, the progress of internal trade was none the less remarkable. It was not so much that the market grew by the extension of the national frontiers, as that business between the inhabitants of the same country increased enormously. The development of international trade, indeed, gave it impetus and shook the old inertia even in the most distant provinces, and the improvement of provincial roads did the rest. After the re-establishment of internal peace, the progress in making rivers navigable, and later the construction of canals, seem to have exercised a decisive influence. Here, too, the water-way preceded the high-road, and for a long time was much more useful. In the absence of a good system of secondary roads, Richelieu and Colbert still not unreasonably considered that the royal high-roads were luxuries.

The growth of the population must also be taken into account. It mattered little if the area of a market did not increase, provided that the density of its population did. In addition, the general increase of comfort doubled both the productive power and the purchasing power of each indi-

---

[1] " The sale of cloth was once only carried on from place to place. To-day travelling is more rapid, and customers must and can be sought all over Europe."—Report of an inspector of French commerce at the end of the eighteenth century. Quoted by Levasseur, *Classes ouvrières*, vol. ii, p. 528.

vidual, and the fashion for "novelties," a manifestation of the increasing comfort, which was particularly marked in the clothing trade, tended to make business more active. "It is notorious," wrote the inspector of commerce quoted above, "that people only buy clothes to-day with the object of buying new ones as soon as their means allow."

The increased volume of internal trade resulted in a change in its organisation. Except in cases where they were, perhaps, necessary to meet the seasonal needs of agriculture, the old periodical fairs were unnecessary now that roads were almost always safe, even for isolated merchants, and now that the population had so increased that there was a steady and permanent demand for supplies. The cities played the part of continuous fairs. Even markets—that is to say, exhibitions of local produce held at short intervals—tended to decline. The cultivator no longer took all his produce to the market-hall, but contented himself with showing samples of it in the square, and the bulk of the goods was taken direct from his barn to the purchaser's shop. In the case of manufactured articles the commercial traveller, taking his sample cases from shop to shop, began to replace the pedlar, who still hawked his ill-stocked baskets round the farms. This transformation, which produced a new mobility in commerce, presupposed that the articles offered for sale had been produced in large numbers, and were identical in price and quality—briefly, that industrial organisation had also been changed.

During the period we have studied, industry was, from all points of view, subordinated to commerce, on which it depended both for its raw materials, which were brought from increasingly wide distances, and for its markets, which continually widened too. The appearance of the cotton industry, among others, was very significant, for hitherto the textile industries had found their raw material close at hand; but this one depended entirely on supplies brought first from the remote shores of the Mediterranean, and later from across the Atlantic. The small master-craftsman was not rich enough to command these distant supplies and to extend his clientèle in proportion, and therefore the big manufacturer stepped in. The same process had already appeared in a less accentuated form in the smaller field of purely national trade. Thus, even before any modification in technique appeared, a certain amount of concentration took place in industry. It was a social concentration which was usually accompanied by geographical concentration, for the big manufactures grouped themselves in districts which were most conveniently situated for receiving their raw materials and for despatching their products.

Sometimes the development of commercial capitalism entailed simply the union into one business of several allied crafts, which had hitherto been quite distinct and which, moreover, continued to preserve their own processes. But usually this collection of many workmen employed in a complicated manufacture under one management could only be carried out by the introduction of professional specialisation among them. "Workmen occupied constantly on the same process," wrote Messance ten years before Adam Smith, "become more skilled and waste less material."[1] And as we have already shown, this reduction of the work of each man to a series of comparatively simple actions, which never changed and soon became mechanical, led directly to the adoption of machinery. But machines in their early days were very expensive. The small master could not as a rule afford them, and this gave the big manufacturer a further advantage by which finally to oust his small competitor.

This was only a stage in the growth of industry. Commerce assisted in its development, and under its auspices industry grew steadily, so that gradually among the nations which had taken the lead in economic progress industrial exports became more important than agricultural exports. This was the case in France, for example, towards the middle of the eighteenth century.[2]

Since industrial development depends on the concentration of capital, it was natural that certain types of industry should develop more quickly than others. Thus the metallurgical industries, with few exceptions, developed later than the textile industries because they required more machinery and therefore more initial outlay of capital. They must not be confused with the mining industries, which, in the early stages when they were simply extractive and only worked

[1] Quoted by Levasseur, *op. cit.*
[2] If one leaves out of account the re-export of colonial produce.

the shallow deposits, had a precocious enough development. In Russia and Sweden they grew up even earlier than the cloth manufacture. Among the mining industries, moreover, a distinction must be made between the extraction of minerals and the extraction of coal, for the latter was held back for some time by the abundance of wood fuel. Among the textile industries those which found their raw material on the spot naturally developed first; the manufactures of silks and cottons came after those of cloths and linens.

The connection between the fundamental types of industrial production was not so close as it afterwards became. Since heavy machinery, with the steam-engine, had not been introduced into the cloth manufacture, it remained almost independent of the progress of metallurgy. But between the different stages of the same manufacture there was a very intimate connection. For example, the spinner worked for the weaver and must produce only as much thread as the latter needed for his cloth. Any increase in speed by the one soon brought about a corresponding improvement in the industry of the other. But we must guard against praising a natural harmony which exists only in our imagination. This marvellous harmony was only achieved at the price of incessant efforts at adaptation, and on many occasions the indispensable equilibrium was cruelly broken. In the same way, if we try to represent the progress of English metallurgy through these three centuries as a regular and continually rising curve, we shall be far from the truth. In the early years of the eighteenth century the British iron industry was at a very low ebb. It was only by the violent reaction of human labour against the apparent exhaustion of natural supplies that it was raised to a height far above its old summit.

Although European agriculture was not yet dependent on industry for its machinery nor on commerce for the improvement and fertilisation of the soil, it was at least indebted to commerce for the increased market facilities which alone could insure bigger profits and therefore encourage more enlightened methods. For technical progress in agriculture depended on the specialisation of soils and climates, as in other industries it implied the specialisation of labour, and this specialisation was only possible when the cultivator was sure of a quick sale independent of the local markets. On the other hand, the improvement of agriculture, as of industry and commerce, demanded an increase of capital, and this could only come to it from those branches of economic activity whose development had been earlier. The progress of agriculture seems always to be slower than that of other forms of human activity, precisely because in it labour has to deal with an unchangeable foundation, and the very spirit of the men who work in the fields comes in the end to share something of the immobility of the seasons which regulate their labour.

This progress, such as it is, can be measured both by the extension of land under cultivation and by the increased yield of the land, not to mention the increase of the nett produce, which resulted in part from the second of these facts and was one of the determining causes of the first. But without attempting to go into details here, it may be said that agricultural improvements spread over Europe, passing from Italy or Flanders to Holland, from Holland to England, and from England to France. This was almost the same course which was followed at first by commercial predominance.

Let us try to see what part was played by each branch of rural economy in the common progress. Horticulture played a very important part. Gardens, even pleasure gardens, were valuable testing-grounds, laboratories where were evolved discoveries which were later to transform the practices of commercial agriculture. Luxury and art are more closely united to utilitarian work than is sometimes supposed, and this is one aspect of their solidarity.

The connection between stock-farming and arable farming was rather more complicated. It is quite certain that during the period we are studying animal manure was the most valuable fertiliser, but at the same time it was necessary, to secure any appreciable benefit from it, that the cattle should not wander at will over the fields, and that their pasture should not absorb an undue proportion of the land under cultivation. That is to say, to be really profitable breeding should depend, at least in part, on fodder crops and artificial grasses, and the animals should be mainly confined in stables. Otherwise the flock must be regarded as a redoubtable enemy of the plough, especially where, as in Spain, it was a question of semi-nomadic sheep-breeding. But whatever form it took, the advance of stock-breeding always marked a further stage in capitalist agriculture. Extensive breeding was the method of exploiting the soil which demanded least labour, and, moreover, every head of cattle represented an easily realisable value. The word *pecunia* (money) comes from *pecus* (herd). Similarly in intensive breeding the size of the flock is a sign of the wealth of the cultivator. The word *cheptel* (cattle), once so common, was a synonym for capital.

Our last task in this sketch of general economic evolution is to prevent a misconception as to the place of agriculture in it. Because it has been convenient to treat agriculture last, it must not be supposed that it did not fill an immense place in the society of that time. Let us not forget that in France in 1790 the rural population was officially estimated to form 78 per cent. of the total population, and that even in England at the end of the eighteenth century the value of the products of the soil far exceeded that of the products of industry, and that the population living on the soil formed four-fifths of the whole working class.

§ 4. Economic Classes.

The history of industry is not only a picture of the different processes by which men have extracted from Nature everything necessary to the fulfilment of their needs, but also deals with the way in which the common task and the common profit have been shared among them.

During the greater part of the Middle Ages, although society as a whole had been divided into two distinct and (so to speak) opposite classes, the nobles and the commoners, there had at least been a certain amount of equality among the latter. Let us consider, for example, the townspeople, workers in commerce or industry. Either they were grouped in gilds where the general rule was that journeymen should sooner or later become masters, or else they were free workers among whom there existed very little inequality of fortune. But from the beginning of modern times we have seen that the mastership tended to become a sort of hereditary monopoly, inaccessible to most of the journeymen, and in the free crafts, and still more in the new industries, the very conditions of production raised an insuperable barrier between the workmen and the big manufacturers. Thus was formed the class of wage-earners who never succeeded in possessing the raw material and tools for their work, whose only property was their strength and skill, and who were forced to hire these out in order to live.

The position of the agricultural workers was rather different. They had never, by any title, had full and entire possession of the soil they worked, but at least they had possessed in common the full enjoyment of vast stretches of pasture and wood. But gradually everywhere the progress of clearings and the division of the common lands reduced the importance of this collective domain, so that although they gradually became free from the personal bonds of serfdom, they, too, were destined to be deprived of all immediate right to the soil which was the raw material of their labour. And although most of them did not live only for the day, like the industrial workers, since they drew the reward of their labours direct from the annual routine of agriculture, none the less their position became more precarious, and the gulf which separated them from the landowners became wider. Moreover, the formation of big estates led to the growth of a class of country labourers whose position was parallel to that of the wage-earners in the towns.

Thus there already existed, especially in the industrial world, what may justly be called a proletariat. It was to a certain extent conscious of its separate existence and of its own interests, which were often opposed to those of its employers, but this consciousness was incomplete and varied from time to time. In the sixteenth century conflicts between masters and men were purely local, affecting only a small number of workers and rousing no echo in the rest of the country. But already in the following century large bodies of workmen were concentrated round the big manufactures. We must not forget that at that date industry had not been invaded by machinery, and that therefore a much larger proportion of labour was necessary then than is required to-day. Thus the concentration of manufacture entailed a concentration of the new proletariat. The result was that, particularly in France, trade unionism developed. The workers, even those in the gilds, felt the need of organising themselves outside the gilds and fraternities, which had become the strongholds of the masters. The progress of industry, the instability of the new manufactures and the rapid alternations of prosperity and ruin condemned masters and men throughout the kingdom to perpetual hostility. The journeys of the workmen's *tour de France* did as much as the concentration of labour round the new industries to create the solidarity of labour.[1] This solidarity, however, did not extend beyond the limits of the nation. Foreign workmen were still regarded simply as competitors.

What was the destiny reserved for this new social class, for example, in France, where its vicissitudes were particularly marked? In the first place, the wage-earners were commons, *roturiers*, whose principal function, in the eyes of the king, was to pay taxes. They therefore bore a heavy share of the royal expenses, in direct taxation, over and above feudal charges. Thus the glory of the monarch and the power of the state cost them dear, and periods of military hegemony and political supremacy did not, during the régime of absolutism, necessarily correspond for them with periods of prosperity. It may be objected that the prosperity of their class was intimately connected with the general prosperity of the kingdom. But this is more than doubtful, for what historians describe by the latter term is often only the wealth of the upper classes, which may be partly built up out of the poverty of the common people. If we pursue the matter still further, we shall see that the wages system contained two striking anomalies.

When the lot of the wage-earners improved, their number tended to increase, but, other things being equal, this caused greater competition among them, which soon resulted in a drop in wages.[2] Wages, however, rose in periods of comparative depopulation such as France experienced at the end

[1] In this work of national labour organisation the initiative seems to have been taken by the most intelligent and best paid workmen, such as printers, and chiefly by the sedentary professions, which, no doubt, were most favourable to the exercise of reflection.

[2] " In all our history there had not been a time when the land was so well cultivated and so valuable, and when the condition of the country folk was worse. It is only right to add that at no time had the population been so large as at the moment of the Revolution."— D'Avenel, *Paysans et ouvriers*, pp. 65-67.

of the religious wars or in the last years of Louis XIV's reign. Depopulation had to be carried to the point of national extinction—as in Spain during the seventeenth century—for it to involve the industrial or agricultural proletariat in the universal ruin. Moreover, if we consider the industrial workers separately, they could feel the effects of excessive competition without a general increase in the population taking place, for they had to meet the new competition of rural industries and of women's and children's labour.

On the other hand, what was the result for the wage-earner of technical progress in industry, of the introduction of machinery or even of the division of labour? "The worker was, indeed, paid less by the piece," wrote Messance; "but as he could manufacture a greater quantity of stuff he found himself better off and in the long run received more money during the year." This would, indeed, always have been so, but for the ever-present risk that the speeding-up of work thus entailed might bring about a sudden reduction in the number of workmen required, a reduction which would be only slowly compensated for by the increased demand, resulting from the economy realised in the cost of production and from the lowered price. Moreover, are we to count for nothing the species of physical and mental decline, which work, at once more mechanical and more intensive, brought to the workman? All this, added to his ignorance of the complex commercial conditions which regulated the selling price of articles, of which his own fragmentary share in their production did not allow him to estimate even the cost, made him incapable of discussing with any advantage to himself the terms of the contract imposed on him.

Face to face with the working class—in the broad sense of the term—was ranged naturally the capitalist class. This included, on the one hand, great landowners or landed capitalists, and on the other hand the commercial, industrial and financial capitalists. The power of the former dated back to the distant Middle Ages and remained stationary, but that of the latter, of more recent origin, was constantly increasing. The extension of the use of precious metals was undoubtedly favourable to them, but in any case the development of commerce in the sixteenth century made a monetary revolution indispensable, and if the mines of the New World had not been discovered it would have been accomplished by the earlier adoption of paper money.

Between these two main divisions of the capitalist aristocracy there existed a certain community of opinion concerning their treatment of the workers; but measures which would increase landed revenue were not always favourable to the success of industrial or commercial enterprises. The opposition in England at the end of the seventeenth century between the " landed interest " and the " moneyed interest " is well known, and the same difference appeared, though less markedly, in France during the eighteenth century. The moneyed capitalists themselves were not entirely united. The bankers and financiers in particular had not precisely the same interests as the captains of industry, nor had the latter those of the gild masters, while the merchants often wanted a quite different policy from the manufacturers, the former continually demanding free trade while the latter insisted on a protective system. For example, during Louis XI's reign the Lyons merchants opposed the development of silkworm breeding in France rather than give up the import trade in Italian silks. In the seventeenth century the great merchants of Leipzig, for fear of reprisals, opposed all protection in favour of German industry.

But all sections of the moneyed aristocracy were alike in the rapid and extraordinary growth of their wealth. Just as in the past a sense of their omnipotence had led the landed aristocracy to the worst excesses of pride and violence, so an inordinate increase of wealth caused profound demoralisation among these new *parvenus*. Colonial trade at first, as we have seen, had its *Conquistadors*, who were no more famous than the others for their respect for justice and humanity. It is unnecessary to recall the fever of speculation and of the corruption of public and private morals which reigned in France at the time of the Regency. The same was the case in England during the first half of the eighteenth century until the very excess of evil was its own cure and the vigorous moral and religious reaction of methodism set in.

Modern society, however, was not divided between these two extremes of wealth and poverty. Between the capitalist aristocracy and the working proletariat were several inter-

mediate classes. In industry they were not numerous, for
neither managers nor foremen, properly speaking, formed a
class. In agriculture, however, *métayers*, if not farmers at
a money rent, were almost as numerous as the labourers. It
is true that these general terms covered very diverse realities;
many *métayers* were as poor as labourers, while some of
the big farmers were wealthier than many of the small landowners. Amidst this confusion of ranks voluntary alliances
appeared; the small landowners, small farmers and labourers
had common sympathies, while the big farmers, who owned
plenty of cattle and excellent agricultural implements,
formed a sort of rural bourgeoisie with the big landowners.

§ 5. Governmental Intervention.

We must now consider the part played by governments
in this profound transformation of European society. Their
economic policy, naturally, throughout so long a period, was
not always inspired by the same motives. At first, and
especially in France, it was dominated by political motives.
The establishment of a postal system, for example, facilitated
the prompt execution of royal orders. The development of
luxury trades increased the power of a wealthy bourgeoisie
devoted to the king, and at the same time exhausted the
resources of the nobles and checked their last efforts at
independence. On the other hand, the policy of the
administration was often directed by purely fiscal interests;
the increase of trade would result in increased Customs
returns. Further progress towards a clear understanding of
national economy was made in the theory of the balance of
trade, which taught governments to stimulate exports and
to diminish imports in order to attract into and retain in the
country the largest possible amount of bullion.

The administration in reality lagged behind public
opinion. For as early as the time of the Renaissance the
very simple truth had taken root in some minds that whatever increased the wealth of the subject also, indirectly but
surely, increased the wealth of the sovereign. This idea,
however, only began to enter into the plans of governments
towards the end of the seventeenth century, and first of all in
England. It did not spread generally throughout Europe

until the second half of the eighteenth century, when it became one of the characteristics of " benevolent despotism." The appearance of the new science of political economy, born of financial preoccupations, synchronised with the final adoption by governments of the more liberal ideas of the bourgeoisie, and their decision to extend their protection to the various enterprises in which the capital and labour of their people was engaged. This protection varied, indeed, in wisdom and in efficiency, but at least it was given without any thought of immediate profit.

With regard to the various types of capitalists, their attitudes were so complex, and varied so widely in the different countries, that it is impossible to generalise about them here. But they all showed the same attitude towards the working classes. On the one hand their many bonds with the bourgeoisie and the natural aversion which they felt towards the turbulence of the lower classes[1] did not predispose them to look favourably upon the claims of the new proletariat; and we have already seen that in general, when conflict broke out and when questions of rights arose between employers and employees, the government did not intervene in favour of the latter. But it must also be remembered that the question of food supplies, which had been one of the main preoccupations of feudal princes and city republics, had not been entirely dismissed by the governments of the great states. It was a matter of public order and safety that the poor should not die of hunger, and the government felt that its dignity, if not its duty, was involved in seeing that the poor could obtain the minimum of food necessary to existence, even if it were at the price of exhausting labour.

II.—COMPARATIVE EVOLUTION OF THE CHIEF STATES

The order adopted in this book shows the order in which European states developed, for they did not all develop at the same time. Perhaps it will be convenient to make some general comparison between them, and, above all, between

[1] In France the government showed itself more favourable to rural than to urban democracy, undoubtedly because only the latter gave it any anxiety.

the two great nations which were the leaders of economic and social evolution.

In the first place, England was the country which was least hampered by feudal survivals. From the dawn of modern times all the peasants possessed unrestricted civil liberty. The cruel serfdom practised until 1775 in some Scottish mines and salt-pits was only an exception.[1] Fiscal equality reigned uncontested, and economic unity, like political unity, had been realised at an early date. Defended by the sea, the military expenses of the kingdom were very low; its land army was small, and even its fleets were manned exclusively by volunteers.

Free from all attack, this island was fitted to be the cradle of political liberty. At the very time when absolutism was being established on the Continent, the royal power had here been strictly limited, and the nation found itself henceforward protected, not only against fiscal exactions, but against the excessive interference of the crown in economic affairs. Henceforward the aristocracy and the upper middle classes themselves directed the business of the nation through their representatives in Parliament. The result was that capitalism flourished and brought about a magnificent and spontaneous growth of individual enterprises. It was private individuals who undertook the great drainage works and made the first canals, and who for a long time helped in the upkeep of roads by paying for the use they made of them. This did not mean that national interests were neglected, for England, indeed, protected her commercial interests more jealously than any other nation. Nowhere was protectionism more rigid in principle and more mischievous in application than in this country where smuggling was made almost impossible by Nature herself.

Another result of her insular position was that development in England was continuous; for three centuries there was no invasion and no serious disaster. There were revolutions, indeed, inspired by hatred of despotism and religious passions, but they did not interrupt economic progress. If Cromwell was not the originator of British commercial im-

[1] " They were bound for life to the soil of the mines and salt-pits and could be sold with them. They even wore collars on which their owner's name was engraved."—Mantoux, *Révolution industrielle*, p. 54.

perialism, he at any rate prepared the way for it, and in this respect the Restoration only carried on the work of the Revolution. When Puritanism died down, the passion for wealth again came to the fore. The succession of William of Orange marked the triumph of the capitalist classes, and the wars of the eighteenth century raised this vigorous nation, small as it still was in territory and in population, to the rank of a world power. The sagacity of the people and the blunders of their enemies removed all danger of foreign superiority. Spain herself had destroyed the competition of Antwerp. It was only with difficulty that Holland, in the period between the reigns of Elizabeth and William, succeeded in winning, or at any rate disputing, the supremacy of the seas. Amsterdam eclipsed London only for a very short time, while France compromised her colonial prospects by long Continental wars.

The progress of capitalism was more complete and peaceful in England than elsewhere. The Whig party, which was its Parliamentary representative, represented not only bankers, merchants and manufacturers, but also the big landowners, and agriculture was hardly less advanced than industry. It was in this small state, every part of which was within easy reach of the sea, that the geographical concentration of industry in certain special districts and in some of the big towns was most marked. From the end of the sevententh century London occupied a more important place in England than was filled by any other town in any other country. And, perhaps, too, in English society more than elsewhere there were already to be seen the greatest inequalities of fortune, the keenest opposition between the new aristocracy of wealth and the new proletariat.

Perhaps because her territories were more extensive, France was slower than England in achieving political unity. Some provinces still preserved an administrative independence which was an obstacle to economic unity. The country was still cut up by internal Customs barriers which, in addition to the feudal tolls, hindered communication; and the spirit of municipal particularism still existed strongly in parts, such as Marseilles. The nobles still retained various fiscal privileges which, directly or indirectly, hindered production. As a result of its natural position or of the personal ambition of its princes, the kingdom was exposed to invasions or dragged into wars of conquest. Many wars had to be waged and paid for, and the professional army, whether voluntary or mercenary, had to be supplemented by a national militia.

Moreover, while England had begun with a sort of absolutism which had gradually been transformed into an organised sovereignty of the people, in France the nation seemed to be embodied in the king. Thus the central power interfered in all the details of economic life, and that not only by the exercise of an unwise and arbitrary fiscal policy. It instituted a minute technical inspection of all arts and crafts. It created state manufactures or invested such private enterprises as pleased it with exclusive privileges. It was the state which first organised and controlled large scale industry, which in England had grown up on its own strength and had even overthrown the barriers raised against it by traditional legislation. The great commercial companies founded in France were almost all, to a greater or less extent, state companies; the king himself often issued appeals for capital, and, indeed, it was precisely the fear of indiscreet interference by the government which paralysed investors. These enterprises, which needed freedom to develop, were stifled by bureaucratic centralisation. One of the few companies which really succeeded was that founded at Marseilles in 1741 for the African trade; the greater part of the capital was subscribed in Marseilles, and the local Chamber of Commerce directed operations.[1]

Between the French monarchy and private capitalism were formed more or less successful alliances, which are one of the original features of French history. The monarchy forced the heads of companies to share the profits of their monopolies with it. It used the farmers-general for the collection of indirect taxes. It instituted the monopoly of licensed victuallers and corn merchants in order to secure the provisioning of the army and to regulate the corn trade. No sooner had Law's bank begun to prosper than the Regent transformed it into a royal bank, with the result that the Bank of France did not really come into existence until a hundred years later than the Bank of England. Even barge

[1] Lavisse, *Histoire de France*, vol. ix, pp. 225-226.

and waggon transport was for a time[1] organised as a public service in the same way as the posts. With more reason the state almost always took charge of big works of public utility; the constructor of the Canal des Deux-Mers was commissioned by the government, and troops were used in making the Loing Canal. In 1455 the Lyonnais and Beaujolais mines were confiscated from Jacques Cœur and worked by the state; the decree of May 14th, 1604, stated that mining concessions granted to private individuals were revocable.[2] While British India was to remain for another hundred years under the almost unchecked control of a private company, Choiseul, when he tried to colonise Guiana, did not even ask for help from private capitalists. The state itself carried on the slave trade, sent out colonists and stocked them with provisions.

The more the state interfered in economic life, the less active private initiative became. While the best of the British aristocracy divided their time and their money between agriculture, industry, commerce and politics, the French nobility were absorbed, save in time of war, in the life of the court, where they wasted their own revenues and those of the state instead of working to increase them. Pride of birth prevented them from enlarging their order and from introducing new blood into it by the admission of the most distinguished members of the manufacturing or commercial classes. The latter also were in another way the victims of absolutism. From the time of the Renaissance they suffered from two evils " from which the Renaissance had been powerless to deliver them : the plague of officialdom and the scorn which was felt for industrial and commercial careers."[3] As the bureaucracy and governmental centralisation established themselves more firmly, they seemed to lose their bold spirit. French merchants were certainly more daring in the sixteenth century and in the reign of Henry IV than during the most splendid years of the personal government of Louis XIV, and it was not until the early years of a freer century that their old spirit awoke once more. Moreover, the sentiment which we may perhaps call economic patriotism or nationalism was

[1] Under Henry IV and Richelieu.
[2] See Fagniez, *Économie sociale sous le règne de Henri IV*, p. 35.
[3] Pigeonneau, *Histoire du commerce de la France*, vol. ii, p. 176.

much less active in France than in England. Prohibitions and protective tariffs were never so rigidly applied there, and foreign merchants found it easier to establish themselves in French than in English ports.

Lastly, the course of French prosperity suffered many abrupt checks and many periods of decadence. Civil wars, aggravated by foreign intervention, did far more harm in France than in her rival in wealth. This is true not only of the religious wars, which lasted for over thirty years, but also of the ridiculous and apparently insignificant revolt of the Fronde. There followed Louis XIV's policy of provocation and persecution which ended in disaster. Between 1685 and 1715, even if the ruin of the kingdom was not so complete as has sometimes been said, it cannot be estimated to have lost less than a million subjects, a twentieth of the total population. Later the terrible reverses of the Seven Years' War reduced foreign trade by a half.[1] The Revolution and the Napoleonic empire reduced it still further, and not until 1835 did it again reach the total which it had attained in 1789.

Industry and agriculture fared no better, for each in turn was more or less cruelly sacrificed. Sully opposed the establishment of new manufactures. Colbert and his successors, until the middle of the eighteenth century, neglected the interests of agricultural production. The result of this policy at home and abroad was that France, who in territory and population was so far ahead of England, was behind her in every branch of economic development. Moreover, the utilitarian spirit, the genius for practical commerce, were less developed in the country of Descartes than in the country of Bacon. The passion for pure science and for art for art's sake are often obstacles to the acquisition of mere material riches.

But on the other hand social inequalities were less marked in France, especially in rural society. Even Dr. Rigby testified (1789) that " although less wealth is to be seen there, the members of the lower classes are less often clad in rags and given to idleness and misery."[2] The reason was that small scale agriculture, which often presupposes the

---

[1] From 616 millions it fell to 322.

[2] See Babeau, *Vie rurale dans l'ancienne France*, pp. 141-142.

existence of small peasant proprietors, was more widespread in France, particularly in the neighbourhood of the towns and in the vine-growing districts. The French monarchy, too, pursued a juster—one might even say a more democratic—agrarian policy than the English Parliament, in all that concerned the division of common lands and the exchange of holdings. Social equality originated in France as political liberty in England.

Among the other states, which played only a secondary part in the economic history of Europe, Holland is worthy of a place apart and near the great leading nations. For half a century, indeed, it was she who took the lead in economic progress, and she exercised an effective supremacy, founded on the combination of boldness and prudence which distinguished her bourgeoisie, and on the hard work and persistent economy of her people. But at any rate from the political point of view her position was less favourable than that of England, for she was involved in Continental affairs and vulnerable by land. For this land of river deltas and peninsulas, as for ancient Attica, it was a misfortune not to be an island. Moreover, as we have shown, however marvellously cultivated and thickly populated the country was, it was, nevertheless, too small in area. The division of the old Low Countries into two different and even hostile nations compromised their futures for a long time to come.[1]

While the monarchies of North-Western Europe had already in the fifteenth century achieved political unity, and one of them had even established a form of national representation, the great central states were still in process of formation. Their economic development felt the effects of this delay. If from the seventeenth century onwards Hamburg had been backed up by a united Germany, it might have rivalled London. If Austria had not been obliged to maintain the European equilibrium against France, to reconquer Hungary from the Turks, and to defend Silesia against Prussia, she might have become a great Mediterranean power. Internal divisions and uncertain frontiers prevented these two empires of the future from opening up access to the sea and the roads to commercial expansion. So

---

[1] Flanders had been further decreased by the territories annexed to France.

both in the Danubian monarchy and in the kingdom built up of scraps of land here and there on the middle courses of the German rivers, rural economy continued to prevail. The Duchy of Prussia, Brandenburg, and many provinces of Austria-Hungary were barren lands which had to be cleared and populated—in fact, colonised—before industry could take root there. When industry did at last prosper there, it was thanks to a system of narrow protectionism, which elsewhere was out of date. Even agriculture rested on certain archaic social relations, whose survival showed the near neighbourhood of even more backward nations. East of the Elbe, bondage to the soil, forced labour for the lord, and domestic service of children in the lord's house existed until after Jena, while in the Danube basin many of these relics of the past survived until 1848.

In the north the Scandinavian countries suffered from the long civil and foreign wars in which they became involved; but the chief explanation of their slow development lies in natural disadvantages—the general poverty of the soil and the harsh climate—the consequences of which were aggravated by certain retrogressive measures in political and social life.

The economic history of the southern states can be summed up as almost continuous decadence for 200 years, from the middle of the sixteenth century to the middle of the eighteenth. The last rays of a once dazzling artistic splendour, the luxury, elegance and refinement which remained until the end in a few brilliant cities, should not blind us to this fact. Italy languished, not so much because she was divided internally and far from the Atlantic, as because her people seemed to have lost their capacity for labour at the same time as their military activity. The rich lived on the wealth which they had acquired in the past. Elsewhere capital was used actively in the promotion of commerce or industry, and thus increased rapidly, but in Italy it was only used half-heartedly, if at all, in industry, or more often maintained itself by international financial operations which benefited only a few families. The gild system of Florence reached its maturity at the end of the fourteenth century, when the distinction between large and small traders, and between traders and craftsmen, was clearly marked. Thereafter it declined slowly for 400 years, and during that time no large scale industry grew up to take its place.

The economic destiny of Spain seems somehow to have miscarried. Her history is a sort of melancholy miracle; the very events which ought to have assured her prosperity were, in the end, fatal to it. No sooner had she achieved political unity by conquering the last stronghold of the Moors, than she threw away the fruits of victory by brutally expelling her most active subjects, on the pretext of finishing a holy war. No sooner had she become the biggest monarchy in the West than she fell under the government of ambitious sovereigns who ruined her by pursuing the chimera of imperial or Catholic hegemony. Just as she was beginning to awaken to modern economic life she had the misfortune, by giving the signal for European expansion, to become mi tress of immense colonial possessions and of the richest mines in the world. The American market which she reserved for herself, that El Dorado from which galleons crammed with gold and silver sailed into her ports, conferred upon her subjects a fatal right, which many of them were only too ready to exercise—the right to idle. The result is well known. In the seventeenth century Spain had fallen to a point which England had already begun to pass in the thirteenth; she exported her raw wool to more industrious countries, from which she bought cloth. She had enjoyed more than a century of political, military, literary and artistic glory, but this brilliant and short-lived prosperity had poisoned the future economic life of the nation. Portugal also collapsed under the weight of its apparent triumph, which its territory was too small to bear.

Russia forms a world apart, not only because of her immense expanse and her racial affinity to Asia, but also because her development followed a peculiar and very complex course. Although she seemed to have realised territorial unity almost as soon as the Western States, she did not possess a modern political organisation until the beginning of the eighteenth century. Thus from the economic and social point of view Russia entered the new era in a condition so unimaginably backward that it is difficult to estimate. " The history of Muscovy in the seventeenth century reproduces to a great extent conditions which the

Barbarian Invasions had brought about in Western Europe a thousand years earlier."[1] At the beginning of the sixteenth century the bourgeois of the towns were in exactly the position from which those of the West had freed themselves in the twelfth century. And up to the present day, in spite of English, Dutch, German and French penetration, commerce, and especially foreign commerce, has held only a secondary place in this half of the Continent.

The abyss between Russia and the rest of Europe was made still wider by a definite retrogressive movement in social organisation. "Towards the end of the sixteenth century, when throughout the West the bonds attaching the agricultural population to the soil were being broken or at any rate relaxed, Russia, on the contrary, was busy forging these chains which hitherto had not existed there!"[2] Until the beginning of our own times serfdom grew steadily more firmly established and more burdensome. Yet this empire, heterogeneous as it was, was not in decline. Slowly, in spite of this social retrogression, as political organisation improved, economic progress followed in its course. When Poland relapsed into anarchy and all her towns decayed, Moscow, St. Petersburg and Riga were quite ready to undertake the work of great markets, which devolved on them as a result of their position midway between East and West, henceforth closely connected.

III.—THE PRELUDE TO CONTEMPORARY SOCIAL ECONOMY

The second half of the eighteenth century is marked by the beginning of a threefold revolution, which by simultaneously transforming the system of production, circulation and distribution of wealth, opened the way for the present economic age.

In the first place, such technical changes took place or were foreshadowed in industrial production that this form of economic activity became far the most important, or impressed its own characteristics on the rest. The moment had

[1] Waliszewski, *Le berceau d'une dynastie*, pp. 43-46.
[2] Waliszewski, *Ivan le Terrible*, p. 22.

come when hand-driven tools could and must give way to power-driven machinery. On the one hand, machines had become so complex and, so to speak, intelligent that the application of blind force was enough to work them with scarcely any help from skilled workmen. And on the other hand they had become so complicated and heavy that human strength was not enough to give them rapid movement. But a motive power had to be found which should be more easily handled and more mobile (in the state of knowledge which then prevailed) than the force of waterfalls. This was found in steam.

Savery's and Newcomen's machines, which, properly speaking, were pumps and not motors, only used the force of the vacuum made by the condensation of water-steam. As early as 1681 Denis Papin had undoubtedly discovered how to use the expansive force of vaporised water to drive a piston, but his famous *marmite* was only a kitchen pot. The first steam-engine worthy of the name was constructed by the Scotsman James Watt in 1769. In 1781, furnished with a movable slide-valve and a ball regulator which controlled the passage of steam into the cylinder, and provided with joints which converted the alternate into a circular movement, the steam-engine could be turned to many uses. Plenty of fuel was needed to work it, and Europe, along the chains of the Hercynian hills, and, above all, England on both sides of the Pennine Range, possessed rich deposits of coal. The industrial revolution was imminent.

It was in mining that the new machine was first used, to guard against floods. Then almost at once it was adopted by the forge-masters. It worked powerful bellows, which permitted an economy of a third to be effected in the coal used for making coke, it worked rolling-mills and hammers. Metallurgy made great strides with its help, and in turn improved it by giving it a stronger frame, more exact gears, and pistons which fitted the cylinders exactly. Finally, in 1785 Cartwright adapted it to cotton spinning, and four years later it was used in weaving at Manchester. Soon " two steam looms, watched by a boy of fifteen, wove three and a half pieces of stuff in the same time that a skilled weaver took to make one with a flying shuttle."[1]

[1] *Cf.* Levasseur, *Histoire des classes ouvrières*, vol. ii, p. 525.

The steam-engine, which enabled cheap articles to be produced even when labour was dear, was soon introduced into France, where, thanks to the efforts of Jacques Constantin Périer, the great manufacturer and member of the Académie des Sciences, it soon became well known. In 1779 Watt and his partner Boulton constructed the famous Chaillot steam pump at Paris. The English " iron king," Wilkinson, in 1788 installed on one of the islands of the Lower Loire a steam boring-mill capable of boring seven cannons at once out of solid metal. At the Montcenis works, formerly at Creusot, where cannons and water conduits were made, six steam-engines supplied the power for big cylindrical bellows, boring machines, the old hammers and tilt-hammers used in forging iron, and also for hoisting coal (1785).[1] In 1791 the Anzin mines possessed twelve steam pumps.

At the same time that metallurgy was undergoing a development which was later to be of use to agriculture, industrial chemistry also came to life. This was the age when Le Blanc succeeded in extracting soda from sea salt, when Thénard found a way of producing white-lead in bulk, when Berthollet discovered the bleaching liquid known as *Eau de Javel* (1785), which Watt introduced into England, and when Lebon made decisive experiments in the dry destructive distillation of wood and later of coal.[2]

Science now took over the direction of industry. Newcomen and Hargreaves had been only artisans, Arkwright and Cartwright only chance discoverers, but Watt was a real *savant*, whose encyclopædic knowledge recalled the scholars of the Renaissance. The eighteenth century, especially in its second half, differed from the preceding century precisely in this, that it did not give exclusive predominance to pure science and that it cared more for the practical application of science. The age of empiricism was close at hand.

In face of the universal changes in old processes and the prodigious growth of industries hitherto unknown, the old gild organisations were simply barriers to be swept aside. In

[1] The steam engine was introduced into Germany at exactly the same time.

[2] See Renard and Dulac, *L'évolution industrielle et agricole depuis cent cinquante ans*, p. 29.

England the gild system had already begun to fall into disuse in the seventeenth century. We have seen how peremptorily Parliament condemned its principles in 1753. The Statute of 1563 remained a dead-letter until it was definitely repealed in 1814. On the other hand, let us take two states, such as Tuscany and France, where the organised crafts survived much longer, though their fall was no less rapid when it came. In Florence, the city of the old *arti*, two successive edicts of February, 1770, suppressed the mastership fees, authorised craftsmen to become members of more than one gild, and abolished the gild courts. This example was soon followed in Milan (1771) and Sicily (1786).[1]

In France from the beginning of the eighteenth century the great merchants of Bordeaux and Nantes declared against the gild monopolies through the agency of their Chambers of Commerce : " They may have been useful and well-organised institutions to begin with, but now they show nothing but abuses which it would be impossible to reform and which call for their complete suppression."[2] In 1752 the Council of Commerce rejected a demand for the amendment of their statutes put forward by the carpenters of Caen, on the grounds that it was " only a plan to check public freedom and to make themselves masters of the goods and money of individuals."[3] In 1770 the Department of Commerce expressed the wish that the number of journeymen in each business should no longer be limited, and that the length of time a man had to spend as a journeyman under the same master should be reduced to one year.[4] Finally, Turgot, by one of his famous edicts of 1776, considering that " citizens of all classes are deprived of the right to choose the workmen whom they wish to employ and of the advantage in lower prices and improved manufactures which competition would give them," proclaimed freedom " for all persons, of whatever sort and condition they be, and even for foreigners . . . to embrace and exercise throughout the kingdom . . . any profession or craft they choose, or even to exercise several

---

[1] *Cf.* Renard, *Syndicats, trade-unions et corporations*, pp. 148-149.
[2] Chambre de Commerce de Bourdeaux, 1716. *Cf.* Fagniez, *Corporations et syndicats*, p. 54.
[3] *Cf.* Levasseur, *op. cit.*, p. 452.
[4] *Cf.* Germain Martin, *Grande industrie sous Louis XV*, p. 334.

together." The reaction which followed the reformer's down-fall did not revive the gilds in their old form. Wo. ien, as well as foreigners, ceased to be excluded from organised crafts. A man was still allowed to exercise more than one craft, and all limitation of machinery or of the number of men a master might employ was swept away. The exclusive class of " masters " was only a shadow of its former self and vanished completely at the beginning of the Revolution.

The modern monopolies created by the French monarchy to encourage the development of new industries survived no longer than the old ones, which dated back to the Middle Ages. From 1750 onwards exclusive privileges were only granted in exceptional circumstances, and the Declaration of December 24th, 1762, limited their duration in all cases to fifteen years.[1] In the same year the Controller-General Bertin declared that " nothing was more contrary to his principles than to continue the granting of bounties."[2] Occasionally even the monopolists themselves—as, for instance, the Van Robais, who for a hundred years had held the sole right of manufacturing fine cloth at Abbéville—" gave up their monopoly and sang the praises of freedom."[3]

In this atmosphere of liberty and progress all technical regulations crumbled away, not only those which had been enforced by the gilds, but also those which had lately been decreed by royal authority. From 1754 onwards the stocking knitting industry spread unopposed throughout all the towns and provinces, and French hosiery began to be famous. From 1763 onwards paper manufacturers were allowed to use any machine which they thought might be useful. Inspectorships given to men like Gournay, Vaucanson and the Irishman Holker were of real help to national industry instead of hindering it by trying to standardise it. Necker himself in 1779 was forced to simplify rules and formalities, and although he maintained the system of stamping by inspectors, he allowed manufacturers to sell freely all kinds of new articles, provided only that they were clearly marked as such.

But the provincial assemblies which he had just created

---

[1] Cf. Weulersse, *Mouvement physiocratique*, vol. ii, pp. 242-243.
[2] Cf. Levasseur, *op. cit.*, pp. 494-496.
[3] Lavisse, *Histoire de France*, vol. viii[2], p. 346.

for the most part pronounced against any inspection and any stamping, for at this time the new doctrine of *laisser faire* was becoming popular, conquering first of all public opinion, and finally the government itself. Colbert himself, the first great organiser of industrial monopolies, had never been ignorant of their disadvantages. He had regarded them as " expedients," as " temporary crutches," indispensable for putting young industries on their feet. He had hoped that the official companies which he had created would soon break up into a number of private societies. " Il faut laisser faire les hommes," he himself wrote.[1] Moreover, the economic policy of the eighteenth century, like the despotism of which it was one manifestation, was enlightened and liberal. " In the past we cherished soldiers," wrote Gournay to Trudaine; " now we must cherish labour. How? By honouring it, by giving it the protection to which it has a right, and especially by applying to it the powerful spur of competition."[2] Some twenty years later the Physiocrat Bandeau wrote: " The only distinction between the manufacturers or master-craftsmen and the ordinary labourers should be the knowledge, the wish and the ability to set up a workshop."[3]

But it was of little use to free production if trading facilities, which ought to have grown with it, were still hampered by traditional obstacles.

" Anything which tends to restrict the freedom and the number of merchants is worthless," wrote Colbert in 1671. As a matter of fact, wholesale trade, even in France, had always been free and open to nobles as well as to commoners, so that the edict of 1765 only acknowledged an established fact. We have shown how even the corn trade succeeded in escaping to a great extent from the wearisome control of the government. Turgot, like Leopold at Florence, suppressed the merchants' gilds as well as those of the craftsmen; and in Tuscany, at least from 1770 onwards, all internal Customs dues and even the state monopolies of salt and tobacco were abolished.

In external commerce the question of freeing colonial trade presented most difficulties, for it was usually the

[1] Lavisse, *Histoire de France*, vol. vii[1], p. 221.
[2] Levasseur, pp. 569-570.
[3] *Introduction à la philosophie économique*, p. 431.   1771.

creation either of the state or of some privileged company. As early as 1669, however, Colbert had listened to the complaints of the colonists of Canada and the West Indies against the monopoly of the West India Company. Exactly a century later, with the loudly expressed approval of the chief towns in the kingdom, the East India Company was in turn suppressed, and trade with the East, which had now become much easier, made a great advance as soon as it was thrown open to competition. Even in Spain the privilege of trading with overseas possessions, which had hitherto belonged to Seville, Cadiz and Santander, was extended to fifteen ports, and in 1774 her colonies were authorised to trade directly with each other. Purely foreign trade had never been subject to absolute monopolies between nationals of the same country. In 1670 the men of Marseilles opposed the grant of any private monopoly to the new Levant Company, and in 1759 their own port lost the privilege of being the sole port of embarkation for the Ottoman Empire.

Between nations, however, there was much less freedom, for even to-day the era of a free international economy seems scarcely to have begun, if indeed it is ever destined to come. But precious modifications were introduced in the system of prohibition and protection. The " commercial truce " made at Picquigny in Louis XI's reign had already set up some measure of free trade between France and England. A similar effort, inspired by political motives, was made in 1606, but since the English observed the new treaty only in so far as it was favourable to them, this attempt at economic disarmament was a failure. The French merchants, however, still demanded a liberal policy. " When Henry IV wished to reserve the French market for the French by strengthening the Customs tariffs, all the corporations which he consulted were in favour of the plan. Only one protest was made. This came from the mercers, who sold everything, though they manufactured nothing, and whose trade depended to a great extent of foreign merchandise."[1] Thus the past stretched out a hand to the future, and the individual cosmopolitanism of the old merchants gave promise of the free trade internationalism of certain modern states. Moreover, protection often defeated its own ends. Thus the policy pursued by the different states of enticing away the best

[1] Renard, *Syndicats, trade-unions et corporations*, p. 92.

workmen from neighbouring countries ended in the rapid diffusion of the most jealously guarded craft secrets.

When Cromwell passed the Navigation Act, French merchants protested against Fouquet's measures of reprisal. Fifty years later their demands were definitely formulated and shortly afterwards were granted. In 1711 the facilities granted to the Dutch by the Treaty of Ryswick were extended to the English, the Danes and the Hanse towns. In 1713 formal commercial treaties were made with the United Provinces, the Austrian Netherlands and Prussia. With England a general agreement was made, implying the reciprocal application of the "most favoured nation" system; but at the request of the manufacturers of London and Lancashire Parliament refused its ratification.[1] At last, when industry was becoming all-important in England while agriculture was returning to favour in France, an agreement was arrived at. The Eden Treaty (1786) arranged that import duties should be lowered in England on French agricultural produce, and in France on British manufactured goods.

Neither of the two governments was yet converted to the doctrine of full commercial liberty. Walpole, however, had already conceived the idea of making England a vast *entrepôt*, which the merchandise of the whole world might enter freely, for subsequent redistribution among the nations. The profits of this immense traffic would more than compensate for the small loss which foreign competition could inflict on a country whose economic development was so advanced. The revolt of the American Colonies (1776) relaxed the stringency of a colonial system, the futility of which was demonstrated by Adam Smith in the same year. Learning by experience, France opened the ports of her remaining colonies to foreign ships. Even Great Britain began to relax her traditional rigour in the enforcement of the Navigation Act, and in the last twenty years of the century the amount of her foreign trade was more than doubled.

While artificial barriers in the path of commerce were thus being removed or lowered, the circulation of wealth, which had been made more active, notably by the development of mining and metallurgy, was being transformed by

[1] See Lavisse, *Histoire de France*, vol. viii[1], p. 261.

the use of new means of communication, which were the direct result of recent industrial discoveries.

The new motive power, mastered and disciplined at last, was first applied to water transport. Long after the first attempts of Papin, but almost twenty years earlier than Fulton's successful experiments, the Marquis de Jouffroy introduced steam navigation on the Doubs (1776). As early as 1769, indeed, Cugnot, a military engineer, had made, for carrying ordnance stores, a powerful but very slow and heavy steam-waggon, which may be called the ancestor of our automobiles. But mechanical transport did not enter into general use until a much more level road was substituted for the ordinary carriage road. As early as William III's reign wooden railways had been used in the Newcastle mines to facilitate the transport of coal, though the first iron rails did not appear in England until the year in which Watt constructed his first machine. About 1785 at Montcenis in France five or six leagues of special track were laid to carry coal to the blast furnaces, both the rails and the truck wheels being of cast-iron. The track was ready for Stephenson's locomotive.[1]

The increasing control of man over Nature and the attitude of *laisser faire* henceforth adopted by governments opened the way to a new society in which capitalists and workers formed two widely separate classes, who were to co-operate in the work of production, but were to come into conflict over the division of profits.

Although stanch defenders of the gild system tried to preserve in all cases the necessity of making a "masterpiece," while on the other hand one of the advocates of free industry proclaimed, without much thought, that when setting up a workshop it was not enough for a man to have skill and willingness to work unless he had money, nearly everyone agreed in regarding the separation of the masters and the wage-earners as a natural and necessary process. For example, Turgot described the birth, or rather recognised the existence, of the modern proletariat in these concise words :

[1] Note in passing the mechanical striking of the coinage, another instance of the innumerable applications of steam-power. It was introduced into England in 1790, and, by making counterfeiting more difficult, gave fresh security to commerce.

" That class of men who, having no property but their labour and industry, have therefore the need and the right to use their sole means of livelihood to the fullest extent."

In France as in England capitalists increased the scope of their enterprises by joint action. If necessary they went into partnership, and thus, either in their own names or under cover of a joint-stock company, they succeeded in establishing financial control over a whole group of industries. De Wendel and Wilkinson, the first directors of the Creusot Company, also controlled the Blanzy glass-works and the foundries at Indret and Ruelle; in addition de Wendel had an interest in the works at Hayange, Charleville and Tulle, and thus controlled the greater part of the heavy metal industry of France. These two men represented such a huge accumulation of business and were so powerful, that they gained a sort of dictatorship over the hundreds of workmen whom they had collected from all over the province to construct blast furnaces and forges at Montcenis.

Against this formidable concentration among employers the workers were condemned to helplessness. The edict of 1776 which suppressed gilds in France forbade " all masters, journeymen, workmen and apprentices to form any association or assembly with each other." In Tuscany the Grand Duke Leopold also prohibited all trade societies. Nominally this legislation, which carried economic and social individualism to its furthest limits, held the balance even between capitalist and wage-earner. But actually the wage-earner was the humblest and most helpless of individuals, while the capitalist was a host, an association, in himself. The apologists of free industry took to task those capitalists who had too narrow a conception of their scope and functions : " A few men who have capital, and who as a result of their exclusive privileges encroach on their brothers' livelihood,[1] think that they are doing well; they do not realise that freedom, which would double the activity of every worker, would greatly increase the profits of capitalists. They stupidly fetter the arms which ask nothing better than to work to bring them riches."[2] And it must be remembered

---

[1] He is talking of the masters of the gilds.

[2] Dupont (de Nemours), quoted by G. Weulersse, *Mouvement physiocratique*, vol. ii, p. 396.

that in this unequal contest the strong always had a powerful ally in machinery, which robbed more and more workers of their employment and thus increased competition.[1] As early as 1744 the introduction of Vaucanson's machines at Lyons had roused such fury that he was forced to flee in disguise. In 1789 the Caen spinners complained bitterly against the introduction of English machinery: " These machines employ only one-tenth of the workmen and thus rob the other nine-tenths of their livelihood. It is barbarous to rob the poor of their present employment, which is their only property, without giving them at least some assured and daily compensation."[2]

The one resource left to these outcasts of the capitalist system lay in their numbers, if they could be brought to unite. Even in the eighteenth century one class of French workmen seems to have conceived the plan of a national organisation of workers against masters. Letters patent of February 26th, 1777, stated that " the workers in the paper-making industry throughout the kingdom have united in a general association, by means of which they control the industry as they please and decide the success or failure of the manufactures."[3] Their weapons were strikes, riots and rough handling of masters, and they were so successful that even machinery had to retreat before them. " The Montgolfiers assert that their father had had cylinders made at Annonay and that his workmen forced him to return to the old method."[4] Similarly in England the workers were forming permanent associations which developed into trade unions, and even in 1780 they were protesting vigorously against the evils of the truck system, or payment in kind,

[1] " Wherever labour is expensive," wrote an inspector, " it must be supplemented by machinery. This is the only way of competing with places where labour is cheap. England taught Europe this long ago." *Encyclopédie méthodique*, quoted by Levasseur, vol. ii, p. 525.

[2] The introduction of mechanical looms not only led to a sudden reduction in the number of workmen, but also enabled skilled workmen to be replaced by cheap unskilled labour. In France children of seven and old men of seventy-five were employed in the big cotton industry. See Schmidt, *Revue d'histoire économique et sociale*, 1913, No. 3.

[3] Lavisse, *Histoire de France*, vol. ix, p. 241. In England, at the beginning of the eighteenth century, the wool-combers had formed an association of the same kind.

[4] Levasseur, *op. cit.*, vol. ii, pp. 804-811.

and of the sweating system, or exploitation of domestic industry.

But the workers also appealed to the government, which was forced to intervene in the great social struggle which was just beginning, in order to see that at least the elementary rights of humanity were respected. We have seen why the attitude of the government had not always been absolutely hostile to the working class, and in the second half of the eighteenth century the enlightened despotism of sovereigns and ministers was influenced by new philanthropic ideas. While the Renaissance had been aristocratic in character, and the Reformation had meekly adapted itself to the needs of the wealthy bourgeoisie as well as to the ambitions of princes, the new philanthropy was animated by a sincere pity for the less fortunate members of the human race. At a time when the public was learning at last what marvels of skill were needed for the manufacture of the most ordinary articles, and when economists, with Adam Smith as their spokesman, had just proclaimed that labour—that manual labour which hitherto had been despised as a mark of servility—was the source of all wealth, the wretched condition of the workers naturally aroused universal sympathy.

In France the great industrialists seem to have been intermittently conscious of the obligations created by their new position and to have realised that it would not be in their own interest to neglect them. In the eighteenth century the master-printers agreed to reserve certain funds, which were, however, levied on their staff, for the relief or encouragement of their workmen. Help was to be given to the sick and to the old workmen whom age or weakness had reduced to want; bounties were to be given to those who had been thirty years in the same employment and whose conduct had been exemplary. The Glass Company supplied its employees with food at low prices during scarcity, and in 1760 it instituted ten retiring pensions for their benefit. The Gobelins and St. Gobain workmen, who lived within the enclosure of the factory, had the benefit of a small garden. The directors of the steel manufacture at Noiraye, near Amboise, gave prizes to their best workmen. Henry IV had stipulated that in every mining enterprise one-thirtieth of the nett profits was to be devoted to the maintenance of a service of medical and spiritual help for the miners; chaplains and doctors were always to be at their disposal. A century and a half later the Anzin company spent 100,000 livres every year in giving help to the sick and in pensions to the widows and orphans of those who had died at their work.

The middle and upper classes united with the government in its attempts to help the victims of unemployment by providing relief works. In Louis XVI's reign the Marquis d'Hervilly opened a linen factory for this purpose, and the Marquis de Choiseul-Gouffier a paper factory, while up and down the country charitable institutions and philanthropic societies were founded for the same purpose.[1]

Turgot declared that the workers must have special protection at the very moment when he set them free. Leopold of Tuscany, though he dissolved the gilds, took care to replace them by Chambers of Commerce, Arts and Manufactures, one of the functions of which was to encourage and help the poorer artisans. In France an administrator like Trudaine de Montigny approached that essential problem of the new social economy, the rate of wages, in a spirit sympathetic to the workers. " On the whole," he wrote to the Intendant of Auvergne-Montyon, " wages are too low. It is an advantage to the employers, but a disadvantage to the state. The many are sacrificed to the private fortune of the few. . . . The state already does a great deal for the masters in forbidding or checking foreign competition. It must not help them by keeping down the wages of native workers " (1766).[2] And when, for instance, the Thiers paper manufacturers formed an employers' association with the express object of resisting the workmen's claims, the government gave them only occasional support.[3] In England until 1813 the justices of the peace kept the power, given them by the Statute of Artificers in 1563, of fixing the rate of wages, and for some

[1] Arkwright's spinning machine was quickly adopted by some of these societies.

[2] See Levasseur, *op. cit.*, vol. ii, pp. 803-804.

[3] See Lavisse, *Histoire de France*, vol. ix, p. 242, and Germain Martin, *Grande Industrie sous le règne de Louis XV*. Extract from the statutes of the association: "Article 3: The paper manufacturers shall employ any workmen they choose without protest from the journeymen. Article 5: The paper manufacturers shall take as many apprentices as they like. Article 6: The journeymen shall do their full day's work."

time the rapidly increasing proletariat put their faith in this archaic legislative survival.

If the workers were to incur the dangers of freedom, they ought at least to reap its advantages too. In a century which had heard the eloquent voices of Montesquieu, of the Swedenborgian Wardstrom and of Wilberforce raised on behalf of the abolition of negro slavery, how could it be possible that part of the European race should be oppressed by a hardly less degrading industrial slavery? The English Tories, who were afraid that agriculture would be sacrificed to industry and that landlords would be ruined by the increasing expenses of urban poverty, incessantly denounced the scandal. When an Auvergne manufacturer demanded that two workmen who had left his factory should be brought back by the police, Trudaine did not hesitate to reply " that it is an established principle that workmen are not slaves in France and that they are only bound by their own agreement."[1] Yet in the country districts of this very kingdom there were still thousands of serfs, and even where serfdom, strictly so called, had disappeared, feudal rights still encroached on the economic freedom of the *roturiers*. The edict passed in 1771 by the King of Sardinia forcing the nobles of Savoy and Piedmont to accept the commutation of their rights for money is the forerunner of the famous resolutions which the Constituent Assembly was to pass on the night of August 4th, 1789, and which the armies of the Republic and of the Napoleonic Empire were to enforce throughout the West.

A new era was opening, an era in which the enormous development of machinery, by making commerce worldwide and bringing about huge concentrations of capital, was to revolutionise conditions of labour and for a time to reduce the majority of the workers to a precarious position, despite their newly won freedom. This economic and social revolution, with the agitations which it roused and the interventions which it necessitated, is as much the mark of our own times as is the political revolution.

[1] See Levasseur, p. 667, quoting Trudaine: " The regulations which forbid workmen to be enticed away from their employment are irreconcilable with the principle of their personal freedom."

INDEX

PLATE 1. MANUFACTURE OF CLOTH AT FLORENCE
(See page 262)

PLATE II. MANUFACTURE OF CANE SUGAR AT THE END OF THE 16th CENTURY

PLATE III.   FLEMISH PRINTING PRESS IN THE 16th CENTURY

PLATE IV. THE PORT OF AMSTERDAM IN THE 17th CENTURY

PLATE V. LONDON BRIDGE IN THE MIDDLE OF THE 17th CENTURY

PLATE VI.   FRENCH CANNON FOUNDRY IN THE 18th CENTURY

PLATE VII. "BORN TO LABOUR:" THE FRENCH PEASANT
(From a 17th century engraving)

PLATE VIII. SILK MANUFACTURE IN THE MILANESE

Date Due
